BECOMING SOVIET JEWS

A HELEN B. SCHWARTZ BOOK IN JEWISH STUDIES

THE MODERN JEWISH EXPERIENCE
Deborah Dash Moore and Marsha L. Rozenblit, *Editors*
Paula Hyman, *Founding Co-Editor*

BECOMING SOVIET JEWS
The Bolshevik Experiment in Minsk

Elissa Bemporad

Indiana University Press

Bloomington and Indianapolis

Becoming Soviet Jews has been awarded the Fraenkel Prize in Contemporary History as outstanding work in twentieth-century history.

Published with the generous support of the Helen B. Schwartz Fund for New Scholarship in Jewish Studies of the Robert A. and Sandra S. Borns Jewish Studies Program at Indiana University

This book is a publication of

Indiana University Press
Office of Scholarly Publishing
Herman B Wells Library 350
1320 East 10th Street
Bloomington, Indiana 47405-3907 USA

iupress.indiana.edu

Telephone orders   800-842-6796
Fax orders   812-855-7931

© 2013 by Elissa Bemporad

All rights reserved

No part of this book may be reproduced or utilized in any form or by any means, electronic or mechanical, including photocopying and recording, or by any information storage and retrieval system, without permission in writing from the publisher. The Association of American University Presses' Resolution on Permissions constitutes the only exception to this prohibition.

⊖The paper used in this publication meets the minimum requirements of the American National Standard for Information Sciences—Permanence of Paper for Printed Library Materials, ANSI Z39.48-1992.

Manufactured in the United States of America.

Library of Congress Cataloging-in-Publication Data

Bemporad, Elissa.
  Becoming Soviet Jews : the Bolshevik experiment in Minsk / Elissa Bemporad.
    pages ; cm. — (Helen B. Schwartz book in Jewish studies)
  ISBN 978-0-253-00813-8 (cloth : alk. paper)
  ISBN 978-0-253-00822-0 (pbk. : alk. paper)
  ISBN (invalid) 978-0-253-00827-5 (ebook)
  1. Jews, Soviet—Belarus—Minsk—History. 2. Jews—Belarus—Minsk—Social life and customs—20th century. 3. Jews—Cultural assimilation—Soviet Union. 4. Jews—Soviet Union—Identity. 5. Communism and Judaism—Belarus—Minsk. I. Title. II. Series: Helen B. Schwartz book in Jewish studies.
  DS135.B382M563 2013
  305.892'40478609041—dc23

                                                              2012049483

1 2 3 4 5 18 17 16 15 14 13

דודן,

אהבת עולם אהבתיך על כן משכתיך חסד
ירמיהו לא, ב

PUBLICATION OF THIS BOOK
IS SUPPORTED BY A GRANT FROM
Jewish Federation of Greater Hartford

Contents

	List of Figures	*viii*
	Acknowledgments	*ix*
	Introduction	1
1	Historical Profile of an Eastern European Jewish City	13
2	Red Star on the Jewish Street	31
3	Entangled Loyalties: The Bund, the Evsektsiia, and the Creation of a "New" Jewish Political Culture	51
4	Soviet Minsk: The Capital of Yiddish	81
5	Behavior Unbecoming a Communist: Jewish Religious Practice in a Soviet Capital	112
6	Housewives, Mothers, and Workers: Roles and Representations of Jewish Women in Times of Revolution	145
7	Jewish Ordinary Life in the Midst of Extraordinary Purges: 1934–1939	176
	Conclusion	211
	Notes	217
	Selected Bibliography	253
	Index	269

Figures

1. Map of the Jewish Pale of Settlement, ca. 1900. — *18*
2. Distribution of shoes to children of Jewish homes by the Joint Distribution Committee, Minsk, ca. 1923. — *33*
3. Map of the Belorussian Soviet Socialist Republic (BSSR), 1926–39. — *36*
4. On Nemiga Street, 1923. — *42*
5. The Minsk Central Train Station, 1930s. — *87*
6. At a parade celebrating the tenth anniversary of the Bolshevik Revolution, Minsk, 1927. — *88*
7. Physics class in Yiddish at the Jewish section of the Unified Professional School, Minsk, 1928–29. — *92*
8. At a kosher market stand, Minsk, 1924. — *126*
9. "My wife's aunt came and carried out the *bris*. Of course the father isn't too happy about this." *Oktyabr*, April 17, 1927. — *139*
10. Students of the Jewish Pedagogical Training College learning to shoot, Minsk, 1925. — *164*
11. View of Lenin Street, from Freedom Square to Sovetskaia Street, 1930s. — *178*
12. Belorussian State Jewish Theater, 1930s. — *182*
13. Detail of the Belorussian State Jewish Theater. Performance poster featuring Sholem Aleichem's *Motl Peysi dem Khazns* (Motl, the cantor's son). — *183*
14. From Avrom Goldfadn's play *The Witch*, staged by the Belorussian State Jewish Theater in 1939. — *184*

Acknowledgments

I AM MOST GRATEFUL to all my colleagues, friends, and family, who, in different ways and in different countries, supported me through the ups and downs that the researching and writing of this book entailed. First, I would like to thank Steve Zipperstein, who saw this project through its initial stage and who gave me the support and encouragement to become a better writer of Russian Jewry. I am grateful for his mentoring, his rigor, and above all his generosity. It is a pleasure to thank others who guided my training in Jewish history and Russian history: Valerio Marchetti, who, in my years at Bologna University, first showed me where Russia and Jews meet; Aron Rodrigue, who made me think broadly about issues of emancipation, acculturation, and national minorities in multinational empires; Amir Weiner, who helped me sharpen my ideas about the Bolshevik experiment and who was ultimately responsible for my shift from the nineteenth to the twentieth century when, during a graduate seminar on Soviet historiography, he said to me, "Don't you see how much more interesting Soviet Jews are?"; and Terrence Emmons, with whom I had some of the most engaging conversations on Russian society and historiography of my career. I thank Avrom Nowershtern, David Roskies, David Fishman, and Samuel Kassow, for showing me the exceptional richness of Eastern European Jewish life and culture.

Over the years, a number of individuals have offered useful comments on different sections of this book, or discussed other relevant issues with me that informed my views. Among the many scholars who in many different ways contributed to the making of this book, warm thanks to Evelyn Ackerman, Natalia Aleksiun, Mordechai Altshuler, Eugene Avrutin, Zachary Baker, Yaacov Basin, Elisheva Carlbach, Igor Dukhan, Gennady Estraikh, Olga Gershenson, Zvi Gitelman, Harriet Jackson, Laura Jokusch, Naomi Kadar z"l, Mikhail Kalnitskii, Joshua Karlip, Ben-Tsion Klibansky, Rebecca Kobrin, Misha Krutikov, John Champagne, Cecile Kuznitz, Leonid Katsis, Efim Melamed, Misha Mitsel, Kenneth Moss, Jess Olson, Eddy Portnoy, Alyssa Quint, Per Anders Rudling, Robert Seltzer, Sasha Senderovich, Anna Shternshis, Nancy Sinkoff, Julia Sneeringer, Barry Trachtenberg, Shelly Tsar-Zion, Sarah Tsfatman, Amir Weiner, Debby Yalen, Vital Zajka, Arkadii Zeltser, and Carol Zemel. My heartfelt appreciation to Marion Kaplan (no one has ever read my work as closely as she has), Olga Litvak (the most brutal and brilliant critic on the Russian Jewish street), David Shneer, and Jeffrey Veidlinger, for their comments and suggestions.

The research for this book was enabled by support from a number of institutions, including the Taube Center for Jewish Studies at Stanford University, the National Foundation for Jewish Culture, the Memorial Foundation for Jewish Culture, the Center for Jewish History in New York City, the Mellon Foundation, the American

Councils (ACTR/ACCELS) for International Education Title VIII Research Scholarship, the YIVO Institute for Jewish Research, and the Hadassah-Brandeis Institute. I also owe a debt of appreciation to Jerry and William Ungar for generously sponsoring the chair that makes possible my presence at Queens College.

The research for this book involved more than a dozen archives and libraries on three different continents. In Minsk, I am indebted to the archivists and staffs of the National Archives of the Republic of Belarus, the State Archives of the Minsk Province, the Belorussian State Museum and Archives of Literature and Art, the Belorussian State Archives of Film and Photography, the National Academy of Sciences of Belarus, and the National Library of Belarus. I wish to thank Inna Pavlovna Gerasimova, head of the Jewish Museum in Minsk, who was generous in sharing her knowledge with me. In Moscow, I am grateful to the staffs of the Russian State Archive of Literature and Art, the State Archives of the Russian Federation, the Russian State Archive of Social and Political Research, Former Party Archives to 1945, and the Russian State Library. In Jerusalem, warm thanks are due to the staff of the Avraham Harman Institute of Contemporary Jewry, Oral History Division at Hebrew University, the Central Zionist Archives, the Yad Vashem Archives, and the Jewish National Library. In New York, I thank Misha Mitsel, senior archivist at the American Jewish Joint Distribution Committee. Last but not least, I am immensely grateful to the staff of the YIVO Archives and library, and I wish to thank in particular Marek Web, Krisha Fisher, and Jesse Aron Cohen, all of whom offered their assistance.

I would like to thank my editor at Indiana University Press, Alex Giardino, as well as Janet Rabinowitch and Peter Froehlich, for their insight, assistance, and immense patience in guiding me as I completed this work. Many thanks also to the Helen B. Schwartz Fund for New Scholarship in Jewish Studies of the Robert A. and Sandra S. Borns Jewish Studies Program at Indiana University and the Jewish Federation of Greater Hartford for generously supporting the preparation and production of this book. I am grateful and privileged to see my book included in the superb *Modern Jewish Experience* series.

Throughout the researching and writing of this book I had the loving support of friends and family. My friends and colleagues in the History Department at Queens College make the third floor at Powdermaker Hall a warm and stimulating place to work. Peter Yankl Conzen *z"l* offered friendship and enchanted encouragement, especially in New York and Jerusalem. Nina Rogov and her late, beloved husband, Dovid Rogov *z"l*, have been to me the embodiment of the best traditions of the sister cities of Minsk and Vilna. Tania Novikova and Yaakov Basin made me feel at home every time I traveled to Minsk, even during the most dreary and wintery Belorussian months. There are many close friends who have helped me in big and small ways over the years: my dearest Modena friends, Susanna Beltrami, Giada Chiari, Sibilla Cuoghi, and Davide Manelli; and my Bologna University companions in many exceptional Russian adventures, Simona Bulgarelli, Federica Larini, and Simona Magnani.

I wholeheartedly thank my parents-in-law: Shikl, for teaching the love of *the* language, and Gele, for being such a gifted *bobe*, poet, and archivist. I am blessed to have an extraordinary family: my parents, Arturo and Donna, my brothers, Jonathan and Joel, and my sisters, Hali and Micol. I am indebted to them for innumerable reasons that go beyond the pages of this book, but that made it possible. I am grateful to my son, Elia, and my daughter, Sonia, for their impatience, remarkable creativity, laughter, and playfulness. By the ages of seven and three, respectively, they have visited more countries in Eastern Europe than most people do in a lifetime. I dedicate this book to the main source of inspiration in my life, my husband, friend, and *compagno*, Dovid. I thank him for always being there for me and believing in me, and for making every day about a different color of the rainbow.

BECOMING SOVIET JEWS

Introduction

"This is my revolution."[1]

Becoming Soviet Jews is a study of the acculturation process into the Soviet system as experienced by the Jewish population of Minsk during the interwar period, from the Bolshevik Revolution of 1917 to the eve of the Hitler-Stalin pact of 1939. The book examines the dynamic encounter between pre-revolutionary Jewish life and the new Communist agencies and organizations that the Bolsheviks set up in the city. By focusing on issues of continuity and change in the lives of Minsk's Jews, it analyzes the modernization and social integration of one cultural-ethnic group within an intensely ideological state-system, which wielded on each and every individual an almost inescapable pressure to conform to its tenets, much more than other modern systems did at the time. The exploration of Jewish social, cultural, and daily life under the Bolsheviks reveals the intricacies and inconsistencies of the sovietization process and the patterns of Jewish accommodation. This process was far from linear and hardly ever uniform. It depended on a variety of factors, ranging from the social settings in which the individual operated and interacted with others, to the different views held by the individual and the options that Soviet society proffered to him or her. These factors included enthusiasm for Communist ideology, ambition to succeed, quest for employment, anxiety to fit in, necessity to survive, fear of marginalization and punishment, as well as pressures from family, friends, and fellow city-residents.

Notwithstanding the variety of settings, views, and options, the ways in which all members of the Jewish group experienced their path to sovietization in Minsk was shaped by the character of the city itself. Minsk was a historic Jewish center long before the establishment of the Soviet Union. It was located in the heart of the Pale of Settlement, densely populated by Jews, the area where the majority of Soviet Jews lived until the eve of World War II. The setting of Minsk, a historic Jewish city since the sixteenth century that was transformed into the capital of a Soviet Republic (the Belorussian Soviet Socialist Republic, or BSSR) by the Bolshevik Revolution, influenced the complicated process of give-and-take between Jewish particularity and Soviet universal ideas that characterizes the process of becoming Soviet Jews.

In spite of Lenin's violent rhetoric, and the quick tempo with which the Bolsheviks hoped to revolutionize Russian society and bring Socialism to the world—or at least to one country—the transformation of the core of Jewish life occurred at a slower pace in historic Jewish centers in the Pale of Settlement than it did in the Russian interior, in particular the Russian metropolises of Moscow and Leningrad. Geography curbed the intended radical consequences of the Bolshevik experiment (complete assimilation of the Jewish minority group into the Soviet family of peoples), impinged on the intensity with which the Communist project took hold of the Jewish street, and facilitated the preservation of lines of continuity with pre-revolutionary Jewish life. As this study of sovietization in the Pale indicates, Jewishness in the Soviet Union varied according to local and regional traditions and conditions.

From Russian to Soviet Jews

With a population of more than three million, the Jews who lived in the territories of the Soviet Union constituted in the interwar period the second-largest Jewish community in Europe after Polish Jewry. Beginning with the revolutions of February and October 1917, a small but fiercely committed and highly organized group of Social-Democrats gradually took over the core of the tsarist dominion, including most of the Pale of Settlement. Under the leadership of Lenin, the revolutionary vanguard of the Bolshevik Party began to create a one-party political system, a state-controlled economy and an official atheistic culture wherever it extended its power. In doing so, it brought about many changes in the lives of everyone, including the Jews.

Before the Bolsheviks came to power, Russian society had largely excluded Jews from positions of prominence. While social emancipation existed for some middle-class Jews during the late nineteenth and early twentieth centuries, legal restrictions affected the lives of most. Official curtailments on the admission of Jews into the military and state services, education and local administration complemented compulsory Jewish residence within the boundaries of the Pale.[2] Similar restrictions existed for many subjects of the empire who belonged to national minority groups. But because of their higher level of education and politicization, as well as their quicker pace of urbanization compared to the surrounding population (in Belorussia, for example, more than half of the urban population was Jewish in 1897), the burden of legal restrictions weighed considerably upon the Jewish population. Many enlightened, acculturated, and politicized Jews yearned to belong to the society of their residence, their aspiration being frustrated on a number of occasions, first in the 1860s at the time of the failed reforms of Alexander II and later in 1905, following the abortive first Russian revolution.

With the dissolution of the tsarist empire, the Provisional Government brought into power by the revolution of February 1917—introduced freedom of speech, press, and assembly for all citizens, thereby granting Jews an array of political and civil rights and ending their decades-long social segregation. The Soviet regime confirmed the legal emancipation of its Jewish residents, allowing them to join the political system, become citizens of the state, and participate in the newly established Socialist society without quotas or discrimination. Upward mobility was the most striking consequence of the shift to full-fledged citizenship. The rise in the number of Jews employed in the offices of Soviet government was so remarkable that it gave the impression, mostly at the popular level, of Jewish domination of the new regime. Whereas they formed less than 2 percent of the total population, by the mid-1920s, the Jews constituted 6 percent of the Soviet ruling elite and 10 percent of the leadership of all Soviet economic agencies.[3] A number of Jews held important posts in the high echelons of the Communist Party and the Red Army command.[4] Between 1934 and 1941, Jews held 33.7 percent of the posts in the central apparatus of the People's Commissariat of Internal Affairs (NKVD), 40.5 percent of its top leadership and secretariat, and 39.6 percent in its main State Security Administration (GUGB).[5] In 1939, in the Belorussian Republic (where Jews made up for 6.7 percent of the population),[6] 57 percent of the directors of medical institutions, 51.3 percent of physicians, 53.7 percent of dentists, 49 percent of managers and directors of stores, and 24 percent of directors of agricultural and industrial enterprises were Jewish.[7] Institutions of secondary and higher learning opened up to young Jews. No longer forced to travel abroad to evade the existing anti-Jewish quotas or take a high-school equivalent exam as *externs*, as historian Simon Dubnow and writer Isaac Babel had done, Jewish students swarmed into universities and institutions of higher education.[8]

"This is my revolution," wrote Solomon Grinberg in the autobiography he submitted to the Communist Party of Belorussia (CPB) applying for party membership in 1928. The son of a *melamed* (teacher in a Jewish religious elementary school) and grandson of a carpenter, Solomon was born in Bobruisk, Minsk *guberniia* (province) where, since the age of twelve, he had worked as an apprentice hairdresser, from eight in the morning until eleven at night. With limited knowledge of Russian (his mother tongue was Yiddish), he explained to the party organization that the long workday forced him to remain illiterate and prevented him from understanding anything about the February revolution. As soon as the October revolution broke out, however, "I instinctively felt that this was my revolution. . . . I immediately sided with the Bolsheviks, supported their conspiratorial work . . . [and] enrolled as a volunteer in the Red Army . . . , where I served until 1923. . . . I [now] work as a hairdresser in Minsk." In poor Russian, Solomon concluded the autobiography by beseeching the local cell of the CPB to accept him: "I recognize the party as the vanguard of the working class and believe it the duty of every conscious worker to join it . . . and fight against world capitalism . . . for a world revolution."[9] Whether Solomon applied for party membership out of belief, enthusiasm, conformity, or opportunism, the revolution gave him the option to become part of its elite and open the path to potential success in Soviet society.

But success had a price for all those willing to embrace it. While opening its doors to Russian Jewry, the Soviet regime banned Jewish political organizations outside the Communist Party, denied religious Jews and their institutions the right to continue playing a role in Jewish life, and destroyed a wide range of autonomous Jewish organizations. The Bolshevik leadership conveyed to its citizenry a clear message: those who did not conform to the views and codes of belief of the new Soviet system would suffer the consequences. As early as December 1917, Lenin had called for "a purge of the Russian land from all vermin . . . the idle rich, priests, bureaucrats, and slovenly and hysterical intellectuals." On August 31, 1918, *Pravda* (or Truth, the central organ of the Communist Party) wrote, "The towns must be cleansed of this bourgeois putrefaction. . . . All who are dangerous to the cause of the revolution must be exterminated."[10] During the period known as War Communism (the Bolsheviks' first version of a planned economy), Lenin confirmed his intention by imprisoning, deporting, and sentencing to death thousands of potential or real opponents. According to Robert Conquest, from 1917 to 1923, two hundred thousand people were killed by the Cheka, or the political police, and three hundred thousand as a result of repressive measures, such as the containment of risings and mutinies.[11]

Summary trials against political, religious, and cultural leaders who did not succeed in fleeing the country were followed by mock ones against religion, held responsible for perpetuating "bourgeois" and anti-Soviet behavior among Soviet citizens. With few exceptions, most forms of Jewish particularity, be it allegiance to the Zionist or Bundist movements, observance of religious rituals, or commitment to Hebrew language and culture, were delegitimized as part of the general drive to get rid of political opposition and wipe out clericalism. Supporters of political parties, members of religious communities, and owners of non-Soviet businesses or enterprises were pushed to the margins of society. This also was an expression of Lenin's intent to establish power with no concession to and compromise with the "bourgeois enemy." In the early phase of the revolution, this intent found its high point in the bloody suppression of the Kronstadt Rebellion of March 1921.

The combination of freedoms granted to, and constraints enforced on, Soviet Jewish citizens (albeit in different measures), entailed numerous changes in their political, cultural, and religious identity. Some Jews eagerly embraced the universal possibility of a classless society in which national identity would eventually disappear and be replaced by the Marxist idea of the "merging of nations." They rushed into government offices and institutions of higher learning, and they readily dissociated themselves from all vestiges of their Jewish identity and background. Sons and daughters rebelled against their Zionist, Bundist, or religious fathers and mothers, integrated into Soviet society, and came to form the backbone of the new Soviet intelligentsia. For those Jews who partook in "the Jewish social rise, Jewish patricide, and Jewish conversion to non-Jewishness," integration meant escaping religious, cultural, and political Jewish particularity.[12]

But the straight-forward, rapid path to acculturation into the Soviet system should not be ascribed to Soviet Jewry as a whole. In many of the medium-to-large urban centers with a sizeable proportion of Jews and located in the pre-1917 territory of the Pale (which included the BSSR), the response to the Bolshevik emancipation project in the 1920s and 1930s was multifaceted and not circumscribed to "Communism as anti-Jewishness" and "Jewishness as anti-Communism." In other words, while adapting to the new system, many Jews, whether former Bundists, Yiddish activists, political Zionists, religious practicing Jews, or Russified liberals, remained committed to some expressions of Jewishness, and they attempted to walk the fine line between accepted Soviet behavior and social norms and expressions of Jewish particularity.

Minsk: A Unique or Ordinary Place?

"A close-up look allows us to grasp what eludes us from the overall view, and vice-versa," wrote Carlo Ginzburg in his discussion about the intricate relationship between micro- and macrohistories.[13] The focus on one densely populated Jewish city challenges the widespread view that Soviet Jewry was a homogeneous and easily identifiable group with commonly held aims and aspirations. The local distinctiveness—economic, political, and social—of a specific place expands and diversifies our understanding of the Soviet Jewish experience.[14] At the same time, the study of the Jewish path to integration into Soviet society within the context of one city recaptures some of the general traits of Soviet Jewish life, providing insights into unnoticed features and highlighting the elaborate negotiation process between Communism and Jewish identity experienced by most Jews.

Like all places, Minsk was a unique city, with distinctive and idiosyncratic traits. In the Soviet landscape of urban centers, it was the only Jewish city that became the capital of a republic, as the new political and administrative hub of the Belorussian Soviet Socialist Republic intersected with a historic Jewish center in the Pale of Settlement. The geopolitical transformation of the city produced an intensification of Communist activities, exposing the new capital to a thorough and systematic sovietization process. As a Soviet capital, Minsk attracted a higher concentration of Bolshevik official institutions than other pre-revolutionary Jewish centers did, often serving as a lighthouse to spread Communist ideology to the surrounding cities and towns of Belorussia. This distinct characteristic can therefore reveal aspects of the sovietization process that remain elusive in places that did not house as many party institutions and Soviet administrative offices. The more Communist institutions sprung up in Minsk, the more radical and intense became the thrust to accept, or embrace, Bolshevism. By virtue of its new political status, Minsk also became a much more dynamic, exciting, and appealing place to live than it had ever been in pre-revolutionary Russia, attracting thousands in search of new opportunities.

Despite these exceptional features, in many ways Minsk remained a very ordinary Jewish city. With a large Jewish population throughout the interwar period—which grew from forty-eight thousand in 1923 to seventy-one thousand in 1939, and oscillated between 43 and 30 percent of the total city population—Minsk can be used as a case study to investigate adjustment to and participation in the Bolshevik experiment as it occurred in most urban centers of the former Pale.[15] Many towns and cities in the Jewish heartland shared Minsk's demographic profile, both in Belorussia and in Ukraine. The Jewish density of Minsk, but also of Gomel (30 percent Jewish), Berdichev (37 percent), Zhitomir (31 percent), Vinnitsa (35 percent), and even Kiev and Odessa (one-quarter and one-third Jewish, respectively),[16] fostered self-confidence and comfort about Jewish identity—a feeling that generally did not exist in the cities outside the erstwhile Pale.[17] In this demographic context, family ties and friendship networks made allegiance to Jewish identity more common and multifaceted. And while the most acculturated Jews, many of whom were largely indifferent to their Jewish background, left for Moscow or Leningrad in haste—usually without parents and relatives—the fairly more traditional Jews from the *shtetlekh* poured into the cities, "impacting the urban ecology of the Jewish population."[18] Combined with Jewish self-confidence, demographics yielded a less traumatic version of sovietization, as the centripetal forces of assimilation were countered, or at least tamed, by the centrifugal forces of a heavily Jewish city. In Minsk, as in so many other places, the path to sovietization did not involve a complete denial of or departure from Jewishness, but allowed for the possibility of retaining aspects of Jewish identity that might have otherwise been cast off in the acculturation process. Here, acting as a Jew and a Bolshevik could sometimes coexist, intersect, and harmoniously meet, as the making of Soviet Jews resulted not only from the violent changes introduced by the Communist project, but also by the largely overlooked, lines of continuity with pre-revolutionary forms of Jewish life.

Ruptures and Continuities

The brutality employed by the Bolsheviks to uproot the existing social order led Jewish historians to focus on the rupture that occurred after 1917 and to the ways of life, behaviors, and identities that the revolution persecuted and outlawed.[19] A new historiography emerged following the 1991 Soviet collapse. The opening of most Eurasian archives enabled scholars to take a glimpse in the middle, see what happened beyond destruction, verify the latitude existing in the midst of constraint, assess the importance of gray categories, which complement the black-and-white colors generated by the Cold War discourse, and shift the focus from what the system prevented to what it made possible.[20]

Integrating a discussion of continuities between pre-revolutionary and post-1917 life into the narrative of change, and analyzing the extent to which specific Jewish practices and beliefs persisted under the Soviets, sheds new light on the quandaries of the Jewish response to the Bolshevik experiment. Whether political, cultural, or religious in nature, Jewish particularity endured with different degrees of intensity, passion, and visibility during the interwar period.

Studies on the role and deeds of the Evsektsiia—the Jewish section of the Communist Party—acknowledged the tension between particularity and universalism underlying the Jewish path to sovietization.[21] With the responsibility of bringing the revolution to the

Jewish masses and destroying Jewish "bourgeois" religious and cultural institutions, the members of the new Jewish political establishment no longer appeared as blind bureaucrats who strove to hasten Jewish assimilation and destroy all expressions of Jewish particularity.[22] Rather, in their commitment to bring the revolution to the Jewish street, they also wished to preserve some aspects of its distinctive nature. Similarly, the members of the Soviet Jewish cultural establishment were much more concerned with producing a new Soviet Jewish culture than with rejecting completely pre-1917 Jewish canons and themes.[23]

However, not only members of the Soviet Jewish political and cultural elite experienced this tension. It affected most ordinary Jewish men and women, including workers, young students, mothers and daughters, former Bundists and Zionists, pedagogues and shopkeepers, rabbis and *shohtim* (religious slaughterers). For those who welcomed the changes introduced by the Bolsheviks, civil and political participation symbolized normalcy, security, self-esteem, and empowerment. For those Jews who, for political, cultural, or religious reasons, did not identify with the new regime, participation spewed from necessity, as rejection and social marginalization became harder and harder to bear. Daily life circumstances and practical concerns made participation—and thereby conforming one's behavior to the accepted rules of the new society—inevitable for Jews and non-Jews alike. Without participating, the likelihood of obtaining employment, a source of income, and supporting one's family grew slimmer. Even the members of the political and cultural underground organizations set up in the cities of the Soviet Union during the 1920s and early 1930s, conformed to Soviet behavior and became, at least to some degree, involved in building the system, as they struggled daily to combine Soviet and Jewish values in their lives. In other words, a wide range of possible behaviors existed vis-à-vis the Soviet system, fluctuating between active support and forced adjustment, deviance and defiance. Each behavior confirmed the individuals' ability to express social deviance in the face of a dominant ideology and repressive order. It was possible to participate in the system without giving full support to its values and principles, as a complex civil society—far from static and monolithic—continued to exist, stifled but not wiped out by the system.[24]

Structure of the Book

Each chapter of this book strives to accomplish two goals: first, to tell the "story" of Jewish continuities in the midst of the Bolshevik transformation of society; second, to dispel some well-established myths about the patterns of accommodation into the Soviet system experienced by most Jews in the interwar period. Chapter 1 recreates the historical, cultural, and socioeconomic profile of Jewish Minsk, from the origins of its Jewish settlement until the eve of the Bolsheviks' advent. Approaching the city from the context of its eighteenth- and nineteenth-century geocultural character as a Lithuanian Jewish city and locating it within the context of the geopolitical setting of tsarist Russia, it highlights some of its specific traits and recaptures the nature of its Jewish neighborhoods and inhabitants. It describes the city's century-long relationship with nearby Vilna and anticipates some of the tensions that surfaced between the two cities following the establishment of the Belorussian SSR and the shattering of long-standing Jewish cultural borders. As a prominent center of Jewish religious scholarship and Haskalah (Jewish enlightenment), not unlike other cities in the northwestern provinces of the Russian empire, Minsk saw the growing and relentless politicization of its Jewish residents during the late part of the nineteenth century. A stronghold of Jewish Socialism, Bundism, and different shades of radical Zionism, pre-revolutionary Minsk was not a cradle of Jewish traditionalism and tsarist oppression only. Many of its Jewish inhabitants (much more than its Belorussian counterparts) had entered a restive state long before the revolution came. This restlessness could only have intensified as Minsk became the theater of the stormy events of World War I, was occupied first by the German army and then by Polish troops, and lived through the fierce power struggles interspaced between the February and October revolutions and the Civil War.

Chapter 2 studies the early impact of sovietization on the Jewish street of the Belorussian capital. With higher levels of literacy and politicization compared to the Belorussians, Jews flowed into the new administrative, economic, and cultural sectors of Soviet society at a quicker pace and gained a special status in the city. But the successful acculturation into the new system of many weighed against the social marginalization of many others, who were pushed to the side or persecuted because of their social background and identity. At the same time, Jewish "bourgeois" institutions and organizations, with pre-revolutionary ideas, social networks, and modes of action endured during the 1920s. Jewish university students strove for acceptance and attempted to shake off the social stigma that they inherited from their parents' pre-revolutionary professions, or from their own pre-Bolshevik political affiliation. Most of them embraced the Soviets' appealing message of equality and acceptance for all through Communism. Underground support for Zionism among some members of the younger generation continued during the 1920s and occasionally into the early 1930s, albeit in small and declining numbers due to unyielding persecution. By the mid-1930s, Zionism ultimately gave way to the triumphant yearning to participate in the Bolshevik experiment, as only a minuscule number of Jews continued to support its ideals, even if they actively participated in the Soviet system.

Chapter 3 traces the continuities between the local Bundist tradition of Minsk and the city's Soviet Jewish political leadership. As former Bundists joined the Communist Party and moved into the ranks of the Evsektsiia—the new official overseer on the Jewish street—they attempted more often than not to balance their pre-revolutionary political identity and cultural heritage with their recently acquired Communist faith. The Bundist legacy found expression in their political strategies and cultural choices. As indicated by the Bolshevization of three Bundist institutions and icons—the Central Jewish Workers' Club, the Yiddish daily newspaper, and the legendary Jewish party hero Hirsh Lekert—pursuing Bundist strategies and preserving an ideological continuity with the party's past became rather common among the Communist Jewish elite. The entangled loyalty to Bundism and Bolshevism, and the subtle interplay between the city's political past and its Communist present, influenced the sovietization process of many ordinary Minsk Jews as well. Bundist local patriotism shaped the Bundist imprint on political and cultural tactics and goals. These ranged from a special and conspicuous commitment to Yiddish, to a new political and cultural rivalry between Jewish Minsk—the periphery—and Jewish Moscow—the center. Minsk's Jewish political leaders, literati, and cultural activists disregarded, or even disputed, the directives coming from Moscow, vying with the first city of the USSR for the title of capital of Soviet Jewry. A Soviet Jewish synthesis based on the Bundist tradition could however not be tolerated for long, and the option of maintaining a connection between sovietness and Bundism, as an expression of Jewishness, progressively gave way into the 1930s.

During the interwar period, Minsk grew to be one of the world capitals of Yiddish language and culture. With the support of Soviet nationality policy, the language assumed a position of public prominence that it had never enjoyed before. Chapter 4 maps out the main stages of the Yiddish experiment, or the Jewish *korenizatsiia* campaign to promote the use of the language in the spheres of bureaucracy, culture, education, and everyday life on the Jewish street. It considers the new public space in which Yiddish made its appearance weighing it against the status of the Belorussian language, and the campaign to support the use of Belorussian, and comparing it to Russian's "patrician" role of established literary and political language in Minsk. Enshrined in the Belorussian constitution, the new official status of Yiddish, together with the state support for Yiddish cultural, educational, and scholarly enterprises, turned the Belorussian capital into one of the most successful examples of the Yiddish experiment in the Soviet Union. Home to numerous new pedagogic, academic, and cultural institutions functioning in Yiddish, Minsk attracted hundreds of Jews from the cities and *shtetlekh* of the USSR eager to settle in a Soviet Jewish center and partake in Yiddish-language institutions. The Yiddish experiment was a quintessential product of the Bolshevik experiment and grew out of the Soviet nation-state building project, therefore producing, especially in its scholarly output, shades of artificiality. But the support for Yiddish also relied on solid preexisting foundations and was not entirely enforced top-to-bottom. The high proportion of Yiddish-speaking Jews, the deeply rooted Bundist tradition of the region, the relatively small size and provincial character of Minsk, the lack of support for the Belorussian language and the idiosyncratic character of Belorussian nationalism—were all factors that contributed to the relative success of the Yiddish experiment in Minsk, but also, as we will see, to its demise.

Chapter 5 studies the persistence of Jewish religious practices in different public, private, and secretive underground settings in the capital of the Belorussian SSR. Whether forced to adapt to the new system or eager to participate in it, many Soviet Jews combined in their lives deviant attitudes toward various aspects of religious observance and identification. Religious practices and customs deeply embedded in the daily life of the city often defied the Soviet's agenda of making a tabula rasa of the past and erase century-long traditions. Providing a religious education to one's child, attending synagogue, purchasing kosher meat, or circumcising one's newborn son not only depended on the intensity of antireligious persecution and discrimination. It also varied according to the individual's perseverance and ability to camouflage his or her compliance with religious tenets, as well as on the social networks in which he or she operated. A wide array of social and political forces and pressures—at times conflicting ones—contributed to the persistence or decline of Jewish religious practices. Some originated from the state, the party, and the workplace; others from friendship networks and family ties. Religious Jews—and Soviet citizens who were committed only to a number of Jewish rituals—could count on the support of other family members or city residents to abide by religious practices. While Soviet discrimination against Judaism made the observance of Jewish rituals more complicated, the number of Jews who participated in religious life, together with those who supported the institutions that made religious practice possible, remained remarkably high through the early 1930s. By contrast, the antireligious struggle of the Bolshevik policy mapped onto existing social, generational, and economic divides in the Jewish community that predated the revolution. Disputing rabbinical authority was not entirely uncommon before 1917. These existing tensions, combined with the official harassment of religious practice, led to the inevitable waning of religious life. By the second half of the 1930s, social networks and family ties, while not wiped out, were both loosened and reconfigured. Jewish identity moved increasingly away from religious authority and normative Orthodox Judaism and took on a new "ethnic" imprint, as the sovietization of the second postrevolutionary generation began to bear real fruit.

By focusing on the ways in which one specific group of Jews negotiated between Communism and Jewish identity, Chapter 6 chronicles the distinctive path to sovietization of Jewish women. The modus operandi of the Minsk Communist agencies responsible for drawing Jewish women to the revolution, and the strategies they envisioned to solve "the women's question," provide evidence of the many challenges Jewish women faced when attempting to modernize according to Bolshevik guidelines. A wide range of responses to and patterns of participation in the Bolshevik experiment marked their experience in the new Soviet system. These were also shaped by the different visions that men and women held of Jewish women's path to sovietization and integration into Bolshevik society. These visions influenced the gender discourse on the Jewish street and affected the shifting roles that women came to play in the political, cultural, and social life of the city. Female empowerment, which would have been a natural outgrowth of the Soviets' commitment to gender equality, eventually met and collided with male empowerment, as Jewish men began to view the "new Soviet Jewish woman" as a dangerous threat to their status. Male anxiety enhanced the tension between the public and private spheres of women's lives, a strain that had first emerged during the latter part of the nineteenth century, albeit at a much smaller scale. Beyond the specific gender context of the Zhenotdel, or Women's Department of the Communist Party, which generated a new elite of Soviet Jewish women in the 1920s, only a small proportion of Jewish women held positions of power and responsibility in party organs and Jewish institutions during the 1930s. Without rising to positions of leadership, a large number of Jewish women still contributed significantly to the sovietization of the Jewish street. But the tension between their public role as "agents of revolution" and their role as mothers and wives who guarded the hearth grew exponentially. In particular, the tension was deepened by the largely unsympathetic, or at least indifferent, attitude of male Jewish party members, who in light of Stalin's patriarchal views of female duties of the late 1930s, tended to ascribe to Jewish women traditionally "bourgeois" roles.

Finally, Chapter 7 recaptures Jewish ordinary life and manifestations of identity in the late 1930s, at the height of Stalin's Great Terror. The existence in Minsk of compact Jewish neighborhoods, combined with the ongoing influx of *shtetl* residents and the role of Yiddish in the public sphere, contributed to the preservation of an intensive Jewish ethnic identity. Despite the violence and thoroughness with which the purges impinged on the Jewish street, they did not constitute the end of Jewish life. The Terror's vigor, enhanced by the geopolitical character of the city (and the Belorussian SSR in general), wiped out the bulk of the Jewish cultural elite and institutions in Minsk, perhaps more than anywhere else in the Soviet Union. But the Terror mostly affected the party, professional and intellectual leadership. Furthermore, the knowledge of what was happening to Jews in "fascist" Poland and Nazi Germany in the late 1930s, combined with the awareness of the absence of official anti-Semitism in the Soviet Union, sustained Jewish self-confidence and built up the self-perception that Soviet Jews embodied the true vanguard of world Jewry. As never before, the seemingly opposite factors of Soviet patriotism and commitment to Jewishness converged rather harmoniously. Elapsed continuities of solidarity with other Jewries also resurfaced during the late 1930s. The sense of Jewish commonality and fellow-feeling that had distinguished pre-revolutionary life emerged once again. As Jews looked toward the West with growing concern, they experienced the forgotten sense of belonging to world Jewry as a whole.

A Note on Sources

This study of Soviet Jewish life in Minsk is based on a wide range of sources and documents from archives and libraries in Minsk, Moscow, Jerusalem, and New York. In order to reconstruct Minsk Jewry's profile during the interwar period, providing quantitative and qualitative data as well as details about everyday life, I used primarily autobiographies, correspondence, memoirs, personal accounts, statistics, party-cell minutes, and meeting proceedings. Soviet archival sources about (or by) Jews become flimsier during the second part of the 1930s: the national category "Jew," which appears consistently during the 1920s, fades away from most official documents. This was most likely determined by the Soviets' confidence that the "Jewish question" had been solved, as well as by the 1930 liquidation of the body in charge of recording the different aspects of the sovietization process of the Jews—the Evsektsiia. The gap in sources also grows out of the almost complete destruction of the city at the hands of the Germans during World War II (and the burning of thousands of documents that the Soviets failed to evacuate to the East before the Wehrmacht set foot in the city). To meet the challenge of recapturing Jewish life in the 1930s especially, I have relied extensively on interviews as well as on the Soviet official press. With very few exceptions, I have refrained from using interviews conducted in the twenty-first century: the rendition of the events by the informants would be obfuscated not only by the trauma of war and loss, but also by the test of time. When possible, I preferred using interviews conducted in the late 1960s and early 1970s (and occasionally 1980s), housed in the Yad Vashem Archives and, more often, in the Oral History Division of the Hebrew University's Institute for Contemporary Jewry in Jerusalem. Some of these interviews, albeit in their abridged translated version, were included in the encyclopaedic memorial book (*yizker bukh*) titled *Minsk ir va-em* (Minsk, city and mother) compiled in the aftermath of the Holocaust to memorialize the Jews of Minsk and edited by Shlomo Even-Shoshan and David Cohen, both natives of Minsk who left the city for Palestine in the mid-1920s. As a rule, I made use of the original version of the interviews rather than their abridged published texts. I have tried to be very cautious and critical in my reading of the local Soviet press—in particular, the Yiddish newspaper *Oktyabr*, the only Jewish daily issued in Minsk throughout the interwar period. Like all official party publications it is swamped in the quagmire of Soviet propaganda and party-line style and content, but a careful reading of it can elicit details about Jewish life in the late 1930s unattainable through other sources.

A Note on Transliteration

I have transliterated most foreign words according to the Library of Congress system for Hebrew, Russian, and Belorussian. The names of famous personalities are spelled as they are commonly used in English (for example, Maxim Gorky, not Gorkii, and Dubnow, rather than Dubnov). Yiddish words are romanized according to the system established by the YIVO Institute for Jewish Research. Well-known personalities, such as Mendele Mocher Seforim, are spelled as they are usually spelled in English, without reference to the YIVO rules of transliteration. All foreign words are transliterated without diacritic marks. I have chosen to use the simplified version for the transliteration of Belorussia (and Belorussian), over Byelorussia (and Byelorussian). All translations are mine unless otherwise indicated.

1 Historical Profile of an Eastern European Jewish City

In Eudoxia, which spreads both upward and down, with winding alleys, steps, dead ends, hovels, a carpet is preserved in which you can observe the city's true form. At first sight nothing seems to resemble Eudoxia less than the design of that carpet, laid out in symmetrical motives whose patterns are repeated along straight and circular lines. ... But if you pause and examine it carefully, you become convinced that each place in the carpet corresponds to a place in the city and all the things contained in the city are included in the design, arranged according to their true relationship, which escapes your eye distracted by the bustle, the throngs, the shoving. ... An oracle was questioned about the mysterious bond between two objects so dissimilar as the carpet and the city. One of the two objects–the oracle replied–has the form the gods gave the starry sky and the orbits in which the worlds resolve; the other is an approximate reflection, like every human creation. ... But you could ... come to the opposite conclusion: that the true map of the universe is the city of Eudoxia, just as it is, a stain that spreads out shapelessly, with crooked streets, houses that crumble one upon the other amid clouds of dust, fires, screams in the darkness.[1]

In the Beginning

Home to Polish aristocrats and landlords, Jewish merchants and artisans, Russian-Orthodox and Uniate (Greek Catholic) merchants, and a small community of European Muslims, or Tatars, Minsk was located in the heart of Belorussia, the region enclosed by historic Russia to the northeast, Lithuania to the northwest, Ukraine to the south, and Poland to the west. Over the centuries, the city moved across geopolitical borders, which resulted in altering its geocultural profile. Part of the Grand Duchy of Lithuania since the fourteenth century, the city was incorporated into the Russian empire at the end of the eighteenth century. It rested surrounded by villages and rural settlements inhabited primarily by Orthodox peasants who spoke Belorussian, and Jewish merchants and artisans who spoke Yiddish. While the official documents of the Grand Duchy of Lithuania were drafted in Old Eastern Slavonic, or Ruthenian (a predecessor of modern Belorussia), under Polish-Lithuanian rule Polish became the official language used by the aristocracy and royal administrators in Minsk. When the tsar stepped in, in 1793, Russian replaced Polish as the linguistic medium employed by the new government's bureaucracy. Built by the Poles in the fourteenth century, inhabited by the Jews since the sixteenth century, and administered by the Russians since the late eighteenth century, until the end of the nineteenth century the streets of Minsk echoed mostly with Polish, Yiddish, and Russian.

The Minsk Jewish community dated back to the early sixteenth century, when Polish King Stefan Batory granted a few Jewish families their first charter allowing them to trade within the city limits in exchange for liquid assets.[2] Mostly engaged in tax collection, lease-holding, and handicrafts, from the beginning Jews played a prominent role in the city's commercial life. Not unlike the rest of early modern Europe, however, their prosperity depended on their competition with the local Christian merchants, who pressured the king to invalidate the charter rights. In a few instances the king gave into the demands of the local Orthodox population. But practical judgment and economic profit ultimately guided his decision concerning the status of the Jewish population. Throughout the seventeenth century, the Polish-Lithuanian crown granted the Jewish community permission to buy land for a cemetery, acquire real estate on the city market square, and engage in commerce without noticeable restrictions.[3] When the merchants of the bigger and wealthier Jewish community of Brisk (Brest-Litovsk) (which had jurisdiction over the Minsk Jewish community in religious and fiscal affairs) tried to prevent Minsk Jews from attending the fair in Mir—a major commercial hub at the time—King Jan III personally intervened and ruled in favor of the Minsk merchants. This unusual case of the crown meddling with internal Jewish affairs reflects the extent to which Minsk Jewish businessmen served the king's interests in the region during the seventeenth century.[4]

Statistics from the eighteenth and nineteenth centuries confirm the economic standing of the Minsk Jewish community. In 1797, 10,625 Jews (and 7,008 Russian Orthodox) belonged to the urban lower-middle-class social estate (*meshchane*) and engaged in small trade and commerce; 322 Jewish merchants (and 226 Russian merchants) engaged in wholesale trade in the city.[5] In mid-nineteenth century, 253 Jewish merchants in Minsk (and only 10 non-Jewish merchants) belonged to the third merchant guild.[6] In 1886, 88 percent of the merchants living in the city and district of Minsk were Jewish.[7] Besides controlling almost entirely the lumber trade in the Minsk Province (*guberniia*), Jews owned some of the largest factories in the city, including the Botvinnik and Ashkenazi glass factory, the Karlip and Ginzburg tobacco factory, the Lekert brewery, and the Kaplan, Tasman, and Grinblat typographies. This was a noteworthy accomplishment given the lack of industrial resources and general economic backwardness of the Belorussian region.

Following the 1793 second partition of Poland, and its incorporation into the Russian empire, the city became the capital of the Minsk Province and grew into an urban center of sizeable political importance. It became a Russian administrative center, home to tsarist deputies and officers. The city also grew into an important bureaucratic center for the supervision of Russian Jewry: here, state officials argued over the different paths to the solution to the so-called Jewish Question in the northwestern provinces of the empire.[8] The geopolitical transformation of the region also generated a change in status of the Russian language. Following the 1831 and 1863 Polish revolts, the northwestern provinces of Minsk, Vilna, Grodno, and Kovno were exposed to an efficient—and at times violent—Russification campaign intended to stifle the Polish independence movement and its local supporters.[9] Sponsoring the use of Russian in lieu of Polish, tsarist functionaries hoped to ensure the political loyalty of the Minsk population to the Russian empire.

The shift from Polish to Russian as the language of the political and cultural life of the city affected the Jewish population as well. With such a high proportion of Jews concentrated in the region's urban centers, Russian authorities were forced to address the Jewish population as part of their political schemes. From the end of the eighteenth century to the end of the nineteenth century, the number of Jews living in the city had constantly grown, increasing from 1,322 in 1776, to 12,976 in 1847 and 47,562 in 1897, or 52.3 percent of the city population.[10] Expecting Jews to be pragmatic and shift to the language of those in power, tsarist bureaucrats hoped to turn them into rivals of the Polish independence movement and supporters of Russian language and culture in the northwest.

This policy was relatively successful in the Jewish milieu.[11] While the bulk of the Minsk Jewish community was trilingual—Yiddish being its spoken language, Hebrew its written one, and Russian, instead of Polish, the language used to communicate with the surrounding non-Jewish population—a number of Jews started using Russian only. They were significant not in their number but in their influence and wealth. By the end of the nineteenth century numerous Jewish institutions, societies, and philanthropic organizations of the growing urban bourgeoisie operated primarily in Russian. These included a private modern school, an elementary school, two dental schools, a trade school for boys and girls, a library, an agricultural farm, a hospital, and the local branches of the Society for the Promotion of Enlightenment Among the Jews of Russia OPE (Obshchestvo dlia rasprostraneniia prosveshcheniia mezhdu evreiami) and the Society for the Protection of the Health of the Jews OZE (Obshchestvo zdravookhraneniia evreev). When comparing Minsk to Vilna, Daniel Charny—brother of the distinguished literary critic Shmuel Niger—underscored Minsk's "Russianness." "Minsk was always 'half Yiddish and half Russian,'" wrote Charny, "[so much so that] a Jew from Vilna would feel in Minsk almost like a foreigner, . . . as if he was staying in a hotel, where it's good to spend the night only."[12]

The linguistic Russification and embourgeoisement of certain sectors of the Jewish community of Minsk, in particular its commercial and entrepreneurial elite, led to acculturation, social interaction with the Russian officialdom sent in from Russia proper, and, in some cases, even conversion to Russian Orthodoxy. Born in Bobruisk in 1833, in a traditionally observant Jewish family, Pauline Wengeroff married a successful tax-farmer from Minsk, who in 1871 became vice director of the Commercial Bank in the city. Chonon Afanasii Wengeroff became such a prominent figure that following the assassination of Alexander II in 1881 he was the only Minsk resident besides the city mayor to be invited to St. Petersburg to lay a wreath on the grave of the deceased tsar.[13] The Wengeroffs, who in the words of Pauline led a "well-to-do and elegant life in Minsk," were also very active in the local Jewish community: with the help of Rabbi Chaneles and contributions by wealthy local Jews, they founded a Russian-language vocational school for Jewish boys and a Russian-language trade school for Jewish girls, supported by the Jewish Ladies' Club of Minsk.[14] In spite of this commitment to Jewish communal life, when writing her memoirs in the first decade of the twentieth century, Pauline lamented the rampant assimilation in her household and her children's conversion to Christianity. One became a well-known scholar of Russian literature; one the owner of a preserves factory; and one a celebrated pianist.[15]

The majority of Minsk Jews were, however, craftsmen (primarily shoemakers, tailors, hatters, and turners), small traders, and members of the growing Jewish proletariat, typically employed as skilled workers in light industry, carpentry, and blacksmith workshops. The proportion of Jews engaged in shoemaking, tailoring, carpentry, and turnery in the city reached 71.2 percent at the end of the century.[16] Most of them lived in poverty. When visiting Minsk in the early 1880s, the Russian economist Andrei Subbotin described the abject life conditions of the Jewish poor of Yatke and Shlos Streets, and of the Komorovke, Blote, and Liakhovke neighborhoods (as they were known in Yiddish), "who tasted bread and butter only in their dreams, ate potatoes and onions throughout the week, and like most inhabitants of the Pale suffered from protein deficiency because of the higher price of kosher meat."[17] Most of the members of the Jewish working force attended synagogue, sent their children to a traditional Jewish elementary school, or *heder*, and were predominantly Yiddish-speaking. Only a thousand Minsk Jews, or 2 percent of the total Jewish population of 47,562, did not declare Yiddish their mother tongue in 1897. This proportion was almost half of that in the rest of the Russian empire.[18]

The modest urbanization and industrialization process that swept through Russia during the nineteenth century left a mark on Minsk as well, as the city assumed some of the aesthetic traits of a modern city. By the early 1890s, Count Chapskii, mayor of the city at the time, introduced trolley cars, built a slaughterhouse, and had a number of streets paved.[19] Minsk had two main train stations—the Brest Station and the Vilna Station—not too busy and located in small wooden buildings.[20] With their passenger and freight cars heading to and coming from Moscow, they connected Russia with the northwestern regions of Lithuania and Poland.[21] The publicist and traveler Shpilevskii—who wrote extensively for the periodical *Sovremennik* (The contemporary)—described Minsk as "one of the biggest and most beautiful cities of Western Russia. Thanks to the commodities and the reconstruction work carried out after the 1835 fire . . . , Minsk can be considered the capital of Belorussia. It is bigger and more stylish than Mohilev and Vitebsk."[22]

In Shpilevskii's description, most buildings were made of brick and had tiled roofs, and most streets were paved and tidy. Walking through the streets of Minsk in the mid-nineteenth century, visitors would have noticed the groves and alleys of the city garden, the building of the New Market (Novyi rynok), with its squared boulevard, post office, and Lutheran church; the High Market's square (Vysokii rynok) with its Russian Orthodox and Catholic churches, Bernardine monastery and bazaar; and finally, the Low Market (Nizkii rynok), where the City Hospital, with its oval shape of a "Greek temple" stood.[23] The most modern section of the city was the New Market, or New Place. Here, city residents had access to imported goods from Vilna, Odessa, Moscow, and Warsaw, together with the local goods produced in the Minsk clothing and shoe workshops, "praised throughout Belorussia and exported to Kiev during the winter."[24] Book dealers from Moscow would come to this section of the city, where the Minsk public library stood, and furnish local bookshops, well-supplied with Polish, French, and German books, with the latest Russian publications. The city's leisure institutions were clustered in the High Market: the casino, which hosted parties during the Carnival, the theaters, the acrobatic performances, the inns, coffee houses, and the most popular restaurant of all, Fogel and Tsybulskii.[25]

Besides overemphasizing the quintessential Russian Orthodox character of the city and, at the same time, downplaying its Polish and Catholic past, Shpilevskii acknowledged, with a hint of regret, the Jewishness of Minsk. Not devoid of the anti-Jewish prejudice typical of nineteenth-century Russian conservatives, his vivid portrayal dwelled on the Low Market, also known as the Old City (Staryi gorod). This was the city's main Jewish quarter, dominated by the Jewish square, its small businesses, and on the Sabbath, the distinctive odors of the holiday meal.[26] The High Market was also overwhelmingly Jewish: the residence of wealthy Jewish merchants who traded in clothing and silk, and the site of the first Jewish state school established in the city. Situated next to the cathedral, at the corner between Bernardinskii and Sobornyi Streets, the school was inaugurated in 1845 thanks to the initiative of some of the most prominent Jews of Minsk as well as the support of civil authorities. Despite the staunch opposition of the local Orthodox establishment, which in 1841 had forced out of the city through "curses and snowballs" the *maskil* Max Lilienthal for trying to establish a Jewish state school, the Haskalah dream of secular education was eventually realized.[27] The Ministry of Education introduced Russian and arithmetic into the school's curriculum, and Minsk became one of the most prominent Haskalah centers in the northwestern provinces of the Russian empire.[28]

The demographic nature of Minsk contributed to its perception as a Jewish city. Although the publicist Shpilevskii did not explicitly call Minsk a "Jewish city," the reader of his essay is left with the impression of a city inhabited primarily by Jews. With their merchandise, their Sabbath, their streets, and their institutions, Jews—and not Russians, Poles, or Tatars—seemed to dominate the city landscape. Pauline Wengeroff captured a snapshot of Minsk's Jewishness in the late nineteenth century: Walking through a busy street at the time of the 1881–82 pogroms that devastated the Jewish

Figure 1. Map of the Jewish Pale of Settlement, ca. 1900.

communities of the empire, her husband Chonon suddenly heard someone shout "Jew, get off the sidewalk!"

> As he turned around he saw a Russian, his face full of hatred. The street was crowded with Jews. One man lifted his cane and called out to the anti-Semite, "What are you thinking of, to speak like that, to speak so scornfully? The street is free for everyone." In a moment the anti-Semite was surrounded by furious Jews. He disappeared very quickly.[29]

The city's demographic nature countered therefore the gravity of anti-Semitic incidents. Sometime in the 1910s, Leybush Rozenbaum attended a State Gymnasium in Minsk, where a significant proportion of students was Jewish (fifteen out of forty in his class), while most teachers were not. The math teacher, of German background, once asked Leybush why he refused to answer when called upon. The student explained that his name was not Lev (the Russian version of his name)—as the teacher called him—but Leyb (a Jewish name). The teacher replied that such name did not exist, especially in written form, to which Leybush retorted "check my birth records and you will see that my name is Leyb." The math teacher kicked him out of the classroom. As Leybush recounted the incident at home, a heated discussion broke out between his parents: while the father advised moving him into a Jewish gymnasium, the mother favored going to battle with the anti-Semites. It was eventually her position that prevailed. The father went to school with his son's birth records as proof of the name and demanded from the school administration that he be called only Leyb.[30]

On the eve of World War I, 51.9 percent of the 102,000 inhabitants of Minsk were Jewish.[31] Upon his arrival in Minsk in 1915, Saul Liberman, the distinguished Talmud scholar born near Pinsk in 1898, noticed, "[It] made the impression of a large city where everyone was Jewish. I had not yet seen such a Jewish city." He recalled a hot summer day, strolling with his elderly uncle—a rabbi from the nearby *shtetl* of Lohoisk—in Minsk's Old City on a narrow street known in Yiddish as Tsvishn di kromen (Amongst the Stores). Because of the heat and the small number of customers, the shopkeepers were sitting outside their stores and chatting. As his uncle approached the shops, one by one the shopkeepers stood up and, out of respect for the rabbi, formed around him a long line "as if they were soldiers." "I had never seen anything like that anywhere else. This was a rabbi they did not know, but recognizing him as such, because of his garments and appearance, they . . . remained standing until he crossed the street."[32]

Remapping the Geocultural Character of a Lithuanian Jewish City

Located in the heart of the Pale of Settlement, Minsk lay 160 kilometers southwest of Vilna, capital of the Lithuanian Grand-Duchy until 1791. Since the sixteenth century Vilna had developed into an important cultural and commercial center in Eastern Europe and into the cultural and religious hub of Jewish Eastern Europe. "As far as Jewish population goes, Vilna occupies a second position compared to Odessa or

Warsaw," wrote a Jewish historian in the early twentieth century, "[But] as far as . . . its historical role of cultural and religious center . . . which has existed for more than four centuries, Vilna occupies the first place."³³ Known for its rabbinic scholars, in particular the Vilna Gaon, Elijah of Vilna, chief opponent of Hasidism, Vilna became the symbol of Litvaks, cold, rationalist and *maskilic* Jews.

Minsk also developed in the *litvish* (Lithuanian) tradition, favoring the analytical and rationalist approach to Jewish lore over the mystical one endorsed by Hasidic rebbes, generally more rooted in the southern provinces of Poland and Russia. In the course of the seventeenth and eighteenth centuries, the city turned into a well-known center of religious scholarship, competing in fame with other major Torah centers in Eastern Europe. Yehiel Heilprin, a distinguished Talmudist, cabbalist, and author of historical chronicles, moved to Minsk and taught in the city's first yeshiva. In 1733, the Talmudist Aryeh Leyb b. Asher Ginzberg, author of the treatise *Shaagat Aryeh* (The roar of the lion—Bialystok, 1805), established the second yeshiva in Minsk. At the end of the nineteenth century, Jeroham Judah Leib Perelman, known as "the great scholar of Minsk" (Minsker godl) served as a rabbi in Blumkes kloyz, which housed one of the largest yeshivas in Minsk.³⁴ Of the eighty-three synagogues, houses of prayer, and *minyonim* in Minsk at the end of the nineteenth century, only three were Hasidic.³⁵ Minsk developed in the same cultural tradition as Vilna not only in its approach to religious scholarship. The success of the Haskalah and of Socialist-oriented movements was also a specific trait of the Lithuanian region. At the end of the nineteenth century, Minsk became one of the largest centers of Jewish Socialism (Bundism and Socialist-Zionism alike) in the Russian empire.

Daniel Charny also captured the close, but at the same time, hierarchical relationship existing between the two Jewish cities referring in his memoirs to the popular Yiddish expression "*A shtub mit a kamer.*"³⁶ Meaning "a house with a chamber" (the house being Vilna and the chamber Minsk), the phrase denoted the supremacy of Vilna over Minsk, but also the interdependence and familiarity between these two historic Jewish centers. Such hierarchy emerged from Vilna's prestige as a cultural and political center in the world of Polish-Lithuanian and later Russian Jewry. Vilna served as the center of Jewish book-printing in the region, housing one of the most important Jewish typographies in Eastern Europe, the Romm typography, founded in 1795. Vilna was the hometown of the Vilna Gaon, who, by the time of his death in 1797, was already a legendary figure overshadowing the fame of other Jewish scholars and Talmudists from the northwestern provinces. Minsk, by contrast, was not a traditional center of Hebrew and Yiddish printing, and although it was the native town of many renowned scholars, their fame could not even begin to compete with that of the Vilna Gaon. In the words of Rabbi Shimon Yakov Gliksberg, a student of Jeroham Judah Leib Perelman, "When compared to Vilna, Minsk was considered the second city," its fame obscured by Vilna's reputation.³⁷ This hierarchical relationship stemmed also from the different level of economic growth in the two cities. Unlike Vilna, which was the largest commercial center of the northwestern region, Minsk was surrounded by a poor agricultural area and a few industrial structures of no major commercial importance.

The geopolitical status of Minsk—a Polish-Lithuanian city in the sixteenth century with a small Jewish settlement and the capital of a Russian province in the eighteenth and nineteenth centuries with the fourth-largest Jewish community in the Pale of Settlement—changed once again during the second decade of the twentieth century. The end of World War I and the Bolshevik Revolution resulted in the creation of new borders that broke up the territories of the Russian empire, dividing and transforming preexistent cultural and political landscapes. Historic Lithuania, home of Lithuanian Jewry, was divided in three distinct political entities. The northern provinces constituted themselves into an independent Lithuanian state, with Kaunas (Kovno) its capital city; the Vilna (Wilno) region was incorporated into the newly restored Poland; and the southeastern district became Soviet and was called the Belorussian Soviet Socialist Republic, with Minsk its capital. The partition of Lita and the lack of diplomatic ties among the three states had a strong impact on Jewish cultural geography leading to the rise of new Jewish centers and generating new perceptions of Jewish regional identities.

As the capital of a Soviet republic, Minsk became one of the main centers in Soviet Jewish life, and in some respects a much more vital center than it had ever been in prerevolutionary Russia. The change of status altered the city's relationship with Vilna, on whose periphery Jewish Minsk had developed for centuries. The severing of the link between the two cities led Minsk to develop different cultural endeavors independently, no longer as a "second city." By becoming part of "fascist" Poland, Vilna lost, at least in part, its value as a positive cultural reference point for Jews in Minsk and was replaced by Moscow, the political heart of the new Soviet system. The geopolitical transformation of the region gave rise to a new relationship between Minsk and Moscow, the latter being not only the new capital of the Soviet Union, but also, for the first time, the administrative and, at least in title, cultural center of Russian Jewry.

On the Road to Revolution: 1890–1920

By the end of the nineteenth century modern political ideologies had penetrated large sections of the Jewish communities of Russia, promoting the rise of radical social and political visions among many Jews. During the first decade of the twentieth century newly established Jewish parties, committed to solving the "Jewish question" and, at the same time, improving Russian society, attracted loyal supporters from across the socioeconomic spectrum of the Jewish community. If in absolute terms the most successful political movement was Zionism, the support for Socialism was particularly strong among the Jews of the northwestern regions of the Russian empire. This was not only because of the demographic nature of the region, which included a higher proportion of Jews in the workforce than Ukraine or Poland did, where most of the proletariat was Christian. But also because leading Jewish Socialists in Lithuania and Belorussia were less assimilated, and thus more likely to be sensitive to the needs of the Jewish masses, than it was elsewhere where they tended to be active in the Russian milieu.[38]

Minsk became a stronghold for the activities of Jewish radical groups and played a pioneering role in spreading Socialism through the region. Led by Michael Rabinovitsh-Charny, who later migrated to America and became active in the labor-oriented organization *Arbeter Ring* (Workmen's circle), the very first campaign of Socialist propaganda to address Jewish workers was held in Minsk in the 1870s.[39] Members of the Jewish intelligentsia were reading and studying about Socialism already in the 1880s. When Vilna overtook Minsk as the center of Jewish radicalism in the 1890s (especially at the time of the establishment of the Jewish Labor Party Bund in 1897), a tense rivalry developed between the Socialist groups in the two cities. As the Vilner turned to creating a mass movement, the Minsker formed an opposition to its methods and tactics. One of the leaders of the so-called Minsk opposition, Abraham Liessin (born in Minsk in 1872), also thought that Jewish Socialism should reject the "cosmopolitan" view embraced by most Jewish radicals in Vilna and favor a more "national" approach, which merged a passion for Socialism with a profound connection to Jewish history.[40] Before leaving for New York in the late 1890s, and eventually becoming the editor of the Yiddish literary and political journal *Di Tsukunft* (The future), Liessin served as an inspiration and guide to a generation of future Bundists in the city.

One of the first political hectographs in Yiddish, *Arbeter bletl* (The worker's leaflet), was issued in Minsk in mid-1897;[41] and one of the first underground typographies in tsarist Russia was set up in the city. Here, the Minsk Bund Committee published its organ *Der minsker arbeter* (The Minsk worker). In 1897, one thousand Jewish workers in Minsk were politically organized and active in underground Bundist circles (in Vilna they were fourteen hundred; in Bialystok, a thousand).[42] At the Sixth Congress of the Socialist International, held in Amsterdam in August 1904, the Minsk Bund Committee represented twelve hundred Jewish workers from the city. While the figure was significantly lower than the number of Jewish workers represented by the Vilna Committee (three thousand), it was higher than the one represented by the Bialystok (seven hundred) and Lodz (one thousand) committees, and equaled the number of Jewish workers from Warsaw (twelve hundred; with a Jewish population of 277,787).[43] On the Bund's initiative, the founding congress of the Russian Socialist Democratic Party (RSDP) was convened in Minsk in 1898. It took place at the location of the Bund's Central Committee, recently transferred to Minsk because of the mounting anti-Socialist crackdown and arrests in Vilna.[44] During 1903–5 Minsk became therefore a prominent site of political demonstrations, meetings in synagogues, protests against the wave of anti-Jewish pogroms, arrests, strikes in factories, and terrorist assaults on local authorities. This opposition movement was largely coordinated by the Bund. In its attempt to reach out to the religious constituency and sway to the Socialist cause as many yeshiva students as possible, local Bundist activists issued propaganda brochures in Hebrew as well—and not only in Russian or Yiddish, which was standard Bundist practice—and smuggled them into the Minsk yeshivas.[45]

While the Bund had an impressive grasp over the Minsk region, overall, Zionist parties wielded the greatest influence in the city. With the goal of purchasing land in Palestine, Kibbuts Niddehei Israel (Ingathering of Jewish Exiles) was organized in Minsk in 1882, alongside with groups of Hovovei Zion (Lovers of Zion). The young Nachman Syrkin, a native of Belorussia and one of the future founding fathers of Socialist-Zionism, moved with his family to Minsk in 1884. Here, as a gymnasium student, he joined the local branch of Hovovei Zion that was quickly gaining popularity in the city.[46] By the end of the nineteenth century Minsk became one of the largest centers of Labour Zionism in Russia. The Zionist Workers' Movement (Poale-Zion, or Workers of Zion) emerged in different Russian cities in the 1890s; the first group was established in Minsk in 1897 (the party was formally established by Ber Borochov in Poltava in 1906). Here it produced a specific local version, or "Minsker Tolk" (Minsk School), of Poale-Zion, which, in opposition to the later Poltava period under Ber Borochov's leadership, rejected the social-political struggle in Russia and downplayed the role of class conflict among Jews in the diaspora. The first convention of the Zionist Labor organizations in tsarist Russia was held in Minsk, in late 1901.[47]

In August 1902, with the permission of the Russian Ministry of Internal Affairs, the Second Conference of Russian Zionists convened in Minsk. A total of 526 delegates from all over Russia participated. The well-known Minsk lawyer and Zionist activist Semyon Rozenbaum, who arranged the permit to convene the conference, and who was later elected as the Minsk province deputy to the First Russian Duma (1906), gave the opening speech. At the time of Herzl's Uganda proposal to create a Jewish homeland in East Africa (1903), Rozenbaum—who lived in Minsk until 1915—held speeches at his home as well as in the city's synagogues attacking the territorialist supporters of this plan. In one instance, at the Tailor's Synagogue on Yatka Street, the Jewish lawyer spoke in favor of the Jewish National Fund (established in 1901 to purchase land in Palestine for Jewish settlements). Here, he explained with great passion how average Jews could raise funds to purchase land in Palestine: "If every Jew offered what he spends on tobacco; if every Jewish woman offered what she splurges on feathers for her hats; and if every worshipper offered what he pays for decorations on his *tallit* . . . with these millions of rubles we could buy all the land of Palestine."[48]

Chanan Goldberg, who became one of the founders of the Minsk Zionist radical group Ha-poel He-haluts (The Working Pioneer), described his path to Zionism during the 1910s. Upon graduating from the Minsk Jewish gymnasium in 1912, he made contact with some local Zionist leaders and went from reading only the Russian classics Lermontov and Pushkin to becoming acquainted with the nationalist-oriented Russian Jewish writer Sh. Frug and reading Bialik in Russian and Yiddish translations. During World War I, he began to study Hebrew and check out Hebrew books from the Minsk Central Library. He attended meetings organized by Dov Ber Malkin, a war refugee from the Minsk Province, who spoke about Yiddish literature and Zionism, and who always carried with him three books, one in Russian, one in Yiddish, and one in Hebrew. He also joined the informal gatherings held on the Sabbath in the home of Eliezer Kaplan (who would eventually become the first finance minister of the state of Israel). Here Kaplan spoke in Yiddish about Zionism. At times, young Bundists and Socialist-Zionists, who lived in the same poor neighborhood of Komorovka, would walk to the city center and have fun together. But most times, the young members of the two Socialist parties came to blows or disrupted each other's meetings in the city. At the time of Lenin's 1917 coup, during a gathering of the Yugend-Bund (Young Bund) held near the Governor's House, Chanan suddenly took the floor and criticized the Jewish labor party.[49]

Zionist groups won significantly at the elections to the Russian Constituent Assembly, organized following the events of the 1917 Russian revolution and held in November 1917: in the Minsk *guberniia* the Jewish nationalist coalition made of Zionist and religious parties obtained 65,046 votes against the 11,064 of Jewish Socialists.[50] The forty-one delegates to the Conference of Jewish Soldiers on the Western front, held in Minsk in late 1917, included twenty-one general Zionists, ten Poale-Zionists, one Bolshevik, and five Bundists; the elected Western Front Committee included four general Zionists, two Poale-Zionists, and one Bundist.[51] The 1918 elections to the council of the Minsk *kehillah*, the legal body of the local Jewish community, also resulted in a Zionist victory: Zionist groups accumulated a total of 53 percent of the votes, whereas the Bund reached only 20 percent.[52] The Bund's proposal that Jewish schools no longer be under the jurisdiction of the Jewish community but be managed by the municipality was among the reasons for its defeat.[53]

Despite its distance from the revolutionary centers of Petrograd and Moscow, Minsk also became the theater of stormy events and fierce power struggles during the months between February 1917 and the October revolution. Excitement, unrest, and fear quickly spread through the city. A Jewish worker in a local printing factory remarked that joy and panic simultaneously seized his fellow workers as reports about the February revolution reached Minsk. While most workers cheered the revolution, many initially refused out of fear to participate in the demonstrations in favor of Lenin scheduled to take place in Minsk. Eventually, as support for the revolution grew, fear subsided, and workers' demonstrations moved from the factory kitchen to the city theater, and onto the street.[54]

Taking advantage of freedom of speech, press, and assembly introduced by the Provisional Government (brought into power by the revolution of February 1917) Zionists issued in Minsk the Yiddish weekly *Dos yidishe vort* (The Jewish word), the Yiddish biweekly *Der yid* (The Jew), and the Russian-language publication of the Zionist youth group, He-haver. On the other end of the political spectrum, the Bund consolidated its position through the support of prominent local leaders. In June 1917, it issued the party's central organ, the Yiddish daily *Der veker* (The alarm), and the organ of the local section of the youth organization Yugend-Bund, the Yiddish journal *Der yunger arbeter* (The young worker). In the fall of 1917, Minsk held the official celebration for the twentieth anniversary of the Bund's establishment, with concerts, plays, a public session of the Central Committee, and a street demonstration.[55]

Despite the absence of a strong Bolshevik faction at the time of the February revolution, and the appearance of a separate Bolshevik group in the Minsk Soviet only in May 1917, Lenin's supporters easily defeated their opponents.[56] On November 7, following the Bolshevik coup in Petrograd, Minsk joined the revolution. That morning the workers of the Kantorovich wallpaper factory gathered by the plant's gate and spilled out onto the streets excitedly discussing "what was happening in Petrograd."[57] On November 8, local Bolsheviks organized the Revolutionary Committee and declared all power to the Soviets, while different factions of Mensheviks, Bundists, and Socialist-Revolutionaries issued a declaration condemning the revolution and called for the transfer of authority to the Municipal Duma, headed by Bundist Arn Vaynshteyn.[58] On November 9, the whole city was an armed camp and a bloody clash between the Bolsheviks and those who opposed them seemed inevitable. But encouraged by the Social-Democratic group "Committee for the Salvation of the Revolution," the two sides ultimately reached a compromise and signed a truce—the Bolsheviks fearing a setback in case of a direct clash with their opponents. But as soon as they got hold of reinforcements from Red Army soldiers on the western front, they broke the truce and reinstated the Revolutionary Committee. On November 22, with a majority of 115 votes against 29, the Minsk Soviet of Workers and Soldiers dissolved the Municipal Duma.[59]

But the Bolsheviks were not in power for long. In early February 1918, after declaring war on Russia, the Germans approached Bobruisk from the west, defeated the Red Army, and headed toward Minsk. While the local Bolshevik organizations quickly evacuated to Smolensk, a small group of Belorussian intellectuals and political leaders established the Belorussian *rada*, or council, tried to gain control over Minsk, and declared the formation of the Belarus National Republic, a short-lived body eventually overthrown in early 1919. Both Bolsheviks and Germans never recognized the Belorussian Council as a legitimate political entity. Belorussian nationalists also faced the opposition of the Poles who, relying on the support of Polish Minsk residents made every effort to set up their headquarters in their "Polish city." Unlike the Poles, the Belorussians could not count on much political support in the city: besides a small minority of Belorussian intellectuals active there, most advocates of the Belorussian cause lived outside the city.

As the Germans approached, and the fear of a possible civil war grew among large sectors of the local population, panic took hold of the city.[60] Jews in particular worried that the imminent clash between Belorussians and Poles would result in anti-Jewish violence. Because of the sheer chaos, some political activists even considered fleeing the city.[61] Under German occupation, however, the economic and social conditions in Minsk improved somewhat, especially when compared to the early years following the outbreak of World War I. During the war many businesses had closed down, stores had little or no merchandise, and the cost of living had increased dramatically; the number of war refugees and invalids "who went from home to home begging for help, or simply stood on the streets was unbelievable."[62] Thousands of war refugees sought a safe haven in Minsk, as the city population grew from approximately 100,000 to 140,000. During the most critical phases of the war on the eastern front, it happened that synagogues abstained from holding holiday prayers in their buildings and instead gave shelter to the large number of needy Jewish refugees pouring into the city.[63]

While the German occupation of Minsk brought some respite to the economic and social crisis in the city, it stifled its political life. German authorities monitored all political activities in the city: The organ of the Socialist-Revolutionaries *Delo truda* (Workers' cause) was closed down, and the Bund's *Der veker* underwent severe censorship; no political meeting could be held without official German authorization; and finally, the Duma, which had resumed its functions, was dissolved once again.[64]

On December 10, 1918, after nine months of occupation, German troops left Minsk in haste propelled by the news of an impending revolution in Germany. The Red Army temporarily regained control over the region and entrusted the Revolutionary Committee with full authority. On January 1, 1919, the Bolsheviks created the SSRB, or the Soviet Socialist Republic of Belarus. It was disbanded soon thereafter, when its territory merged into the Lithuanian-Belorussian Soviet Socialist Republic (LBSSR). The latter was subsequently divided into two parts: large sections of its western provinces were seized by Poland in the summer of 1919, and the remaining eastern regions eventually became the Belorussian SSR.

During this brief period of Bolshevik rule, Zionist activities were greatly curtailed. In a letter to Yitshak Gruenbaum in Warsaw, the union of Minsk Zionists asked to receive information about Zionism in Poland, "as we have been kept in the dark for the past three months." "Please send us also a few issues of *Yudishe folk* [The Jewish people; the Yiddish Zionist publication in Warsaw]," solicited the authors of the letter, "so that we can distribute them to our community."[65] Minsk continued to be a center of Labor Zionism, as Poale-Zion feverishly organized events in the city. Because of its pro-Bolshevik orientation at the time, the organization faced no political repression. In early February 1919, the Second Extraordinary Conference of Poale-Zion in Soviet Russia took place in Minsk. At the end of the conference, the delegates joined the members of the local Poale-Zion organization to mourn the recent death of German Socialist Karl Liebknecht.[66] A few weeks later, from March 8–10, the Second Plenary Session of the Central Palestine Commission of Soviet Russia also took place in Minsk.[67] And in late March, the Poale-Zion organized in the city courses for party activists, instructors, and propagandists, with lectures on Marxism, Palestine as a territorial center, and Poale-Zionism as the ideology of the Jewish proletariat. Course participants received a monthly stipend, room, and board.[68]

The influence of Jewish Socialist parties in Minsk, combined with the lack of popular support for the Bolshevik leadership, prompted some of the resolutions taken by the Soviets as they resumed power after the Germans left. After all, the Jews in Minsk, more than the Belorussians and to some extent the Poles, already had a well-developed Socialist political and cultural leadership that could be employed in state and party institutions.[69] In order to build Communism the Bolsheviks relied heavily on the Bund, perhaps more than they did elsewhere in Russia. When the Revolutionary Committee resolved to close down all publications in the city, it made only two exceptions, the Communist Party organ and the Bund's central organ.[70] *Veker* became therefore the only newspaper in Minsk that never ceased publication during these years of turmoil, from 1917 to 1921. Despite the Bund's resistance to Bolshevism, two Bundist leaders were called upon to occupy important public offices: Arn Vaynshteyn became minister of social affairs and Ester Frumkin minister of education. When in April 1919, during the Polish-Soviet War, the Revolutionary Committee resolved to create a body to hold off the approaching Polish Army, it welcomed volunteers from the Bund and Poale-Zion. As the Polish troops conquered Vilna and advanced toward the cities of Belorussia, leaving behind a trail of pogroms, the Bund and Poale-Zion mobilized their supporters into two Jewish military units linked to the Red Army. The Borochov unit—named after labor Zionist leader Ber Borochov—enrolled primarily members of Poale-Zion, while the Grosser unit—named after Warsaw Bundist leader Bronislaw Grosser—enrolled mostly members of the Bund.[71] Another Jewish battalion was established in May 1919. Called the "First Minsk Guard Battalion," it consisted of Labor Zionists, Jewish Communists, Bundists, and Jewish workers with no political affiliation from Minsk, Bobruisk, Vitebsk, and Gomel.[72] In the words of union activist Grigory Aronson, "From an ideological vantage point the Bund . . . dominated . . . [Minsk's] life, shaping it with its own colors and directions."[73]

On August 8, 1919, as the Polish troops approached the gates of Minsk, the Red Army withdrew from the city. Minsk remained under Polish occupation for eleven months, until July 11, 1920. In the process of taking over the northwestern region, the Polish army carried out a number of anti-Jewish pogroms throughout the cities and *shtetlekh* of Belorussia, including Minsk, Bobruisk, Borisov, Koidanov, and Slutsk. Despite the violence, Jewish political groups, communal institutions, and cultural organizations of all stripes were active under the Poles. In September 1919, the Zionist organization of Belorussia issued the Yiddish daily *Farn folk* (For the people). The Bundist daily appeared under the name of *Der minsker veker*. At the communal elections of January 1920 the Zionists triumphed again: the seventy-one members elected to serve in the committee included nineteen General Zionists, six Poale-Zionists, four Tseirei-Zion (Young Zionists), and three Mizrachi (religious Zionists).[74]

Under Polish rule, General Zionism, which was non-Socialist and did not identify with the Bolshevik Revolution, resurged. In March 1920, the Herzeliah People's House on Rakovskaia Street organized a "Palestine evening" with Jewish national dances, an Italian-style orchestra, and speeches by Zionist activists. Local organizations held memorial events following the death of prominent local Zionist and cultural activist Avraham Kaplan. The Zionist youth organization He-haver (The Friend), which arranged Hebrew-language courses for youngsters in Minsk, decided to honor Kaplan by hanging his portrait in its club and collecting funds to sow plants in Palestine in his memory.[75] Hundreds of Minsk Jews attended the tribute to Kaplan held in the Choral Synagogue, which saw the participation of Jewish communal leaders, including the head of the Jewish *kehillah* Dr. Feldshtein and the economist Dr. Chayim Dov Hurwitz.[76]

Events surrounding the traditional Jewish holidays (which were discouraged under the Bolsheviks) abounded. The Committee for the Distribution of *matsah* for Passover, managed by the Minsk *kehillah*, and located on Koidanov Street, offered low-priced unleavened bread to poor *melamdim*, and dispensed it free of charge to Jewish soldiers. In May 1920, thousands of Jewish children joined the march organized by the School Committee of the Minsk *kehillah* on the occasion of the Jewish holiday of Shavuot. Holding flags with the blue and white Jewish national colors, students from the Talmud-Torah, state schools, the three Zionist schools in the city marched toward Cathedral Square. Middle-school students and Jewish scouts gathered at the He-haver club to play music and sing national songs. "The only nuisance at this grandiose rally," commented a local Jewish newspaper, "was the Agudat Israel school administration that forbade its children to take part in the event."[77]

Encouraged by the widespread suspicion that Jews supported the Bolsheviks, anti-Jewish violence reached its peak at the time of the Polish army's retreat from Belorussia, in early July. In Minsk, the feverish evacuation of Polish civil institutions and military units culminated in a violent pogrom with causalities, an extensive fire that destroyed forty to fifty houses, and looting of Jewish property.[78] On July 11, Rabbi Yechezkel Abramsky described Polish brutality in Minsk as follows:

> Miserable, I walk through the ruined streets, without the strength to keep my head up, buried under the burden of destruction, freshly spilled blood and cries of orphans . . . theft and murder in every section of the city and in every neighborhood touched by the Polish army, I doubt that the world will ever believe that such horrendous crimes were committed by human beings. Who will believe that [the Polish] nation . . . began its independent existence with such horrifying actions from the middle-ages. Can one believe that people elegantly dressed . . . with European manners, act like the Haydamaks [Ukrainian paramilitary bands], killing, looting and starting up fires against people, horses and the luggage of those who try to flee Minsk?[79]

The violence endured by the Jewish population under the Poles encouraged popular support for the Red Army, as Jewish public opinion welcomed the establishment of the Belorussian SSR. A few months after the Bolsheviks came to power in Minsk, a proclamation issued in a local Communist Jewish publication reminded "Jewish workers of what will happen if you fall again in the murderous hands of the Polish 'aristocrats.' Pogroms . . . slavery and abuse . . . Take the rifle and sword into your hands and set out in a heroic struggle for the final victory against your bloody enemies."[80]

Sore Rejzen—younger sister of the better-known cultural activists Avrom and Zalmen Rejzen—hailed the revolution with great passion in a poem published in the local Jewish Communist newspaper in September 1920:

> Nu, oyb krig to zol zayn krig
> Undz iz lang farshprokhn zig
>
> Vayl zi veys dokh vos zi vil
> Vayl vi zunen helt ir tsil.
>
> Vayl dos iz ir letster shtrayt
> Un di mentshhayt iz bafrayt
>
> Internatsional undz ruft
> Vi a bas-kol in der luft.[81]
>
> [Well, à la guerre comme à la guerre
> Our victory is long-since guaranteed
>
> Because we know what we want
> Because our goal shines bright like the suns
>
> Because this is our last struggle
> before humanity is freed
>
> The International calls to us
> like a heavenly voice from on high.]

Many Jews equally suffered from persecution in the aftermath of the reestablishment in Minsk of the Bolshevik regime. In a letter dated late 1920, a prominent local Zionist activist remarked, "Our [Zionist] educational and cultural activities are being hounded . . . our elementary school, which existed for years, was taken from us. The teachers and many of the students left the school because a decree was issued forbidding the teaching of Hebrew . . . Some of our teachers are living in great poverty and don't even have bread."[82] The commotion of everyday life in the city continued during the Civil War years, for Jews and non-Jews alike. Attempting to build up Communist institutions in Minsk, a Jewish activist lamented in October 1920:

> The population is in a state of chaos because of the plundering and violence. . . . [C]ity stores are empty or closed. . . . One pound of bread costs 1.500 rubles, a pound of butter 20.000 rubles. . . . [T]here is no wood. . . . I turn to the Central Bureau [in Moscow] with a personal request. I know it is not appropriate, but I have no other choice. I have no coat, no blanket and . . . no warm clothing [which] makes it impossible for me to work.[83]

Conclusion

Like elsewhere in Russia, a fairly large section of the Minsk Jewish population supported the revolution out of fear for the White Army, its allies—including the Poles—and the anti-Jewish violence they promoted. While few shared the political views of the Bolsheviks, the news of massacres perpetrated against the Jews in Belorussia, and in the cities and *shtetlekh* of Ukraine especially, led many to take sides with the Soviets. Ukraine suffered much more acutely than Belorussia (with the number of pogroms and Jewish causalities in Ukraine reaching at least twice the number of pogroms and causalities in Belorussia).[84] Moreover, while in Ukraine pogroms were usually carried out by local nationalist groups and Cossack bands tied to the tsar, in Belorussia the Polish army set off the anti-Jewish violence, generally without the collaboration of the local peasant population.[85] Even though the massacres in Belorussia can hardly compare to the ones perpetrated in Ukraine, they still strengthened Jewish pro-Bolshevik tendencies wherever they existed. In its commitment against anti-Semitism, viewed as the abhorrent legacy of tsarist autocracy, the Red Army usually acted in defense of the Jews and as a result was viewed by the Jewish population as a positive, or at least not a threatening, force.[86] In Minsk, finally, the understandable choice of "the lesser of two evils" was fueled by the sense of utter powerlessness experienced by Jews more than others during the frenzy of 1917–20, with the Bolsheviks in power, then the Germans, then the Bolsheviks again, then the Poles, and finally the Bolsheviks once more. The sense of relief and security experienced by most Minsk residents with the 1920 establishment of the Belorussian SSR was probably more intense among Jews than others because of the official condemnation of the anti-Jewish pogroms. Immediately following the end of the Civil War, Soviet authorities in Belorussia encouraged the systematic documentation of the massacres, the publication of witness accounts and literary works honoring the victims, and the punishment of the perpetrators.[87]

2 Red Star on the Jewish Street

Sovietizing Jewish Minsk: Struggles and Compromises

When the Bolsheviks began to municipalize private businesses across the city, the owners of the eighteen bookstores in Minsk (including one Judaica bookstore), petitioned the local authorities. They promised to follow Soviet instructions and apply "Soviet tenets" to the book business if the Bolsheviks returned the bookstores to the management of their owners.[1] Yudl Shapiro, who owned a bookstore on Alexandrovskii Street, pleaded to the Executive Committee of the Belorussian Soviet of Workers, Soldiers, and Peasants not to take over his store. This would deprive his family of their only source of income. He even begged to be employed as a clerk in "his own bookstore."[2] But the Bolsheviks brushed aside similar petitions. In their sweeping move to sovietize the city and remold it in the spirit of Communism, they disrupted the lives of many Minsk residents, Jews and non-Jews alike.

The sovietization of Minsk involved an onslaught against Jewish life. Shortly after taking over the city in July 1920, the Bolsheviks dismantled most existing Jewish institutions. Many religious and educational institutions such as synagogues and *hadorim* (Jewish religious schools) as well as the Minsk *kehillah*, all of which had formed the core of Jewish life before the Bolshevik rise to power, were closed down and their buildings municipalized. The Jewish cemetery on University Street was requisitioned from the Jewish community by the Land Commission of the City Executive Committee and turned into a grazing field for goats. "All Minsk residents who live in the center of town and own goats must obtain the permission from the city and pay a ruble and 50 kopecks a year per goat to have access to the field," read an announcement in the local press.³ Zionist publications were shut down. With the exception of Poale-Zion and He-Haluts (The Pioneer), all Zionist organizations discontinued their legal activity; some went underground. The Bund, which functioned as an independent party until March 1921, was forced to merge with the Communist Party. The words of a worker employed in the Minsk tobacco factory on how to punish counterrevolutionaries echoed the growing intolerance toward non-Communist parties and organizations during the Red Terror campaigns of mass arrests and executions: "Their place is the gallows!"⁴

The main sovietizing agency on the Jewish street was the Evsektsiia, or the Jewish section of the Communist Party. The Central Bureau was established in Moscow in 1918.⁵ In Minsk, the first Evsektsiia was organized in 1919, but as the Polish army neared the border with Soviet Russia its members were drafted into the Red Army and the section collapsed.⁶ In 1920, after Minsk became the capital of the Belorussian SSR, headquarters of the Belorussian Communist Party, and administrative and bureaucratic hub for the new political system, the Main Bureau of the Evsektsiia was established once again. It became operative on August 8, as the Main Bureau of the Evsektsiia of Belorussia.⁷ Its mission was to sovietize the Jewish population through Yiddish, the language accessible to most Jews, and "vanquish" all pre-revolutionary Jewish parties and communal organizations. Besides destroying the foundations of pre-revolutionary Jewish life, the Evsektsiia also strove to create new educational, political and cultural institutions that would—so it hoped—replace the role that Judaism, Hebrew culture, and Zionism had played for Minsk Jews.

* * *

The sovietization of the Jewish street also involved taking over and incorporating into Bolshevik organizations existing "bourgeois" institutions. After all, Lenin's official position vis-à-vis pre-revolutionary society envisioned the employment of the professional "bourgeois" force—the *spetsy* (specialists)—and the exploitation of their knowledge to build the new Soviet society. In May 1921, the Minsk branches of prominent pre-revolutionary Jewish communal institutions were placed under the supervision of the Jewish section of the People's Commissariat for Nationality Affairs and transferred to the Soviet agency's locale.⁸ For example, the Minsk ORT (Obshchestvo rasprostraneniia remeslennogo zemledelcheskogo truda sredi evreev) was supposed to attract the local Jewish population to "productive work," easing the transition of Jewish workers and artisans from small private workshops to large-scale plants, factories, and agricultural cooperatives.⁹ By virtue of the authority it still enjoyed among the local Jewish population, the old leadership could lend some credibility to the Soviet enterprise.¹⁰ But despite Communist supervision, these institutions were excluded from the state financial budget, and their activities became contingent upon foreign relief funds, especially aid from the American Jewish Joint Distribution Committee, or JDC.¹¹

Figure 2. Distribution of shoes to children of Jewish homes by the Joint Distribution Committee, Minsk, ca. 1923. Courtesy of the American Jewish Joint Distribution Committee Archives (Collection 21/32 Russia).

The JDC sponsored a vast number of welfare, medical, industrial, and cultural enterprises throughout the city. With their lives disrupted by years of war, many Minsk residents (Jews and non-Jews alike) required assistance: hundreds of war refugees still needed to be fed daily as late as 1923.[12] The JDC assisted university students—most of whom were Jewish—who had access to very little food and lived in deplorable conditions: with as many as ten lodging together in one small room with no ventilation, they slept on boards with no linen or blankets.[13] Relief was provided to university professors. After inspecting the newly founded Minsk university, the JDC chairman of the western provinces "was convinced that . . . the shabby manner in which the professors dressed provided enough evidence that they were badly in need of clothes."[14] In 1923, the JDC paid to heat the locale of the Jewish section of the Belorussian Drama Studio.[15] Throughout the 1920s and early 1930s, the JDC managed to provide some support (both legally and illegally) to religious Jews, sending parcels with *matsah* flour, kosher meat products or financial aid for underground religious education.[16] In agreement with the Social Security Department, the JDC allocated $2,000 for the construction of a new Jewish old-age home in the city, which would accommodate Jews only. Inaugurated on November 1, 1923, the Minsk Jewish old-age home was the only institution of its kind in the USSR, where Jewish elderly had a separate and distinct home from non-Jewish elderly.[17] Finally, the American organization subsidized at least eight institutions in Minsk—including public kitchens, children homes,[18] and vocational schools for teachers, shoemakers, and metalworkers.[19] In spite of the nonsectarian agreement with Soviet authorities, most of the JDC subsidy recipients were Jewish.

* * *

The Bolshevik Revolution promised freedom only to those Jews who met specific socioeconomic and political criteria. Zalman Y. Basok, who after resettling in Minsk during World War I became a prominent board member of the Jewish community, was immediately arrested by the Bolsheviks in 1921 and sentenced to death, without a trial. The sentence was not carried out only because the Jewish commissar designated for the job had recognized him as someone who had helped his family before the revolution and secretly released him.[20] Most "bourgeois Jewish elements" who escaped the death sentence, but did not manage to flee the USSR, came under the new Soviet category of *lishchentsy*, or citizens disenfranchised from Soviet electoral rights. From the Russian *lishchit'*, to deprive, this new political category designated all "former people," or *byvshie liudi*, of nonproletarian background and connected to the "bourgeois putrefaction," as Lenin put it. This category included therefore members of the pre-revolutionary elite, former officers or high-ranking bureaucrats in tsarist state service, religious functionaries, and those who profited from hired labor ("exploiters"). *Lishchentsy* typically became outcasts: even if only one member had been disenfranchised, the entire family experienced restricted access to housing, education, and medical assistance.[21]

Being labeled a *lishchenets* entailed, first of all, public branding: local newspapers and the entrance to the Minsk City Soviet building displayed the names of the social outcasts. On March 26, 1925, the chairman of the Construction Workers' Committee, Mikhail Shkliarik, complained to the electoral commission of the Minsk City Soviet, "My wife and I are offended for having been included on the 'Black' list and deprived of the right to vote in the elections. I demand a public refutation in the press. . . . I ask the party organs to . . . call to account those who provided the false information."[22] The chairman of the workers' committee knew very well that a *lishchenets* stigma would jeopardize his position in Soviet society. The reasons for being included on the black list ranged from contraband, prostitution, and alcoholism, to holding a market stand or owning a small house.[23] Of the 482 people included in the Minsk City Soviet black list in 1930, the majority had Jewish names.[24]

Because of their pre-revolutionary occupation, more Jews than non-Jews faced legal restrictions under the new regime. According to one source, 40 percent of Jews and 5 percent of non-Jews were disenfranchised in the Minsk Province. With no bread cards, expelled from cooperatives and other industrial enterprises, many *lishchentsy* could often rely only on the support of JDC, which made every effort to resettle them on land or absorb their children into new industrial plants.[25] Many relied on help from relatives in America. As Nokhem Khanin noted after his trip to Minsk in the late

1920s, "Wherever I met a Jew and asked him what his source of livelihood was, I got the same answer: American relatives send me money."[26] Others dealt with their loss of income by turning to profiteering and black marketing, often ending up being arrested by Soviet authorities.[27] And even those Nepmen (as small businessmen were labeled during the mixed economy of the NEP years), who earned a comfortable livelihood in spite of the persecution of private trade and the burden of exorbitant taxation, ultimately became tired of being considered pariahs. Their children were last on the list for school matriculation and stood little chance of entering government service because of their parents' status of "nonworking element."[28] Some desperately tried to get out of the *lishchentsy* category by minimizing their past as former traders. Kh. Levin explained that he had turned to trading as the only way out of abject poverty. "For an illiterate person like me, with no specialization, under tsarism . . . commerce was the only choice." He was "forced" to open a small stand in the marketplace (or *lavka*) with his wife. And when during the 1919 occupation the Poles destroyed his stand and apartment, commerce became once again the only solution. Levin somehow restored his small business, which he ran until 1928, when he went bankrupt because of the soaring taxes. He now appealed to Soviet authorities to include him in the city job register so that he could become employed and support a family of six: "I don't think that [my past as a merchant] should be the cause of rejection," he wrote.[29]

Besides lack of food and housing (only trade union members had access to co-op stores and housing allotment), disenfranchised "bourgeois" Jews had no right to free medical services. If a family member fell ill, he or she would not be treated in the city hospitals, unless they paid high fees.[30] The *lishchentsy* condition prompted a group of Minsk Jewish doctors to come together and establish a new medical organization. Under the leadership of Dr. Z. Levin, who at the time worked for OZE assisting victims of war and pogroms, the Minsk doctors established EMSO (Evreiskoe Meditsinskoe Sanitarnoe Obshchestvo), or the Jewish Medical and Sanitary Society, in mid-1926. The founders intended it as a complement to the general City Committee for Mutual Aid, which did not provide medical aid to "bourgeois nonworking elements." EMSO assisted therefore the Jewish poor and *lishchentsy* of the city. When the doctors first organized themselves, setting up their own administration and regulations, they operated independently from Soviet agencies and outside the supervision of the official voice on the Jewish street, namely the Evsektsiia.[31] So much so that one year after EMSO's establishment, the Minsk District Party Committee was still trying to figure out who had given permission to organize the society.

Before the revolution, most EMSO doctors had worked in the OZE local branch or in the other Jewish medical organization in Minsk—the Society for the Assistance of Poor and Sick Jews—established in the city in 1909.[32] Besides performing medical services, the doctors lectured on health and hygiene issues in clubs and movie theaters.[33] The society had its own clinic and it also provided financial support for those in need. A Jewish Red Army soldier turned to EMSO when his parents could no longer support

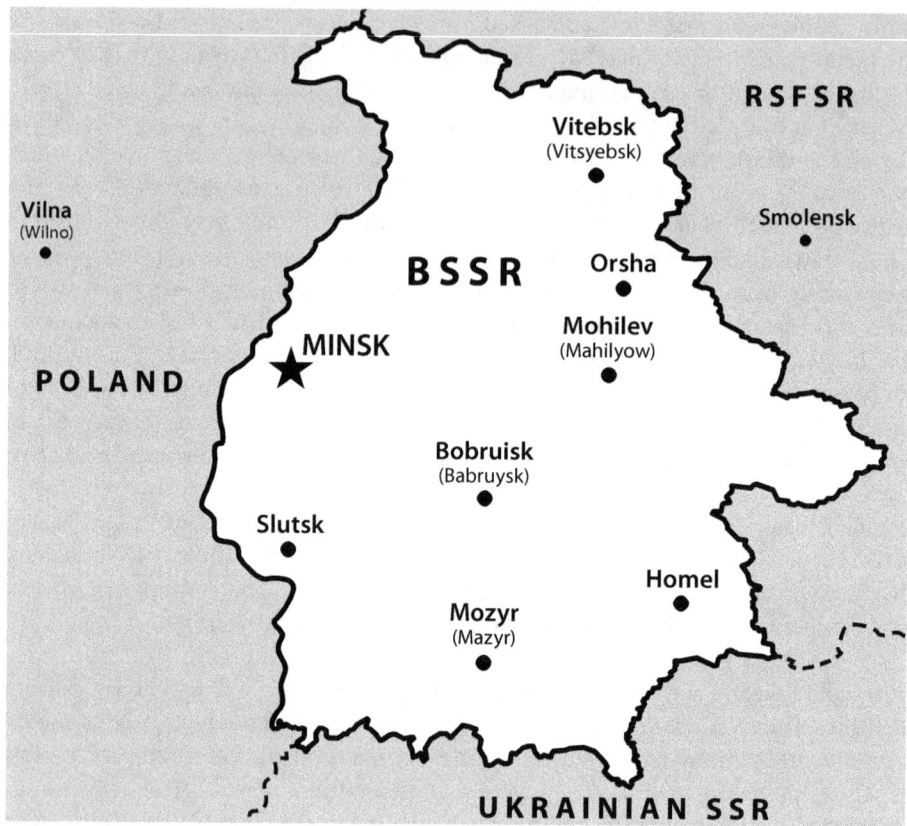

Figure 3. Map of the Belorussian Soviet Socialist Republic (BSSR), 1926–39.

his two brothers enrolled in a local Soviet Jewish school. In the same appeal, soldier Levin asked EMSO to pay for his mother's dental plate, as the family did not have adequate means to buy her the missing teeth.[34] Intended as a Jewish organization, EMSO began to offer medical treatment to the poor of other ethnic groups only in late 1928.[35]

Fearing that the Jewish society might start offering medical assistance to the working class as well, therefore spoiling its "immaculate nature with bourgeois lies," Communists began to attack it.[36] In late 1927, Jewish Communists warned that Mizrachi leaders had joined the society and that "EMSO . . . could turn into the old Kahal." To avoid this, the Evsektsiia struggled to ensure Communist influence on the society, encouraging party members to join its administration.[37] At the end of that year, nine Communists joined the fourteen doctors (who were nonparty members) on the board of directors.[38] By November 1928, the number of Communist and non-Communist board members was roughly equal, with twelve nonparty members and eleven party members.[39]

Among the Jewish organizations established under the Soviets, EMSO was in many ways unique. In sheer disregard of official Soviet guidelines of internationalism, which were strictly applied by the Bolsheviks to other social service and philanthropic organizations, EMSO was established solely as a Jewish institution with the purpose of bringing assistance to the marginalized Jewish population of Minsk. Although the Jewish Medical and Sanitary Society eventually came under the Evsektsiia's influence, it outlived the Jewish section of the CPB, liquidated in 1930, by one year. It existed in the city until 1931, where it functioned primarily as a clinic for the Jewish poor. Second, the fact that a group of Jewish doctors organized EMSO without consulting with the Evsektsiia and obtaining its authorization suggests that grassroots organizations were still possible in the 1920s. EMSO doctors relied on preexisting social networks to establish their society. At least during the NEP years, these networks escaped full control from the party and the state. EMSO's existence (however brief) reminds us once again that the Soviets did not hold sway over society as a whole during the 1920s. Finally, EMSO was one of the few Jewish organizations that did not adhere, at least in the beginning, to the principles of Soviet nationality and language policy. Like other pre-revolutionary Jewish societies established by the Russian Jewish intelligentsia, EMSO's language was not Yiddish—the Soviet designated Jewish national language—but Russian. After all, the Jewish doctors who founded it and devoted themselves to the interests of the Jewish population of Minsk used Russian as their primary language. As Soviet influence over EMSO grew, the language of correspondence, meeting minutes and literature progressively shifted to Yiddish.[40] This enterprise remains a revealing example of the scope of pre-revolutionary ideas, social networks, and modes of action within the constraints of the new system.[41]

The Altering Jewish Landscape: Demographic, Socioeconomic, and Political Changes

At the onset of the Bolshevik experiment, the Jewish population of the growing capital of the BSSR experienced momentous demographic, socioeconomic, and political changes. Some of these changes predated the Soviets by a few decades and were merely intensified by the establishment of the new revolutionary regime.

The Jewish population of the Minsk District began to drop during the late nineteenth and early twentieth centuries, mostly as a result of overseas' migration to America and internal relocation from *shtetlekh* and villages to larger urban centers. In 1897, in the Minsk Province, 38.7 percent of the total Jewish population lived in the cities and 61.3 percent in towns and villages. By 1917, the proportion reversed itself as 64.5 percent of the Jewish population lived in the cities and 35.5 percent in towns and villages.[42] Triggered by the economic crisis that hit the Belorussian town and village at the turn of the century, internal migration was directed primarily toward Minsk. The economic backwardness, the dearth of natural resources, and the primitivism of agricultural structures compelled many Jews to leave their place of residence and settle in larger urban centers where the growing industrialization and the newly established factories offered wider opportunities of employment and livelihood. Jews and non-Jews alike were much better off in Minsk, the new economic, political, and administrative capital of the region, than in the towns and villages.

Throughout the 1920s and 1930s, the Belorussian capital absorbed thousands of newcomers from the surrounding *shtetlekh*.[43] Born in 1906, after graduating from middle school in the *shtetl* of Lohoisk, Morduch Kapilevich moved to Minsk to make a livelihood; in the city, he worked as an apprentice photographer from 1924 to 1927 and in 1928 was employed by Belgoskino, the Belorussian state film industry.[44] In 1929, 236 young Jews like Morduch left the *shtetl* of Uzda; of these, 125 went to Minsk (53 percent), 54 to Moscow and Leningrad, and 35 to Mohilev and Vitebsk. In 1931, of the 1,309 Jews who left twelve different Belorussian *shtetlekh*, 52.5 percent moved to other cities in Belorussia, 27.9 percent relocated to the Russian Republic, and 9.3 percent to Ukraine. The overwhelming majority of those who moved to other areas in Belorussia settled in Minsk.[45]

Despite the constant stream of migrants into the capital, however, overall the proportion of Jews in the city decreased. If in 1897 the Jewish population reached 52.3 percent (47,562) of the total city population, in 1923 it made up 43.6 percent (48,312), and 40.8 percent (53,686) in 1926.[46] The remarkable growth of the non-Jewish population, which increased three times more than the Jewish population and reached 78,217 in 1926, partly affected the drop in the percentage of Jews in the city.[47] The decline was also determined by the outbound migration movement. In the early 1920s, many Jews tried to leave the country, some more successfully than others.[48] While Itka Sulskaia was about to receive her travel permit to the United States and ship voucher through the company Balt-American Lines, her daughter Rachel was denied an exit visa.[49] From January to June 1923, the American representatives of the Minsk branch of Yidgezkom (the Jewish Public Committee to Aid Victims of War, Pogroms, and Natural Disasters) processed the travel permits of five hundred registered migrants from Minsk and surrounding *shtetlekh*.[50]

Many more Minsk Jews relocated to other Soviet cities as a way to escape legal restrictions associated with the social stigma of disenfranchised citizens. As soon as the administration found out that Hershl Rozin had lied about his father's social background on his application, he was expelled from the Faculty of Math at Belorussian State University in Minsk. Hershl's sister Sonia, who admitted on the application that her father had been a "small lumber dealer," was also expelled from Belorussian State University. Their younger brother Aron Rozin, by contrast, decided to circumvent his siblings' experience and moved to Leningrad to attend university: "[Here] I will not have to fear that they discover . . . my social origin."[51] Like Rozin, many young Jews seeking to "fit in" moved to larger Russian cities.[52] Moscow and Leningrad, in particular, became the preferred destination of hundreds of disenfranchised Minsk Jews who had lost their income. During the mid-1920s the proportion of unemployed young Jews in the city surpassed the proportion of unemployed non-Jews. In 1927, 63.4 percent of the unemployed under eighteen were Jews, and 46.4 percent of the unemployed between eighteen and twenty-three were Jews.[53] That same year, nearly 80 percent of the members of the youth labor exchange were Jewish.[54] The large out-migration from Minsk was therefore driven not only by the infinite opportunities existing in Moscow and Leningrad but also by unemployment in the Belorussian capital. Lured by the perspectives of income, success, and status, thousands of Jews settled in the two Russian metropolises.

Despite the number of Jews who left Minsk—and the ensuing overall decline of the Jewish proportion of the city population—Jews remained the single largest national group in the capital of the BSSR after the Belorussians throughout the 1930s. In 1928, Belorussians made up almost 42.5 percent of the Minsk population and Jews almost 41 percent.[55] In the urban landscape of the USSR, this proportion was indeed remarkable, especially when compared to other capitals of Soviet republics. It might not be that surprising therefore if the *Wehrmacht*'s assessment of the demographic features of the city in 1939 noted that the city inhabitants of Minsk were "Jewish. [B]esides them, Belorussians, Russians, Ukrainians, Poles and other nationalities [lived in the city]."[56]

The revolution left a deep impact on the socioeconomic makeup of the Jewish population of Minsk, altering its role in the city economy as well as granting unprecedented upward mobility to many of its members. If at the beginning of the twentieth century nearly 85 percent of all local merchants and small traders in the city were Jewish, by 1926 only 7 percent of the Jewish population was engaged in commerce; and by the mid-1930s the category of private merchant had essentially disappeared. The proportion of Jews employed as craftsmen remained significant, dropping from 71.2 percent in 1897 to 60.5 percent in 1926. If in 1897 only nineteen Jews were employed in the public sector, which traditionally excluded Jews, in 1926 local Soviet agencies employed nearly three thousand Jews. Jews represented 56 percent of clerks employed in commercial enterprises, 54.6 percent of those employed in industry and manufacture, and 71.2 percent of those employed in light industry. They played a key role in the movie industry and in the management of the republic's economy: in 1926, eight out of the ten Belgoskino employees were Jewish; three years later, thirty-eight out of the fifty-five employees were Jewish (or 69 percent).[57] In the mid-1920s, more than 50 percent of the staff in the Supreme Soviet of the National Economy of Belorussia (VSNKh BSSR) was Jewish (thirty-eight out of seventy employees).[58]

Some threads of continuity with the pre-revolutionary reality countered these changes. Jews continued, for example, to be largely absent from specific sectors of the economy, such as transportation, communication, and heavy industry. With twenty-one Jews employed in 1897 and forty-eight in 1926, the railroad industry in Minsk remained a non-Jewish domain as it had been under the tsar.[59] The new Soviet regime targeted primarily the "capitalist class" of business owners. During the NEP years, most private enterprises in the city were requisitioned from their legitimate owners and usually leased by the state to the highest bidder. If the majority of factory owners in Minsk were Jewish before the revolution, in the postrevolutionary years most lessees and managers of these same factories—now turned into Soviet businesses—were Jewish as well. In 1923, the VSNKh of Belorussia leased the leather factory on Red Street to Goldberg and Kershtein, the iron foundry "Metal" to one Lichterman, and the jam factory on Novaia Komarovskaia Street to Goder and Goldberg.[60] Set by the Soviet agency in charge of leasing state enterprises, the terms of the contract were rarely to the lessee's advantage. In June 1924, for example, the Soviet leasing agency resolved to lease the tobacco factory on Nemiga Street, formerly owned by Tsukerman, to Leitman and Levin: the lease would last one year, and the lessees were expected to renovate the building and purchase new equipment for the factory.[61] While the factory owners and their relatives were usually dismissed as exploiters of the working class,[62] in some cases a relative or the owner himself became the new manager or lessee of the Soviet enterprise. For example, the tobacco factory formerly owned by Karlip and Ginzburg was leased to Karlip and Burk, while the cigarette factory formerly owned by Falkson was leased to Falkson himself. In spite of Soviet intentions, a degree of continuity in "family businesses" persisted during the NEP years.[63]

In the context of the political revolution that swept through the city, Jews came to form a large proportion of the party professional and administrative apparatus. In 1922, they represented 45.9 percent of the entire membership in local party committees, and in 1923, 48.3 percent of the party technical apparatus. In 1922 and 1923, respectively, Jews formed 50.7 and 47.9 percent of the delegates to the Executive Committee of the CPB, and 34 and 37.9 percent of the members of the Executive Committee of CPB. In 1923, ninety-two Jews headed different commissariats.[64] Jews also became quite active in the city party leadership. Of the twenty-five party cells existing in the Minsk City District in 1924, nineteen had Jewish secretaries (not one was headed by a Belorussian).[65] In 1926, 50 percent of the members of the Minsk Pioneer Organization were Jewish.[66] In 1927, there were thirty-four *otriadi*, or detachments of young Communists, in the Minsk City District: Jews represented the overwhelming majority, counting 852 members out of a total of 1,189 members. For the first time in the history of the city, the Minsk chief of police was Jewish, as was the deputy chief of police.[67]

Strolling Through the Streets of Minsk

In September 1925, during his Minsk sojourn, Yiddish writer H. Leyvik wrote a letter to his wife in New York, noting the impressions of his trip to the Belorussian capital.

> As I walk through the streets, I see the ... changes ... I also see a good deal of injustice, hear complaints and grasp the ... poverty of many.... Here people dress very modestly, and with my bright-colored suit I am simply ashamed to walk on the street. So I don't wear it. Nobody suffers from hunger here, it is possible to eat and drink in abundance.... Food is very inexpensive. There are mountains of fruit ... meat and

dairy products. The aspect of life where you notice poverty is clothing. But in fact the Minsk region and its *shtetlekh* have never been very fashionable—one family always shared one pair of boots.[68]

Leyvik's words echo those of Nokhem Khanin, a prominent figure in the Workmen's Circle and the Socialist Federation in New York City, who traveled to Minsk—the city in which he grew up—in the late 1920s:

> I look at the street I once knew so well, and every little stone speaks to me about hardship, desolation, and need.... [Everyone] looks at me with astonished eyes ... at my hat, my white collar ..., my coat ... elegant shoes.... I don't know why they called me the American Doctor. Probably because of my clothes, which ... sparkled like diamonds compared to their tatters.... When I walked through Minsk, I was the only one wearing a white collar and a whole coat.... people would look at me wondering "where does he come from?"[69]

But it wasn't only "hardship, desolation, and need" that the two writers might have noticed as they strolled through the streets of the city in which they had once lived or had often visited during their youth. Walking toward the Jewish neighborhood of Nemiga in the early 1920s, the two writers might have crossed over the Novokrasnaia quarter, which still held houses of ill repute; they would have passed through one of the Jewish cemeteries in use at the time; and then, between the Vilna and Brest train stations, come across the neighborhood of the Jewish *balegoles*, or carters, who carried passengers or merchandise across the city. They might have walked from Nemiga toward the High Market and seen the crowds of Jewish artisans, brushmakers, shoemakers, tailors, carpenters, chimney sweepers, and painters who had coated the roofs of Minsk in green or red—most of whom were being reorganized in small and large cooperatives.[70] And then, once they reached the corner between Soviet and Engels streets, they might have noticed the former restaurant Vengrezshetski—requisitioned by the Communists in 1923—where Minsk residents enjoyed breakfast or lunch, or simply sipped a hot chocolate, while listening to the string orchestra or playing billiard.[71]

Because of their interest in Jewish culture, Leyvik and Khanin might have walked by the box office of the Belorussian State Jewish Theater, Belgoset, and purchased tickets for Sholem Aleichem's play *Kasrilevke*.[72] About 572 people on average viewed the twelve plays performed by Belgoset in Minsk in the early months of 1928, with a total of approximately 7,000 viewers (661 of them purchased their tickets at the main box office, 1,614 at the workers' box office, 250 saw the shows for free, while the large majority, about 4,000, obtained tickets at a reduced price through their trade unions or other political and cultural organizations in the city).[73] Leyvik and Khanin might have also visited the reading room and children's division of the Y. L. Peretz Minsk Central Jewish Library. (This was the former Nofech Jewish Library, established in pre-revolutionary Minsk by the local philanthropist and Zionist activist

Figure 4. On Nemiga Street, 1923, with the dome of the main synagogue in the background. Courtesy of the Belorussian State Archives of Film and Photography (0–38532).

Yehuda Zeev Nofech.) Chatting with its readers about the Peretz library holdings, they might have gathered information about the rich belletristic and political collections of Soviet and foreign books, as well as about the poor selection of Russian literature in the Jewish library.[74]

Inaugurated in 1925, the Jewish Department of the Belorussian State Museum consisted of several permanent exhibitions. These included displays of antiques, manuscripts, some of the first Jewish books printed in Belorussia, the model of a typical Jewish home from the 1880s, and religious objects. The museum devoted one of its rooms to Jewish arts and crafts produced in Dubrovno, Minsk *guberniia*, and in particular to the manufacturing history of *talitot* (prayer shawls) and parchment for sacred books in that specific *shtetl*. Finally, the Jewish museum devoted a special section to the Yiddish writer Mendele Mocher Seforim (born in Kapulye [Kopyl], a *shtetl* in the Minsk *guberniia*), with facts and objects related to his life and work; a section about the history of Jewish household objects; and a section with photographs of old Jewish tombstones. A number of Jewish religious books were located in the Jewish section of the museum's library.[75] Besides visiting the permanent exhibition, Leyvik and Khanin might have taken a look at the special exhibits "Ancient Jewish Silver—the Work of Jewish Artisans from the Seventeenth Century" and "The History of the Jews of Minsk," set up by the museum staff in 1928. At the time, the museum curators were also planning an additional section about the "new Jewish lifestyle," which would display the work of

Soviet Jewish artists, material from the Minsk Central Jewish Court, and facts about Jewish settlement on land.[76]

During their journey through the Belorussian capital, Leyvik and Khanin might have met the young Chayim Zaretskii. Born in 1906 in Kapulye, in 1924 Chayim enlisted in the local firefighters and was appointed chief trumpet fireman. He joined the Komsomol in early 1926 and was dispatched to Minsk to work in the administration of the Belorussian State School of Music. Chayim might have eagerly shared with them that he planned to apply for membership in the Communist Party and proudly told them that during summer and winter vacations he returned to his home *shtetl* to carry out propaganda work on behalf of the Komsomol.[77] A former Bundist mother, by contrast, fervently hoped that her twenty-year-old son would never join the Komsomol because of the sheer careerism that drove its members. Actively involved in Bundist conspiratorial work in Minsk in the early 1900s (she helped embroider the red flag that hung on the city boulevard during the first revolutionary demonstration in Minsk), this mother opposed the Bolsheviks. "As bad as it was under the tsar," she confessed, "[now it is worse]: in order to get a better position even Communists are willing to become informers and betray kith and kin."[78]

A woman by the name of Mariasha assessed the new regime quite differently. Also an advocate for the Bund, in the pre-revolutionary years she lived in the poorest neighborhood of Minsk, the so-called Blote, or Mud, home to the Bundist underground movement before 1917. While she did not live in lavishness and was still illiterate after the revolution, Mariasha cherished great hopes for her children, who under the Soviets joined Communist organizations, became educated, and most importantly no longer suffered from the stigma of poverty. "I am not a party member," she admitted, "but my heart applauds the Bolsheviks because they take care of the poor turning them into human beings. . . . [If we stay here and cannot join our family in America] then it's much better to have a Bolshevik regime."[79] While walking through the streets of Minsk and meeting some of its residents, Leyvik and Khanin might have sensed the intricate ways in which the sovietization process affected their lives, with its complicated outcome of fascination and violence, conciliation and hostility, adjustment and lack of alternatives. As Rosa, a young woman employed in a local factory, explained, "[My husband and I] know that our newspapers don't write the truth and that they might even make up events; and yet we read them every day, and have already stopped to doubt and began to believe."[80]

Gateway to Utopia: Jewish University Students in Minsk

"S'iz shver tsu zayn a yid [it's hard to be a Jew]," complained Hershl Shneerson—one of the heroes of Sholem Aleichem's 1913 homonymous play—upon realizing that completing a gymnasium with a golden medal was no guarantee of admission to Kiev University. In order to join his Russian peers and become a university student he would have to face the existing Jewish quota on higher education. Shneerson eventually evaded the quota system by pretending to be a Russian and taking on the identity of his fellow student Ivan Ivanov, while the latter, who wished to prove to his Jewish friend the absence of legal discrimination against Jews in Russia, took on Shneerson's identity, and to his surprise, was enveloped by anti-Jewish measures typical of late imperial Russia. Many young Jews resorted to less complicated devices than the one used by Shneerson: they traveled abroad to attend university or converted to Russian Orthodoxy for the sake of admission, some of them even reverting back to Judaism upon obtaining their university degree.

This situation changed radically with the collapse of the tsarist empire, when resolutions passed by the Provisional Government, and confirmed by the Bolsheviks, put an end to Jewish exclusion from Russian higher education. The first resolution affecting Jewish life, which predated the March 20th decree abolishing all national and religious restrictions for Russian citizens, was the March 4 decree "abolishing the percentage quota for Jews entering schools." With the removal of legal barriers on education, during the 1920s and 1930s young Jews moved to Soviet cities and streamed into universities and institutions of higher education. The access to higher education created unprecedented opportunities for young Jews.

Under the Soviets Minsk became, for the first time, a university city. Before Belorussian State University opened its doors, in September 1921, youngsters committed to higher learning moved to other cities in Russia, as the Bundist leader-to-be Vladimir Medem did when he left Minsk for Kiev to attend university. From the very beginning, the demographics of the student body at Belorussian State University marked this institution as a largely Jewish milieu, as Jews rushed to enroll in all faculties. In the first academic year, the number of Jewish students enrolled at the university was 500, or 67 percent of the 737 students (193 were Belorussians; 24 Russians; 2 Poles). By 1923, the number of Jewish students increased more than twofold and reached 1,246 (Belorussians counted 658 students, Russians 125, Poles 41); and by 1924, the number of Jewish students in all faculties at Belorussian State University grew to 1,500 (Belorussians counted 1099, Russians 170, Poles 12).[81] Even though the proportion of Jewish students eventually dropped as a result of the "affirmative action" programs and preferential admissions for the indigenous nationality, that is, Belorussians, launched by the government during the mid-1920s, their share remained remarkable. In 1927, Jews made up 44 percent of the total student body in the Faculty of Medicine; 30 percent in the Pedagogical Faculty; and 47.7 percent in the Faculty of Economics. In 1928, Jews constituted 37.5 percent of all university students in Minsk.[82] This notable proportion became an important social factor in the preservation of Jewish identity, whether Jewish students were consciously committed to it or not. In other words, Jewish students at Belorussian State University were not escaping their Jewish background and environment in order to attend university and become part of the surrounding society, as Jewish students had often done in imperial Russia and were doing in Moscow in the 1920s. On the contrary, young Jews who enrolled at Minsk university would run into, socialize with, and sit next to other Jewish students in the classroom, on a daily basis, whether they wanted to or not. In other words, here the path to sovietization and acculturation into the system did not require a denial of or departure from Jewishness.

The proportion of Jewish students at Belorussian State University confirms the striking upward mobility of young Jews, eager to embark upon successful careers and serve as the new Soviet specialists in the fields of pedagogy, engineering, medicine, and economy. However, the Jewish "obsession" with education, not dissimilar from that of their American counterpart in the 1920s, originated from social aspirations and not necessarily from ideological devotion to Communism. Social ambition and devotion to education did not necessarily imply dedication to the Communist Party. An inspection about the fulfillment of party directives among Jewish university students in Minsk showed that during the 1928–29 academic year, only 158 of the 975 Jewish students enrolled at university were members of the Communist Party. The inspection's conclusions noted, "The number of Communists and members of the Komsomol among Jewish students is not significant enough."

The Secret Place of Zionism

During the 1920s, the humanities curriculum at Belorussian State University included also traditional Jewish subjects, such as Bible and Talmud. Most interestingly, it included Hebrew language, making the university the only public setting in the Belorussian capital in which Hebrew still found a place following the 1921 ban on "the language of Zionists and clericals." Students specializing in Jewish studies, with a focus on literature or history, studied the language in order to read manuscripts and documents in Hebrew. They made a Jewish choice within the context of higher education. But whether they planned on becoming members of the Minsk Soviet Jewish intelligentsia or not, they opted for an officially sanctioned synthesis between Jewishness and Sovietness that excluded Zionism. Virtually no student who enrolled in Hebrew courses at Belorussian State University supported Zionism, secretly or publicly. We can in fact assume that not one of the students who in late 1928 petitioned the dean of the Faculty of Pedagogy protesting against the anticipated cutback in Hebrew-language instruction and its merging with semitology belonged to a Zionist group.

Members of underground Zionist youth groups deliberately avoided taking courses in Jewish studies, above all in Hebrew language. The presence of informers, who checked on the students' background, and the arrest by agents of the OGPU (GPU; All-Union State Political Administration) of the language instructor Merlis, suspected of being active in local Zionist circles, made young Zionists very cautious.[83] By contrast, they enrolled in large numbers in the courses on economics taught by Chayim Dov Hurwitz, journalist, Zionist activist, and economist, as well as speaker at the 1902 Russian Zionist conference in Minsk and former editor of the Yiddish-language central organ of the Zionist organization of Belorussia, *Farn folk*.[84] Because of Hurwitz's standing in Zionist circles, his classes (which he taught primarily in Yiddish) attracted mostly Zionist students and auditors, creating an unofficial Zionist subcommunity. Hurwitz's courses often gave young Zionists a chance to secretly carry out political propaganda as they warily strove to enlist in the movement the unaffiliated students who came together during his lectures.[85]

Those secretly involved with underground Zionist groups faced constant harassment from Soviet authorities. The obsession of Jewish Communists with the "dangers" of Zionism ranged from accusations of a Menshevik-Zionist "united front," to the existence of an alliance between the Zionists and Petliura, the Ukrainian nationalist responsible for the death of thousands of Jews during the pogroms carried out at the time of the Civil War.[86] Jewish Communists also blamed Soviet authorities for their lack of rigorousness in dealing with Zionism, noting that the legal existence of Poale-Zion and He-Haluts—tolerated until 1928—encouraged the activities of other illegal Zionist groups.[87] And they might have been right.

Until the mid-1920s left Zionist organizations remained relatively active in postrevolutionary Minsk, reaching more than five hundred members by 1925.[88] In the early 1920s, some maintained a semilegal status: among them, the Communist-oriented Kadimah, or Forward (originally established in 1917), and Hitpathut, or Development (established in 1919), which because of their positive interpretation of Marxism and Communism, even received from the authorities a space to set up a club for theater, music, and sporting activities.[89] A third semilegal Zionist youth organization active in Minsk was the student association He-haver. In 1923, Kadimah, Hitpathut, and He-haver joined forces under the local branch of the umbrella organization EVOSM, or United Organization of Zionist Youth in Russia.[90] Members of Zionist youth groups would come together mostly in unofficial venues, such as the private homes of local Zionist activists. The home of the Susanski family, for example, became a meeting point for youth group members, who could come together and listen to Zionist interpretations of Sholem Aleichem's work, or browse through the Hebrew and Yiddish book collection held in the family's private library.[91] Youth group members were recruited among students in Soviet middle schools. In 1923, at the age of thirteen, Aron Rozin attended a Soviet Russian school, where 60 percent of the student body was Jewish.[92] A classmate approached him and convinced him to join the Zofim, or Scouts, of the Minsk youth organization of Ha-shomer ha-tsair, or the Youth Guard, the Zionist group banned by the Soviets in 1922.[93] Together with other members of this group, Rozin would secretly distribute pro-Zionist flyers through the streets of the Jewish quarter of Nemiga and toss them in the air in the central synagogue courtyard or inside the synagogue buildings during the Sabbath service.[94]

While all Hebrew-language publications in the city were closed down shortly after the Bolsheviks came to power, Hebrew books remained available to Soviet citizens until the mid-1920s. In late 1921, the Pushkin Central Library held a collection of 600 Hebrew books, and the Peretz Jewish Library held a collection of 1,266 books in

Hebrew, mostly belle-lettre and scholarship, and 346 Hebrew periodicals.[95] By 1924 the Hebrew book collection in the Peretz Library had expanded, reaching 2,900 books.[96] During that same year, children were still checking out Hebrew books from the Peretz Library.[97] The fact that they made use of books in Hebrew, a language associated with "bourgeois" political organizations and a religious lifestyle, suggests their parents' support for some form of Zionism. Through the help of the JDC, Minsk parents also had access during the 1920s to underground structures for the study of Hebrew language and culture. Small study groups gathered illegally in cellars or nearby forests to teach children Hebrew.[98] During 1928–29, thirty small classes, with a total of 150 students and fifteen teachers, regularly met in Minsk.[99]

In the mid-1920s, the Minsk Zionist youth groups suffered a severe blow. Many young activists were arrested by GPU agents. Berta Levin, who was only sixteen at the time, chose to take her life rather than inform the secret police on her fellow comrades.[100] Nahum Goldin joined Kadimah in 1923, then He-haver in 1924, and was a member of the EVOSM Minsk governing board since 1924. Arrested on February 2, 1925, with eighteen fellow activists, he was expelled from the Soviet Union.[101] A member of the underground Zionist group Hashomer ha-tsair, the teenager Ruva Gelfand served as a kind of art director for the organization's handwritten illegal publication. When the GPU found the publication at the Gelfand residence, they arrested Ruva and deported him to Kirghizia.[102] In 1927, the Pushkin and Peretz libraries finally removed their Hebrew-language holdings making the access to Hebrew-language material almost impossible for most city residents.[103] Only a tiny proportion of those who kept Hebrew books or books about Zionism on their bookshelves could read them in the private sphere of their home. Until 1937, when he was arrested and purged as an "enemy of the people," Marc Zhitnitskii, who worked for the Belorussian State Publishing House in Minsk, kept in his home works by Ber Borochov, founder of Labor Zionism.[104]

In spite of the ongoing bullying by authorities and peers, some young Jews strove to become Soviet while maintaining an allegiance to Labor Zionism, officially tolerated until the late 1920s. In 1927, a group of Jewish students celebrated the twenty-fifth anniversary of the establishment of Poale-Zion by marching in front of the building of Belorussian State University, with the party's flags and banners.[105] While Poale-Zion remained a legal organization in the Soviet Union until the summer of 1928, open support for a political party other than the Communist Party in a public space departed from Soviet norms and was considered behavior unsuitable for students at a Soviet university.[106] After all, upon graduating these university students would supposedly join the new professional cadres in charge of building Socialism. Being affiliated with Labor Zionism and remaining marginal to society was one thing, being a member of Poale-Zion and participating or being employed in state organizations was quite another. As someone asked during the 1927 Minsk Conference of nonparty Jewish workers, "Why are members of the Poale-Zion allowed to work . . . if they are considered Zionists?"[107]

A year later, political inspectors investigated the implementation of party directives at Belorussian State University. The ensuing report disapproved of the presence of students enrolled at the university who belonged to Zionist organizations, in particular Poale-Zion, and concluded that "during the past and current academic years the absence of serious admission procedures led to the acceptance of Zionist students. A more vigilant and thorough selection process... is indispensable for the future."[108] That same year, another inspection to check the party-mindedness of the student body accused some students associated with Zionism of having tried to infiltrate Communist organizations such as the Jewish Workers Club. Luckily they "were rejected by the club's board because they were not Communists." And yet some students did manage to graduate from university while secretly remaining involved with Zionism. Two brothers, who in search for a better living moved to Minsk after the revolution, eventually joined and became active in the illegal Zionist group Zeire-Zion even as they attended and graduated from Belorussian State University.[109]

On June 28, 1928, the Poale-Zionist movement was officially banned. Its members were asked to sign a document, reproduced in the Minsk Jewish daily, which acknowledged the counterrevolutionary nature of Labor Zionism. Like former Bundists a few years earlier, former Poale-Zionists who signed the document could join the Communist Party without recommendations and candidacy period.[110] With the ban on Poale-Zion, the last legal vestige of Zionism in the Soviet Union disappeared. Soviet citizens would now be able to express their support for Zionism only in a clandestine fashion, limiting their connection to the Zionist idea to the privacy of their homes, to the few, if any, Zionist publications still in their possession, to the secretive conversations with restricted groups of friends. Some Zionists attempted to leave the Soviet Union and reach Palestine.[111] But the great majority, who did not manage to leave and could no longer face the burden of social marginalization, decided to conform. As the youth groups progressively disappeared during the second half of the 1920s, many young Zionists joined Communist youth organizations in a reasonable attempt to fit in. Even when their previous association with Zionism made their political loyalty to the party questionable, with occasional complaints about Zionists who joined the Komsomol, most youngsters enrolled in the Communist Youth League, attracted by the universal message of the ideology and tired of feeling rejected.[112] Many publicly acknowledged their mistakes in the local press, as Isak Rubenchik, member of the Minsk Left He-Haluts, who asked to make known "that after nine months in Palestine, I have returned and no longer am a member of He-Haluts."[113]

Finally, a small minority maintained a secret allegiance to Zionism while successfully partaking in Soviet society well into the 1930s. Born in abject poverty in 1910 in Uzlian, Minsk *guberniia*, after the revolution Aron Rozin moved with his family to the Belorussian capital. By 1935, at the young age of twenty-five, he was appointed head of the Bread Production Planning Department for the entire Belorussian Republic. Despite his prominent position in the city economy, Rozin remained a Zionist.

His whole family was active in different Zionist groups: one brother and sister were members of Zeire-Zion until 1930, two brothers were active in illegal groups linked to He-Haluts; and one sister was in the Young Poale-Zion.[114] Rozin spent twelve years as an activist in different Zionist organizations in and around Minsk: in 1923, he joined his first underground Zionist movement, the Minsk organization of Ha-Shomer ha-tsair. In 1925, he became secretary of the Minsk organization of the Young Poale-Zion, and following the Soviet banning on the party, he joined the underground group. The secret group did not organize any subversive action against the state, nor did it publish pro-Zionist literature, but rather limited its activities to bimonthly meetings with debates on Zionist ideology and issues related to Jewish life in the Soviet Union.[115] As Rozin pointed out, by the mid-1930s, "Zionism was in a state of agony and was dying out quickly in the Soviet Union."[116] In 1935, the Minsk underground Poale-Zionist circle counted only eight members.[117]

Even if limited, Rozin's activity in the underground Poale-Zion accompanied his professional path through and successful integration into Soviet society. Like other Jews, he attempted to negotiate between "acting Bolshevik" and "acting Jewish," between universal Communist practice and a particular Jewish identity. His behavior, which balanced deviance with conformity, did not necessarily denote an opposition to the system. As he admitted, he did not become overly critical of the Soviet regime until his arrest, in 1935. Rozin was, however, exceptional in the form of deviance he practiced. Compared to other expressions of social deviance, such as religious practice, for example, which the Soviets intermittently tolerated or persecuted less fervently, Zionist deviance became much more uncommon in Soviet society, where authorities violently inhibited any political deviance. As Ester Frumkin poignantly noted, "No Jewish Socialist party . . . fought for its principles with as much vigor and devotion as these Jews wrapped in their prayer shawls."[118] This remark by the former Bundist and Jewish Communist leader not only conveyed the depth of her antireligious feelings. It also acknowledged the nearly accomplished defeat of Jewish political movements—Zionism in particular—compared to the fairly dynamic life of Judaism throughout the 1920s and mid-1930s.

The Jerusalem of the BSSR

Jewish history is often viewed as the succession of hegemonic centers that, at different historical times and following Jewish migratory movements, emerge as important nuclei that come to influence the course of Jewish history. Minsk's rise to new Soviet Jewish center was quite remarkable. Unlike those centers that grew over time, following waves of Jewish migration and long-term socioeconomic factors (as was the case of Odessa in the nineteenth century), those centers that arose because of political upheavals (revolutions, wars, or change of borders) were created abruptly. The transformation of Minsk from provincial capital to capital of a Soviet republic, and its subsequent development into a political and cultural center, occurred suddenly and was therefore more dramatic. The revolution, which elected Minsk the capital of a Soviet republic, led to the reassessment of established perceptions of center and periphery in Russian Jewish life. Separated from its historic territory of Lita, Jewish Minsk replaced its traditional orientation toward Vilna with a new relationship with Moscow.

The geocultural character of the urban centers of Belorussia—a small, economically backward region without a well-established and historically rooted national culture and identity—helped Jews gain a special status in the political and cultural life of the city. With their overall higher level of literacy and politicization compared to Belorussians, Jews flowed into the economic and cultural sectors of society at a quicker pace, frequently sovietizing quite smoothly. But the successful acculturation into the new system of many weighed against the social marginalization of many others, which resulted from their social background or claims of national-cultural identity. Most marginals, however, eventually chose to—or were forced to—adapt to the new Soviet codes of behavior and partake in the system. In a way the geocultural nature of Minsk alleviated this thorny process: the city's Jewishness made the transition into Soviet society easier as it allowed for the possibility of retaining aspects of Jewish identity that might have otherwise been cast off in the acculturation process.

Compared to the surrounding cities and towns of Belorussia, such as Mozyr, Gomel, Slutsk, or Vitebsk, Minsk acquired some of the traits of a large modern urban center, especially by virtue of its new standing as Soviet capital. New wide streets ran from one side of town to the other, more efficient public transportation carried its residents and electrification lit a number of its neighborhoods, as "three-colored lanterns" appeared at the main crossroads. Yet, when compared to other major cities in the European region of the Soviet Union—like Leningrad, Moscow, and Kiev—Minsk remained a provincial Jewish city of limited size, more similar to Berdichev or Zhitomir, with some of the features typical of a large *shtetl*. As the new Soviet capital intersected with the historic Jewish center of the Pale of Settlement, Minsk remained "the Jerusalem of Raysn," the Jewish term for the region of Belorussia. When describing Minsk in 1928, at the crossroad of major geopolitical and geocultural changes, the Yiddish writer and journalist I. J. Singer exposed the features of a Lithuanian Jewish city: "Everyone agrees that Minsk is a happy, lively city. Still evident is the charm typical of Lithuanian Jewish cities near the border, where ideas and smuggling, fearfulness and lawlessness, religiosity and heresy, modesty and dissoluteness, antiquity and modernity are compressed together in the grubby alleys and houses, and fill the city with life, dynamism and hope. Here, one is still a little provincial, a tad old-fashioned and therefore more believing."[119]

3 Entangled Loyalties

The Bund, the Evsektsiia, and the Creation of a "New" Jewish Political Culture

> Let it be said clearly and precisely at this, the last moment, that whatever happens to the name of the Bund, to the form of the Bund, whatever the conference should decide—Bundism will live as long as the Jewish proletariat lives, Bundism will live—and will be triumphant.[1]

> We face the dilemma of independent existence or sections [Evsektsiia], with the hope that we will be able to remake the sections and suit them to the needs of the Jewish proletariat.... We remain loyal to this outlook. This is our Bundism, this is the Bund. Not a single one of us has ceased to be a Bundist, nor will any of us cease to be. Therefore I can close my speech with the cry "Long live Bundism, long live the Bund!"[2]

> Jewish workers! The Bund is not leaving you. It remains with you. It leads you under the banners of the All-Russian Communist Party. Jewish workers! Carry your love, your trust, your fidelity to the Jewish Labour Bund into that great alliance [bund] in which the organization of the Jewish proletariat will in time emerge.[3]

During the NEP, the New Economic Policy inaugurated by Lenin in 1921, when less stifling restrictions were enforced on Soviet citizens, it was relatively easier to express publicly the commitment to specific aspects of Jewishness and balance them with the Soviet vision of universalism. At the end of the NEP, with the launching of the Cultural Revolution and the 1929 industrialization campaign, expressions of Jewishness that were not consistent with Soviet ideals were banished from the public domain of institutions and organizations and became more and more confined to the private sphere of the home. However, while the Bolsheviks continued to ruthlessly mold the lives and consciousness of individuals according to Communism, within the historical constraints of the day Soviet citizens (Jews and non-Jews alike) still managed to assert their allegiance to specific aspects of pre-revolutionary political and cultural life, albeit quietly and cautiously for the most part.

The persistence in Soviet Minsk of political and cultural strategies peculiar to the local pre-revolutionary Bundist tradition of the city provides a noteworthy example in the study of continuities. After Vilna, Minsk was the largest Bundist center in the northwestern provinces of the Russian empire. During the late nineteenth century, with the growth of the Jewish proletariat in the northwest, where 40 percent of adult Jews were engaged as workers in handicrafts and factories, revolutionary activity expanded rapidly.[4] The growth was so impressive that the Jewish labor movement developed two idiosyncratic features in most of the northwestern region: first, in the nearly complete absence of non-Jewish Socialist parties, the Bund was not exclusively organized for Jews and by Jews, but often conducted revolutionary agitation among Belorussian and Russian workers as well. (True for Minsk or Kovno, this was not true of Vilna, where both Polish and Russian Social-Democratic parties were active and enjoyed popular support since the end of the nineteenth century.)[5] Second, in this region only, the Bund had more members than the Zionist movement during the early years of the twentieth century (24,440 Bundists in 1906 versus 18,760 Zionists in 1903).[6] In 1897, Minsk counted 1,000 Jewish workers members of the underground trade unions, called *kassy*, which planned strike activities, economic struggle, and political opposition to the tsar. This was an extraordinary number at the time, second only to Vilna.[7] *Kassy* members and leaders carried out conspiratorial work in forests, private homes, and factories as well as organized public rallies. The so-called Kurlovskii shooting, one of the bloodiest events in the northwestern region, took place in Minsk during a workers' demonstration organized by the Bund, when tsarist troops opened fire on a mass rally in late October 1905, killing fifty-seven people, forty-two of them Jews.[8]

In Minsk as elsewhere, the Bund had fought for the ideals of Socialism, civil equality for Jews, and the creation of autonomous institutions that would support the development of Yiddish language and culture. Politically in line with the Mensheviks, Bundists believed that a capitalist-bourgeois regime should precede the dictatorship of the proletariat and unanimously condemned October 1917 as a Bolshevik coup d'état. But in 1921, following the liquidation of the Jewish party, many Bundists throughout the Soviet Union agreed to join the local bureaus of the Evsektsiia.[9] Joining the ranks of the Communist Party and becoming members of the Evsektsiia, former Bundists were able, for the first time, to exert real political power on the Jewish street.[10] In doing so, however, many continued to express their loyalty to specific principles of their political past, at times publicly, at times in a more subtle way, reverting to Bundist subtexts.[11] For some, the commitment to Bundism was deeply ideological. For others, it originated from a natural familiarity with the Bundist political discourse they had grown accustomed to over time. While numerous former Bundists lashed out against the Jewish party and, in order to overcome the distrust of local Communists, promoted the campaigns that led to the arrests of the so-called Right Bundists (who had voiced their opposition to the Jewish party's merging with the Bolsheviks), many were unable to fully renounce, overnight, the political convictions they had fought for before the revolution and ended up developing a twofold loyalty to Bundism and Communism.

Compared to other regions of the Soviet empire, the new Jewish political leadership in Minsk succeeded in remaining closely associated with the Bundist tradition at the personal, institutional, ideological, and cultural level also as a result of the city's geographic position and nature. Operating in a place that was far from Moscow and, albeit capital of a Soviet republic, in many respects still a provincial city, during the 1920s the Jewish political leadership enjoyed more autonomy here than it did elsewhere. It relied not only on the pre-revolutionary local strength of the Bund, but also on the weakness of local Communist organizations. The proportion of members of the Jewish labor movement (in 1904 the Bund had twelve hundred members in the city of Minsk alone) was significantly higher than the proportion of Belorussians, Russians, and Jews together, who were active in the city's Communist organization.[12] As of 1921, the CPB had only approximately two thousand members, while the average Russian *guberniia* at the time included twelve to fifteen thousand party members.[13] The statement made by the Bundist leader Ester Frumkin at the time of the disbandment of the Jewish party—"Bundism will live as long as the Jewish proletariat lives, Bundism will live—and will be triumphant"—had real implications in Minsk.[14] Here, more than elsewhere, the Bundists who ultimately embraced Communism could envision the Evsektsiia as something more than a mere section of the Bolshevik Party, as something truly akin to an autonomous Jewish organization.

Establishing Power: The Evsektsiia Takes Over

At the beginning of the twentieth century Belorussia was one of the least developed regions of European Russia. With an industrial production amounting to half of Russia's and 74 percent of the population engaged in agriculture, it had one of the highest rates of illiteracy in European Russia.[15] Marxism, which in Belorussia bore almost no relation to the Belorussian national movement, spread rather slowly and late in the territories of the future BSSR, at least among Belorussians.[16] The first political circles devoted to Marxist ideas were largely organized by Jews and, to some extent, Poles. Founded in Smolensk in May 1917, by the Bolsheviks who had served in the ranks of the Western division of the Red Army, the Communist Party of Belorussia was primarily made up of Russians and run in Moscow.[17] As stated during the First Congress of the Belorussian Communist Party, held in Smolensk on December 30–31, 1918, the CPB functioned as a section of the Russian Communist Party.[18]

The early months following the defeat of the Polish troops were marked by a close and yet problematic relationship between local Communists and the Minsk Bundist leadership, generated mostly by opportunism on both parts. Because of the lack of support for the Bolshevik cause, to gain control over the region and form a strong local government Communists had no choice but to negotiate with local Bundists. Many Bundists, however, yearned to be involved in the new power structure. During the 1920 electoral assembly of the Minsk Soviet, for example, Communists and Bundists came to an agreement that eight Soviet members would be elected from the Bolshevik faction and seven from the Bundist Party.[19] Similarly, during the 1920 electoral campaign, the official instructions for local elections explicitly encouraged Bundist candidates to run on the CPB election lists (while rejecting candidates from the Poale-Zion). In several instances, the Central Committee of the CPB recommended that Communists refrain from engaging in polemics with Bundists.[20]

Not unlike the CPB, in the early stages of its establishment the Evsektsiia was in dire need of support from the Bund and relied heavily on the Jewish party to organize propaganda activities, appointing from its ranks the new Communist cadre. In August 1920, the Minsk Evsektsiia organized a Committee for Public Assistance: besides two Evsektsiia members and one member of the Revolutionary Committee, the Executive Committee included one Bundist as well.[21] In early September, the Evsektsiia convened a meeting together with the Bund's Central Committee to set up the Jewish sections of the People's Commissariat for Nationality Affairs and the People's Commissariat for Education.[22] And in mid-September, as part of the effort to promote Jewish conscription in the Red Army, the Evsektsiia invited the Bund to participate in the Week for Recruiting Jewish workers on the Western front. The public speakers—among them Yankl Levin, member of the Bund's Central Committee—were all Bundists.[23] This was an unusual case of collaboration with an independent political party: in Moscow, at the time, the government was entirely based on a one-party system.

Some Communists voiced their concern about the mounting power struggle between the Evsektsiia and the Bund, and their fears about the separatist nature promoted by Bundism.[24] In September 1920, two members of the Minsk Evsektsiia, Moshe Kiper and Mikhail Levitan, called for the Bolsheviks to quit negotiating with the Jewish party and dismiss all Bundists who held leading positions in the local Soviet government. "The most important commissariats... such as the Council of National Economy (Sovnarkhoz), Social Security Department, Commissariat for Public Health (Zdravoobraz)... are in the hands of Bundists. [One] has the impression that the Bund, and not our party, is in power... these commissariats shun the control of the party and appear as Bundist organs, not party organs."[25] The Evsektsiia accused Bundist Arn Vaynshteyn (Rakhmiel), president of the Belorussian Council of National Economy, of carrying on Bundist petit-bourgeois ideals in the economic life of the cities of Belorussia, and held him responsible for the ineffectiveness of the nationalization process of the Belorussian industry.[26] With no Communists in its leadership, the People's Commissariat for Education was also controlled by Bundists. "It is impossible to start an offensive against [the Bund] when it represents Soviet authority in all of its most prominent institutions," commented the head of the Evsektsiia Levitan (himself a former Bundist).[27]

Whether the absolute dominion of the Bund was true or largely overstated, it still appears clear that, insofar as Communists lacked political support and committed activists, collaboration with the Bund was necessary and inevitable. Setting up the whole Soviet administrative and bureaucratic system weighed on the shoulders of a few comrades. The Minsk Evsektsiia regularly contacted Moscow asking to dispatch personnel to take over positions held by Bundists and carry out work in the city trade unions, traditional Bundist strongholds.[28] As Kiper pointed out the reconstruction task was huge, especially following the Polish invasion and the Bolshevik evacuation of Minsk, when Soviet organizations were completely destroyed and the city was left a "deserted place."[29] "There is nobody here who can do anything," wrote Kiper, "there is not one local comrade who will commit to serious work." Kiper himself could not focus exclusively on the work on the Jewish street as he was also active in building the general party infrastructure, "as the plenipotentiary of the Central Bureau of the Party."[30]

By March 1921, the Bolsheviks' ambition for absolute control over the political life of the country resulted in the liquidation of all political parties and factions within the Communist Party. The struggle by local Bund leaders—even those who in 1920 had joined the Left Bundists, or Kombund—to preserve organizational autonomy for the Jewish proletariat,[31] together with the written protest of several hundred Jewish workers in Minsk who voiced their opposition to the merger with the Communist Party, were of no use.[32] The Bund's demand to coordinate separately the Jewish working force was, in the eyes of the Bolsheviks, simply unacceptable. As the suppression of the Kronstadt rebellion clearly showed, the party would not tolerate criticism, opposition, or factions.[33]

Held in March 1921, in Minsk, the Extraordinary All-Russian Bundist Conference was forced to endorse the proposal of the Comintern Committee to merge the Bund with the Communist Party. The Central Bureau of the CPB advised all local Communist organizations to welcome into their ranks the members of Bundist organizations, "in order to eliminate, as quickly as possible, the sense of alienation . . . [and] . . . animosity resulting from the . . . [Bundist] separate organizational existence." Scheduled to take place in Minsk on April 19, 1921, the actual merger of the Bund with the Communist Party was marked by a dramatic ceremony, as Bundists marched with their banners to a local theater and handed them over to representatives of the CPB.[34] The ceremony was supervised by a special commission formed by a member of the Central Bureau of the CPB, a member of the Bund's Regional Committee, and a member of the Minsk Evsektsiia. Power negotiation took place as a merger condition: one member of the Bund's Regional Committee would become a member of the Central Bureau of the CPB, and two members of the Bund's Regional Committee would become members of the District Committees of the CPB. As for the rank and file, those Bundists who wished to could automatically join the Communist Party, without recommendations or a period of candidature, simply by filling out a questionnaire. Their party service would begin in April 1921, and their party card would register their previous party affiliation and revolutionary service.[35]

Other Bundist organizations merged with general Belorussian Communist institutions as well. The Bundist youth organization Yugend-Bund joined the general Communist youth organization, the Komsomol.[36] A commission of members from both organizations coordinated the merger, emphasizing that, "because of the major role played by the Young Bund in the region, many of its activists [should] serve in the local and regional Jewish sections of the Komsomol."[37]

The Minsk Evsektsiia admitted that, following the liquidation of the Bund, propaganda work among the local Jewish population was carried out more effectively. With 234 Bundists joining the ranks of the Communist Party of Belorussia, the situation in Minsk—stated the Evsektsiia—"greatly improved."[38] During the early months after the dissolution of the Jewish party numerous former Bundists came to serve prominently in the Minsk Evsektsiia, so much so that the Jewish section emerged as the Bund's heir. In this early phase, the separation between the Soviet Jewish agency and the dissolved Jewish party was blurred, to say the least. Two months after the Bund's liquidation, the Evsektsiia devoted a special issue of the local Jewish organ of the CPB, *Veker*, to celebrate the twenty-year career of Arn Vaynshteyn in the Bund's Central Committee.[39] In other words, a Communist newspaper celebrated the anniversary of someone's activity in another, now-defunct political party. As late as November 1921, the halls of the Jewish workers' clubs in Minsk, now under the supervision of the Evsektsiia, were still adorned with Bundist flags.[40] And in the summer of 1922, the Minsk Evsektsiia determined to celebrate in the city the twenty-fifth anniversary of the birth of the Jewish workers movement, that is, the founding of the Bund, in 1897.[41]

From the start, the Evsektsiia was conceived as an administrative body of the general CPB and not as an independent Jewish institution. However, Bundist-style autonomous leanings easily seeped through. The 1922 circular letter addressed by the Central Committee of the CPB to all local party branches in the republic, unambiguously prescribed the nature of the Evsektsiia and its relationship with general party organizations, reminding its leaders of its absolute lack of autonomy: "*The Evsektsiia cannot independently admit a new member or expel members . . . nor does it issue separate party-membership cards* [emphasis added]. . . . In trade unions, factories, and institutions with a large proportion of Jewish workers, the Evsektsiia does not organize separate cells or factions, but conducts propaganda work through the general party cells."[42] The fact that two years into the establishment of the Evsektsiia, and a year after the merger of the Bund into the Communist Party, the Central Committee of the CPB was still sending out nonchalant reminders about the absolute lack of self-rule on the part of the Jewish section, is an indication of how widespread the autonomous trend reminiscent of the Bund still was at the time. So that it might have been quite common for Evsektsiia members to admit or expel other members independently from the Communist Party or even to claim that separate membership cards should be issued for Evsektsiia affiliates.[43]

Minsk was seemingly more reluctant to break away from its Bundist past than were other Jewish centers. Here, former Bundists who had joined the new Soviet leadership did not feel compelled to distinguish between their Bundist past and their new Soviet career. Born in Gorodishche, a *shtetl* in the Minsk *guberniia*, Rebecca Gimmelshteyn had joined the local Bundist organization in 1904 and remained active in the party until 1920. In 1923, while she was head of one of the largest cooperative stores of the Minsk Central Workers' Cooperative, Rebecca wrote her autobiography. She traced the main stages of her career and referred to her pre-revolutionary political activity in the Bund with pride. She even emphasized that she personally knew, since 1904, two prominent former Bundists, members of the Bund's Central Committee, who at present held high offices in the city. One of them was Arn Mordukhovich (Vaynshteyn), whom she called only by name and patronymic, an indication of how well-known he was in Minsk.[44] Rebecca's words reveal that in 1923 the association with the Bund could be considered a positive factor in the life of Soviet citizens: she was not expected to wash out her connection with the Jewish party. Similarly, in the mid-1920s, the author of the official history of the Minsk tailors' union did not conceal that conspiratorial work in pre-revolutionary Minsk was carried out under the capable leadership of local Bundists, who still lived in the city at the time: "When the Bund got involved, then 90 percent of the strikes succeeded."[45]

Conducive to this acquiescent approach to Bundism was the continuity between the Evsektsiia and the Bundist leadership at the personal level. After all, the most prominent members of the Minsk Evsektsiia were former Bundists who had worked in the pre-revolutionary local organizations of the Jewish party: Avrom Beilin, Vulf Nodel, Bunin,[46] Yankl Levin,[47] Elye Osherovitsh,[48] and Ber Orshansky.[49] This continuity led to the emergence of entangled loyalties between Bundism and Communism. Yankl Levin, a young carpenter who became one of the Bund's top organizers in Minsk, became the Evsektsiia's secretary. In attempting to leave untouched the revolutionary nature of the Bund, Levin distinguished "Left Bundists," who had welcomed the merging with the Communist Party, from "Right Bundists," who had disparagingly rejected to join the Bolshevik Party. By emphasizing the difference between the two factions, he could separate "good Bundists" from "bad ones," and blame only the "rightists" of counterrevolutionary behavior. In April 1922, by warning Jewish Communists against the dangers of Zionists groups and their negative influence on the local Jewish population, Levin indicated that among its allies Zionism counted the White Army, the rabbis and "Right Bundists."[50] The Evsektsiia secretary refrained from using the more general term "Bundists," which allowed him to maintain a veiled allegiance to the party he had fought for before the revolution.

While in Minsk the local Jewish political leadership remained largely unchanged after the revolution, in other major Soviet Jewish centers, such as Moscow, Kiev, Kharkov, or Odessa, which had not been Bundist strongholds prior to the Bolsheviks, the degree of continuity was less prominent. In addition, only in Minsk the personal continuity was matched by an exceptional institutional continuity, absent elsewhere. The two most well-known Bundist institutions in the city—the Bronislaw Grosser Workers' Club and the Yiddish newspaper *Veker*—were preserved in the early Soviet period. They marked the Jewish street with a specific cultural legacy, which, in light of Soviet politics, should have been eradicated in 1921 at the time of the dissolution of the Bund.

"Bundist" Institutions

The Central Jewish Workers' Club and the central Jewish organ of the CPB became the two chief institutions employed by the Evsektsiia to popularize Communism on the Jewish street. The Bronislaw Grosser Club and the newspaper *Veker* had been Bundist institutions in Minsk long before the dissolution of the Jewish Labor Party. Both represented legendary emblems in the history of the Jewish workers' movement in Russia and Poland. Not only did the names "Grosser" and "Veker" evoke some of the most salient moments in the history of the Jewish party. For many Bundists they also embodied the very spirit of the Jewish party. When the "new" Jewish political leadership took over the two Bundist institutions, it did not rename them according to the usual Bolshevik practice. While many Bundists embraced Communism as an ideology, they still remained committed to the Bundist idea of a separate Jewish organization and a distinctly Jewish political identity. Maintaining the original Bundist names became a symbolic continuation, or at least an expression, of the Bundist organizational autonomy and political principles.

Born in 1883 in Miechow, near Cracow, Bronislaw Grosser became a prominent Bundist in Warsaw.[51] Together with Vladimir Medem he was one of the key spokesmen for the Bundist "neutralist" position on the national question, which maintained that only time (in the form of the will of the masses) would determine whether assimilation (and use of Russian) or a national revival (and use of Yiddish) would mark the future of the Jewish proletariat. When Grosser died—in December 1912—he was quickly hailed as a Bundist icon and legendary combatant for the good of the Jewish working class. So much so that following his death it became quite common in interwar Poland to name educational, cultural, and health institutions after Grosser, including the famous Bronislaw Grosser Library in Warsaw.

The new Soviet regime gave prior consideration to changing pre-revolutionary names into Communist ones, especially if the newly occupied "bourgeois" spaces had played a central role in the life of the city before the revolution.[52] The act of renaming symbolized taking possession of a space, revolutionizing it, and making it Communist. It is therefore surprising that the name of one of the supposedly central Soviet Jewish institutions in the city, expected to spread Communism among the Jewish masses of the Belorussian capital, preserved such a quintessential Bundist name.

The name question had been one of the core issues debated by the Bund in its negotiations with the Bolsheviks. On the eve of the merger, the leaders of the Jewish party argued in favor of the preservation of the word "Bund" in the official designation of the Communist Party.[53] Among the conditions, which, on January 29, 1921, the Bundist delegation presented to the committee for the unification of the two parties, was that "the Bund and the Evsektsiia are united in the Communist Party under the name of General Workers' Union of the Bund." As the Jewish Commissar Semion Dimanshteyn admitted, "For the Jewish masses . . . the word 'Bund' had a mystical meaning."⁵⁴ Of course, all the requests presented by the Bund's delegates, including the solicitation to preserve the name "Bund," were turned down by the Communist Party. Once it became clear that they would have to give up both organizational autonomy and the name Bund, the focus of Minsk's former Bundists shifted to other names of institutions and personalities that had played an important role in the party's history. As a precondition to join the Communist Party, many Bundists demanded that the name of their Grosser Club be maintained.⁵⁵

The club's name was so closely associated with the Bund that its preservation tricked some into believing that the Jewish labor party still existed. Complaints were issued from nearby Mozyr and Slutsk, voicing the astonishment with the Bund's protracted existence and the Grosser Club's activity as the central Soviet Jewish club in Minsk.⁵⁶ For the most part sporadic and inconsequential, these protests countered the official position of the Evsektsiia, which was clear and firm. When in March 1922, comrade Shekht suggested to merge the Grosser Club with the general Party Club because of dire financial conditions, Yankl Levin resolutely replied: "The Grosser Club represents the only major Jewish cultural institution in all of Belorussia. . . . It must be preserved at all costs."⁵⁷ Less than a month later, the Evsektsiia reiterated in a definitive way that "the further existence of the Grosser Club is absolutely necessary."⁵⁸

After the Bund's merger with the CPB, the Minsk Grosser Club found itself at the junction between old and new, between the Bundist past and new Communist foundations. If the club's director Salmon had to join the Communist Party in order to retain his position,⁵⁹ the club maintained a connection with its Bundist tradition by housing the library of the Bund's Central Committee. The Evsektsiia relocated the library from the Jewish Central Party School to the Grosser Club, so that evidence of the Bundist past would now be preserved in the city's central Soviet Jewish club.

Under Bundist management, the club's nature had been both of a political organization as well as a cultural institution: it had a library and organized classes and literary programs, as politics was pursued under the cover of culture. Here, the Bund had held its party meetings and the party's Central Committee had met on a regular basis. After its official reopening on December 22, 1921, the club quickly developed into one of the main Jewish cultural centers in Minsk. It attracted Jews from all over the city not only as a political institution, with *kruzhki* and lectures on Marxism, but also as a place where Jews spent leisure time and came together to converse. The club housed several divisions, including musical, theatrical, sporting, and artistic divisions, and regularly organized literary soirées and concerts. The main events sponsored during the month of August 1922 included a chess tournament, with the participation of one hundred people, and a literary evening with a lecture on Yiddish theater by Moshe Rafalskii and readings of Peretz's work by the Yiddish studio cast—on the newly built stage—with the participation of three hundred people.⁶⁰ The club's library included 1,368 Yiddish and Russian books.⁶¹ Approximately 5,000 readers visited the reading room every month. In 1924, the club counted 237 members (only twelve of them being

Communist Party members).⁶² Between 100 and 150 members attended the club daily, but as a report on the club's activities stated, "Unfortunately, our older party members [that is, Jews who had joined the Communist Party before the liquidation of the Bund] rarely visit the Grosser Club."⁶³

During the early 1920s the Grosser Club developed into one of the best organized workers' clubs in the city. Located in the impressive four-story building of the former Hotel Europa, on Freedom Square, in the city's historic center, in November 1923 it also became the home of the Jewish Folk University (Evreiskii Narodnyi Universitet).⁶⁴ Also referred to as the Minsk Workers' University, it was an evening school for adults designed to replace the political study groups that regularly met at the Grosser Club. Classes were open to one hundred students, met three times a week, and were taught in Yiddish.⁶⁵ In 1924, the Jewish Workers' University was described as follows: "Its goal is to provide the working masses with a solid political knowledge, acquaint them with the foundations of natural sciences, . . . giving them . . . a Marxist worldview. . . . [It] serves not only Minsk, but is a cultural center for the whole republic. . . . The university [has become] an exemplary institution for Jewish workers throughout Belorussia."⁶⁶ The number of members in the Grosser Club increased over time, reaching 397 by 1926, with an average of 300 people attending the club daily. The number of those members who belonged to the Communist Party also increased. Of the 397 members, 100 were Party members and 59 belonged to the Komsomol.⁶⁷ While most people no longer associated it in their minds with the Bund, the club remained an important Jewish cultural institution in Minsk throughout its existence, until the mid-1930s. Ironically, however, the mere fact that Jews came together in the former Bundist club was considered by some hard-core Jewish Communists as a manifestation of Jewish parochialism, national separatism, and perhaps even Bundism. In 1926, some Jewish Communists voiced their concern about Jewish workers attending exclusively the "Jewish club" ("*evreiskii klub*"): "It is a fine club, managed by a fine group of activists. But if you take a look, you will see that . . . those who visit the club don't go to any other club, even though many activities are organized elsewhere as well. They love to gather in their Jewish club." The worker Dvorkin replied to the criticism, explaining "when you go . . . [to the Jewish] club you meet your usual circle of friends, with whom you can talk, in the Karl Marx Club [the general Communist club] there is no one to talk to. This is why [Jewish] workers are drawn to the [Jewish] club." Another worker added that it was not the allegiance to the Bundist tradition that attracted Jewish workers, but rather a question of habit, combined with the unique variety of cultural activities available in the Jewish club.⁶⁸ In the early 1930s, these activities included a chorus, a string-instrument circle, a shooting circle, a literary circle, an antireligious seminar, and a photography circle. It was Jews who participated in the club's activities; sometimes they shared a common Bundist memory. But more often they simply enjoyed spending leisure time in the company of other Jews, in what possibly remained one of the most vibrant Jewish social settings in the city until the mid-1930s.

* * *

Name and space continuities tied to the Bundist tradition were retained also with regard to the local Jewish Communist newspaper. Situated in the locale of the Grosser Club, the city's former Bundist newspaper, *Der Veker*, became in 1921 the official publication of the Evsektsiia of the Belorussian SSR.[69] Compared to the other two main Jewish dailies published in the Soviet Union—*Der Emes* (The truth) issued in Moscow as the official organ of the Central Bureau of the Evsektsiia, and *Komunistishe fon* (The Communist banner) issued in Kiev and later replaced by the Kharkov-based *Shtern* as the organ of the Main Bureau of the Ukrainian Evsektsiia—the Minsk newspaper had been a well-established institution in the city since the earlier phases of the Provisional Government. In the summer of 1917—the opening issue appeared on May 12—*Der Veker* became the first Bundist newspaper legally published in Minsk.[70] Its origin was deeply rooted not only in the local Bundist tradition of the city, but also in the more general tradition of the northwestern region of the tsarist empire. Issued in Vilna during the 1905 revolution, *Der Veker* was the name of the first Bundist newspaper to be legally published anywhere in tsarist Russia,[71] thereafter becoming a potent symbol of Bundist heroism and appearing as the name of a number of Bundist publications in Poland and America. When the Bund was forced to liquidate in April 1921, its local organ was not closed down but simply turned into a Communist newspaper overnight. Unwilling to fully part with the past, the new (old) Jewish leadership asked and obtained approval that *Veker*, and not the first Bolshevik Yiddish newspaper issued in Minsk, *Der Shtern*, become the organ of the CPB Evsektsiia. As the Jewish Communist Shmuel Agursky pointed out, *Veker* "was our worst enemy during the revolution. . . . [Later it] became a propagator of the Communist doctrine; and yet, each Communist could not forget the [Bundist] role played by *Veker*."[72]

This continuity was rather unique in the context of Soviet Jewish and non-Jewish institutions alike. Considering the power struggle between Lenin and the Mensheviks, and the fact that the Bund shared the same revolutionary doctrine of the Mensheviks, it is remarkable that the main organ of the Evsektsiia, in the capital city of a Soviet republic, maintained its original Bundist name. To be sure, nowhere in Soviet Russia was there an equivalent case of a Menshevik newspaper or institution, which, taken over by the Communists and transformed into an official party institution, retained its pre-revolutionary name.

The association between Bund and *Veker* was ensured also by the remarkable stability in the paper's editorial office. Elye Osherovitsh served as the editor of the Minsk daily from 1919 to 1937. Born in 1873 in the Minsk *guberniia* and active in the Bund's city organization since the early 1900s, Osherovitsh reached the highest ranks of the Jewish political leadership in Minsk. Director of the Jewish Folk University since 1923 and secretary of the Evsektsiia in 1924, he was appointed editor-in-chief of the newspaper in 1922. During the early 1920s, all but one of the other members of the newspaper's editorial staff were former Bundists.[73]

The social and economic crisis unleashed by the Civil War disrupted Soviet life as a whole, affecting also the operation of institutions that had existed before the revolution. The editors of the newspaper had to struggle for its existence. To face the publication's deficit and improve its circulation throughout Minsk and the surrounding district the National Minorities Bureau of the CPB appointed agents for a marketing campaign.[74] Press Committees in the Evsektsiia bureaus of the region were in charge of enlisting subscribers and making sure that in each "workshop, factory, and party cell with a large percentage of Jewish workers, every Jewish party member . . . [and] conscious worker subscribed to *Veker*." To increase the newspaper's circulation, in mid-1922 the Evsektsiia called for "each party member to subscribe to a newspaper individually or as part of a collective; for each party member to convince at least two nonparty members to subscribe to the newspaper; and for party cells to organize collective subscriptions at every institution and factory."[75] A network of agents working on commission was also organized. They traveled to the cities and *shtetlekh* of Belorussia and advertised the subscription to the Jewish daily.[76]

Despite the initial financial difficulties and the rather small circulation of the newspaper, *Veker* became one of the most read Yiddish dailies in the Soviet Union. Even though never really impressive, especially when compared to the circulation of the Polish Yiddish press of the same period, the circulation of the Minsk Jewish daily, during specific years, roughly matched the circulation of the Moscow Jewish daily. But while the Minsk-based daily had a local and, to some degree, Belorussian character, the Moscow daily had mostly an All-Union feature and was largely distributed outside Moscow and the Russian republic. In July 1922, *Emes* had a circulation of three thousand copies; *Veker* of twenty-five hundred;[77] in May 1925, the Moscow daily had a circulation of six thousand; the Minsk daily reached that same circulation one year later.[78]

The heavy Bolshevization that permeated the pages of the former Bundist publication, while fending off many potential readers, did not prevent the Minsk daily from becoming an important social and cultural institution for the local Jewish population. At times, it even served some communal functions traditionally carried out by the Jewish community before the revolution. It was, for example, through the pages of the Yiddish daily that hundreds of Minsk Jewish residents with relatives in America found out about letters, visas, or packages sent to them from overseas during the 1920s. When Meyer Pishkin decided to make contact with his cousin in Brooklyn, he published a message in the only Jewish newspaper in the city.[79] The only way I. Zofin could find out that money from his American relatives awaited him at the Minsk post office was by reading the Yiddish daily.[80] As advertised in the announcements regularly posted in the newspaper, to retrieve parcels or information about their relatives Jewish citizens had to turn to the local Yiddish press, which in the absence of other institutions had become one of the cornerstones of the new Soviet Jewish community.

* * *

The personal and institutional continuity between Bund and Evsektsiia was too apparent and began to arouse complaints. How could the two official organs of the Jewish section of the CPB still be called with their original Bundist names? In February 1925, a group of seventeen Jewish Communists petitioned the CPB and the Evsektsiia asking to rename the two institutions, thrusting aside the Bundist past once and for all. The petition signatories argued that Bundist traditions slowed down the Bolshevization of the Jewish workers, who continued to heed exclusively their former leaders [Bundists] and ignore the new Communist elite. In Belorussia and in Minsk, in particular—continued the petition—the legacy of the Grosser Club and the Yiddish daily *Der Veker* prevented the Jewish masses from fully embracing Communism. The letter provided examples of true Communist Jewish personalities whose names should be used in lieu of Grosser and *Veker*; these included the names of Shimilievich-Raisen, who had fought against the Poles, and of Zalman Khaikin, editor of the first Communist Yiddish newspaper published in the region (*Der Shtern*). Both had joined the Bolsheviks as early as 1917. The name issue was addressed as follows:

> [The name of] the club of the Right Bundist comrades-in-arms of Abramovich, in Poland, is "Bronislaw Grosser." ... [This fact] has ... a negative effect on the political émigrés from Poland [who settle in Minsk]. ... [T]he central Yiddish organ of the Communist Party should be called with the Old-Bolshevik name *Der Shtern*, the first to illuminate the road to Communism for the Jewish proletariat, rather than *Der Veker*, ... which has "suspicious namesakes" on the other side of the border ... [and is] a daily supplement to the American Jewish *Forverts* [Forward] ... after a five-year permanence in our party, these old names and traditions have become obsolete.[81]

The Evsektsiia endorsed the name-change request several months later, on October 7, 1925, when the words *Der Veker*, a shameful trace of the Bundist heritage, were erased from the daily. The reaction to the allegation of preserving Bundist traditions entailed a more radical resolution than the one suggested by the petitioners. The club and newspaper were in fact not renamed with the Jewish, albeit Communist, names of Khaikin and *Der Shtern*, but with purely Communist names. The Grosser Club became the Lenin Club—after the Bolshevik mythical father—and *Der Veker* became *Oktyabr* (October)—as a way of celebrating the eighth anniversary of the October revolution.[82] It was hard to get more ideologically correct than that.

An ensuing name-change campaign swept through other Jewish institutions in and around Minsk. The organ of the Jewish section of the young pioneers, entitled *Der Yunger Veker* (The young Veker), was renamed *Der Yunger Leninets* (The young Leninist), while "Veker" collective farms that existed in the surrounding region changed their name to "Oktyabr." In the first issue of the Jewish daily with the new untainted title, the former Bundist and member of the Evsektsiia, Moshe Shulman, explicated the grounds for the name revolution:

> For the Jewish worker of our region *Veker* represented a tradition [the Bundist one], ... this name is connected to the memory of those years.... The Bund disappeared and only the name *Veker* remained.... the new *Veker* was transformed into a Bolshevik organ.... And if the content of *Veker* was a Communist one then ... why keep the old name, which reminds the Jewish worker of his youth errors, his earlier mistakes, ... his traditions, which have already lived their lives to the end? ... *The name of a newspaper is not a hollow sound, but rather a program, a slogan, a path* [emphasis added] ... we could not have chosen a better name: nowhere else in the Soviet Union is there a newspaper with such a name, a simple one with an important content. The shift from *Veker* to *Oktyabr* represents yet another step forward in the Bolshevization process of the Jewish masses.[83]

Recognizing the name of an institution not as a mere "empty sound," but rather as the echo of a definite political program, was at the heart of the decision to preserve the original Bundist names. Maintaining "Grosser" and "Veker" until 1925 represented the attempt on the part of the new leadership to pledge for the continuity of the Bundist tradition within the new Soviet context.

The Lekert Cult and the Construction of a Soviet Jewish Hero

Another legendary figure loomed over the Bundist historical memory of the city, perhaps even more than Grosser. Born in 1880, in Hanushishok, Grodno *guberniia*, after his father's death Hirsh Lekert moved to Dvinsk where he worked as a shoemaker and joined the local Bundists.[84] He carried out propaganda work among Jewish tanners and shoemakers, spreading political appeals and leaflets. From Vilna, where he moved to in 1895, he embarked on conspirative work on behalf of the Bund. Arrested in 1900, Lekert spent several months in Petersburg's "Kresti" Prison and in Ekaterinoslav, eventually returning to Vilna in 1902, illegally.[85] The Vilna Bundist organization was officially opposed to political terrorism, a weapon used to fight tsarist authorities by other Socialist groups such as Narodnaia Volia (The People's Will), for example. But after the events of May Day 1902, when the Vilna Governor General Viktor Von Wahl ordered the flogging of Jewish and Polish workers for participating in a political demonstration, a group of Bundists—among them the members of the Central Committee—called for revenge. It was Hirsh Lekert who attempted to assassinate Von Whal. Even though he only wounded the Russian official, Lekert was sentenced to death and hung on June 10, 1902. Recognized as a martyr for the Jewish workers' movement, he was instantly introduced in the pantheon of Bundist heroes.

Like every other nationality in the Soviet Union, Jews were also entitled to their national heroes, so long as these did not clash with Soviet ideals. The classical authors of Yiddish literature, for example, lent themselves well to play the role of new Soviet Jewish heroes. Cultural events to celebrate the birth or death anniversary of Sholem

Aleichem and Mendele Mocher Seforim were regularly organized across the city.[86] In September 1927, on the occasion of the tenth anniversary of Mendele's death, besides holding festive celebrations and hanging the writer's portraits in schools and cultural institutions throughout Belorussia, the inspector for Jewish culture of the BSSR, Osherov, suggested to rename Mendele's native town Kapulye (Kopyl) Mendele-shtot.[87] Similarly, in 1936, to commemorate the hundredth anniversary of Mendele's birth, the secretary of the Central Committee of the CPB, Gikalo, commissioned the Writers' Union of Belorussia to organize a literary evening dedicated to the writer's work, the editorial staffs of newspapers across the republic to write articles about him, and the Belorussian State Publishing House to issue his best works both in Yiddish and Belorussian.[88] Unlike Sholem Aleichem, who was the recognized "Jewish folkwriter" par excellence throughout the USSR, Mendele was celebrated as a kind of Jewish regional hero: he was born in Belorussia and spent his youth there.

The Minsk Jewish leadership chose, among others, the Bundist icon Hirsh Lekert. With his social background—a poor shoemaker—and his active struggle against tsarist authorities that cost him his life, Hirsh Lekert had the potential qualities for becoming the perfect Soviet Jewish hero. Bundist political leanings were the only blemish in Lekert's life. The solution was thus to remove these "counterrevolutionary" incidents from his biography and rewrite him into the framework of the general workers' movement. Interestingly, local Jewish activists did not even consider selecting as a heroic figure on the Jewish street Hesia Helfman—the Jewish woman from Mozyr (a *shtetl* much closer to Minsk than Vilna) who, with no Bundist blotch to hide, in 1881 collaborated in the assassination of Tsar Alexander II.

In May 1922, the Minsk Evsektsiia turned to the Executive Committee of the CPB with the proposal to "immortalize the memory of Lekert" by erecting a monument in the Belorussian capital.[89] The presidium of the Central Executive Committee of the CPB endorsed the proposal at once and finalized the idea of building in Minsk a monument to honour Hirsh Lekert on May 18, 1922, with the following resolution:

> June 10 is the twentieth anniversary since the day of the execution in Vilna of Hirsh Lekert . . . an illiterate Jewish shoemaker . . . [who] attempted to assassinate the Vilna Governor Von Wahl. . . . For his attack on Von Wahl Lekert paid with his life. [He] was one of the many fearless fighters, who during the early period of the revolutionary struggle sacrificed their lives for the workers' cause. The Central Executive Committee of Belorussia resolved to build a monument for Lekert in Minsk where, almost at the same time as in Vilna, dozens of . . . revolutionaries . . . were sentenced to flogging. . . . The memory of Lekert must be immortalized. This is the cause of all conscious workers, peasants, and Red Army soldiers.[90]

While Lekert's Jewishness was openly acknowledged, his specific Bundist affiliation and identity were not mentioned. He was presented as a universal hero who fought for the general proletariat and could therefore fit in harmoniously with the ideal of Soviet universalism. Ironically, however, the erection of Lekert's monument on Freedom

Square, in lieu of the pre-revolutionary monument to Alexander II "The Tsar-Liberator," produced for the first time in Soviet Minsk a uniquely "Bundist" space.[91] Whether the location was a coincidence or not the monument stood in the same square as the former Bundist institutions, the Grosser Club, and the editorial office of the daily *Veker*.[92]

A campaign to collect the funds for the monument's erection was launched in the summer of 1922. "If on June 10, 1902, Lekert was led to the gallows in silence, on July 10, 1922 a monument to honor him [will] be erected at the thunderous sound of the International," avowed the party cell of a local Jewish institution.[93] Comrade Bunin—a former Bundist and a member of the Evsektsiia—spoke in front of the party cell of the Sewing Industry Workers' Union (where most workers were Jewish and shared a Bundist past) and called on each comrade to make a contribution toward the monument's erection.[94] Even though it was not mentioned, the Bundist background of the Jewish martyr was well-known to most. A number of Jewish union members might very well have experienced in person the events of 1902, while the younger ones had most likely heard about Lekert from comrades or family. Hirsh Lekert remained first and foremost a Bundist hero.[95]

During the 1922 campaign, meetings were held throughout the city to collect donations for the monument. The Shveiprom tailors' union convened a meeting, in Yiddish, for three hundred comrades; the Grosser Club organized a conference, where former Bundist Moshe Rafes, drawing from his book *Hirsh Lekert*, issued that same year in Minsk, spoke about his recollections about the Bundist martyr;[96] and the Central Executive Committee of the CPB called a ceremonial meeting in the city theater, during which three comrades took the floor in Yiddish. Overall, sixteen meetings were held in Russian, with the participation of a large segment of the city's working force. The railroad workers' meeting alone saw the participation of six hundred people.[97] At the general meeting of the "House of Mother and Child" organization, women workers "stood in memory of the deceased fighter."[98] According to one source, six thousand people participated in the nineteen Lekert assemblies held in the city during the month of June.[99]

The Evsektsiia received subventions toward the monument's erection also from places like Slutsk, Vinnitsa, and Orenburg. These contributions were in turn allocated to a special fund in the Financial Department of the CPB.[100] Even though Lekert was introduced as a universal revolutionary hero who sacrificed his life for the good of the general workers' movement, the funds were collected primarily among Jewish workers, with the assumption, it seems, that they would contribute more than others to the erection of the monument to a Jewish—and for many Bundist—hero.

Moscow and Minsk joined forces in the Lekert endeavor, not only financially. With the intention of bestowing on the Lekert monument an all-Union status, the Minsk Jewish leadership consulted with the Moscow Evsektsiia.[101] Some former Bundists in Moscow, in particular those natives of the Lithuanian region, home to the Jewish labor movement, were drawn by the idea of creating a Jewish revolutionary monument and perhaps, unconsciously, a Bundist niche. This was possible in Minsk, but unfeasible in Moscow. In her popular account of Hirsh Lekert and the Jewish workers' movement, in which she attempted to integrate harmoniously the history of the Bund into the history of Lenin's RSDP, Ester Frumkin (from Moscow) hailed with passion the Soviet canonization of Lekert in Minsk. Published in Moscow in 1922, the book starts off with a reminder of the intimate relation—as well as the new hierarchy—existing between Vilna and Minsk,

> The city of Vilna, where Lekert fought and died, together with the military field where his bones lie hidden, are still in the hands of our class enemy. But just a few hours away from Vilna, the Soviet Union comes into sight, with Soviet Belorussia and its capital Minsk, which has always been Vilna's sister-city, as life throbbed with the same heartbeat here and there.... What cannot be accomplished in Vilna is being carried out today in Minsk ... near the High Market, [by] the former Governor's House ..., close to the warped dome of the big *besmedresh*, surrounded by even older shuls ..., in the middle of this square, a small boulevard leads to the statue of Alexander II.... Now the square is called Freedom Square, the Governor's House is the Central Executive Committee ... the former richest hotel in town is the Jewish workers' club [Grosser] ... and the only thing left of Alexander II is stone ... and there are people who once worked with Lekert, fought with him.... Hirsh Lekert lives! Hirsh Lekert has been brought back to life![102]

The Lekert monument was eventually put up in the second half of the 1920s, initially as an extension to the old monument to Alexander II (a large plate with "Lekert" engraved in Hebrew golden letters was placed in lieu of the tsar's head), and later on as a separate bust crafted by sculptor Abram Brazer, who was living in Minsk at the time.[103] The existence of such a Jewish urban space in a Soviet city appears unique. Perhaps nowhere else in the Soviet Union—or for that matter in Eastern Europe—was it possible to come across a monument to a Jewish (or Bundist) hero.

A simultaneous movement to rename streets and institutions after the Jewish martyr accompanied the Soviet canonization process of Lekert in Minsk. The Tanner's Union petitioned the Executive Committee of the CPB to rename Liakhovskii Street, Lekert Street. It also asked permission to hang a portrait of Lekert in the room of the union's board of management; distribute to union members small medals with his portrait; and name the Children's Home and the Professional School for Shoe Manufacturing in Minsk after the "new" Soviet hero.[104] In 1924 three city streets were renamed after Lekert.[105] Until the late 1930s, the mixed Belorussian-Jewish Soviet school no. 24 was located on Lekert Street.[106] A variety of institutions and organizations throughout Belorussia (such as the collective farm in the *shtetl* Liadi, the children's home in Mohilev and the Soviet Jewish school in Gomel) were renamed after Hirsh Lekert, and they retained the name until the late 1930s.[107] At the same time, cultural events celebrating the new Soviet Jewish hero were held in the city, and Yiddish popular songs about him occasionally performed.[108] His history was also retold to students of the Minsk Soviet Jewish schools in its untainted version, well into the 1930s.[109] The 1931 fourth year textbook for Soviet Jewish schools in Belorussia, for example, included a detailed account of the 1902 events that led to the execution of the "poorly dressed . . . barely twenty-year-old Jewish worker . . . , whose statue stands in Minsk." It also featured Lekert's portrait. The account, followed by questions to be answered by students (such as "Why did the Soviet Union put up such a monument for Lekert?"), also included traces of the Bundist version about the alleged encounter and exchange between Lekert and the Vilna state rabbi moments before the execution.[110]

Two more cultural projects on the subject of Hirsh Lekert got underway in Minsk. Belgoskino produced a movie about his life. Entitled *Zayn Exelents* in Yiddish, and *Ego prevoskhoditelstvo* in Russian (His excellency), the movie was based on the screen adaptation by Minsk Yiddish writer Tsodek Dolgopolskii,[111] and it was directed by Grigory Roshal in 1928.[112] It was shown in movie theaters across the city, with intertitles in Yiddish or in Russian.[113] One of the few Soviet film productions to portray the economic and cultural life of the Jewish working masses, the movie focused on the participation of Jews in the revolutionary struggle through the idealization of the main character: as a hero of the international proletariat who happened to be Jewish, Lekert had no association with the Bund.[114] To the contrary, the Bund was depicted as an evil force operating on the Jewish street together with the wicked rabbi who, in the film, instigated Lekert's execution. In a complaint to the Moscow Society for Playwrights and Composers for the modest movie royalties, Dolgopolskii criticized the film director's reading of the events: "As a contemporary of Lekert, and a brushmaker who actively took part in the workers' movement of that period, I collected material in the course of several months . . . and now Roshal comes by and denies having used my work. . . . Roshal is not acquainted with the Lekert era . . . and . . . was unfortunately not able to make good use of my material."[115] It might be that the Yiddish writer was hinting here at the extreme sovietization of the Jewish worker and the fierce attack on the Bundist context of the day.

A similarly pungent anti-Bundist narrative appeared in the play *Hirsh Lekert*, performed by the Belorussian State Jewish Theater. Based on the drama by Soviet Yiddish writer Aron Kushnirov,[116] specially written for Belgoset, the play opened in Minsk on March 23, 1928, and was performed eleven times from 1928 to 1929.[117] Unlike the renditions of poets such as Avrom Rejzen, A. Leyeles, Avrom Sutzkever, and H. Leyvik, who before him took the life of the legendary Bundist martyr as the subject of their work,[118] Kushnirov's version was fiercely anti-Bundist. It included several negative characters disparagingly referred to as "Bundovke" or "Bundovets," who resisted the proletarian hero Lekert. In addition, the play presented the idea of taking revenge against Von Wahl for lynching the workers as originating exclusively from Lekert and a Polish worker, and in sheer disagreement with the Bund's Central Committee. The local Yiddish press greeted *Hirsh Lekert* as one of the most successful plays performed by Belgoset. Rafalskii himself thought of Lekert as a true revolutionary and Bolshevik-to-be hero, and he intended the play as a celebration of the tenth anniversary of the October revolution.[119] As late as 1936, the first play of historical content mentioned in the list of notable performances by Belgoset was *Hirsh Lekert*.[120]

In spite of the emphasis on Lekert's membership in the international proletariat, his concealed Bundist past reemerged in the late 1930s: he was rejected as an unreliable Soviet symbol and banned from the Minsk stage. His monument was demolished in 1937, in the wake of the Terror. The attempt to reshape Hirsh Lekert into a Soviet Jewish hero was, however, rather successful. Besides Sholem Aleichem (and perhaps Mendele Mocher Seforim) this became the most thriving experiment in recasting a Jewish hero into Soviet fashion. Drawing on their political and cultural "usable past," the Jewish leaders of the Belorussian capital rescued a pre-revolutionary Bundist hero and sovietized him. They erected a monument and named streets and institutions after him, something that the Jews of Vilna, under the Polish government, could not hope to accomplish. Similarly the Moscow Jewish leaders, possibly also interested in the erection of a monument to a Soviet Jewish hero in a Moscow square, did not turn to the Central Committee of the Communist Party requesting a Lekert memorial, as was done in Minsk. They knew that this would hardly have been accepted in Moscow. In Minsk, Jews enjoyed more autonomy and power, were far from the union's political center, and could claim Lekert an integral part of the city's local history and folklore. The Lekert myth in Soviet mold of the interwar period is, however, mostly forgotten. Unlike the Sholem Aleichem myth, Lekert was purged during the Terror, covered up by the destruction of the war and forgotten in the postwar oblivion of Jewish life in the former Pale of Settlement.

Bundist Imprint on Political and Cultural Strategies

Among the cultural strategies inherited from the Bund and promoted by the new leadership, the most visible, powerful, and less problematic one was—quite obviously—the support for the Yiddish language. Over time, the Bund had become more and more committed to Yiddish and Yiddish culture, regarding them as the true essence of the Jewish proletariat's national identity. The commitment to Yiddish and the right to use the language in all Jewish institutions was so rooted among Bundists that even Vladimir Medem, the theorist of the "neutralist school," endorsed this idea toward the end of his life: Yiddish was the quintessential manifestation of the Jewish nation.[121] This support—which remained fundamental for most former Bundists after the revolution and became partly responsible for the success of the Yiddishization campaign in Minsk—was in harmony with the 1919 official Soviet endorsement of Yiddish as the national language of the Jewish minority.

The debate among Minsk Evsektsiia members over the future role of Yiddish in the life of the Jewish workforce originated from the Bundist legacy of the city. The two key positions held by pre-revolutionary Bundist leaders (namely, Ester Frumkin's "nationalist school" supporting the use of Yiddish in all fields of Jewish life as the repository of Jewish national consciousness, and Medem's "neutralist school" supporting the masses' freedom of choice to make use of Yiddish or shift to Russian) resurfaced in the Soviet context of the Evsektsiia meetings.[122] While Medem's neutralism was short-lived and did not develop into a full-fledged school of thought in the Bund, the nationalist/Yiddishist position eventually became the mainstream view among the Jewish party leaders. Under the Soviets, the Bolshevik-internationalist position contested the Yiddishist stance.

Participants in the December 1921 Evsektsiia meeting in Minsk offered one explanation for the state of predicament in the process of Bolshevizing the Jewish street: the widespread tendency among Jewish workers toward *"sliianie"*—or amalgamation with the general work—and their inclination to study Russian. The Evsektsiia/Bundist nationalist position argued that this negative tendency, which resulted from the aspiration for upward mobility, interfered with the political education and consciousness building of Jewish workers. Their political development could be attained through Yiddish only: "Even when he knows a little Russian, the Jewish worker still remains an intellectual cripple . . . his real maturity can be achieved only in Yiddish." This position, shared by Arn Vaynshteyn, who favored enforcing the use of Yiddish in all Communist institutions, represented a sequel to the Bundist national stance. The counterposition supported by former Bundists in the Evsektsiia was voiced by Ber Orshansky, who praised the desire to know Russian as a healthy manifestation on the part of Jewish workers. The Evsektsiia's slogan, continued Orshansky, should be "work in two languages with a tendency to shift to . . . Russian." This position, which discredited the Yiddishist one, stemmed from the internationalist view of the Bolsheviks.[123]

At times, the commitment to Yiddish among former Bundists produced "separatist tendencies"—as Communists might have disparagingly called them—which clashed with their allegiance to Communism. The Evsektsiia faced the somewhat elusive task of easing the tension between the particular nature of being a Jewish section (which meant using Yiddish) and its general character of party section (whish meant using mostly, but not exclusively, Russian). These "separatist tendencies" emerged, for example, in the relation between some predominantly Jewish party cells in the city and the Red Army, one of the vital institutions of the Bolshevik experiment and the most efficient "School of Communism."[124] In July 1926, the party cell of the Komsomol Jewish section of the Printers' Union noted that despite a number of programs conducted jointly with the Red Army the collaboration with the Soviet institution was inadequate because "our cell operates in Yiddish."[125] Similarly, during the meeting of the brushmakers' factory party cell, held in November of that same year, the war committee remarked, "The question about work in the Red Army has been debated over and over again, and yet we were not able to gain any support . . . primarily because our cell operates in Yiddish."[126] While the members of both party cells acknowledged that the collaboration with the Red Army was dysfunctional because of the linguistic difference, no one suggested shifting to Russian in order to encourage the relationship with this quintessential Communist institution.

One of the most compelling examples of the commitment to Yiddish is dated March 1927. The party cell of the heavily Jewish factory Minshvei operated exclusively in Yiddish: the meeting minutes were drafted in Yiddish and only upon the request by general institutions were they translated into Russian. Historically linked to the Bund, the Minshvei party cell aspired to interact with the Red Army solely in Yiddish. So much so that on the occasion of the Red Army's tenth anniversary, it refused to work in partnership with the Soviet institution since this entailed using Russian. "Because our party cell is a Jewish one, and operates in Yiddish," explained the resolution, "we cannot assist ... the Red Army in Russian. ... [T]he question of creating relations with the Red Army should be removed from the agenda."[127] The commitment to Yiddish, to speaking and using the language within the context of Soviet institutions, thereby creating a separate setting for Jews, was a vestige of the Bundist tradition and remained the single necessary (and available) trait to guarantee the national existence of the Jewish proletariat.

Bundist political and cultural strategies were also reflected in the new rivalry that emerged between Minsk and Moscow. The changes in demography, occupational patterns, and social life experienced by Minsk Jewry in the aftermath of the revolution were accompanied by a new awareness, on the part of the leadership especially, of the city's different geopolitical status. With the creation of Soviet administrative and bureaucratic infrastructures, cultural and political agencies, and the establishment of new borders, provincial Minsk developed into the political, economic, and cultural hub of the Belorussian Republic. In the Jewish context, this meant that the newly established Jewish agencies in the capital, in particular the Evsektsiia, imparted orders and dispatched instructions to the local Evsektsiia bureaus in surrounding towns and *shtetlekh*;[128] that young activists from Gomel and Bobruisk would move to the capital and enroll in the newly established Jewish institutions; that Jews from the *shtetlekh*, distraught by the economic crisis of the Belorussian village, would abandon their place of residence and look for employment opportunities in the republic's capital.

The new geopolitical status of Minsk entailed setting up relations with cities outside the immediate Belorussian region, most importantly with the capital of the Soviet Union. With Moscow as the political and administrative center of the Soviet Union, and Minsk as the capital of the Belorussian republic, new relations developed between the Jewish elites of the two cities. Jewish Minsk replaced its historic orientation toward Vilna with a new one toward Moscow. This orientation, however, was not only marked by loyalty and compliance. Generated by a distinctively Jewish vision of the surrounding region (absent in other Soviet Jewish centers, such as Odessa, Kiev, or Kharkov), the orientation toward Moscow was also shaped by conflict. The tension with the Moscow Jewish agencies responsible for monitoring and supervising Jewish life throughout the Soviet Union was missing from non-Jewish local organizations as well: both

Belorussians and Russians living in the Belorussian capital were not in direct conflict with Moscow. On the contrary, Russians and Belorussians had a long-established tradition with Moscow and/or St. Petersburg at the top of the hierarchy, and Minsk at the periphery. Due to the existence of the Pale of Settlement, Jewish geography was different. As a result, while depending politically and administratively on Moscow, the Jewish institutions of the Belorussian capital revealed a tendency to disregard, or even dispute, the directives coming from the capital of the USSR.

The tension between Minsk and Moscow was both a legacy from the past (Minsk being a Jewish historical center and Moscow not being one) and the product of the new system. For the first time in a position of exercising power in the region, the political and cultural leadership of Minsk Jewry was well aware of the historical role that the city had played in the past of Russian Jewry. The Jewish community of Moscow, by contrast, was a fairly new one, which had not influenced the religious, cultural, and political history of Russian Jewry: from a Jewish vantage point Moscow had no recognized status. Minsk was also the only Jewish city in the Soviet Union to become a Soviet capital, in which the numerical difference between the main national group, the Belorussians, and the second national group, the Jews, was minimal.[129] But the most relevant factor accountable for the confrontation of the political and cultural resolutions coming from Moscow, and the tendency to come to decisions autonomously from Moscow, was the Bundist local patriotism embedded in the Minsk Jewish leadership. Closely intertwined with the Bundist claim for autonomy, local patriotism originated from the idea of "*doikayt*" (in Yiddish, commitment to stay here), a principle dear to Bundism. The rivalry, which built upon Minsk's status of historic Jewish city in the heart of the Pale of Settlement, expressed itself throughout the 1920s and early 1930s among Evsektsiia leaders, literati, and cultural activists who worked in theater and research institutions.[130] Whenever Minsk rebuffed instructions from Moscow, it justified its actions by emphasizing "the different local specificities."[131] Because of its Bundist and Jewish past, and its densely Jewish population, Minsk, in the Soviet periphery, aspired to become the real capital of Soviet Jewry rivaling Moscow, the center.

This situation was further complicated by the intricacy of Soviet bureaucracy. As has been noticed, "Besides the central, republic, regional, city and local committees, each nationality had its own chain of command and hierarchy which at times overlapped and created conflicts over authority."[132] In other words, it was not clear whether the members of the Evsektsiia in Minsk should report to the Central Committee of the CPB, to the Central Bureau of the Evsektsiia in Moscow, or to both agencies. Because of this ambiguity, Jewish activists in Minsk could easily challenge the tendency to bring Jewish geography in line with Soviet geography by turning Moscow into the center of Soviet Jewish culture.

From the very beginning there were regular exchanges between Jewish activists in Moscow and Minsk on different issues, ranging from the liquidation of pre-revolutionary Jewish organizations to the formation of local Evsektsiia bureaus.[133] In their struggle to preserve a degree of independence from the center, Minsk activists tended to adopt resolutions about Jewish questions without the consultation with or approval from Moscow, sometimes disregarding orders from the capital, as was done after the dissolution of the Bund in March 1921. In November 1921 the Evsektsiia Central Bureau in Moscow criticized Minsk for having Alef Litvak—the Vilna Bundist who opposed the merging of the Bund with the Communist Party—as the president of the committee for the study of the history of the Jewish workers' movement. Moscow ordered Minsk to remove him from office.[134] In August 1922 the Moscow Central Bureau instructed Minsk to abstain from carrying out the resolution passed a few weeks before about the celebration of the twenty-fifth anniversary of the birth of the Jewish workers movement, that is, the founding of the Bund in 1897.[135] Whether the Jewish political leadership in Minsk complied with the directives coming from the Moscow Evsektsiia at once is not known. The documents do reveal, however, that being more reluctant to separate from its Bundist past, the Minsk Evsektsiia tried to act independently from its Moscow counterpart.

At the meeting of the Minsk Evsektsiia held on June 24, 1921, the cultural activist Yudl Frankfurt informed about the resolution endorsed by the Jewish section of the Belorussian People's Commissariat for Education. Not only did the resolution call for the organization in Minsk of a Jewish Department at Belorussian State University, it also proposed the creation of a central Institute for Jewish Culture, "which should be established in Minsk, and not in Moscow," declared Frankfurt putting into words the rivalry with the Soviet capital. The plan to organize an Institute for Jewish Culture in Minsk was approved.[136] While the Jewish Department at Belorussian State University and the Jewish section of the Institute for Belorussian Culture were eventually established, the Institute for Jewish Culture was not. The initial support for this resolution, however, reveals the assumption that Minsk, and not Moscow, should be the capital of Jewish cultural life. It also echoes the attempt to establish the primacy of Jewish cultural geography over Soviet geography.

Hersh Smoliar, who settled in the Soviet Union from Poland in 1921, captures the expression of this supremacy when he highlights the sense of entitlement that the Minsk Jewish leadership experienced, especially when compared to other Jewish centers: "I have been connected to that quintessential Jewish city for many years. In the beginning, only from far away.... [T]he whole local environment there ... with its demonstrative Soviet Jewishness [*yidishkayt*] differed visibly from the atmosphere in Kiev, Kharkov, and other cities in Ukraine."[137] This "demonstrative Soviet Jewishness" marked the rivalry between two of the most prominent Jewish cultural institutions in Moscow and Minsk, namely, the Moscow State Yiddish Theater, or Goset, and the Belorussian State Jewish Theater. In October 1921, the Minsk Jewish troupe became the Jewish section of the Belorussian State Theater and was brought under the supervision of the Evsektsiia.[138] It soon became apparent, however, that Minsk lacked the proper institutions and personalities to set up a Yiddish theater and train its actors. From 1922 to 1926, the Jewish section of the

Belorussian People's Commissariat for Education sent the troupe to Moscow to study under the tutelage of the Moscow Yiddish Theater and its director, Alexander Granovsky, with the understanding that it would eventually return to Minsk and develop a theatrical tradition and repertoire in its home republic.[139]

Upon returning to Minsk in 1926, the Jewish troupe was upgraded from studio to theater. Reacting (at least partially) to the fact that "the provincial theater had been coached by the central one," from the outset Belgoset tried to produce an independent and exemplary revolutionary canon that would distinguish the Minsk performances from the ones put on stage in Moscow. In the words of a Belgoset actor, "From the beginning the Moscow theater based its repertoire on the classics of Yiddish literature, whereas the Minsk theater based its repertoire on works of Soviet political content."[140] In particular, Moshe Rafalskii, a native of Kiev who had moved to Minsk during World War I and founded the theater Undzer vinkl (Our Corner),[141] became committed to producing original plays without the biblical heroes and *shtetl* fables prominent in the Moscow theater. Director of Belgoset from its establishment until 1937, Rafalskii repeatedly complained about Granovsky's ambition to control the artistic production of the Minsk studio and turn it into a branch of Goset. Insofar as it was supposed to become "a theater for Belorussia," argued Rafalskii, the Minsk studio should maintain a degree of autonomy from the Moscow theater.[142] In this early phase, the actors themselves emphasized the innovation of their theater vis-à-vis Goset: with twenty *komsomoltsy* and a party cell, their studio was a true collective. "It is not a coincidence if we call ourselves the first Jewish Workers' Theater, not only in form but in content as well."[143] Striving for independence from Moscow, the Minsk artists came under the influence of the extreme left proletarian culture and drew inspiration primarily from political works by contemporary Soviet writers, Jewish and non-Jewish alike, who glorified the Soviet regime. As a reaction to Moscow's canon, which was thematically more nationalist and ethnographic, Belgoset distanced itself from Jewish themes and selected a more internationalist repertoire.[144]

These two remarkably different approaches to Soviet Jewish theater originated also from the dissimilar realities of the two cities. The Jews of Minsk remained, so to speak, in the *shtetl*, among Jews, in a historic Jewish center. They could remove themselves and their cultural activities from that reality while remaining, at one and the same time, part of it. Hence, the possibility of choosing a more Communist and internationalist repertoire: functioning in a predominantly Jewish milieu, Minsk Jewish Communists did not need to draw inspiration from it, but rather wished to distance themselves from it. By contrast, most Moscow Jewish artists, originally from the cities and villages of the Pale of Settlement, had moved away from the *shtetl*. From Solomon Mikhoels, who was born in Dvinsk, to Benjamin Zuskin born in Ponevezh, most directors and actors of Goset had physically departed from a quintessential Jewish environment. In Moscow, they performed for a largely non-Yiddish speaking audience, arguably "the most assimilated segment of the Jewish population of the Soviet Union," and often for a non-Jewish audience.[145] Being removed from Jewishness, they confronted the nostalgia (or the absence of such a place) striving to recreate the emotional, historical, and national bond with their Jewish past: hence, the preference for nationally oriented plays and the commitment to the Jewish content of Goset. Moreover, while the Moscow audience—made primarily of assimilated Jews and non-Jews—was drawn to a Jewish theater to see "Jewish" performances, the Minsk audience—made largely of Yiddish-speaking Jews living in a Jewish city—was not necessarily enticed by plays with a Jewish content, but might have been more curious about the recently available European and Soviet plays.

The tension between centralization and regionalism is also reflected in the confrontation between the main Soviet Jewish publications of the two cities. The controversy between the official Yiddish party organs, the Moscow *Der Emes* and the Minsk *Der Veker*, began as early as 1921. In October of that year, the editor of the Minsk daily Elye Osherovitsh addressed a letter to the Evsektsiia in Moscow complaining about the attacks on *Veker* promoted by Moshe Litvakov, editor-in-chief of *Emes*. According to Osherovitsh, Litvakov wrongly accused the Minsk publication of ignoring questions of political economy and using "*Ha-melits* [antiquated flowery language] disguised with proletarian phraseology." In response the Minsk-based activist reproached Moscow: if the capital was not satisfied with *Veker*, then it should send specific guidelines and instructions as to how to properly organize provincial newspapers.[146] While provincial Russian- or Belorussian-language party newspapers did not publicly attack central ones,[147] the Jewish press in Minsk, caught up in the dispute between center and periphery, did attack central Soviet Jewish institutions in Moscow. The rivalry between the two newspapers carried on throughout the 1930s and reached its peak during the Great Terror campaigns of 1936–38 when both editorial staffs accused each other of bourgeois nationalism and Bundism.[148]

The question of which newspaper served the center and which one the periphery, and more generally of which geographic area represented the main Jewish center, was formally addressed in 1926. At a general party meeting held in Moscow in March of that year, it was suggested to relocate the editorial office of the Moscow newspaper to the "Pale of Settlement," namely, to Minsk or Kharkov. Not only did *Emes* circulate primarily in Belorussia and Western Ukraine, but the cost for supporting the editorial staff in Moscow was high. However, it was the perception of Soviet geography, with Moscow as the political and administrative capital of the Soviet Union that prevailed in the end over Jewish cultural geography.[149] The final resolution called for leaving in Moscow the newspaper of the Evsektsiia Central Bureau. In the Soviet capital, stated the resolution, *Emes* would retain its "leading character and All-Union significance," which were very different from the local features intrinsic to the Minsk newspaper.[150]

The conflict swayed the political front as well. When, in the mid-1920s, Soviet authorities began to argue in favor of the establishment of agricultural settlements for Jews in one region, Minsk opposed the creation of a territorial base outside Belorussia:

it supported Jewish settlement in loco and resisted the proposal to create Jewish colonies in Crimea, Ukraine, or Birobidzhan.[151] The disagreement between Minsk and Moscow on this issue persisted until the end of the 1920s.[152] Moscow, as well as other major Jewish centers such as Kiev or Kharkov, where the Zionist and territorialist heritage was more conspicuous than the Bundist one, favored the project of Jewish resettlement elsewhere. Minsk, however, showed a firm commitment to Belorussia and produced a local variant of the territorial project, adopting as a priority the commitment to the reconstruction of the *shtetl* on new economic foundations. So, for example, the Jewish Department at Belorussian State University conducted several demographic and economic research projects about the *shtetl* and the possibility to reorganize it in accordance with Soviet principles, without dismantling it.[153] This element of "local patriotism" manifested itself politically, culturally, and scientifically as the outcome of the reelaboration of the concept of "*doikayt*" within the Soviet context.[154]

For Minsk, thus, the Autonomous Jewish Region of Birobidzhan never really became an integral part of Jewish cultural geography as it did (at least officially) for the Jews in Moscow, Kharkov, and Kiev. Indeed, the Minsk Jewish leadership attempted, as long as it was possible, to contest the Birobidzhan enterprise altogether. This tendency appears among the general Jewish population of Minsk as well. In 1928, 829 families (with 4,146 individuals) from the city of Minsk and the Minsk District registered to move to agricultural settlements. Of these, 785 families registered from seventeen different *shtetlekh* around Minsk and 44 registered from the city of Minsk. Only 182 of the 829 families agreed to settle on land located outside Belorussia. The following year, 129 families (with 566 individuals) from the city of Minsk registered to move to agricultural settlements; of these, only 70 agreed to settle outside Belorussia.[155]

Since Moscow Jewry was itself a population of transferred migrants from Belorussia and Ukraine, the Moscow Evsektsiia could easily conceive of building a new Jewish center in a place previously uninhabited by Jews (Birobidzhan). Moreover, Jews in Ukraine had suffered significantly during the Civil War pogroms, much more than the Jews living in Belorussia, so that it became more plausible for them to search for a territorial solution elsewhere. But Minsk Jews were rooted in a Jewish center and the local Evsektsiia was eager to retain it. For them emigration to Birobidzhan meant the dissipation of their center. They already had a Jewish territory in Minsk. And indeed both in absolute numbers and in percentage of the total local population there were more Jews in the one city of Minsk than in the entire Jewish autonomous region. Jewish activists in Minsk (and elsewhere in Belorussia) were often driven by a sense of superiority compared to Jewish activists in Ukraine, who had to fight for the existence of the Jewish sections, and in Moscow, who rarely had access to general party leadership. This assertiveness, combined with the inclination to respond to current challenges by exploring their Bundist past, ultimately explains the frequent absence of consultations and negotiations with the Moscow Jewish leadership.[156]

Branding Counterrevolutionaries

At the end of 1923, the Central Bureau of the Evsektsiia in Moscow invited Yankl Levin, secretary of the Minsk Evsektsiia, to take on a position in Kharkov in the local Jewish section.[157] A few years later, at the same time of the renaming of the Grosser and *Veker* institutions, Levin indeed left Minsk for a different location. The suspicion that he had been forced to leave the Belorussian capital because of his loyalty to Bundism quickly spread through the city. Some rejected the insinuation as false and tried to discredit the rumours by pointing out that Levin was "a 100% Bolshevik, . . . [as he] had shown in his tough Bolshevik orientation of his Minsk work."[158] While it is hard to confirm with absolute certainty, it does seem plausible that Levin was transferred because of his political past and the suspicion of his ongoing allegience to the Bund. As a matter of fact, even after embracing Communism former Bundists were often haunted by their Bundist past and branded as counterrevolutionaries. During the second half of the 1920s, the branding consisted mainly of suspicion and vigilance on the part of true Bolsheviks vis-à-vis former Bundists, who could still be rescued and restored to society. During the second half of the 1930s, however, the link to Bundism was viewed as an irredeemable sin and critically impinged on the social status of the individual, often resulting in a matter of life or death.

From the very beginning, the Communist Party kept detailed records of the pre-revolutionary political affiliation of each new party member. This left room for and gave rise to suspicion toward the political integrity of all former Bundists (as well as Zionists, Mensheviks, or Socialist-Revolutionaries), who joined the party. The 1923 figures about the "quality" of the members of the Belorussian Communist organization show that the overwhelming majority of those who used to belong to other parties were Bundists. Out of a total of 1,106 party members and candidates, there were ten Mensheviks, thirteen SRs, thirty-seven Poale-Zionists, two anarchists, nine Jewish Socialists, and three hundred forty-seven Bundists.[159] As the number of young party members grew over time, the proportion of "descendents" (*vykhodtsy*) from the Bund decreased. In 1928, in the Minsk District party organization, out of a total of 2,133 Jewish party members and candidates, former Bundists amounted to 216 only. In the party organization of the municipal district, out of a total of 841, former Bundists were 107.[160]

But in spite of this decline, the attacks against the Bund and its former members increased. A systematic campaign of Bolshevization—and de-Bundization—of the Jewish street kicked off following the renaming of the Grosser Club and *Veker*. In 1926, the Central Committee of the CPB issued a political letter (*Politpismo*) addressed to its local and regional organizations, condemning Bundism and calling for the eradication of the Bundist tradition in the area.[161] More specifically, the letter called for the suppression of the "Idealization of the Bund" (*Idealizatsiia Bunda*), or the conviction that certain aspects of its history could be rescued and celebrated—first of all its pioneering role in the establishment of the workers' movement in Belorussia.[162] Meetings to discuss the nature of Bundism, Bundist names and symbols took place throughout the city: the political letter was debated in more than fifty different party cells in Minsk in 1926. Some comrades defended the revolutionary nature of the Jewish party, attempting to preserve its integrity. At the Tanner's Union party-cell meeting, comrade Kantsler argued, "In Belorussia . . . [the Bund] was a revolutionary party. . . . [W]ithout the Bund our party could never have accomplished what it did among Jewish workers. . . . Bundists led the struggle. I remember how the meetings were held in the synagogue's courtyard . . . in Yiddish and in Russian."[163] Others acknowledged the existence of a strongly rooted, and consequently dangerous, Bundist tradition in Minsk, and warned against the widespread tendency to view the Bund as the organizing force of the Jewish proletariat. The fact that many comrades openly voiced their opposition to the renaming of the Grosser club and *Veker* newspaper, argued comrades Kozhebrodski and Levita, revealed how intensely Bundist traditions still resonated in the city. At the closed-door meeting of the Belorussian People's Commissariat for Work, comrade Erofeev echoed this view, stating, "[T]he Bundist heritage can hardly be wiped out at once. It is difficult for them [former Bundists] to become 100% Leninists and be born again."[164] But comrade Penzner retorted admitting that he could not quite understand why the Bund had suddenly come under attack. "Bundists played a major role in the revolution. . . . [T]his was never . . . a counterrevolutionary party," he declared.[165]

The letter issued by the Central Executive Committee of the CPB stirred up fear, suspicion, and confusion throughout the city. Some warned against the danger of using the term "Bundist" as a synonymous of "Jewish."[166] Many complained against the tendency to consider former Bundists unreliable Communists and to bar them from filling executive positions in Soviet institutions; in some cases, former Bundists were dismissed from their positions and replaced by Belorussians.[167] The question asked by one comrade Shadchin—"Is it possible to have a former Bundist work in the Komsomol?"—is indicative of this tendency.[168] In 1929, two former Bundists courageously refused to publicly denounce the counterrevolutionary nature of the Bund. Instead, they rejected the value of the Politpismo. Of course, they were fired on the spot.[169] The political letter did not, as its promoters had anticipated, "eradicate" all traces of Bundism, nor did it clarify once and for all the official position regarding the nature of the Jewish party and the role it had played in the history of the Jewish proletariat. As late as 1930, workers around the city were still debating the revolutionary nature of the Bund.[170]

The accusation of "Bundism" became synonymous with a broad and multifaceted number of accusations, including national-chauvinism, pessimism, and territorialism. So preferring Yiddish to Belorussian; urging a Jewish child to attend a Yiddish school instead of a Russian or Belorussian school; objecting to the growth of non-Jewish workers in a predominantly Jewish factory; or marrying only Jewish women, all were deemed the outcome of "Bundist behavior."[171] In March 1929, with the launching of the *samokritika* (self-criticism) campaign, comrade Zusina was expelled from the party because she did not behave as a party member on the shop floor of her factory and made chauvinistic remarks about a Russian worker. In other words, "She did not shake off her Bundist traditions."[172]

Even after the most visible (and some of the most subtle) traces of Bundism had disappeared from the public life of Minsk, the attack on the Jewish party continued. The accusation of "idealization of the Bund" became widespread in the early 1930s, in a campaign that seemed to anticipate the Great Terror of 1936–38. At the Municipal Party Conference held in 1932, as part of the criticism against Jewish chauvinism, historian Israel Sosis, professor at Belorussian State University and former Bundist, was accused of tainting his research through the "idealization of the Bund."[173] On July 23, 1933, the first issue debated at the meeting of the party cell of *Oktyabr*'s editorial staff was the "idealization of the Bund." Agursky pointed out that despite the struggle launched in 1925 against Bundism some Communists (former Bundists) still idealized the Jewish party in the literature, the press, and during the party purges. "This can be explained," continued Agursky, "with the fact that the idealization of the Bund has always been openly voiced."[174] Izzy Kharik, the Soviet Yiddish poet and member of the Central Committee of the CPB, cautioned against the new Bundist menace: "The Bund finds itself now in a new stage. . . . There are party members, even devoted ones, who still talk, to this day, about the Bund with enthusiasm. . . . to them the counterrevolutionary nature of the Bund is still unclear."[175]

Conclusion

With ambivalence and subtleness, in late 1925 former Bundist Sholem Levin admitted his entangled loyalty to the past and the present:

> When I heard about the change of name, I . . . recalled the days when the Bund was on the verge of being liquidated. Even back then there were . . . groups of comrades (including myself) who, while already standing with both feet in the party, still cried out "have pity and let us at least have the name Bund, with which it is difficult to part." . . . We know how much energy and strength we invested in our Grosser Club, to which we dedicated the best and most beautiful energies we had. However, when the . . . moment came we washed it off with our own hands. . . . The space of the Grosser is now occupied by Lenin. . . . [T]hese names mean much more to us. . . . Why . . . should the shadows from the past appear in front of our eyes?[176]

Not unlike many other former Bundists who chose to participate in the political life of the city, in particular on its Jewish street, Levin yielded to a sort of Bundist-Communist dual personality. In other words, activists (mostly but not exclusively those who had been affiliated with the Jewish party) quickly learned to write, speak, and act in a Communist fashion, while thinking and feeling in another (Bundist) way, especially with regard to questions related to the Jewish population.[177] The inner rift that enveloped so many activists on the Jewish street expanded over time as they came to realize that the more they identified with Communism, the more their past came back to haunt them. Yearning for power—particularly after years of secretive Bundist activities during the pre-1917 era—when given the option to renounce their political past and join the Communist Party, many had accepted. It is hard to say whether they understood at once what this swap entailed.

The extraordinary Bundist nexus recreated in interwar Minsk resulted from the combination of different factors: first, after Vilna, Minsk had been the greatest historic center of the Bund in the Russian empire; second, in March 1921, the Bund's liquidation conference in Minsk came to a close with a commitment to the spirit of Bundism; third, the intense personal continuity on the local level between former Bundists and the new Jewish political and cultural leadership surpassed that of most Soviet Jewish centers; fourth, safeguarding a connection to the Bund's past through the two main Evsektsiia institutions, the Grosser Club and the *Veker* daily; fifth, the effort to reshape a quintessentially Bundist hero into a Soviet one, which enabled to legitimize (albeit not openly) the Bundist tradition into the present; and sixth, the perseverance of Bundist principles in the political and cultural strategies of the Jewish activists, particularly with regard to the commitment to Yiddish and to expressions of a Soviet/Bundist "hereness." But a Soviet Jewish synthesis based on the Bundist tradition could not be tolerated for long, and the option of maintaining a connection between Sovietness and Bundism, as an expression of Jewishness, progressively disappeared. In 1930, with the reorganization of the All-Union Central Committee of the Party the Evsektsiia was dissolved. This marked the refusal of the party leadership to tolerate even the mildest form of separatism and autonomy, in all its manifestations, including the Jewish section, the Polish section, and the Women's section.[178] Aspects of Bundism did live on even after the liquidation of the Evsektsiia into the 1930s. Ultimately, however, the Bundist tradition could not fit into the Soviet universal paradigm, and the allegiance to the Bundist past had to retract more and more from the public sphere. The creeping shadow of the Bundist heritage, which probably never completely left the Jewish political and cultural leadership of Minsk, was crushed in the repression of the Great Terror together with its former affiliates and icons.[179]

4 Soviet Minsk

The Capital of Yiddish

Korenizatsiia in the Belorussian Context

> Many comrades don't even know where to begin [to replace Russian with Yiddish]. We have no typewriters and have to rewrite the bookkeeping in Yiddish; it's a little "strange." We are used to carrying out secretarial work in Russian, . . . [now we must] change into Yiddish the membership cards, the registration tags and receipts.[1]

Following the June 1919 decree, when the Bolsheviks selected Yiddish as opposed to the "clerical" Hebrew and the "bourgeois" Russian, as the official language of instruction for all Soviet Jewish schools,[2] Yiddish became the preferred instrument of propaganda to reach the adult Jewish masses as well, and the ideal language of political, cultural, and scholarly Soviet Jewish enterprises. This preference had two main components. On the one hand, the sovietization of society and the politicization of everyday life led to the functional use of Yiddish, which became crucial in spreading Marxist ideology among the Jewish masses with little or no knowledge of Russian. On the other hand, as the native language of most Jews living in the Soviet Union, Yiddish represented one of the officially accepted categories for establishing the existence of a Jewish nationality in the USSR. The Soviet nation-building process involved reshaping the former Russian empire into a Socialist federation of nationalities and transforming the peoples of tsarist Russia into modern citizens of the newborn Socialist society. If the category of religion had been delegitimized as a determinant of nationality for all peoples in the USSR, the category of territory, or residence in a specific republic, was hardly applicable to the Jews because of their lack of a major territorial concentration.

The linguistic category became therefore an important element of national identification for Jews more than it did for Ukrainians or Belorussians, who could ground their national identity on territory as well. The shift toward the twofold function of Yiddish as an instrument of propaganda to reach the masses and as a defining trait of Jewish national identity resulted in Yiddish assuming a new status in the political, scholarly, and everyday life of Soviet Jews.

In Belorussia, and in its capital Minsk, this preference for Yiddish was officially mandated and enshrined in law. Only here did Yiddish enjoy the official status of a state language, something which it did not in other Jewish centers, such as Odessa and Kiev, or other large cities with major concentrations of Jews, such as Moscow and Leningrad. As one of the languages of the four main national groups in Belorussia, together with Belorussian, Polish, and Russian, Yiddish became an official state language of the BSSR. The 1920 Declaration of Independence of the Belorussian Republic proclaimed "Full legal equality of languages (Belorussian, Russian, Polish, and Yiddish) with respect to government agencies and in organizations and institutions of public education and Socialist culture."[3] The declaration guaranteed every citizen—no matter what his or her nationality—"the right and the actual possibility to use his mother tongue in dealing with any kind of organ and institution in the Republic." Every nationality could have schools of its own and every public agency or organization should have the "appropriate number" of Yiddish-speaking employees.[4]

A thriving separate Jewish culture in Yiddish, as well as, for example, courts of law operating in the Jewish language, were in the best interest of the promoters of the so-called *korenizatsiia* (indigenization) policy, a campaign to favor the use of Belorussian and Ukrainian (over Russian) in the political agencies and cultural institutions of the Belorussian and Ukrainian republics. The campaign to neutralize the authority of Russian, which had come to symbolize the oppressive nationalism of the tsarist empire, the political foe of the Bolshevik regime, and to gain the support of non-Russian national minorities was launched in the first half of the 1920s. It was known as Belorusizatsiia, or Belorussianization, in the BSSR, and Ukrainizatsiia, or Ukrainianization, in the Ukrainian SSR.[5] Local Belorussian authorities hoped that by supporting the use of Yiddish in cultural institutions and official party organizations they would dissuade the Jewish population from using Russian, the language preferred by the Jewish intellectual elite during the nineteenth century and imposed from above by tsarist administrators to counter non-Russian nationalism.[6] Similarly, local leaders hoped that by gathering support for minority languages (in Belorussia, Yiddish and Polish), they would encourage the use of Belorussian among Belorussians, thereby neutralizing the authority enjoyed by the Russian language particularly in urban centers.

The commitment of local authorities to Yiddish was stronger in Minsk—and in other Belorussian urban centers—than it was in Ukrainian cities, where the Ukrainianization process was generally less inclined to support the cultures of national minorities. Unlike Ukrainian nationalism, which was relatively well established and rooted before the birth of the USSR, Belorussian nationalism was, in many ways, the outcome of the Soviet experiment on the territories that in 1920 came to be known as the BSSR.[7] The awareness of concepts such as "Belorussia," "Belorussian language," and "Belorussian history"—the notion of a shared Belorussian past, language, and culture—remained uncommon and tenuous, in the cities in particular, until the establishment of the Soviet Union and thereafter. Before the revolution, Ukrainian nationalism, which emerged as a political and cultural movement during the nineteenth century, could count on a fairly strong Social-Democratic organization, on a movement to modernize the Ukrainian language, and on a futurist and symbolist literary tradition, in Ukrainian. By contrast, not only was a Belorussian version of European modernism missing, but within the family of Eastern European nationalities, the Belorussian Social-Democratic Party was one of the last ones to be founded, in Vilna in 1903. In general, illiteracy, poverty, and insufficient education hindered the creation of a modern national Belorussian identity.[8] As Francine Hirsh has noted, "From the start, the creation of the Belorussian Republic was an example of nation-making 'from above': not only did the so-called 'Belorussian people' react with indifference or opposition to the establishment of the republic, but some party members expressed concern that the party was 'artificially cultivating' a Belorussian nationality which did otherwise not exist."[9] A 1921 appeal to ethnic Belorussians living outside of Belorussia, signed by the head of the Central Executive Committee of the BSSR I. Adamovich, and the Deputy People's Commissariat for Education Ester Frumkin, confirms the attempt to forge a Belorussian national identity among an intelligentsia that lacked one. The appeal addressed "scholars, literati, pedagogical, and . . . cultural activists, who were natives of Belorussia," asking them to return to Belorussia and contribute to the creation of a new Soviet culture in the Belorussian language. While acknowledging that "the working conditions in the Belorussian language are especially difficult," the petition heartened Belorussian cultural activists by pointing out that "you should not be embarrassed if you do not know well enough the Belorussian language. Here . . . you will remember the language of your childhood and you will study it."[10]

While driven by Moscow, the *korenizatsiia* campaign in the republics was therefore also influenced by specific regional idiosyncrasies. Not only did the weakness of Belorussian nationalism shape the *korenizatsiia* policies in Minsk, encouraging local authorities to provide additional support for the cultures and languages of the national minorities living in the republic. But the position that the culture and language of a specific national group occupied vis-à-vis Russian also marked the evolution of the *korenizatsiia* campaign in the Belorussian capital. In the case of the Jews, for example, the commitment to Yiddish was stronger in Minsk and other Belorussian cities than it was in Ukraine, because many leading Jewish Communists in the Belorussian capital were former Bundists and deeply supported the development of Yiddish as the Jewish national language. Furthermore, the Bund—historically much weaker in Ukraine—had championed national-cultural autonomy, which put language at the center of Jewish national identity (unlike the Zionists and territorialists, who stressed the significance of political sovereignty and autonomy). The intense involvement with Yiddish of many Jews became therefore another key factor in the Belorussianization campaign in Minsk.

Belorussian and Yiddish

> We don't like the Belorussian language; students flee the class of Belorussian.... [T]here is no need [for it]. There is the Belorussian Pedagogical Training College, may they study it there and teach the Belorussian language to the village.[11]

In early 1924, the People's Commissariat for Internal Affairs, the NKVD, approved a resolution promoting the linguistic Belorussianization of the administrative apparatus and political agencies throughout the BSSR. The resolution anticipated that by early 1925 all regional and central offices, agencies and institutions throughout the republic would replace Russian with Belorussian. Dictated by the Soviet nationality policy, the resolution aimed first of all at neutralizing the supremacy of Russian, which had stifled the languages and cultures of other nationalities. To make up for the oppression endured under the tsar, non-Russian nationalities were entitled to special assistance in the form of preferential treatment in education and employment. Moreover, promoting the knowledge and use of Belorussian in the city had an additional ideological justification linked to the political principle of *smychka*, or the joining of ranks between the city and the village. The success of the dictatorship of the proletariat ultimately depended on the alliance between the proletariat and the peasantry, something that could be achieved only once the urban working class learned Belorussian, the language spoken by the poor peasants in the villages. The NKVD recommended therefore that all employees study Belorussian and carry out office work in Belorussian.[12]

The campaign for the promotion of Belorussian in the administrative and political agencies of the country spurred a parallel campaign for Yiddish, as Yidishizatsiia (or Evreizatsiia in Russian) became the Jewish analogue to Belorusizatsiia.[13] Previously disparaged as low-status vernaculars, and considered devoid of literary standing, Yiddish and Belorussian suddenly became official state languages, which would serve the patrician domains of politics, scholarship, and culture. However, in their path to officialdom in the Belorussian capital the two former "jargons" came across a number of obstacles, ultimately generating some shades of artificiality.

First of all, the Belorussianization campaign faced a critical lack of popular support. The Belorussian language enjoyed a low prestige among city-dwellers, Jews and non-Jews alike, especially when compared to the Ukrainianization campaign and the relatively widespread support for Ukrainian in medium-to-large urban centers in Ukraine. The resistance to the Belorussianization campaign was common among a large number of Belorussian, Russian, and Polish city-dwellers who, having lived in Minsk all of their lives, generally identified Russian as their mother tongue.[14] In

October 1926, at the party-cell meeting of the factory Varshavianka, one member (possibly even a Belorussian) argued that, while "no one doubts that . . . at some point there was a Belorussian language . . . , in our time, the Belorussian language and culture per se do not exist."[15] He also complained about the financial burden that the campaign for Belorussian entailed, pointing out the excessive cost of issuing newspapers, journals, and textbooks in Belorussian, as well as funding cultural and educational institutions. Finally, he argued that forcing students in institutions of higher education and secondary schools to study Belorussian was a waste of time, especially for Russian and Jewish students.[16] In the 1920s, there were no similar remarks about the Yiddish language and culture and the newly established Yiddish institutions in Minsk.

Many Jews resisted the linguistic Belorussianization of their workplace. In January 1925, the party cell of the Minsk Sewing Industry Workers, which operated exclusively in Yiddish, met to debate the abovementioned 1924 NKVD resolution to introduce Belorussian in local Soviet agencies.[17] Many of the workers, all of whom were Jewish, voiced their opposition to Belorussian.[18] One party-cell member pointed out that the peasant in the village not only spoke a version of Belorussian utterly incomprehensible to the city inhabitant, but the peasant was himself likely to understand Russian better than the city version of Belorussian. Another member compared Belorussian to Ukrainian and emphasized that the Ukrainizatsiia campaign was much more reasonable since, "Ukraine has its own history and heroes, something that is missing here in Belorussia." Of course the party cell eventually resolved to comply with the official guidelines and called for the study of Belorussian and the liquidation of illiteracy in Belorussian among Jewish workers.[19] In most cases, however, party directives recommending that all political and cultural activists in the city be literate in Belorussian were considered a formality and in most cases ignored. In early 1927, at the height of the Belorussianization campaign, for example, three applicants were considered for employment at the Jewish Pedagogical College that trained teachers for Yiddish-language schools. Alexander Vitkin, who applied for the position of library director; Evsei Bialyi, who applied for the position of gymnastics instructor; and Anna Raskina, who applied for the position of first-year Yiddish teacher. When asked whether they knew Belorussian, all three candidates admitted they had no knowledge of the language. They were hired anyway.[20]

Many members of the Jewish intelligentsia who had graduated from Russian-language institutions in pre-revolutionary years, and had therefore become more familiar with Russian as their language of communication and intellectual creativity—refused to learn or use Belorussian. Gezov, a Jewish teacher in the local professional school for tailors, who also taught Belorussian in a Belorussian school to make ends meet, disdained so much the Belorussian language that he asked the students "to address him only in Russian."[21] The young Nina Shalit-Galperin, who grew up in a Russian-speaking Jewish home, remembered walking through the streets of Minsk as she recited and, at the same time, made fun of the "weird" translation of Pushkin's *Evgenyi Onegin* into

Belorussian, which she had to learn in school.[22] But the Communist Party of Belorussia warned against the dangers of resisting Belorussianization (*soprotivlenie* Belorusizatsii) in Soviet society and blamed the old Russified bureaucracy and the pre-revolutionary intelligentsia, made up of doctors, lawyers, and financial experts, for waging a war against Belorussian.[23]

The interplay between the official status of the Jewish language, the low prestige of Belorussian, and the official disfavoring of Russian led many Jews to be positively inclined toward the Yiddishization efforts and the use of Yiddish. Taking the floor in Yiddish at general party meetings to speak about general topics became a relatively common practice among Jewish activists in Minsk in the 1920s and well into the second half of the 1930s.[24] Born in the *shtetl* of Igumen (Ihumen), where most residents were Jewish, Nikolai Goloded, the first secretary of the BCP from 1925 to 1927 (and later chairman of the Belorussian Council of People's Commissars), a Belorussian by nationality, had some knowledge of Yiddish. The fact that one of the political leaders of the republic knew Yiddish conferred some prestige on the Jewish language among Jewish city residents.[25] If Yiddish was to a larger or smaller degree accepted in general non-Jewish settings, it was often seen as the exclusive linguistic channel for Jewish settings. In November 1928, at the party-cell meeting of the heavily Jewish clothing factory Minshvei, which counted 155 Jewish members and six Belorussians, one comrade was interrupted when he tried to address the meeting in Belorussian. As another member reproachfully commented, "Shmidt did not behave properly when he spoke in Belorussian at a Jewish meeting."[26] Local Jewish bodies applied Yiddishization as an absolute principle within Jewish ethnic settings like the Minsk factory and refused to conduct any work in Belorussian (or Russian).

Minsk became an ideal location for the thriving of Yiddish: on the one hand, the financial support from the state; on the other hand, the lack of competition with Belorussian, the language that the party "ascribed" to the majority of the population of the republic, even to those Belorussian city residents who did not know it. The weakness of Belorussian only strengthened Yiddish. In this Jewish city, perhaps more than in other major Soviet Jewish urban centers, Yiddish had enjoyed a distinctive standing that predated the implementation of Soviet nationality policy and the launching of the Belorussianization campaign. Indicative of the exceptional status of the language in the city was the inaugural ceremony of Belorussian State University, held on July 15, 1921, when the secretary of the Evsektsiia welcomed the event by addressing the large audience in Yiddish.[27] It is hard to imagine something similar taking place in Moscow, or in any other capital of a Soviet republic, during the inauguration of a state university.

Yiddish in Soviet Urban Public Life

The Jewish version of the *korenizatsiia* campaign, which entailed government support for institutions and agencies operating in Yiddish, as well as the employment of

Figure 5. The Minsk Central Train Station, 1930s. Courtesy of YIVO Institute for Jewish Research (Collection R1 Minsk 1).

Yiddish-speaking clerks, brought the Jewish language to the forefront of the public life of the city with a new intensity, not known in pre-revolutionary years.[28] The language was displayed in public spaces in Minsk and for the first time became more visible in the everyday life of the city. On the building of the Central Train Station of Minsk, the name of the city appeared not only in Belorussian, Russian, and Polish, but in Yiddish as well. Passengers, who traveled to the city and saw the Hebrew letters on the building, were reminded of the official status of the language and the Jewishness of Minsk. Upon arriving in Minsk in 1928, the Warsaw-based Yiddish writer I. J. Singer noted with surprise, "These four languages, Belorussian, Russian, Polish and Yiddish, meet me at the train station. They look down at me from the grey wall. . . . I come across them at every step, in every commissariat, office, everywhere there are signs in the four languages." The fact that Yiddish appeared in public spaces on the streets of the city, continued the writer, "is now something normal. The only one who marvels at this is probably me."[29] Passing through the Soviet Union in 1931, a Polish-Jewish journalist confirmed Singers's impressions as he noted the difference between Minsk, with the big Hebrew letters visible from the train as it approached the station, and Odessa, "which became entirely Ukrainianized." "The captions on

Figure 6. At a parade celebrating the tenth anniversary of the Bolshevik Revolution, Minsk, 1927. Courtesy of YIVO Institute for Jewish Research (Collection R1 Minsk 56).

the signboards of stores and institutions are in Ukrainian, and only sometimes in Russian," noted the journalist, concluding that very "rarely will you see a sign in Yiddish."[30]

In Minsk, by contrast, a number of important institutions, such as Belorussian State University, displayed their official name on their building in Belorussian and Yiddish. The language was heard on the Belorussian state radio,[31] and it was seen in the intertitles to the films in the movie theaters of the city.[32] During local elections, electoral notices were distributed in Yiddish;[33] the city's Executive Committee of the Communist Party received written correspondence in Yiddish,[34] and applications for party membership or candidacy were submitted to local party committees in Yiddish.[35] Used for communiqués, protocols, and correspondence between the members of the Evsektsiia, Yiddish became an integral part of the city's public political life. In 1926, five Minsk party cells fully or partially operated in Yiddish,[36] and twenty-three pioneer detachments used Yiddish as their language of communication.[37]

On May 7, 1924, the administration of the Central Post and Telegraphic Office of Minsk addressed the district and city party committees with a notice, which appeared in the local press a few days later. The postal service was looking to employ clerks who were able to read, speak, and write in the local languages. The notice explained with meticulous detail the system through which the mail that reached the post office was to be delivered to the recipient of a parcel or letter. Letters written in a local language, such as Polish or Belorussian, were usually addressed on the left side of the envelope, while the right side of the envelope was typically left blank by the sender; this allowed the clerk to translate the address into Russian on the right side of the envelope. The job guidelines included a specific feature related to Yiddish. Because addresses written in Yiddish usually took up the whole surface of the envelope starting from the right side and moving leftward, and no blank space was left for the translation, the clerk was instructed to translate the address on the other side of the envelope.[38] As these instructions to prospective post-office clerks illustrate, the language's constitutional equality not only introduced Yiddish to the pettiness of Soviet bureaucracy. It also incorporated the language in the everyday life of the city and surrounding region, perhaps making this the only area in Eastern Europe in which letters could be addressed in Yiddish.

In all probability, Minsk also became the only capital city in Europe where, as late as 1937, one could see a truck passing through the city streets, distributing bread to local cooperatives, with the word "Bread" written in Yiddish on it. Actually, as someone noticed at the time, lamenting the level of "ignorance and provincialism" of the text on the bread lorry, the writing did not appear in standardized literary Yiddish, but in Litvish Yiddish, or the dialect spoken in Minsk and its environs. (Instead of reading "*broyt*"—or "bread" in standard Yiddish—the text on the truck read "*breyt*," which in the Litvish dialect indeed means "bread" but in standard Yiddish means "wide.")[39]

Courts, Sports, and Classrooms: Yiddish or Russian

Of course, many Jews kept to the Haskalah prejudice that contemptuously viewed Yiddish as a jargon bereft of grammar and did not consider it a viable alternative to Russian. In 1926, the member of a local party cell complained about the obstruction of the Yiddishization campaign in his factory by the middle management. Here, whenever one "submits an article in Yiddish for the wall-newspaper . . . he is told that there is no room for it; the union's secretary argues that the workers understand Russian, when in fact 50 percent of our Jewish workers have a very limited knowledge of Russian; the secretary does not even allow us to campaign for the subscription to *Oktyabr.*"[40] And yet, as one of the languages used to promote the cultural renaissance of the peoples of Soviet Belorussia, Yiddish made its way into the city's top cultural spheres. It made its way into theaters through plays and concerts presented by the Belorussian State Jewish Theater and the Jewish State Chorus, which regularly performed in Minsk.[41] Through the founding fathers of modern Yiddish literature, whose works were interpreted as compatible with the Soviet *Weltanschauung*, the language penetrated the general cultural institutions of the city. The literary soiree celebrating the tenth anniversary since the death of Yiddish writer Sholem Aleichem, took place on May 21, 1926, as a public event at the Belorussian State Theater. The literary critic Nahum Oyslender served as the key speaker and lectured in Yiddish about the works of Sholem Aleichem, to a largely Belorussian audience.⁴²

As part of the Yiddish experiment, Yiddish also entered the legal sphere and became a juridical language. The Minsk Central Jewish Court was founded in January 1926. It functioned in Yiddish and served the whole Minsk District. Criminal cases, conflicts over alimony, and financial arguments were tried in the Yiddish-language court. In 1928, the Jewish Bureau of the District Committee stated that, since the date of its founding, the Minsk Jewish Court had become an integral part of the general Soviet apparatus: "It was the accessibility in terms of language that led the Jewish population of the city and *shtetlekh* to place their trust in this court."⁴³ One of the judges who served in the Jewish tribunal shortly after its establishment reported that 80 percent of Minsk Jews availed themselves of the Yiddish-language court, particularly those tried in criminal cases. The reasons for this success, explained the judge, were "first of all the language—in which one can argue things out—and secondly the milieu: there are . . . trials that require from the judge knowledge of the environment, understanding of the conditions, the customs, even the tone. For these [reasons] one comes to the Jewish court."⁴⁴

But the absolute novelty of a legal institution operating in Yiddish also had its drawback. As it turned out, the Jewish courtroom could not function as fully as its Russian counterpart, which relied on centuries of a well-established legal tradition. While the Jewish court had a legal advisory board that served the Jewish population in Yiddish three times a week, petitions were frequently submitted in Russian and even in Belorussian. In most cases, the lawyers took the floor in Yiddish. But as of May 1928, the public prosecutor often carried out his harangue in Russian. In other words, the deficiency of juridical terms affected the successful operation of the court in Yiddish.⁴⁵ While some lawyers were well-versed in the new Yiddish legal jargon, others had received their training in Russian only and adjusted to the system with some difficulty. In the second half of the 1920s, Singer visited the Minsk Jewish courtroom during the hearing of a conflict over alimony. He noticed that the lawyer representing the former husband, a well-known lawyer "who knows the legal code as well as a religious Jew knows *ashrei* [one of the main prayers in Jewish liturgy], must now speak Yiddish and has trouble doing so." The lawyer began his speech in Yiddish and spoke in a mixture of Yiddish and Russian for the rest of the trial.⁴⁶

* * *

Yiddish had been the language used by most Minsk Jews during social events and leisure-time activities across the political spectrum. "We used to speak Yiddish and read Russian . . . when we met with the girls from our circle, we would speak only Yiddish. Our connection to Russian culture stemmed mostly from habit," commented Chanan Goldberg, describing the language affiliation in his local Zionist youth group in the

1910s.[47] The Minsk Jewish youth group Yung-Skoyt, established shortly after World War I and associated with the Socialist-Zionist movement, organized events for Jewish boys and girls aged twelve to sixteen. With the goal of contributing to their "spiritual development," acquainting them with Jewish folk-creativity, and exposing them to Yiddish cultural treasures, the youth group also coordinated sporting events. The language of these activities, which ranged from gymnastics, hikes outside of the city, and swimming lessons in the river Svisloch, was Yiddish.[48]

While the Jewish scout organization—together with numerous other youth groups in Minsk—made use of Yiddish prior to the launching of the Soviet nationality policy, the creation of accurate Yiddish terms to refer to athletics and sports activities was the outcome of the Soviet Yiddish experiment. In other words, if the language used by the participants in these social events was commonly and nonchalantly Yiddish, the terms they employed to refer to specific aspects of athletics was usually Russian. In August 1921, the statute of the Jewish Sports and Touring Club of Minsk (also a pre-revolutionary Jewish institution legalized by the Soviets in 1921, but liquidated shortly thereafter) emphasized that its official goal was not only the improvement of the physical condition and the training of Jewish youth, but also the formation of a new cadre of instructors for Soviet schools. In line with the requirements of the Soviet educational system, which in the Jewish context entailed the use of Yiddish in every sphere of instruction, the club's leaders stated their commitment to "the creation of a gymnastics terminology in the Yiddish language to be introduced among children with poor knowledge of Russian."[49]

The Jewish Sports Club Hamer, formerly known as Maccabi Club, was officially legalized on December 14, 1921. By early 1922, the club counted approximately one hundred members. These were boys and girls, whose ages ranged between fourteen and twenty, and who assiduously attended the club during its hours of operation every evening from 6 to 10 p.m., except Fridays. On January 9, 1922, the club organized courses for instructors of gymnastics in Soviet Jewish schools. The three-month courses were divided between theoretical sessions devoted to the study of human anatomy and physiology, and practical sessions, which met for physical training three times a week. These courses were specifically designed for instructors of gymnastics in kindergartens and elementary schools.[50] While sporting events for Jews were eventually incorporated into the activities organized by workers' clubs, the Komsomol, and party cells, gymnastics instructors in Soviet Jewish schools continued to train their students in Yiddish.

With the creation of a large network of Soviet Jewish schools, Yiddish became the language of Soviet Jewish education. By January 7, 1924, there were in Minsk ten Yiddish elementary schools with 2,505 students and 141 teachers; eight orphanages with 602 children and 77 teachers; seven kindergartens with 400 children and 34 teachers;[51] a four-year Jewish Agricultural Educational Farm;[52] and a Jewish Pedagogical Training College with 175 students and 29 teachers.[53] All of these institutions functioned in Yiddish.

Figure 7. Physics class in Yiddish at the Jewish section of the Unified Professional School, Minsk, 1928–29. Courtesy of the American Jewish Joint Distribution Committee Archives (Collection 21/32 Russia).

The promoters of the *korenizatsiia* on the Jewish street tried to speed up the tempo of the Yiddishization—bringing it up to pace with the Belorussianization process—and enforce upon Jewish children a Yiddish-language education.[54] The 1924 working plan of the Minsk Central Jewish Educational Bureau contemplated the following resolutions for kindergarten and elementary schools:

> 1. Schools in which the language of instruction used to be Belorussian or Russian, and which have a total of 60–70 percent of Jewish children, are brought under the supervision of the Central Jewish Educational Bureau so that Yiddish can be gradually introduced as the school's instruction language. . . . 2. Jewish children in mixed orphanages and kindergartens . . . are educated in separate Jewish orphanages and kindergartens. 3. Jewish teachers who work in general schools are employed, with the same kind of work, in a Yiddish-language school. . . . [I]n the schools with a smaller proportion of Jewish children (40–50 percent), all Jewish children should be regrouped into one Yiddish-language school.[55]

In October 1924, following the Jewish Educational Bureau's working plan, the Central Executive Committee of the CPB ordered Jewish children whose mother tongue was

Yiddish to attend a Jewish school. The resolution did not however appear to be particularly successful, especially with regard to the city: only one Russian-language school shifted to Yiddish, school no. 7.[56] From 1925 to 1926 the student body of the Minsk Jewish schools grew modestly, increasing only from 3,161 to 3,269. One year later, Jewish activists committed to the success of Yiddish-language schools complained about the lack of enforcement from above, a method that would guarantee Jewish children to attend these schools. "The principle of not forcing at the moment of enrollment has essentially turned into the slogan 'enroll your child wherever you want,'" they commented with frustration.[57]

Many Jews refused to attend Yiddish schools and preferred a Russian, or even a Belorussian school, for a variety of reasons. Children who had studied in a Russian-language school for a few years before the launching of the Yiddish experiment were reluctant to enroll in a Yiddish school. At times, "parents saw in the Russian school a better practical purpose . . . and influenced their children's decision."[58] In spite of their association with Soviet Yiddish culture, some Jewish parents enrolled their children in a Russian school. Anna Gershtein's parents were both actors in the Minsk Jewish Theater, but hoping for a better future employment for their daughter ultimately decided on a Russian-language school.[59]

In order to make Yiddish a language of modern school education, a realm traditionally dominated by Russian, Jewish activists had to cope with the dearth of pedagogical literature and the absence of a well-established secular pedagogical tradition in Yiddish. They faced the challenge of building from scratch something that had little preexisting foundation. As a Jewish activist noted in December 1921, "Our schools are going through tough times. . . . [W]e have no material. . . . [T]here is no serious book in Yiddish."[60] By and large, Jewish pedagogues had been trained in Russian, had used Russian-language textbooks in their pre-revolutionary teaching experience, and had published their articles in Russian-language pedagogical journals. When in May 1921, the Evsektsiia, the Minsk Executive Committee and a group of local activists and instructors organized preparatory courses in Yiddish to train a new cadre of Soviet Yiddish teachers, one of the questions debated was whether knowledge of Russian should be considered a prerequisite to attend the courses. The questionnaire filled out by the applicants, included the following queries: "Do you read Yiddish newspapers and books? Can you read and write in Russian? Do you read Russian newspapers and books?" M. Hoder, who eventually became an instructor of Yiddish literature in the city, argued that knowing Russian was crucial for future teachers insofar as "for specific subjects . . . such as pedagogy . . . we don't have the essential literature in Yiddish." By contrast, Yudl Frankfurt, one of the founders of the Jewish Pedagogical Training College in Minsk, claimed that

> knowledge of Russian is not important to us; more important is that [the future pedagogue] be generally mature and satisfy the rest of our requirements; [the lack of knowledge of Russian] will not hamper his enrollment in the courses, . . . we

will ... translate from Russian into Yiddish specific portions of the literature and ... if worse comes to worse we will ... invite Russian teachers to teach Russian, as long as the Jewish teacher is qualified for the rest of the work.[61]

The creation of a new educational system in Yiddish was especially challenging when it came to teaching scientific subjects. As the Minsk teacher Goldberg pointed out, "There are no appropriate books" to teach math in Yiddish.[62] Math was nonetheless taught in Yiddish, and not only in elementary school, but also in institutions of higher learning. When the Jewish section of the Pedagogical Faculty of Belorussian State University (BGU) was established, at the end of 1921, Yiddish became for the first time a language of instruction at the university level. The Jewish section at BGU was a sort of Jewish studies program to train Yiddish school teachers as well as researchers in Jewish history, Yiddish literature, and linguistics. Both Jewish and general subjects were taught in Yiddish. The 1928 Jewish section's curriculum included not only courses such as "The History of the Jews in Poland, Lithuania, Belorussia and Ukraine," "Economic History of the Jews of Russia," "Modern and Contemporary Yiddish Literature," and "History of the Yiddish Language," but also general courses such as "Political Economy," "Analytical Geometry," "Inorganic Chemistry," and "Math."[63]

Yet the promotion of Yiddish in the Jewish section's curriculum, in particular in scientific courses, frequently clashed with the well-established practice of teaching in Russian. During the 1928–29 academic year 40 percent of the courses in the humanities and 10–15 percent of those not related to the humanities, were taught in Yiddish in the Jewish studies program of the pedagogical faculty.[64] In October 1933, the university's party organization noted that the major shortcoming in the faculty of chemistry was the Jewish section, which lacked instructors and textbooks in Yiddish.[65]

The Construction of a New Center

In the early 1920s, Ester Rosental-Shnayderman, a Yiddish teacher in a Warsaw CYSHO (or TSYSHO, Central Yiddish School Organization) school who moved to the Soviet Union in 1927, complained about the state of Yiddish culture in Poland and the discrimination that Jews and Jewish institutions endured at the hands of the Polish government. As an alternative to Poland she eagerly looked eastward across the border at the blossoming of Soviet Jewish culture, at the publication of pedagogical literature in Yiddish and the state support for Yiddish schools. Rosental-Shnayderman shared the view of thousands of Polish Jews when she wrote in her memoirs:

> For us, Jewish teachers of Poland, used to constant evil decrees against the secular school system, it is new and joyful (and at times almost unbelievable) that *there* [Soviet Union] Yiddish culture not only experienced no persecution, but was actually an official government concern. We literally devour the news about how the Soviet state itself takes care of Jewish cultural institutions equally as it does of all others.... [N]o other state has ever undertaken such an enterprise since the Jews have been living in *goles* [diaspora].[66]

Her perception of Soviet Jewish cultural life was shaped by two factors. On the one hand, her political empathy for Communism, combined with the existence of a nationalistic and often anti-Semitic government in Poland, prompted her to paint the Soviet system only in celebratory colors. On the other hand, the reality of a state that officially and financially supported Jewish culture in Yiddish, thereby accepting the Jewish people as an equal member of the newborn Soviet system, attracted her curiosity and support. Unlike the USSR, where in the interwar period Jewish institutions received full sponsorship from the government, in Poland they were neither funded by the state nor perceived as integral to society. Of course, interwar Polish Jewry enjoyed a degree of cultural, political, and religious autonomy unknown to Soviet Jews. But these autonomous institutions and activities remained confined to the margins of society as most Poles rejected the possibility of Jewish integration.[67] The exclusive position of Polish society toward the Jews stood out sharply, especially for the younger generations, against the inclusive approach of the new Soviet order at least vis-à-vis those Jews who accepted the main tenets of the new system.

This novelty, which deeply impressed the young Yiddish teacher from Warsaw, was welcomed by most Soviet Jews who, marginalized from Russian society throughout the pre-revolutionary period, strove now with passion to belong. In the early 1920s, the absolute innovation of government support for Yiddish generated high hopes for the future development of Jewish cultural and scholarly institutions in Minsk. The editors of one of the finest academic publications in Yiddish to appear in the USSR, *Tsaytshrift* (Periodical), issued in Minsk from 1926 to 1931, conveyed with pride the potency of this initial dream: "For the first time in the history of Jewish culture, scholarship and research are no longer supported by individual patrons nor by independent cultural institutions and organizations. For the first time in the history of Jewish culture, our scholarship is directly sponsored by the state."[68]

Partly dictated by the ideological discourse of the time, the enthusiasm and sense of belonging also grew out of the unusual prestige that Jewish pedagogical, literary, and scholarly publications in Yiddish achieved in the Soviet Union during the 1920s. The unprecedented financial support offered by the Soviet state to young scholars legitimized their work and symbolized the official acknowledgment of the existence of the field of Jewish studies, something unthinkable in tsarist Minsk. As pointed out in the 1924 resolution of the Central Executive Committee of the Belorussian Republic, "Traditionally neglected and treated with ridicule, the Belorussian and Yiddish cultures have now gained the right to an independent existence and to further development; slighted in the past, these cultures require now special and long-lasting attention on the part of the state."[69]

In the tsarist empire, the most important Jewish cultural and scholarly enterprises were carried out in Russian and, to some extent, in Hebrew, in institutions located in St. Petersburg and Odessa. The Bolsheviks' rise to power put an end to Hebrew-language scholarship and institutions and by the early 1920s removed the language from the realm of Jewish culture and *Wissenschaft*. While some Russian-language Jewish scholarly institutions continued to exist after the revolution mostly outside of the former Pale of Settlement,[70] they had to struggle for survival and faced the hostile labeling of "bourgeois organizations." These institutions could no longer rely on the financial support of Jewish patrons—who had disappeared from Soviet Russia—and as "bourgeois organizations" they did not qualify for state funding.

As Yiddish replaced Russian and became the new language of Jewish scholarship, the geography of Jewish cultural and scholarly centers was transformed. The focus shifted toward Ukraine and Belorussia, where the large majority of Jews resided, and Yiddish was mostly spoken. St. Petersburg, home to prominent Russian Jewish organizations, such as OPE and the Jewish Historical-Ethnographic Society, was ousted in its role of leading cultural center by the new rising centers located in the historic Pale of Settlement—an area regarded until then as the periphery of Jewish scholarship. In 1924, as the Jewish section of the Institute for Belorussian Culture grew into a Jewish Department, the St. Petersburg Institute for Jewish studies, where historian Simon Dubnow had taught before fleeing the Soviet Union, was closed down. The well-known literary critic Israel Tsinberg, who edited the "bourgeois" Russian Jewish journal *Evreiskaia Starina* from 1928 to 1930, published a relatively positive review of the first volume of the Minsk *Tsaytshrift*, in spite of his criticism of Marxist Jewish scholarship. He acknowledged that Minsk, together with Vilna, had become the new center for Jewish scholarship in Yiddish.[71] In a second review published in the same "bourgeois" Russian-language publication in 1930, Tsinberg drew a brief comparison between the Kiev Yiddish-language *Shriftn* and *Tsaytshrift*, implying that the Minsk periodical was superior.[72] A rather marginal place in the history of Jewish scholarship before the revolution, in the interwar period Minsk became the Soviet Jewish cultural capital, particularly of *Wissenschaft* in Yiddish.

The growing interest in Jewish scholarship in Yiddish, combined with the state-funding program, attracted to the Minsk assembly many scholars who had been intellectually active in other parts of Russia. The Marxist Jewish historian Israel Sosis had engaged in political and cultural activities in Odessa, Vilna, and St. Petersburg/Leningrad before moving to Minsk;[73] the philologist Mordechai Veinger had studied and worked in Warsaw, Moscow, Kharkov, and Tashkent until 1923, when he moved to Minsk;[74] and the literary historian Nahum Oyslender had studied in Berlin and Kiev and worked in Moscow before moving to Minsk.[75]

The correspondence between Oyslender, who moved to the Belorussian SSR in 1925, and Sh. A. Gurshtein, a Moscow-based literary critic who contributed to the Minsk publications throughout the 1920s and 1930s—reflects the image of the city as a new literary and cultural center. In a letter to Oyslender dated May 1925, Gurshtein complained about Moscow: comparing the Soviet capital to Minsk he referred to Moscow as a "literary exile" (*literarishe goles*) where it was hard to locate the latest Yiddish publications ("in all of Moscow there is not even one issue of *Di royte velt* [The red world] . . . "); he also contrasted the promising status of Yiddish studies in Minsk with their uncertain status in Moscow ("what will be in Moscow, and what it will turn into, I cannot foresee").[76] This image of Minsk as a new place for scholarship, built rapidly almost from scratch, is confirmed by the editors of *Tsaytshrift* who acknowledged the difficulties encountered in issuing the first volume of the scholarly journal: "The greatest hardship we faced was determined by the conditions of the printing shops in Minsk, none of which was equipped for printing academic publications."[77]

Not only scholars moved to Minsk. In search for employment opportunities in Yiddish, Jews from throughout the Soviet Union moved to the Belorussian capital during the 1920s. Here, they hoped to serve as teachers or cultural activists in the newly established Soviet Jewish schools and institutions. Writing from Nizhny Novgorod in 1923, Solomon Volovitsh responded to a newspaper ad inviting applications for positions in Yiddish-language institutions. With long-standing experience in teaching Jewish culture and Yiddish literature, which he had taught in Vilna, Warsaw, and Nizhny Novgorod, Volovitsh asked to be employed as a cultural activist in Minsk.[78] From Tcheliabinsk, Samuil Baksht, with a twenty-five-year teaching career in schools, evening courses, OPE institutions, and the local party school, wished to move to Minsk—a university city, he emphasized—and be employed in an administrative position in Yiddish.[79] That same year a teacher from Warsaw, together with two young political émigrés from Latvia, who graduated from a high school in Riga and joined the Komsomol, applied to work as school activists "preferably in the capital Minsk."[80] Miryam Margolin, author of *Mayselekh far kleyne kinder* (Stories for small children), wrote from Berlin in December 1923 hoping to be employed in a Yiddish-language preschool or school in Minsk.[81] In September 1924, B. Epshtein wrote from Moscow, where he was completing a two-month preparatory Yiddish course, searching for employment as a teacher in one of the Yiddish institutions of Minsk; a graduate from the State Jewish Teachers Institute in Vilna in 1915, he had worked in a Yiddish school in Velzher, Vitebsk *guberniia*, since 1916.[82] From Odessa, the math teacher Rubinshtein searched for employment in a Yiddish-language school in Minsk;[83] from Samara, the teacher Yosif Ravin, who had worked in the Yiddish school movement in Lodz for seven years, and regularly published in *Grininke Beymelekh* (Little green trees), the Vilna Yiddish children's periodical, searched for employment in Minsk;[84] and again from Moscow, the Russian-language teacher P. Efron applied for a position in a Yiddish-language school in Minsk because of the Jewish atmosphere of the city.[85]

Some applicants were rejected: Roza Peker's knowledge of the language was deemed limited, as can be inferred from the mistakes in her application letter.[86] Another applicant had no knowledge of Yiddish at all: she wrote her letter in Russian and wished to teach Russian.[87] Elke Hurevitch, who knew Yiddish, but not too well, received the option of working in a Yiddish-language kindergarten.[88] Searching for better employment conditions, perhaps attracted by the Jewishness of the city, but most importantly excited about the idea of participating in the Yiddish experiment, many Jews from across the Soviet landscape and nearby Poland relocated to Minsk.

Institutions in Red

> We had no traditions. In the whole world—and in Russia especially—there was no Yiddish scientific state institute of an academic kind. We had no one to take example from and had to . . . grope in the dark.[89]

Established in November 1921 as a four-year seconday school, the Jewish Pedagogical Training College (Evpedtekhnikum in Russian, and Yidpedtekhnikum in Yiddish) produced a new cadre of "Red Teachers" who served as instructors in preschool, elementary, and adult educational institutions in Minsk and the surrounding *shtetlekh*.[90] The language of instruction was Yiddish. During the 1921–22 academic year, 133 students—mostly from indigent families—enrolled in the Pedagogical Training College, many relocating from different districts in Belorussia, from Soviet Ukraine, and from Poland.[91] With the goal of creating a Jewish proletarian culture, the Evpedtekhnikum's curriculum included Yiddish, math, physics, geography, gymnastics, chemistry, music (classical, workers' songs, and folk-songs), mechanics, and agronomy. Belorussian was introduced during the second year of study. The entry exam, in Yiddish, consisted of questions addressing different topics such as, "Why do you wish to become a pedagogue?" "Describe the most salient moments in Jewish history," and "Are you familiar with the Yiddish classics? And with Russian literature?"[92] The social and cultural events organized by the institution in 1922 ranged from an evening commemorating the anniversary of writer Y. L. Peretz's death, with an audience of more than five hundred people; a lecture by Ester Frumkin on Communist ethics; and a lecture by the literary critic Moshe Litvakov on modern Yiddish literature.[93]

Similar to the other Jewish institutions in the city—and not unlike the newly established Belorussian ones—the Evpedtekhnikum had to cope with the critical shortage of qualified personnel, searching for a director who "must be able to guard the college from Menshevik influence,"[94] or a cleaning lady with sufficient knowledge of Yiddish.[95] The college's biggest challenge remained however balancing among the students the reality of Russian—which in spite of the Belorussianization campaign continued to be the strongest language of the outside world—with the utopia of Yiddish—which was supposed to become the only language of the newly sovietized Jewish street. Based on the resolution passed by the Evpedtekhnikum's party cell in 1925, the study of Russian was deemed necessary.[96] After all, it was the language of a great culture. With Belorussian, however, "one could barely manage in the village."[97] The 1925 data about newspaper and journal subscriptions in the Training College confirms the prominent role played by Russian among the students, with subscriptions to Russian-language publications significantly exceeding those to Yiddish-language publications.[98]

For the first time, Jewish institutions of higher learning appeared in Minsk. The most impressive one was the Jewish section of Belorussian State University, a Jewish studies division that offered courses in Yiddish. The People's Commissariat for Enlightenment endorsed the establishment of a Jewish section in June 1921,[99] and in October of the same year the Evsektsiia resolved to organize a Jewish section in the Faculty of Pedagogy (comprised of four different departments: social history, natural sciences, literature and linguistics, and physics-mathematics).[100] The organizers and supporters of the university's Jewish section struggled to find lecturers and professors who would move to Minsk to teach. In late 1921, Minsk activists consulted with Moscow and Petrograd to attract Jewish scholars to the city. Their goal was to bring to the Belorussian capital two of the most well-known Jewish scholars in pre-revolutionary Russia, historian Simon Dubnow and literary historian Israel Tsinberg. The fact that a newly established Communist institution contemplated hiring two scholars who had—Dubnow in particular—vigorously criticized the Soviet system, confirms that the absence of local academic resources made collaborating with "politically incorrect" scholars conceivable.[101] With the exception of two local scholars (Mikhl Rabinovitch and Merlis, who applied for the position in Yiddish literature and folklore), most candidates contacted in the early 1920s by the Commission for the Organization of the Jewish section at Belorussian State University lived either in Moscow or Petrograd.[102]

In March 1924, the Jewish section of BGU was reorganized into a department and the curriculum became more rigid. The subject of "Local Jewish Studies," Evrevedenie in Russian and Yidkentenish in Yiddish, became mandatory for all students enrolled in the Jewish Department. It studied the history, culture, language, and ethnography of the Jews of Belorussia.[103] Besides the Belorussian language, the study of which was mandatory for all, students who chose to focus on Yiddish language and "specialize in the field of Jewish national culture" could opt between history, literature, philology, natural sciences, or math as a field of concentration and take some of the following courses:[104] "History of the Jews in Russia in the Twentieth Century," "Economic Developments in the Jewish Workers' Movement," "German and Yiddish Philology," "Yiddish Literature," "Hebrew Language," and "Ancient Jewish History."[105] Marxist historians Israel Sosis and Hillel Alexandrov,[106] philologist Mordechai Veinger, literary historian Nahum Oyslender, and historian and folklorist N. Nikolskii were among the professors who lectured in Jewish studies at Belorussian State University in the 1920s.[107]

In spite of the anticipated expansion of instruction in Yiddish (which should have reached 57 percent of the curriculum by 1929) many courses in Jewish studies (particularly the general studies courses) continued to be taught in Russian.[108] Some students in the Jewish Department opposed the complete Yiddishization of the curriculum, a number of them even admitting that they had poor knowledge of Yiddish, chose Jewish studies by default—having been rejected by other departments—and that ultimately wished to move to the Russian republic.[109] Not unlike most Jewish students enrolled in universities throughout the world today, only a minority chose to focus on Jewish studies. In 1927, sixty-five first-year Jewish students enrolled in the Jewish Department at Belorussian State University, while two hundred enrolled in the general department.[110] Most of those who chose to focus on Jewish studies were committed to teaching in a Soviet Jewish school, serving in a cultural institution on the Jewish street, or becoming scholars in one of the fields of the new Jewish *Wissenschaft*.[111] Born near Warsaw in 1903 and a teacher in a Yiddish school in Poland, Sara Aizenberg moved to Minsk and enrolled in 1923 in the Jewish Department, specializing in Yiddish philology, to pursue a teaching career in a Yiddish-language school.[112] Others, like Ruvim Ginenskii who, born in Novogrudok (Novohrudok) in 1892, served both as teacher and director of Soviet Jewish school no. 24, specialized in history in the Jewish Department at BGU probably in order to improve their rank on the Jewish street (and salary).[113] Yet others, like Rivka Rubin, born in Minsk in 1906 and a graduate of the Evpedtekhnikum, applied to the Jewish Department hoping to become a scholar or writer. Rivka was eventually accepted into the small graduate program in Jewish studies at Belorussian State University, as an *aspirant* (postgraduate student) in Yiddish literature.[114]

In 1932, the Pedagogical Faculty at Belorussian State University was transformed into the Gorky Belorussian Higher Pedagogical Institute, a four-year institute, which included a Jewish and a Polish section for the training of elementary and secondary-school teachers of literature, language, and history.[115] A number of aspiring Yiddish poets and writers, such as Lipe Heller and Motl Dekhtiar, attended the institute in the 1930s. Even within this structure, however, the Jewish studies program continued to be short on local lecturers. Yiddish language was taught by the well-known philologist A. Zaretsky, who commuted to Minsk from Moscow. In 1936, Jewish history disappeared from the curriculum. Attempts to get Hillel Alexandrov—who in the meantime had moved to Leningrad—to teach Jewish history at the institute fell through.[116] In 1937, the Jewish section managed to reach a short-term agreement with the Moscow-based historian Tevye Heilikman to teach Jewish history for the academic year.[117]

* * *

Founded in 1921, the Jewish section of the Institute for Belorussian Culture (Institut Belorusskoi kultury or Inbelkult) became the first incorporation of Jewish studies into a Soviet institution of academic research. The official description of the institution read as follows:

> The Institute for Belorussian Culture is a . . . state-sponsored academic institution in Belorussia, under the supervision of the People's Commissariat for Education. Its goal . . . [is] the research of Belorussia from the vantage point of language, literature, ethnography, history, nature, economics. . . . A Jewish section is established for the research of the Jewish language, literature, history and ethnography. . . . The Institute for Belorussian Culture may open museums, libraries, archives, publishing houses, research centers . . . publish scholarly journals and monographs of scholarly, artistic and popular nature. . . . All the publications of the Institute must be issued in Belorussian. . . . The Jewish section publishes its works in Yiddish.[118]

the absence of a Belorussian military terminology, for example, Inbelkult had to turn to Ukraine—where a military vocabulary in Ukrainian existed—and, based on the common Slavic roots of both languages, took the Ukrainian military terminology as a model and constructed a Belorussian counterpart.[125]

Striving to emerge as the greatest scholarly center for Soviet Jewry, the Jewish Department at Inbelkult sought to draw to Minsk not only scholars from other areas in the USSR, but from abroad as well. In 1925, the department's secretary addressed two well-known Jewish scholars who lived in New York at the time, the folklorist Y. L. Kahan and the linguist Yehuda Joffe. Not only were they asked to contribute to the department's academic journal *Tsaytshrift*, but were also invited to work at Inbelkult in the field of Yiddish research. "Tell us exactly when you plan to move to Minsk for permanent scholarly work," stated the invitation made to Joffe.[126] The list of participants in the first Belorussian Academic Congress organized by Inbelkult and scheduled for December 1925–February 1926, confirmed this attempt by the Jewish Department and the scholars linked to it to create a world center of Yiddish scholarship. The list included some of the most well-known scholars in the field of Jewish studies in the twentieth century, such as Max Weinreich and Zalman Rejzen from Vilna, Sh. Birnbaum, Nahum Shtif, and Mark Wischnitzer from Berlin, Shmuel Niger and Yehuda Joffe from New York, and Meir Balaban from Lvov.[127] Finally, the names of illustrious scholars from outside the Soviet Union who published their work in the 1928 volume of *Tsaytshrift*, the institute's Yiddish-language academic publication, also corroborates this aspiration for international acknowledgment on the part of the Jewish cultural elite in Minsk.[128] But the ambition to become the world center of Jewish studies clashed with the difficulty in attracting to Minsk stellar scholars. When Yiddish writer Singer met with some of the cultural activists employed in the Jewish Department in the second half of the 1920s, he was told, "We would like to get scholars like Dubnow . . . so that the world would have the greatest trust in our scholarly academy . . . We will forgive them all [of their] sins, as long as [they] come and work for us."[129] The transformation of the city from periphery to capital of Soviet Yiddish *Wissenschaft* often seemed precarious and entailed a constant struggle for recognition.

In December 1928, the Institute for Belorussian Culture was transformed into the Belorussian Academy of Science (Akademia Nauk Belorusskoi SSR), and the Jewish Department became the Jewish division, or Yidsektor, of the new scholarly institution. It was divided into five commissions: a socioeconomic commission, a historical commission, a language commission, a literary commission, and an antireligious commission, which made the struggle against nationalistic and clerical tendencies among the Jewish population its chief "scholarly" goal. In 1932, during the first year of its existence, the antireligious commission organized seminars at the Minsk Jewish club, as well as investigated the life of workers and artisans in the Minsk factories and cooperatives to assess the extent of their religious practice.[130] One of the most impressive scholarly products of the Jewish division of the Academy of Science was the demographic

In 1924, following some discussion among the founders of Inbelkult (some of whom even argued that Jewish culture should have its own separate institute "and not be integrated into the Institute for Belorussian Culture") the Jewish section was eventually upgraded to the Jewish Department.[119] Its establishment preceded thus the founding of the Vilna YIVO Institute for Jewish Research, the Yiddish scholarly institution in nearby Poland set up in 1925. Within the context of Inbelkult, Belorussians and Jews became the only two national groups entitled to a department, as Russians and Poles could create commissions and sections only,[120] an indication of the special status that Yiddish and the Jews enjoyed in Minsk at the time.

Subdivided into three main commissions—historical, literary, and linguistic—the Jewish Department studied questions related to the history of Yiddish language and literature, the social history of the Jews in Belorussia, their culture and folklore.[121] Headed by Israel Sosis, the Historical Commission was divided into two subsections: one researched the history of the Jewish revolutionary movement in Belorussia, while the second (also referred to as "*kraevedenie*" in Russian, and "*kantkentenish*" in Yiddish) dealt with the socioeconomic and demographic features of the Jews of contemporary Soviet Belorussia, with a special focus on everyday life. One of the major undertakings of the Historical Commission was the collection and translation into Yiddish of rabbinical *responsa*, seen as a precious source for the investigation of Jewish daily life. The commission relied on the collaboration of the scholar Yehiel Ravrebe as well as the former rabbi of Bikhov, I. Manes, who upon rejecting his rabbinical title in 1925, decided to devote his erudition to the scholarly cause of the Jewish Department.[122]

Headed by Oyslender (and following his departure from Minsk by Ber Orshansky), the Literary Commission also included two subdivisions: one devoted to the history of Jewish theater and drama and the second to the research of Jewish folklore. The folklore subdivision relied on tens of correspondents who, from across Belorussia (and the USSR in general), collected Yiddish folksongs, jokes, and proverbs and mailed them to Inbelkult.[123]

The Language Commission was headed by Mordechai Veinger. It included a special section for the creation of a Yiddish academic dictionary, which by 1927 had managed to collect 157,000 words by Yiddish writers and 3,000 by "the common folk," putting together the work terminology of tailors, *katsovim* (butchers), and *klezmorim* (klezmer musicians). Under Veinger's supervision, the Language Commission also worked on the so-called *Atlas of Yiddish Dialects*: by sending out thousands of postcards with questions about regional variations in pronunciation, it collected valuable information about the Yiddish dialects spoken in Belorussia. Finally, the Language Commission dealt with issues of Yiddish terminology, creating a new Yiddish legal, chemistry, physics, and agricultural vocabulary, as well as enforcing spelling and orthographic rules for Yiddish.[124] Incidentally, the same concern for a standardized writing system in Yiddish was voiced by the Belorussian linguists of Inbelkult, who from the beginning strove to yield common rules for Belorussian orthography and terminology. In and socioeconomic study *Yidn in BSSR: statistishe materyaln* (The Jews of the BSSR: statistical material), published in 1929.

From 1932 to 1935, the Jewish division—which in 1933 was renamed Institute for Proletarian Jewish Culture, like the Kiev Jewish studies institution established in 1929—issued the scholarly publication *Afn visnshaftlekhn front*.[131] Shmuel Agursky served as editor-in-chief of the new publication and as prolific "scholar" in most of the projects undertaken by the institute's commissions; Yiddish writer Moshe Kulbak served as stylistic editor for the institute's publication, as well as senior researcher in the literary department, where, among other things, he edited and translated Russian classics into Yiddish;[132] head of the literary commission, literary critic Yasha Bronshteyn taught seminars for doctoral students in Jewish studies at the institute.[133] An example of the "Communist-driven Red scholarship" produced in the Academy of Science in Minsk in the late 1930s was L. Holmshtok's dissertation, which he defended in May 1937. (At this point the Institute for Proletarian Jewish Culture had been closed down and replaced, once again, by a Jewish division—Yidsektor—of the Academy.)[134] Entitled *The Kahal in the First Half of the 19th Century in Belorussia as an Instrument for the Exploitation of the Jewish Working Masses*, the introduction of Holmshtok's study attacked the "bourgeois" historiography of Jewish historians like Dubnow, Balaban, and Wischnitzer, and compared Nicholas I Jewish military reform of the first half of the nineteenth century to Hitler's fascism.[135] In spite of the overbearing shadow of ideology, which heavily stifled the scholarly output of the mid-1930s, some glimmers of creativity (such as the plan to produce a lexicon of Soviet Yiddish writers, initiated in 1934), or sophisticated academic research (as the 1935 study on the origins of Yiddish theater in Belorussia), turned up in Minsk, against all odds.[136]

A New Focus for Yiddish Culture, or the Creation of a Belorussian-Jewish Identity

Expressing the need to "territorialize" Jewish culture and connect it to the territory of the republic, the editor of the Minsk Jewish daily, Elye Osherovitsh, wrote in 1924:

> The Jewish worker in Belorussia feels himself a citizen . . . of the USSR in general, and not of Belorussia where he actually lives. . . . [O]ur first task is to make the Jewish worker a citizen of Belorussia, so that he should feel that Belorussia is his own. . . . From this it follows that our culture should become "territorialized," so to speak. [It must] gain a local coloration, it must mesh with Belorussian culture which has shown signs of growth in the last few years. This is possible and necessary because Belorussian culture is manifesting tendencies toward becoming not a national-personal culture, but a national-territorial one, that is, not a culture of Belorussians as a people isolated in themselves but a culture of Belorussians as citizens living in the given territory.[137]

While Belorussianization was met with a great deal of resistance in the city, it still profoundly influenced the realm of Yiddish culture, literature, and theater, producing an innovative focus on Belorussia. Restricted by the condemnation of Hebrew language and culture, the assault on religion, and the Stalinist notion of "Socialist in content and national in form," Yiddish culture and scholarship were additionally curtailed by territorialization. The latter resulted from the cultural ideology of the Jewish elite, as well as the general Soviet politics applied to the Belorussian context during the 1920s and early 1930s. The emphasis on the Belorussian region emerged, for example, in the literary themes explored by the Minsk Yiddish literary group Yunger Arbeter (The Young Workers). Established in December 1924, it joined the All-Union Association of Proletarian Writers (VAAP), and the All-Belorussian Union of Poets and Writers (Maladniak). Its fifteen members, some of whom were students at the Minsk Evpedtekhnikum, organized events across the BSSR. In Minsk, they held literary soirées at the Lenin Jewish Club. As the Evsektsiia positively noted:

> The Yiddish literary group . . . carried out important literary and educational work in Minsk and the surrounding provinces, thus becoming the only . . . Yiddish-language literary organization of Belorussia to be linked to the masses: it organized *kruzhki* . . . and issued a literary collection dedicated to the victims of the White Terror. . . . [But] most importantly we must welcome the emergence of Belorussian motives in the work of the group.[138]

The Evsektsiia also invited Inbelkult to support the literary group and sponsor the publication of a literary collection entitled *Belorussia*. This would expose the artistic strengths of the Yiddish writers of Belorussia; consolidate their relationship with the motherland, Soviet Belorussia; and most importantly, "attract all revolutionary Yiddish writers, who were born in Belorussia, but live elsewhere, both in the USSR and abroad [*vse revolutsionnye evreiskie pisateli, rozhentsy Belorussi, kak iz SSSR tak iz za-granitsy*] to participate in the collection."[139]

The same geographic and cultural boundaries were set for Jewish actors who wished to perform in the Jewish section of the Belorussian State Theater. Only those born in Belorussia could be part of the Jewish section of the Drama Studio of the Belorussian State Theater, established in 1921. The language of instruction of the three-year courses for actors in the Jewish section was Yiddish, and in order to apply, actors should "have knowledge of Belorussian and Yiddish, as well as stem from the territory of ethnographic Belorussia" (*dlia postupleniia obiazatelno znanie belorusskogo iazyka ili belorusskii i evreiskii dlia evreev i proiskhozhdenie iz etnograficheskoi Belorussi*).[140] While before the revolution the Jews who lived in Minsk and its environs saw themselves as culturally part of Lithuanian Jewry, or in some cases of Russian Jewry, they were now encouraged to identify only with the geopolitical reality of Belorussia and see themselves as Belorussian Jews. Besides studying Yiddish literature, the actors in the Jewish section had to take courses in Belorussian studies (Belorussovedenie) and become acquainted with the Belorussian village and way of life (*byt*).[141]

The "territorialization" of Yiddish literary works in Belorussia carried on through the 1920s and 1930s. Moshe Kulbak, one of the most celebrated Yiddish writers in the

USSR, wrote two major works in the capital of Belorussia. Both were profoundly rooted in the city's contemporary Jewish history and folklore. The two-volume novel *Zelmenyaner*, published in Minsk in 1931 and 1935 respectively, took place in the Belorussian capital and told the story of the sovietization of a Jewish family of artisans, the Zelmenyaner, and the revolution in the ethnic space of the courtyard in which they lived. Similarly, Kulbak's play *Boytre*, published and performed on stage in 1936, was based on the story of a Jewish Robin Hood who lived in Minsk in the nineteenth century; a Belorussian "Jewish Pugachev," wrote literary critic Max Erik, who stole from the rich to give to the poor.[142] A well-known legend in Jewish Minsk, the story of Boytre produced a local Yiddish saying to identify a courageous villain: "*er iz a Boytre*" (he is a Boytre).[143] The interplay between Belorussianization and the creation of a new Soviet Yiddish culture possibly led Kulbak to focus on Minsk and Belorussian-Jewish motifs, both largely missing from his pre-Soviet literary career.[144] The tendency to territorialize the literary output (which by the second half of the 1930s might have been seen also as a way to justify the existence of the literature of a national minority) is echoed in the words of Izzy Kharik and Yasha Bronshteyn, editors of the 1935 collection of poems and short stories, *Sovetishe Vaysrusland* (Soviet Belorussia):

> We should not forget that in each republic Soviet Yiddish literature conveys its specificities, its local republican uniqueness.... Yiddish literature in Belorussia brings to the All-Union Soviet Yiddish literature the scent of the Belorussian landscape, the sound of the Belorussian folk-song, the distinctiveness of the Socialist construction in Belorussia.... The goal [of the collection] is to show how Soviet Belorussia is artistically embodied in our literature.[145]

One of the most original outcomes of the encounter between the Soviet nationality policy and Soviet Jewish scholarship in Minsk was the emphasis on the local reality of Belorussia, the Belorussian *shtetl*, and Belorussian-Jewish history, in the academy. Jewish scholars territorialized their *Wissenschaft* limiting it almost exclusively either to the "Belorussian Jewish" or the "Lithuanian-Belorussian Jewish" past, usually breaking it apart from the pre-Soviet Russian Jewish sociocultural and historical commonality. There were two variants of the territorialization when it came to scholarship: the straight focus on Belorussia based only on the current borders of Soviet Belorussia, and the more sophisticated version which studied Lithuanian-Belorussian Jewry as a single cultural identity, which originated in the fourteenth century following the annexation of the region of Belorussia to the Grand Duchy of Lithuania.

Jewish research institutions in Minsk promoted the study of history more than the Kiev and Moscow institutions did during the 1920s. A Jewish Historical Commission of Belorussia existed in Minsk as early as 1921. In its 1923–24 report, the commission described its attempts to develop the field of Jewish history through public lectures on the Jews in Belorussia; it put together lists of religious books (*sefarim*) considered valuable tools for the research of Jewish history in Belorussia; and it issued a call to collect historical material about the Jews in Belorussia—in particular the history of the Jewish workers' movement—entitled *Vos darf men zamlen* (What must be collected).[146] The tradition of collecting (*zamlen*) historical documents with the help of nonprofessional historians (*zamlers*, or collectors) grew out of Dubnow's 1891 brochure *On the History of Russian Jews and the Establishment of a Historical Society*, published in Hebrew and in Russian.[147] The importance of collecting historical documents and building archives to preserve them, emphasized by Dubnow in his call to the residents of the Pale of Settlement, was reclaimed, albeit in a very different geopolitical context, by the Minsk Commission. The latter addressed the Jewish section of the People's Commissariat for Education explaining the significance of collecting documents on Jewish history in Belorussia for the archive of the Jewish Historical Commission in Minsk. The *zamler* tradition also led to the establishment of a Jewish section of the local museum: in 1924, A. Paleyes became the director of the Jewish Department of the Belorussian State Museum in Minsk.[148] While Dubnow viewed the collection of historical material as the first step toward the foundation of a Russian-Jewish national and historical consciousness, the Minsk Jewish Historical Commission reflected the new linguistic and geopolitical reality of Soviet Jews. Not only was the language of the Minsk Commission no longer Hebrew or Russian, but Yiddish, but its aim was the creation of a new regional identity and consciousness closely intertwined with the territory of Belorussia. Moreover, while Dubnow put a stronger emphasis on the historical value of the *Pinkasim*, or Jewish community records, in line with the new political order, the Minsk Commission favored the study of the Jewish workers' movement in Belorussia. In 1923, for example, the commission's director Mikhl Rabinovitch (himself a Zionist activist before the revolution and a lecturer on Jewish folklore at BGU) headed a locally based historical project to collect information about the family, social background, and political activity of Hesia Helfman, the Jewish woman involved in the assassination of Alexander II, and of Nosn Golubov, a prominent local Jewish revolutionary. Both were born and grew up in Mozyr, Minsk *guberniia*. The information assembled by local *zamlers* would be included in a research publication sponsored by the commission.[149]

The attempt to territorialize Jewish scholarship and enclose it within the borders of the newly established Belorussian SSR, and thus forge a new "Belorussian-Jewish" identity, emerged in original studies from the 1920s and 1930s. In 1926, Sosis published the opening article to the first volume of *Tsaytshrift*, entitled "On the Social History of the Jews of Lithuania and Belorussia." Regarded as one of the first Marxist historians to create a socioeconomic narrative of the Jewish past, Sosis emphasized the importance of a local/regional focus in Russian-Jewish historiography over a universal or all-Russian one. Rejecting Heinrich Graetz's *Leidensgeschichte*, Dubnow's romantic nationalism, and Yulii Gessen's juridical approach, he criticized the tendency to study the past of Russian Jewry as a uniform and homogeneous entity. "The need to research the history of the Jews of the Lithuanian-Belorussian area separately is not determined," argued Sosis, "by our national politics, but rather by the objective reality: the Jews of this region have always distinguished themselves through their specific dialect, culture and socioeconomic traits."[150] In a later essay, which appeared in 1929, Sosis added, "The history of the Jews in Lithuania, Belorussia and Ukraine is usually not even mentioned by the Jewish historian: until the partitions of Poland these territories are imagined as an organic part of the Polish Kingdom; after Poland's collapse they are . . . imagined as Russia."[151] According to Sosis, thus, not only had Russian-Jewish historiography removed from its narrative all socioeconomic dimensions of the Jewish past, but it had also overrated the "abstract notion of a universal Jewish history," invalidating the tangible historical conditions of time and place typical of regional history.[152] The progressive shift from a general all-Russian—or all-Soviet—focus to a local one transpired through the contents of *Tsaytshrift*'s 1928 volume, which included seven different articles with a regional emphasis, ranging from a study of the Jewish guilds in Lithuania and Belorussia during the seventeenth and eighteenth centuries, to a demographic study of the Jewish population in the cities and *shtetlekh* of Belorussia.

The new focus on Belorussia materialized in the field of Yiddish linguistics as well. The Inbelkult Language Commission, with the passionate support of its director Veinger, worked on the Yiddish-language *Atlas*. In essays such as "On Yiddish Dialects," "Linguistic Cartography and Atlas of the Yiddish language," and "Yiddish Dialectology," Veinger published in *Tsaytshrift* the results of the commission's scholarly endeavor: the emphasis was clearly on the history of Yiddish dialects spoken in Belorussia. The Language Commission's commitment to establish a close link between Yiddish and the Belorussian territory emerged also in the pamphlet *Research Yiddish Dialects!* published by Inbelkult in 1925. Calling on the students of the Jewish Department to join the effort, Veinger outlined a program to collect information and study the different dialects of the BSSR.[153] Once again, the shift toward a local emphasis produced an artificial undertone: the historic subdivision of Yiddish dialects into the geographic areas of Lithuania, Poland, and Ukraine certainly did not include a "Belorussian-Yiddish" dialect.

The interplay between the Soviet nationality policy and Jewish scholarship generated a Jewish version of "regional studies" on the contemporary history of the Jews of the Belorussian SSR. Through a microscale approach, the field of "regional studies" focused on the history, demography, economy, and folklore of one geographical area in which the *kraeved* (student of *kraevedenie*, or regional studies) collected documents ranging from ethnographic material to rare documents on the origin of a village. Author of numerous demographic studies about the Jews of Minsk and other Belorussian cities and *shtetlekh*, Hillel Alexandrov became one of the leading scholars in Jewish regional studies at the time. In 1928, Inbelkult issued his brochure *Research Your Shtetl!*, which illustrates the meaning of *kraevedenie/kantkentenish* in the Jewish context. Like Veinger before him, Alexandrov turned to the members of the new local Soviet Jewish intelligentsia calling on them to participate in his program to investigate the *shtetl*: "We hope that our local leaders—teachers, agronomists, . . . students . . . — will support the task of researching the shtetl, thus helping the state, as well as our social and scholarly institutions."¹⁵⁴ Alexandrov emphatically noted that the establishment of a serious scholarship on the Belorussian *shtetl* assisted the Soviet state in carrying out its social engineering project and adjusting the socioeconomic structure of the Jewish population to the needs of collectivization and industrialization. In other words, by researching the origin of one town, its population, economy, pre-revolutionary culture, and political organizations, scholarship served the honorable goal of building a new Soviet society.

Along the same lines of *Research Your Shtetl!*, in 1929 Alexandrov published a textbook for the Jewish schools of Belorussia, entitled *Undzer kant* (Our region). Defined as "the first attempt to put together a *gegnt-bukh* [a book about the region] for Jewish schools," the goal of the two-volume work was to promote the knowledge of the history, geography, economy, and climate of the Belorussian SSR among generations of young Jews. Through the study of this textbook Jewish children were being exposed to a new regional identity, the core principle of which lied in the axiom: "The city or shtetl in which we live belongs to the land called Belorussian Soviet Socialist Republic."¹⁵⁵ The new emphasis on the Belorussian region in the classroom resulted thus in the attempt to recast (and confine) Jewish identity within Belorussian borders, thereby creating the new Belorussian Jewish citizen of the BSSR.

The rise of Jewish scholarship in Yiddish, which bridged the gap between high culture and mass culture on the Jewish street, was marked by the emergence of new themes generally ignored in tsarist Russia. Previously frowned-upon research topics were now brought to the forefront of scholarship: Yiddish language and philology, old and modern Yiddish literature, and Jewish socioeconomic and cultural history with a Marxist slant. Soviet Jewish scholarship in Belorussia was undoubtedly original both thematically and by virtue of its local focus. The local emphasis on the Belorussian region and the "territorialization" of Jewish scholarship grew out of the Soviet nationality policy: in order to be acknowledged as a full-fledged Soviet national group, the Jews had to provide a territorial justification for their existence and, at the same time, refute the existence of a Jewish people beyond the borders of the USSR. This significantly restricted their research possibilities.

By the second half of the 1930s, Russian regained its uncontested reputation of All-Union language. The downfall of Belorussian, coupled with surging accusations of Belorussian chauvinism and nationalism against the supporters of Belorussianization, affected the Jewish scholarly output as well. The 1935 issue of the academic journal of the Institute for Proletarian Jewish culture included only one article highlighting Belorussia.¹⁵⁶ In general, the new political reality of the late-1930s led to the decline in creative scientific work.¹⁵⁷ To be sure, Jewish scholars (as well as writers and pedagogues) had been pressured into carving a Belorussian niche out of their *Wissenschaft*, novels, or textbooks. But the final product often contained more than a glimpse of originality, as they tried to achieve an impossible balance between scientific research and Communism, as well as between playing a part in a Belorussian-Jewish institution or in a Soviet Jewish institution. In the second part of the 1930s especially, the clash between original scholarship and official ideology became inevitable and, for many, unbearable. A new geographic focus in Jewish literary and scholarly productivity should replace Belorussia: namely, the officially selected Jewish territory of Birobidzhan. Finally, the clash between scholarship and ideology caused the estrangement from the field of Jewish studies of many scholars who came to renounce their careers either by choice or, more often, because of charges of "national opportunism."

Conclusion

The official status of Yiddish, the state support for cultural, educational, and scholarly enterprises, the establishment of a Jewish Department at Belorussian State University, and the creation of a Jewish division in the most important academic institution of the republic (Inbelkult, and later the Belorussian Academy of Sciences), made Minsk one of the most successful examples of the Yiddish experiment in the Soviet Union. On the one hand, this experiment was quintessentially Soviet. It originated in the Soviet nation-state building project based on territorial nationalities and on the idea that the Jews, who were lacking a major territorial concentration, could be identified as a national group by virtue of the linguistic category only. On the other hand, the Yiddish experiment was embedded in solid foundations, some of which dated back to the pre-revolutionary period. In addition to the government support for Yiddish, four main reasons promoted the success of the Yiddish experiment in Minsk.

First, by the end of the nineteenth century Minsk had become one of the greatest centers of the Jewish labor movement in the Russian empire. Bundism caught on in Minsk (as well as in other urban centers of historic Jewish Lithuania, which comprised Belorussia) because of the large proportion of Jews in the workforce and the nature of the Jewish political leadership, likely to be less acculturated and Russified in the northwestern regions of the empire than in Ukraine and Poland. The deeply rooted Bundist tradition of Minsk contributed to the use of Yiddish in lieu of alternative linguistic channels, not only among those former Bundists who joined the Evsektsiia after the revolution and strove, with great determination, to build a Yiddish bureaucratic and political system from scratch. But also among Jews who worked in the city post office or in the local clothing factory and who—because of their Bundist background—demonstrated a stronger commitment to the cause of Yiddish than most Jews living in the urban centers of Ukraine or Russia.

Second, the relatively small size of Minsk compared to cities like Moscow, Kiev, or Odessa, together with its provincial character, which the city retained even after its transformation into a Soviet capital, guaranteed the preservation of sizeable Jewish enclaves throughout the 1930s. In Minsk, as well as in most small-to-medium-size cities in the former Pale of Settlement, the Soviet regime did not manage to uproot the historical continuity of Jewish urban spaces, and Yiddish continued to be spoken and heard on the streets of the city until the eve of the war.

Third, there was a direct relation between the socioeconomic background of the Jewish population of the city and their language knowledge and use. While a considerable fraction of Minsk Jewish and non-Jewish residents readily left the city for Russian-speaking Moscow and Leningrad throughout the 1920s and 1930s, the Belorussian capital absorbed thousands of newcomers from surrounding *shtetlekh* and smaller cities who moved to Minsk in search of employment and a better livelihood. They were mostly poor Jews and Belorussians who spoke Yiddish and Belorussian, respectively. In May 1936, for example, the All-City Workers Conference, which convened at the Stalin Club, counted eight thousand illiterate or partly literate workers who had recently moved to Minsk.[158] As Moshe Lewin has noted, the massive urbanization scale "changed the social face" of Soviet cities; with the ongoing peasant influx, new forms of customs and languages marked urban spaces with a rural atmosphere.[159] The steady in-migration of Yiddish-speaking Jews from the Belorussian *shtetlekh* inevitably affected Jewish life in Minsk.[160]

Fourth, the position of Yiddish was enhanced by the Jews' lack of support for Belorussian, a language that, at least in the city, never represented a real alternative for Jewish residents. In other words, Yiddish was never truly in competition with Belorussian as much as it was with Ukrainian in Ukrainian urban centers. As late as October 1935, for example, the instructor of Belorussian language in a Soviet Jewish school in Minsk would speak Belorussian to the students while they would reply in Yiddish.[161]

The strongest evidence of the success of the Yiddish experiment in Minsk can be found in the following statistical data from 1927 and 1939, respectively:

(1) According to the school census of December 15, 1927, in Odessa, where the Jews made up for 36.4 percent of the population, the proportion of students of all school-aged children attending Yiddish-language schools was 9 percent; in Kiev, where the Jews made up for 27.3 percent of the population, this proportion was 8 percent; in Kharkov, where the Jews were 19.4 percent of the population, this proportion was 2.9 percent.[162] In Minsk, however, where the Jews made up for 40.8 percent of the total population, the proportion of students of all school-aged children attending Yiddish-language schools was 55.3 percent for elementary school (*pervyi kontsenter*) and 28.2 percent for middle school (*vtoroy kontsenter*).[163]

(2) The available statistics about the mother tongue of Soviet Jews on the eve of the Holocaust confirm the overall trend indicated by the 1927 school data.[164] In 1939, 22.8 percent of the Jews in Kharkov declared Yiddish their mother tongue, in Odessa—32.2 percent and in Kiev—34 percent. In Minsk, by contrast, almost half of the city's Jewish population, or 49.8 percent, declared Yiddish their mother tongue. This was the largest percentage in any major city of the Soviet Union.[165]

* * *

In the summer of 1937, a complaint about the language used in the Minsk circus appeared in the local Yiddish press. The author criticized the total absence of

Belorussian in the performance and called for the creation of artistic cadres who could speak Belorussian. He also added that "from time to time it would be nice to hear some Polish and Yiddish as well" at the circus performances.[166] Within the context of the rising status of Russian, the low standing of Belorussian in the municipal circus accounts for the absence of the two national minority languages, Polish and Yiddish. In other words, the more Belorussian had to give up its spot to Russian, the less public space was assigned to Polish and Yiddish. If as early as 1935, most of the general and party meetings' protocols at Belorussian State University were drafted in Russian and no longer in Belorussian,[167] it does not seem surprising that Yiddish books appeared upside down in the city bookshop windows,[168] or that most Jewish children in the Minsk Soviet Jewish kindergartens used a mix of Yiddish and Russian, uttering, for example, phrases such as "*idiom v tsimer*" (let's go into the room; half in Russian and half in Yiddish).[169] To be sure, the majority of Minsk Jews were not passionately committed to the Soviet Yiddish experiment in the second half of the 1930s, were not directly engaged in its political and bureaucratic apparatus, nor did they contribute to its scholarly output. Some chose to listen to Russian- or even Belorussian-language radio broadcasts. Yet, a considerable segment of Minsk Jews continued to favor Yiddish over Russian and Belorussian. Those Jews who wished to join the higher party echelons adopted Russian; in search of urban employment, some Jews even switched over to Belorussian. But many Jews chose Yiddish both in public and, as a linguistic channel, in the private sphere of their homes. So long as Minsk remained the capital of Yiddish, this was not a difficult choice.

5 Behavior Unbecoming a Communist

Jewish Religious Practice in a Soviet Capital

The study of the everyday man leads naturally to the study of mentalities, understood as "what changes less" in the historical evolution.[1]

SITUATED BETWEEN THE Low Market and Cathedral Square, and home to numerous pre-revolutionary Jewish religious and communal institutions, the Jewish quarter of Minsk, also known as Nemiga, was the arena of a violent clash in the spring of 1922. The conflict broke out between two factions of the local Jewish population. On one side were the students and faculty of the Jewish Pedagogical Training College, or Evpedtekhnikum, the Soviet institution intended to create a cadre of Communist teachers for the Yiddish schools of Belorussia. The founders of the Evpedtekhnikum set up the new Soviet Jewish institution in a two-story brick building located at the intersection between Rakovskaia and Zamkovaia Streets, or, as the Jews used to call it in Yiddish, *Shlos gas*. This had been the building of the city's Talmud-Torah, the traditional Jewish school built by the local Jewish community for the education of the poorest children in Minsk.[2] Because of its location in a densely populated Jewish area, the former Talmud-Torah was the ideal venue for spreading Communism on the Jewish street.

The other participants in the strife were ordinary residents of the Jewish quarter: mainly workers, artisans, and small peddlers, most of whom were committed to some Jewish religious practices and probably angry at Communist officials for confiscating their synagogues and transforming them into clubs and warehouses. Whether they were strictly observant or lenient in their adherence to Judaism, these "petit-bourgeois" residents of Nemiga viewed the Talmud-Torah as their own collective property, which they and their ancestors had used since its establishment in the early nineteenth century. They expressed their resentment over the seizure of the Talmud-Torah by entering the building's courtyard and disrupting classes.[3]

On May 7, 1922, the students of the new Pedagogical Training College tried to chase out of the Communist institution a number of young Jews who had stepped into the building uninvited. When asked to leave, the young "criminals"—as they were referred to in the official report of the clash—began to throw stones at the students and the windows of the Talmud-Torah's building. As soon as the "red students" caught one of the "criminals" and came to blows with him, a large group of local residents gathered on the street in heated protest. According to one witness, a hundred people surrounded the building, and shouts of "Communists are thrashing children" echoed throughout the street. The uproar ceased only when the college's director instructed the students to end the fighting and return to the courtyard. The "red educator" shut the gate, and the restless crowd slowly dispersed.[4]

The Nemiga strife reflects in microcosm the conflict that erupted in the midst of the Jewish urban population, following the Bolshevik Revolution, between supporters and opponents of the new Soviet system. Similar clashes broke out not only in Minsk but in many Jewish cities and towns across the Soviet territory as well. As intense as the clashes were, however, it would be inaccurate to view their outcome as the sudden demise of religious Judaism and the irreversible rupture of Jewish society into two entirely separate camps: the new Communist Jewish elite, on the one hand, and the observant "ancien régime" Jew, on the other. Although the conflict between those Jews who supported Communism and those who resented the new system significantly influenced the sovietization process of the Jewish population, other factors (social, cultural, and family related) came into play and shaped the dynamics of Jewish everyday life in the 1920s and mid-1930s, especially in the areas of the former Pale of Settlement.

Focusing on the fate of Jewish religious buildings, on Jewish holiday adherence, kosher meat production, and circumcision observance, this chapter explores the changes that occurred in different areas of Jewish religious practice during the interwar period. As the study of the persistence of kosher butchering (*shehitah*) shows, a number of traditional Jewish institutions made the production of kosher meat possible and continued to function throughout the early 1930s, albeit in a "customized" Soviet fashion. By contrast, the practice of circumcision, mainly among Jewish Communist Party members, illustrates how the relationship between party allegiance and family loyalty was a complex dialectic of struggle and compromise. A glimpse into the practice of religious Judaism in a Soviet city reveals that Jewish life did not change radically overnight, in the immediate aftermath of the revolution; even some of the most devoted Communists maintained an allegiance to specific features of Jewish traditional culture. As American Hebrew writer and admirer of the Soviet Union Reuben Breinin stated in 1927, "The [Jewish] community of Minsk is more religious than that of Vilna."[5] While this assertion was probably made to rebut the claim that there was persecution of religion in the USSR, it also suggests the persistence of ancestral mores in a Jewish city undergoing sovietization.

The transformation of the core of Jewish life—of which dietary laws and circumcision were crucial aspects—occurred at a slower pace in Minsk than in Moscow also because of preexisting social networks and family ties that were not suddenly wiped out by the revolution. We may assume, in fact, that a number of actors in the Nemiga strife knew each other, were neighbors, or even relatives. Because staunch supporters of the new regime and those who abided by some religious practice happened to live together under the same roof or on the same street and had to deal with the conflicting pressures of these social settings, they inevitably affected each other's lives, prompting not only conformity with but also deviance from Soviet social norms.

Praying in Minsk

On April 16–17–18, 1922, a group of delegates from the Commission for the Requisition of Church Treasures of the Minsk Region, together with agents of the Belorussian GPU and members of the Evsektsiia, convened to discuss the future of the city synagogues.[6] Acting in accordance with Soviet law, which entitled them to confiscate private property for propaganda and cultural purposes, including schools, clubs, and religious institutions, they strode through the streets of Minsk taking possession of synagogue buildings and ceremonial objects.[7] In some instances, such as in the case of the small house of prayer on Gospitalnaia Street, the synagogue was so modest that they found nothing valuable to remove. In other instances, such as the case of the Great Minsk Choral Synagogue on Volodarskaia Street, they requisitioned precious silver lamps, goblets, and *yadayim* (pointers used for reading the Torah). They walked from Nemiga to the city's outskirts; from the Main Synagogue in the heart of the Minsk *shul-hoyf* (synagogue courtyard) to the Shivah Kruim Synagogue and its Jewish communal library. They requisitioned objects from the synagogue on Klasnaia Street, the ones on Politseiskaia, Mikhailovskaia, Alexandrovskaia, and Staro-Vilenskaia Streets. They paid a visit to the synagogue on Borisovskaia Street; to the Artisans' House of Prayer; to the Shoemakers' House of Prayer, and the Ginzburg House of Prayer; and to the synagogues on Nemetskaia, Rakovskaia, and Novokrasnaia Streets.[8]

Jews had made use of these spaces for religious and cultural purposes for decades, and sometimes for centuries. Each case of requisitioning underscored the "powerlessness" and marginal status in which the new system relegated those who were committed to forms of Jewish religious education and Judaism, which, like attending synagogue, defied Communist zealotry. The requisition and transformation into a Communist institution of one of the most visible Jewish institutions in the city, the Minsk Choral Synagogue, inaugurated on September 1, 1906,[9] and emblem of the city's wealthy Jewish middle-class, symbolized the victory of the Jewish proletariat over religious Judaism, and the defeat of the Jewish bourgeoisie. The conflict took on political and class shades as well, as nothing symbolized the pro-Zionist and well-off Jews in the city more than the Choral Synagogue did. On February 2, 1923, the Minsk Executive Committee ordered "to remove the locale of the Choral Synagogue from the authority of the religious community and to transfer it to the City Department of National Education (Gorodskoi Otdel Narodnogo Obrazovaniia, GORONO) to satisfy the cultural needs of the Jewish working masses of the city." As the Evsektsiia leaders stated with pride, "The greatest victory in the current struggle against clericalism is the occupation of the Choral Synagogue in Minsk. It provides a thrust in the campaign for the appropriation of synagogues in other locations."[10] With the exception of a few ritual objects, which the authorities left behind for the congregants' use in another synagogue, the Soviets requisitioned everything in the building.[11] The Choral Synagogue was initially transformed into the Jewish Workers House of Culture (Evreiskii Rabochii Dom Kultury). With its newly erected stage and film projector, the House of Culture hosted political and cultural events such as conferences on the emancipation of Jewish women and lectures unmasking the counterrevolutionary features of Passover.[12] In 1928, the former synagogue was converted into the Belorussian State Jewish Theater.

By 1924, Soviet authorities had confiscated from their pre-revolutionary owners approximately half of the synagogues and houses of prayer that existed in Minsk before the revolution.[13] It was not the first time in Jewish history that radical Jews seized synagogues and used them for political purposes. During the revolution of 1905, however, when Bundists seized synagogues, their action was temporary, lasting for the duration of a political rally. Moreover, it was not accompanied by acts of desecration, such as the removal or damaging of Torah scrolls, and the rallies were not intended to interfere with religious services. The Bundists convened such rallies in these spaces as opposed to wedding halls or theaters because they wanted to gather a large audience in an important Jewish space, not in a neutral "civil space," and because they tacitly acknowledged that the synagogue was the Jews' communal home, their natural place of gathering; rather than forcibly convert the synagogue into a secular space, they utilized it and then returned it to their owners.

While Communist agencies converted the majority of the city's religious buildings into clubs and Soviet schools, several synagogues remained operative throughout the 1920s and mid-1930s. As of May 1930, the number of religious associations and buildings in use in the city and district of Minsk totaled 249, 129 of which were Russian-Orthodox, 29 Catholic, 2 Evangelical-Baptist, and 89 Jewish.[14] In the city of Kiev, for example, the approximately 65 Jewish religious associations that existed in 1925 were reduced to 12 by December 1930.[15] In Vitebsk, 59 percent of all synagogues and houses of prayer were closed down by early 1931.[16]

Each functioning synagogue (and church) was granted the status of private religious society and officially registered in the Minsk District Executive Committee. According to the 1924 statute of one Jewish house of prayer, the goal of the religious society was "to perform all prayers prescribed by Judaism; to listen to the weekly Torah reading and the explanation of . . . sacred books; and to purchase or manufacture all ritual objects necessary to perform the Jewish prayer. . . . [T]he religious society of this house of prayer organizes religious meetings and administers the property received from the local authorities of the Soviet State."[17] The existence of these official bodies was not always a guarantee for the functioning of the synagogues they represented.

There were several factors that impinged upon their existence, one of them being their proximity to Soviet institutions and the Communists' conviction that a "sacred" Soviet space might become contaminated by a bourgeois institution and its ideologically abhorrent practices. In October 1922, after fifty Soviet citizens and congregants of the house of prayer on Petropavlovskaia Street signed a lease with the People's Commissar of Justice of Belorussia, the Commission for the Separation of Church and State broke the agreement. It argued that the geographic location of the synagogue was illegitimate: it was located in the same courtyard as the Central Bureau of the CPB. The synagogue was closed down, its building confiscated and transferred to the party institutions, and its congregants forced to sign an official agreement legalizing the confiscation. Endorsed by the members of the High Court of the Belorussian Republic, the decision to close down the synagogue read as follows: "It is intolerable for synagogues and houses of prayer of any religious group to be close to Soviet cultural institutions and organizations."[18]

Separating "tainted" religious spaces from "unadulterated" Soviet spaces became a priority in the early years of the Bolshevik experiment. In 1923, the Minsk Construction Workers' Union filed a complaint to the People's Commissar of Justice. The Zeldovich House of Prayer was located on the third floor of the building on Shkolnaia Street, the same building in which the construction workers lived and worked. The union's leadership demanded that Soviet authorities convert the house of prayer into a workshop for the union's members. Almost two years following the submission of the complaint, the People's Commissar of Justice endorsed the union's request: in June 1925, the house of prayer was liquidated and its locale reassigned to the construction workers. The District Commission for the Division of Church and State explained the liquidation of the Zeldovich House of Prayer sanctioning the "sacredness of Soviet space": a non-Soviet institution could not be in the proximity of a Soviet one because of the risk of "bourgeois contamination" posed to the workers.[19] Of course, the implication hidden behind this statement was that some construction workers were attending religious services in the house of prayer, possibly before beginning their workday.

Many buildings in the city, including synagogues, were confiscated and demolished to fulfil the urban master plan of the late 1920s aimed at wiping out Minsk's nineteenth-century provincial architecture and turning the city into a dynamic modern Soviet capital, with wide boulevards, open squares, and gigantic edifices. Located at the corner between Shkolnaia and Ekaterinskaia Streets, in the heart of Nemiga, the Shivah Kruim Synagogue, one of the central houses of prayer in Minsk, still attracted a fairly significant number of congregants after the revolution. While the synagogue building was erected at the beginning of the nineteenth century, the Shivah Kruim Society had existed since the eighteenth century. In the words of its congregants, the building represented for the city "a renowned historical treasure." In 1928, Shivah Kruim was supposed to undergo major renovations. Not only had the congregants received permission from the City Department of Municipal Economy to proceed with the restoration process, but also they had collected the necessary amount to cover the expenses. However, like a number of other private and public buildings in the city of remarkable historic value, the Shivah Kruim Synagogue was incorporated into the plan to expand the city, more specifically to widen the streets surrounding "old" Nemiga. With the endorsement of the Minsk District Executive Committee, the synagogue was demolished at the end of 1928. The committee disregarded the petition signed by the synagogue's congregants, and lest the demolition raise the suspicion of Soviet antireligious discrimination, the City Soviet conducted a campaign in the local press informing the Jewish population that Shivah Kruim had been torn down exclusively to fulfill the urban plan rationale.[20]

During Stalin's Cultural Revolution the battle against religion intensified. Local union leaders and Communist authorities frequently prompted Jewish workers to sign petitions requesting the confiscation of synagogue buildings for their own needs, thus fomenting a staged class-conflict. In November 1929, 503 Jewish workers and artisans from different cooperatives and factories in the city signed several petitions demanding that the house of prayer on Kropotkina Street be converted into a Yiddish reading room to satisfy their cultural needs. The Yiddish reading room met in two small rooms in the building of the Soviet school no. 28 where, as one of the petitions stated, it was impossible to carry out political work for lack of space. By contrast, there were eight houses of prayer in the neighborhood where "clericals harmfully influence the workers by conducting counter-revolutionary propaganda."[21] The Minsk District Commission for the Separation of Church and State endorsed the workers' proposal and converted the synagogue into a reading room. As the District Commission declared, "There are enough synagogues in Minsk [to satisfy] the religious needs of the believers."[22]

Perhaps a more genuine petition, not egged on by the political leadership, was addressed to the Minsk District Executive Committee in July 1929, when a number of Jewish workers protested against the confiscation of a synagogue in Nemiga. Precisely because the building housed one of the only public ritual baths, or *mikvaot*, still existing in Minsk (under the jurisdiction of the City Soviet), the confiscation of the synagogue elicited a wide, and authentic, protest among the Jewish population. In all likelihood a notable percentage of Jews, including members of the working class, was still committed to the religious observance of ritual bathing. The petitioners succeeded and Soviet authorities returned the synagogue to the members of its religious society. But the petition war resumed in 1930, when the Soviet house committee in Nemiga collected more than one thousand signatures by workers' families who appealed to the City Soviet to close down the house of prayer and *mikvah*, "which spread illnesses among neighborhood residents." As the author of a press report on the *mikvah* affair stated, "It is not clear why it is taking so long to close it down and transform it into a cultural institution."[23] The resistance of certain sectors of the Jewish population arguably affected the requisition process, protracting it even when it was instigated by Jewish workers.[24]

For many Soviet Jews, the synagogue not only qualified as a place for religious services but also retained its pre-revolutionary character of social center and neighborhood institution. In other words, it remained a space where Jews, who were not necessarily religious, could come together and spend some leisure time in the company of other Jews. Some chose the synagogue over the club as a meeting point to discuss current events because of the proximity of the building to their home; others as a result of their "nonproletarian" background, which prevented them from obtaining union membership and therefore attending cultural club activities;[25] and others in order to listen to a popular *magid*, or preacher, like the Starye Darogi *magid*, who regularly toured the cities and villages of Belorussia, and who came to Minsk in early 1928 to give sermons in the local houses of prayer.[26] One delegate at the 1929 conference of the Minsk District Executive Committee clarified why some Jews still favored the synagogue over the club as a social venue to meet with other comrades: "Our clubs have not yet reached the desired level [of quality]. They are often located in cold, formal buildings with no *heymishkayt* [cozyness]. This explains why the synagogue often takes the place of the club. The club's activities should be revived through shows and theater plays."[27]

The age of registered synagogue worshippers under the Soviets usually ranged from forty to sixty. Unlike their fathers and grandfathers, who were usually not overly concerned with attaining a prominent position in the new society, younger Jews were under a great deal of pressure to adhere to accepted social behavior and norms on their paths to a successful career. Rarely would they engage in non-Soviet activities such as going to synagogue to pray. Middle-aged and older Jews, by contrast, usually did not give up their religious practices and were likely to remain associated with the synagogue building, regardless of their level of religious devotion. They had little to lose. The Sharlat Synagogue had fifty-five congregants registered on its list of "believers" in March 1927. Almost all were in their fifties, the youngest member was thirty-seven years old.[28] While this list only included the "official" worshippers, and does therefore not provide the full range of Jews who used to hang out in the building or attend religious services on major Jewish holidays, it is still indicative of the age breakdown of Jews likely to attend synagogue.

There were, however, exceptions to this trend. In October 1924, the number of congregants registered in the Tanner's House of Prayer located on Lekert Street reached fifty-seven. The majority were young. Some were eighteen years old; others were in their twenties. Besides a few artisans, smiths, and workers, the congregants were all tanners and resided on Lekert Street. By 1925, the number of congregants grew to sixty-two. While some had been congregants in the Tanners' House of Prayer since 1900, others became members in 1925.[29] As of March 1929 the House of Prayer on Kropotkina Street had fifty registered congregants. Their ages ranged from nineteen to fifty, with an equal proportion of younger members in their twenties and older ones in their fifties.[30]

The fact that young Jews generally avoided becoming registered worshippers of the existing religious societies does not necessarily indicate that they shunned synagogues altogether. Far from being regular *shul*-goers, a considerable fraction of younger Jews attended services, if not on the Sabbath, at least on Jewish holidays. In the fall of 1927, the Minsk Komsomol complained about the number of young Jews who attended synagogue during Rosh Hashanah and Yom Kippur. Of course, what preoccupied the most was the presence of Komsomol members among the worshippers.[31]

In 1933 a new wave of requisitions kicked off in and around the city, with petitions signed by workers and school students demanding the Central Commission for Religious Affairs of Belorussia to turn religious buildings into Soviet institutions.[32] If before the October revolution, there were 657 synagogues in Belorussia, by January 1930 the number dropped to 547. In absolute terms this was a moderate cut.[33] Until 1930, the overall number of functioning religious institutions decreased only slightly since the confiscation process affected primarily larger buildings, while it spared many of the smaller synagogues. Synagogues that seated several hundred congregants on the Sabbath were closed, whereas houses of prayer used by a few dozen people remained open. But at the beginning of the Second Five-Year Plan things changed. The Central Committee of the Bezbozhniki of Belorussia, the League of Militant Atheists, informed the Central Committee of the CPB that by July 1933, 603 Russian-Orthodox churches, 32 Catholic churches, and 417 synagogues throughout the Belorussian SSR would be closed down "to satisfy the workers' requests."[34] Taking advantage of this renewed trend, in September 1933, the Evpedtekhnikum, which in 1922 had claimed the city's Talmud-Torah for its own cultural needs, petitioned the Minsk City Soviet demanding to take over the building of a nearby synagogue. In need of additional space to set up a new dormitory for its growing student population, the Evpedtekhnikum took over the Bricklayer House of Prayer on Zamkovaia Street, located just one block away from the historical building of the former Talmud-Torah.[35] Situated at the center of the synagogue courtyard, the Main Synagogue, or Kalte shul, which together with its imposing dome had appeared in more than one pre-revolutionary postcard depicting late nineteenth-century Minsk also fell victim of one of the confiscation rounds of the 1930s.[36]

The Soviet Korobka and the Underground Educational System

The process that led to the banning of the heder and the yeshivas, and therefore the altering of Jewish traditional education as Minsk had known it for centuries, was set off in June 1922, when the Council of People's Commissars of Belorussia called for "the closing down of all . . . heders, yeshivas, and Talmud-Torahs . . . , and the prosecution in court of those who do not abide by the order."[37] In the months following the decree, a number of *melamdim* and groups of Minsk Jewish residents repeatedly petitioned the Evsektsiia demanding to rectify the heder decree.[38] Passing on to the GPU the names of the petitioners for further investigation, the spokesman for Jewish affairs at the Central Executive Committee of CPB responded that,

> In accordance with the Soviet Constitution and the Criminal Code . . . the instruction of religion to children is forbidden, both in Soviet schools and in private schools and institutions. . . . [T]eaching religion to children is allowed outside school-type institutions. . . . The closing of the heder has nothing to do with religious freedom and in no way should be interpreted as a restriction of religious needs: the education of children is not a matter of religion.[39]

While most *melamdim* closed down their heders, some organized small groups of three to five children, which convened at the home of one of the pupils. After all, teaching religious subjects outside educational institutions remained legal, at least on paper. However, by going from house to house and working seven to eight hours per day the *melamdim* could hardly put together half of the wages they made when teaching a class of thirty to forty children, before the decree.[40] Those who refused to close their heder were arrested, and even those who taught small groups of students were occasionally accused of disregarding the June decree and detained. Troubled by the situation, another Minsk *melamed* petitioned the Evsektsiia describing his position on the heder question. As he explained, the struggle against the heder led to the flourishing of ignorance on the Jewish street: forced to retire, *melamdim* were usually replaced by less qualified teachers, such as former synagogue sextons, matchmakers, and even *balegoles* (coachmen), who had no knowledge of Jewish texts and no pedagogical experience.[41] The Evsektsiia did not take note of the appeal.

While we know a great deal about the ways in which the Soviet system discriminated against religion, making it difficult for Jews to comply with the rituals of Judaism, less is known about the ways in which Jews observed specific religious practices while living and participating in the new society. In spite of the harsh circumstances triggered by the decrees against Judaism and the social pressure to behave as model Soviet citizens, a deliberate rejection of all religious practices was not always the case. Although the June decree represented a blow to Jewish religious education, it did not put an end to it. Jewish religious education did not disappear from the streets of Minsk, but rather was illicitly retained with funds obtained from the production and sale of kosher meat.

Founded in February 1921, the Union of Congregants of Synagogues and Houses of Prayer in Minsk (Soiuz prikhozhan evreiskikh sinagog i molitvennikh domov v Minske) became the official body responsible for supporting Jewish religious practice in the Belorussian capital. Under the direct authority of the Minsk Executive Committee at the time of its establishment the union counted 155 members (most of them Jewish religious leaders).[42] Besides safeguarding the city's synagogues and *mikvaot*, and obtaining *matsah* flour for the Passover holiday, the union served another key function. Point two of its statute asserted the importance of fulfilling "the needs of those who observe the laws of kashrut."[43]

Consuming kosher meat and fowl during the 1920s was relatively uncomplicated in Minsk. The Union of Congregants relied on the same traditional tax system, which, for decades, Jewish communities throughout Russia had imposed upon their members as an indirect levy on kosher meat. Known as *korobka* (or "little basket"), this tax had been the source of constant friction between the Jewish community's leadership, which administered the levy, and the less well-to-do Jews who had to deal with the financial burden. At the same time, the tax enabled the community to meet its debts to the state and to private creditors, and to set aside enough funds to renovate synagogue buildings, look after cemeteries, and finance communal institutions and welfare associations.⁴⁴ The *korobka* system was fundamentally unaffected by the revolution and retained the same modus operandi of its pre-1917 equivalent. The *shohtim* worked under the supervision of the city's rabbi; a *mashgiach*, or ritual supervisor, made sure that the slaughtering process strictly abided by Jewish dietary laws, and collected a tax on each animal slaughtered according to the ritual. The tax was passed on to consumers in the price of each individual chicken or cut of beef. The proceeds of ritual slaughtering were then divided between the ritual slaughterers and the rabbi, while the meat was sold to the local Soviet food cooperatives, at a higher cost than nonkosher meat.⁴⁵

No longer designed to pay for state tax arrears as it was in the nineteenth century, the new Soviet *korobka* was intended for internal Jewish activities only.⁴⁶ It served two main functions. First, it represented the main (and typically only) source of income for rabbis. Together with members of the pre-revolutionary political elite, religious functionaries were included in the *lishchentsy* lists and officially disenfranchised from Soviet electoral rights. They became social outcasts and had restricted access to employment, housing, education, and medicine.⁴⁷ Such limitations affected entire families, even if only one member had been disenfranchised. Gita Gluskina, daughter of the Minsk Rabbi Menachem Mendel Gluskin, recalls that her family was not entitled to live in an apartment because of her father's *lishchenets* status. Kicked out of their residence on Rakovskaia Street, the three daughters, the rabbi, and his wife settled in the main synagogue of the Minsk shul-hoyf, the Kalte Shul, in Nemiga. With no direct access to heating or water, they slept in the women's section of the synagogue. Rabbi Gluskin eventually moved to Leningrad with his family in 1934, where he served as chief rabbi until his death in 1936.⁴⁸

In addition to support the rabbis, the second function of the "red *korobka*" was to subsidize the network of underground religious educational institutions. These sprung up in Minsk shortly after the 1922 Soviet ban on all existing heders, yeshivas, and Talmud-Torahs. The first secret Talmudic institution began operating in Minsk immediately following the decree and was located in the Butchers' House of Prayer. It was not, however, perceived as a permanent institution in the city, but rather as a provisional one that would mostly facilitate the transition to Poland of yeshiva students from different areas of the Soviet Union. It became the residence of about ten students who convened there from Mozyr, Zhitomir, and Kiev, on their way to Poland, where they intended to join the former director of the Miasnikov yeshiva, Rabbi Yoffe, who had moved there after the June decree. Some studied there for a short period of time.

Others just spent the night in the synagogue, where they could count on a hot meal. Once the yeshiva was uncovered, GPU officials arrested the students and their supporters, and they closed down the synagogue.[49]

Under the leadership of Rabbi Yehoshua Tsimbalist, also known as Rabbi Horodner (a native of Grodno who moved to Minsk during World War I), Jewish religious education in the Belorussian capital underwent a substantial resurgence, albeit underground. A highly respected and well-known religious and educational leader, Tsimbalist is described hurrying through the streets of Minsk on Friday afternoon before dusk, informing local Jews about the onset of the Sabbath, and encouraging them not to work but go to synagogue. Because of his popularity in the city, Evsektsiia leaders often tolerated or at least refrained from interfering with his activities on the Jewish street.[50]

In 1924, Rabbi Tsimbalist established an underground yeshiva in the women's section of the Shoavei Mayim synagogue, also located on Zamkovaia Street, near the former Talmud-Torah building.[51] With seventy students, the Minsk yeshiva was the largest one of its kind in the Soviet Union.[52] It attracted students from the Soviet territory as well as from neighboring Poland. Born in Lodz in 1913, Moshe-Zvi Neriyah, who would later become a prominent rabbinic figure in the Yishuv and State of Israel, left his native Poland in 1926 to study Torah in the Minsk yeshiva, at a time when Jewish religious education was officially considered obsolete in Soviet cities.[53]

The Shoavei Mayim yeshiva was only one aspect of the larger underground educational system set up and coordinated by Tsimbalist. Minsk soon became the city with the largest number of yeshivas in the Soviet Union. Besides the advanced Talmudic academy directed by Tsimbalist there were at least three middle-level yeshivas and two lower-level yeshivas. A *yeshiva ketanah* (lower-level yeshiva) was set up on Staro-Vilenskaia Street, with twenty pupils whose ages ranged between twelve and fifteen. Ten students came from outside Minsk. Not only was tuition free, but also the students were provided meals. Minsk families would invite them over for the Sabbath and serve herring and challah.[54] There were four hundred pupils studying in the Minsk underground heders in 1926, most of them officially enrolled in a Soviet school as well.[55] By 1929 the number was still significant and amounted to 324.[56] During the 1920s, a well-organized Tifereth Bachurim organization, or religious youth league, existed in Minsk. It attracted mainly young workers, clerks, and a few university students, who would convene at night, after work, to listen to lectures or engage in conversations on religious topics, get together for prayer and Torah study, and carry out religious propaganda to increase the organization's constituency. If in Leningrad there were thirty members in the local Tifereth Bachurim, forty-six in Moscow, thirty-five in Gomel, and twenty in Kiev, the religious youth league in Minsk counted two hundred members.[57] As Moshe-Zvi Neryah observed, "Rabbis from other cities in Russia would come to Minsk and be surprised by what they saw. Something of this nature in a time like this? How is that possible? They never imagined that there was still such a place. After all, such activity is connected to the dangers of arrest and deportation. From where does one find the courage and strength to do such things?"[58]

While both yeshivas and heders enjoyed clandestine financial support from the JDC, the amount provided from the outside was not adequate to sustain the enterprise. As the records of the 1926–27 reports of the Vaad Rabane SSR, or Council of Rabbis of the USSR, show, the financial need to support the educational institutions amounted to more than 2,200 roubles a month. Minsk received from the JDC only 826 roubles a month. As for the heders, the 1929 report of the Vaad Rabane SSR, confirms that the JDC relief amounted only to 30 percent of the budget for religious education, the rest was being raised within the city.[59] Expenses not only included the *melamed*'s salary, but also covered a monthly wage for a "guardian" to watch over the illegal institution while in use and, in case a teacher was arrested, the financial assistance for the family while he was in prison.[60]

In addition to the support from the JDC and the cooperation of local Jews (who perpetuated under the Soviets the Eastern European Jewish custom of providing meals, clothing, and shelter to yeshiva students, especially those who came from other cities), the continued existence of these institutions depended largely on the *korobka* system.[61] During the 1920s and early 1930s, profits from kosher butchering covered tuition expenses and teachers' compensations, which few parents could pay given the duress of the economic situation and the outlawing of a large chunk of private trade and business. The *korobka* system and the underground educational network were so well entrenched in the everyday life of the city that the divide between permissible and unacceptable was sometimes puzzling and blurry for city residents themselves. At a Minsk Conference of nonparty Jewish workers, during which the practice was to submit queries anonymously in writing to the presidium, the following two questions were asked: "Do the Minsk heders operate legally or illegally?" and "Are the authorities aware of the existence of yeshivas with large numbers of students . . . who are being supported with room and board?"[62] Both questions were asked in all seriousness by perplexed citizens, probably confused by the incongruity between the official persecution of Judaism and the relatively thriving existence of religious education at the time. The questions were posed in 1927, five years after the official closing down of all Jewish religious educational institutions in the city.[63]

The *Shohtim* Trial

While the Soviet system seemed to tolerate, or at least show little interest in the kosher butchering business, the local Evsektsiia leaders attempted to bring the *shohtim*'s activities to an end through intimidation. In their struggle against clericalism, they viewed the performance of this ritual as ideologically repulsive, primarily because it created a source of income for the rabbis.[64] Taking advantage of what seems to have been nothing but a skirmish between *shohtim*, the Evsektsiia organized a show trial against the so-called Gluskin trust, a grouping of twenty-five Minsk ritual slaughterers who worked under the supervision of the city's chief rabbi, Rabbi Menachem Mendl Gluskin.

In early March 1925, in the locale of the former Chorale Synagogue, now the Jewish Workers' House of Culture, in front of three thousand people, the head of the *shohtim*-trust Yankev-Tevye Rapoport was accused of the attempted murder of another *shohet*, one Droykin, who had moved to the Belorussian capital from Lepel, in the Vitebsk Province.[65] Apparently, the newcomer's slaughtering method did not meet the religious standards set by Rabbi Gluskin. Not allowed to be part of the official butchers' trust, Droykin joined another group of *shohtim* who operated independently from the rabbi's supervision and sold their product to the same cooperatives that purchased kosher meat from the *shohtim* working for Gluskin.[66] In addition, by charging less (only five to ten kopeks for one chicken instead of the fifteen to twenty charged by Rapoport), the Droykin group became a threatening competitor for the "Gluskin trust." While Rabbi Gluskin and strictly Orthodox Jews could not accept as kosher the cattle and fowl slaughtered by Droykin (who almost certainly did not make use of the rabbi's ritual supervisor, and who possibly did not comply with the strict rules pertaining to the knife used and the postmortem examination of the animal), many consumers did.[67] Whether they purchased the meat because of its lower price or because of their poor knowledge of the laws and customs of kosher butchering, their action represented the first stage in the breakdown of the historic monopoly of rabbis over the consumption of meat among Jews. In a memorandum addressed to Cyrus Adler at the end of 1928, Samarius Gourary, son-in-law of Rabbi Schneersohn, complained about the chaotic state of *shehitah* in Russia, exemplified by the presence of wandering *shohtim* who traveled from city to city and slaughtered animals without the rabbi's permission.[68] Together with the initial collapse of kosher meat production, the Minsk *shohtim* trial also reveals, perhaps more interestingly, its persistence. As a journalist from Warsaw remarked, "The *shohtim* trial disclosed aspects of Jewish life which we thought had disappeared."[69]

The trial, which began at six o'clock in the evening on Saturday—after the end of the Sabbath—received extensive coverage in the local and foreign press. Possibly the first show trial in the Soviet Union against Jewish ritual slaughter, it also became the subject of a musical satire in Yiddish. Performed on the stage of workers' clubs in and around Minsk, with Yiddish folk songs and traditional religious melodies (including Neilah, typically chanted during Yom Kippur), the play depicted Rabbi Gluskin as the wealthy city villain who monopolized the production of kosher meat in the Belorussian capital.[70] The language of the trial was Yiddish. Rabbis, *dayanim* (scholars of Talmud law), *shohtim*, shopkeepers, underworld Jews, artisans, and workers were cross-examined as witnesses. Recounting the trial for the Warsaw newspaper *Moment*, one reporter pointed out that the rabbinic terminology used to describe the ritual slaughtering process and the Talmudic intonation of both the prosecutors and the defendants could have easily deceived the audience: "If you close your eyes you might feel like you are somewhere in a *shtetl*, in the *bes-medresh*, twenty years before the revolution."[71]

The Jews of Nemiga, or as the Moscow Yiddish daily *Der Emes* defined them, "the foundation of the black market . . . , bourgeois society . . . , contraband, . . . Zionism, . . . [and] the Jewish counterrevolution,"[72] talked about a new "Beilis trial." Numerous protest letters against the "blood-libel" were addressed to the editors of the Russian-language *Zvezda* and the Yiddish-language *Veker*, from throughout the city, the Minsk District, and even Vilna.[73] The public prosecutors Shmuel Agursky, Arn Volobrinskii, and Leyme Roznhoyz (also Evsektsiia members) repeatedly disclaimed that the trial was an attack on the Jewish religion, as the foreign press declared. Rather, they emphasized the criminal nature of the accusations. Drawing parallels with Mendele Mocher Seforim's *Di takse* (The tax), in which the Yiddish writer criticized the *korobka* institution, Agursky stated that all the blame should fall on Rabbi Gluskin, who oppressed poor Jews by forcing them to pay extra for kosher meat, and not on the *shohtim*, who were "just workers in the slaughterhouse." "The fact that religious Jews wish to eat kosher meat does not trouble us," continued Roznhoyz, and he asserted, "We are not *maskilim* who believe the main goal is to struggle against religion. . . . In our system, religion will die out, without violent measures."[74] In the final verdict the prosecutor emphasized the criminal nature of the case, ridiculed the insinuations of religious persecution in the USSR conjured up abroad, and sentenced Rapoport and his accomplices to three years in prison on charges of assault.[75]

The Red Army Eats Kosher Meat

In spite of the 1925 show trial, which the Evsektsiia had intended as a way to attack ritual slaughtering in the city, the production of kosher meat in Minsk continued to thrive. In November 1927, through the support of the JDC, the Minsk Jewish religious leaders were trying to set up a kosher kitchen that would provide a meal to approximately fifty university students, at the cost of twelve rubles a month per student.[76] By early 1928, most beef cattle in the city was slaughtered according to the laws of *kashrut*. The meat distributed in the main food cooperatives of the city—the Central Workers' Cooperative, the Belorussian Meat Trade, and the Belorussian Agricultural Union—had been slaughtered according to the Jewish method. Indeed, when a housewife planned to purchase nonkosher meat, she had to go to one of the city's food cooperatives, approach the shop's counter, and specifically ask the store clerk for *treyf* ("forbidden") meat.[77] The number of cattle killed through *shehitah* traditionally exceeded the demand for kosher meat because of the specific dietary restrictions connected to kosher butchering. More precisely, a portion of animals slaughtered through *shehitah* usually wound up on the general market because of the prohibition to consume animals that, upon further inspection, were found to have blemishes or lesions. However, it was the historic Jewishness of the city, the number of *shohtim* operating therein, and the viability of kosher butchering under the Soviets in the 1920s, that remained accountable for the large amount of cattle slaughtered according to the Jewish ritual.

Figure 8. At a kosher market stand, Minsk, 1924. Courtesy of YIVO Institute for Jewish Research (Collection PO Forward 27177).

A correspondent for the daily *Oktyabr* expressed his outrage after discovering that "the whole population of Minsk is forced to eat kosher meat. Even the Red Army."[78] The Belorussian Agricultural Union, the cooperative that supplied foodstuffs to the Red Army, exclusively sold meat that had been slaughtered ritually.[79] The author of the same article also complained about the absence of high-quality nonkosher meat in the Central Workers' Cooperative: here, he argued, "almost all employees in the meat sector are former *shohtim*." Most kosher meat in the city was sold with a stamp certifying its authenticity. There were *mashgihim* (supervisors of Jewish dietary laws) working in the City Slaughterhouse, sometimes acting as the only veterinary inspectors of the animals, determining whether they were medically fit for slaughter or not.[80] And the *korobka*, the existence of which had very much surprised the correspondent of the Moscow *Der Emes* in 1925,[81] was in 1928 still in effect. For each cattle slaughtered, the *shohet* received one ruble, which corresponded to eighteen hundred to two thousand rubles a month. Forty percent of the ritual slaughterer's revenue went to the rabbi.[82]

With few exceptions, there was little opposition to the production of kosher meat on the part of local Jews. In an open letter published in *Oktyabr*, on February 5, 1928,

Chayim Vilentshik invited Rabbi Gluskin to reimburse him the extra money he paid in the course of several years for unknowingly purchasing kosher meat.[83] In another instance, that same month, a delegation of forty Jewish working women signed a petition to the Minsk City Soviet in which they condemned the extensive production of kosher meat, "eleven years after the October revolution."[84] Although women were more likely to engage in protests when the price of foodstuff was at issue, besides the above-mentioned petition (probably staged by the trade union's leadership or the Evsektsiia), Jewish housewives did not organize a grassroots campaign against the rabbis demanding a just price for meat. In fact, the absence of a popular protest indicates that a large proportion of Jewish women was willing to purchase kosher meat, or at least accustomed to paying a higher price to bring it to their tables.[85]

In the effort to discontinue or, at least, cut the production of kosher meat in the city, the Minsk Evsektsiia turned to Moscow. The Moscow Evsektsiia called for the creation of a Special Commission under the leadership of Bruskin, the deputy people's commissar for trade. In its resolution on slaughtering and meat production in Minsk the commission demanded that "cattle not intended for kosher consumption should not be killed in accordance with [Jewish] ritual laws."[86] There is no evidence that the city agencies actually carried out this resolution. In a place like Minsk, where almost half of the population was Jewish, at least half of the butchers were *shohtim* or former *shohtim*. As a result, slaughtering according to Jewish ritual was deeply embedded in the local meat sector. But the meat industry supervisors had no time to replace a large fraction of workers because of their slaughtering method: their primary concern was meeting the production quota. The Minsk Evsektsiia did however achieve a small victory: the Central Workers' Cooperative agreed to open two shops in which meat would be sold without distinction between kosher and nonkosher quality.[87]

The Evsektsiia was still far from securing its control over the production of kosher meat. In mid-April 1928, for example, a cooperative in Nemiga began selling a new kosher meat product. The official in charge of the manufacture of intestine products at the City Slaughterhouse supported the proposal of the cooperative's chairman to process kosher sausages. The *mashgiah* in charge of verifying that sausage production met the standards of *kashrut* was none other than a relative of the great scholar of Minsk, the famous nineteenth-century Rabbi Jeroham J. L. Perelman.[88]

Soviet authorities did not resist religious slaughtering within governmental structures so long as it did not interfere with the "rationality" of production. On Friday, April 7, 1928, a group of *shohtim* refrained from slaughtering the entire amount of cattle beef ordered by the three main food cooperatives in Minsk because of the imminent advent of the Sabbath. The financial loss inflicted on the City Slaughterhouse by the *shohtim*'s decision prompted the party cell to subsequently employ former *shohtim*, who were now members of the Butchers' Trade Union and probably no longer religious, as slaughterers. The latter slaughtered the cattle in the manner to which they were accustomed, in accordance with the basic precepts of *shehitah*.[89] The shift of *shehitah* from religious supervision to state control symbolized another stage in the progressive loss of authority of the rabbi. Employed as workers, most *shohtim* continued to perform ritual slaughtering following the principles of Jewish dietary laws, generally without the inspection of the rabbi's appointed *mashgiach*.[90] In defiance of rabbinical authority, some *shohtim* claimed they wished to become full-fledged members of the proletariat.[91] From the vantage point of Orthodox Judaism, meat from cattle or fowl slaughtered without the supervision of the rabbi was not kosher. Yet for a significant proportion of consumers such meat was sufficiently kosher, even without rabbinic certification. Many Jews strove to achieve more control over their religious lives and perhaps experienced state interference as a form of emancipation or even empowerment. This combination of the decline of the traditional role of the rabbi and the retention of conventional kosher slaughtering methods generated a new kind of folk-*kashrut*, based on dietary customs and eating habits rather than on traditional religious authority.

By 1930, the "red *korobka*" institution, which had ensured financial support for the rabbis and the illegal educational network throughout the 1920s, began to collapse and slowly gave way.[92] The decline of grassroots religious life was not due only to antireligious persecution but to the general political and economic pressure of the 1930s as well. The regime's turn to rapid industrialization, forced collectivization, and a centralized economy (which caused, among other things, massive food shortages in urban areas) made kosher butchering increasingly difficult. Religious leaders involved in the production of kosher meat were arrested;[93] kosher meat was no longer available in the city's cooperatives; the Minsk yeshiva was closed down in the early 1930s;[94] and Rabbi Tsimbalist, the driving force behind the underground educational network, managed to leave for Palestine in 1933.[95] Whereas cattle slaughtering according to the Jewish method became almost impractical in the 1930s—primarily because the government took control of food production and restricted cattle supply for religious purposes—kosher fowl was easily accessible.[96] Upon the request of individual citizens, state-employed former *shohtim* or unemployed religious *shohtim* slaughtered chicken throughout the mid-1930s, generally undisturbed. As late as 1934, for example, a slaughterhouse for kosher fowl operated on Karl Libknekht Street; Soviet citizens brought their own chicken and the *shohet* performed the ritual slaughter.[97]

In April 1934, kosher butchering in Minsk was dealt a mortal blow and driven to the margins of even smaller underground circles. Yankev-Tevye Rapoport, the same *shohet* indicted in the 1925 *shohtim* trial, was accused of, over the course of three years, raping twelve girls, who were sent by their mothers to the *shohet* with a chicken to slaughter.[98] While Rapoport's absolute innocence is hard to ascertain based on the available sources, the official accounts that portray him as a "monstrous pedophile" who took advantage of the girls are at odds with his reputation among the Jews of Minsk. (Aron Rozin, a young Poale-Zionist not connected with religious circles, spoke very admiringly of Rapoport in his memoirs.)[99] The chief rabbi of Palestine at the time, Rabbi Abraham Isaac Kook, interceded on behalf of the *shohet*, petitioning the Central

Committee of the CPB.[100] It is likely that by publicly exploiting Jewish sexual anxieties associated with the figure of the *shohet*—the only man who in Jewish traditional society had regular contacts with women, often in semiprivate settings—the architects of the Rapoport case were hoping to discredit kosher slaughter in Minsk, for good.[101] Following two closed-door criminal trials (during which Rapoport eventually admitted all the accusations, most likely under pressure), the show trial took place April 2–4. It was held in the locale of the Belgoset—the former Chorale Synagogue and the same venue as the 1925 *shohtim*-trial—in front of a large audience drawn by the lurid details of the rapes.[102] The public prosecutors—Leyme Roznhoyz, delegate of the Central Committee of the League of the Militant Godless, and Chatskl Dunets, deputy people's commissar for education and member of the editorial board of *Oktyabr*—emphasized the relationship between the *shohet*'s religious beliefs (he was linked to the Slonimer Hasidim), his social background (he was a relative of the manager of the Wissotzky tea business in Minsk), and his sexual deviance. The relationship between religion and pedophilia was analyzed in great detail in a booklet on the Rapoport case, entitled *For the Proletarian Court*, published immediately after the trial. The booklet also dwelled on reported cases of rape of minors carried out in the early 1930s by religious Jews in Poland, France, and America. The fact that the trial was organized with such great fanfare, convened in front of thousands of people in the Jewish theater, and followed by a meticulous report of the events, indicates that the trial constituted a major campaign directed against what was still considered by Jewish Communist officials a major problem.[103] Rapoport was eventually sentenced to eight years in prison by the Supreme Court of the BSSR.[104]

The combination between the 1934 show trial and the relentless assault on religious practice under Stalinism led to the decline in kosher fowl consumption during the 1930s. However, the demand for kosher fowl most likely did not subside entirely. After all, Minsk remained the destination of a large and steady migration movement of thousands of Jews from the surrounding cities and *shtetlekh*, where traditional lifestyles were relatively more pervasive, who relocated to the capital in search of employment and a better livelihood. Although it is hard to ascertain how many of these new migrants were religiously observant, it is likely that many of them came from traditional homes and abided by certain religious practices. It took longer for Soviet rule to establish itself in small remote towns, to set up the administrative infrastructure, and to impose Soviet norms. Furthermore, for decades before the revolution Jewish secularization had been slower in small towns than in cities. These were tight-knit communities with social cohesion and social pressures without the anonymity of urban life, so that it took time for Soviet authorities to break these patterns and traditions. *Shtetl* Jews who settled in Minsk were the Jewish counterpart of the Russian peasants who settled in Moscow.[105] Finally, unlike Jews who moved to faraway Moscow, those who settled in Minsk usually migrated as a family and continued to live together as a multigenerational family, chiefly because of the geographic proximity between their *shtetl* and the Belorussian capital. The constant influx of this population into the city probably resulted in the persistence of kosher butchering in Minsk in the second part of the 1930s.[106]

Religion in the Public Sphere: The School

Observing Jewish religious holidays was an ominous threat to the primacy of Soviet principles, especially in the context of Soviet schools. Here conformity to scientific atheism and a nonreligious lifestyle was viewed as crucial in the upbringing of the next generation and therefore placed at the center of the school's curriculum. As the supervisor for Jewish culture of the People's Commissariat of Education in Minsk emphasized in 1928,

> [We must] eradicate the passive attitude toward religion that has dominated the school until now . . . and provide the child with an antireligious education. We cannot talk about . . . [secular] education at a time when the enemy sways children's minds. . . . The whole pedagogical process strives to make the children not only into atheists, but also into active adversaries of clericalism and religion.[107]

But while conforming to most rules set by the new Communist school, both students and teachers frequently deviated from conventional Soviet social norms. Expressions of religious identity in the school's public sphere were more dynamic and widespread than has typically been assumed.

The family embodied the main source of deviance for school children. "Parents are to blame if the heder and shabbos still play a prominent role in the lives of children," stated in 1927 the pedagogical committee of a local Soviet Jewish school.[108] A student in Soviet Jewish school no. 26 recounted in class how her grandmother scolded her after she repeated the antireligious explanations for Jewish holidays she had heard from her teacher. "The teacher lies because he gets paid for it!" commented the grandmother.[109] Soviet schools coped with the "dangerous" influence of the home by organizing parents' meetings to discuss the importance of class attendance on the Sabbath and arranged festive events for the whole family to counter the religious holidays.[110] Seminars for parents explaining the danger that religious holidays posed to their children's upbringing were organized until the late 1930s.[111] The goal was to replace the authority of the home with the authority of the school. In the months preceding Passover, for example, schools geared up for the May 1 festivity—the most important holiday on the Communist calendar—in the hope that the more the students would feel involved in the preparation of the proletarian celebration, the less they would experience the imminent Jewish religious holiday. Instead of the seder, the traditional meal of the first two nights of Passover, school teachers engaged the children in cultural activities in the school club or arranged an outing to the movies or the theater.[112]

In 1928, the Jewish section of the People's Commissariat of Education in Minsk gathered information about school attendance during the Jewish High Holidays.[113] As the collected data shows, the attempt to rescue children from the home's influence, with movie tickets or lectures for parents, was successful only in part. During Yom Kippur school attendance dropped radically.[114] In 1928, the proportion of students not attending classes on that day was remarkably high: in Soviet Jewish School no. 28 more than one-third of the student body did not attend classes;[115] in Soviet Jewish School no. 8, 50 percent of the students did not attend classes;[116] and in Soviet Jewish School no. 10, 53 percent did not attend classes.[117]

Some students, like Leah Gluskina, a second daughter of Rabbi Gluskin, did not attend school on the Sabbath. Enrolled in a Soviet Jewish school, where antireligious propaganda permeated most subjects in the curriculum, by not attending on the Sabbath she publicly stated her observance of religious practice. When in April 1929 the Minsk District Jewish schools' inspector, in accordance with the new antireligious campaign spurred by Stalin's Great Turn, threatened to expel her, Leah wrote a statement explaining that her family's religiosity did not affect her school performance in any way. Her teachers could attest to that. She resolutely argued against the expulsion and wrote, "After two years of being in this school, in the life of which I actively participated . . . I consider this exclusion, two months before the end of the school year, unfair and illegal. In the name of justice I ask you to give me the possibility to complete the seven-year school."[118] While preserving an allegiance to the practices and beliefs of Judaism, the rabbi's daughter was, at the same time, acting as a "good Soviet citizen," actively taking part in school activities and performing well in an institution that did not tolerate religion. With the support of her parents, Leah publicly participated in the Soviet system as a religious Jew as much as it was feasible.[119]

In response to the antireligious campaign of 1929 several students in Minsk were expelled from school because of the observance of the Sabbath. In a letter addressed to a school teacher, a father protested against his daughter's expulsion on the basis of the "Sabbath motive." The tone of the letter is firm and reveals the author's awareness of his rights as a Soviet citizen and the way in which they might be respected. Using the language of an emancipated person, the father wrote, "I protest. . . . As a free toiling citizen of the Soviet Socialist Republic, . . . I cannot allow this to happen. . . . I ask you to give me an official written statement, in which you explain why you do not allow my daughter to attend the school, so that I shall have a juridical possibility to accuse you in front of the higher authorities."[120] While other students attended school on the Sabbath, they refrained from writing on that day. In April 1929, in Soviet Jewish school no. 28, ten students did not attend or write on the Sabbath.[121] That same year, eight students from Soviet Jewish school no. 8 did not attend on the Sabbath.[122] Cases of Minsk students not attending school on the Sabbath and other Jewish holidays were reported in Soviet Jewish school no. 8 as late as March 1937.[123]

The social pressure to conform to conventional behavior in the school—which was not unique to the USSR but certainly more extreme than elsewhere in the modern world—was all the more compelling with regard to publicly performed acts, such as the ritual of *ha-motsi* (blessing over the bread),[124] or the consumption of *matsah* during

Passover. In May 1929, in the aftermath of the Passover holiday, Soviet Jewish school no. 30 adopted a new anti-Passover measure, to be implemented the following year, which would ensure that the food consumed by the students would not be kosher for Passover. Throughout the duration of the holiday the school prohibited children from bringing *matsah* to school and in lieu of this served *beigls*.[125] This indicates that as late as Passover of 1929, many children had been bringing *matsah* to school.

As the case of Leah Gluskina clearly shows, after 1929 it was difficult, if not impossible, to be enrolled in a Soviet school and not attend classes on the Sabbath.[126] There is no indication, however, that children were expelled from school because they did not attend classes on Yom Kippur or Rosh Hashanah. That said, we still have to assume that the political atmosphere of the 1930s, together with the widespread loss of interest in religion among the younger generation, reduced the number of students who did not attend school during those religious holidays.

The way in which students behaved and expressed their religious identity behind the classroom walls also depended on their teachers. Well aware that most instructors did not belong to the party and had been educated in pre-revolutionary institutions, Jewish schools in the city were debating whether nonparty members could adequately fulfill their pedagogical tasks in class. In Soviet Jewish school no. 27 almost all teachers were natives of Minsk. Their years of birth ranged from 1885–87 to 1898–1900. With the exception of the younger ones, most of whom were also enrolled at Belorussian State University, nearly all teachers had worked in pre-revolutionary educational settings. Not one of them was a party member.[127] If we consider the more general picture, it is remarkable that during the school year of 1928–29, out of a total of 178 Jewish teachers employed in the Jewish schools of Minsk only three were members of the Communist Party of Belorussia, one was a party candidate, and thirteen were members of the Komsomol.[128]

Teachers came under constant surveillance by school inspectors. The regional conference on Jewish culture and education held in Minsk in early 1928 reported that a significant percentage of teachers employed in the city schools were politically passive and still abided by "old traditions": some refrained from writing on the Sabbath, others celebrated the seder, others had their baby sons circumcised. In a few instances the deviance from Soviet behavior was more subtle, insofar as it involved going to work on Jewish holidays wearing special clothes, and being dressed up for the occasion.[129] In other instances, such as in the case of a teacher who celebrated the seder at his father's home, nonconformity with Soviet practices was more obvious, although it was carried out in the private sphere of the home.[130] On October 7, 1929, the pedagogical committee of Soviet Jewish school no. 17 debated the case of teacher Dlugina, who had served as a Soviet educator for ten years. Not only had she allegedly been disregarding antireligious work in the classroom, but living together with her father, a rabbi, she regularly observed religious rituals. This was hardly the expected behavior of a Soviet teacher, who was supposed to serve as a role model for the students even in her private life and to convey to children a quintessential Communist education.[131]

The expressions of noncompliance with Soviet practice in the public sphere of the classroom were different. While largely shaped by the degree of constraint enforced by the system, students' observance of Jewish religious practices also depended on the social atmosphere of the specific school they attended, the behavior of their classmates, the teachers' attitude toward deviance. In some instances, the teacher's benevolent or neutral attitude toward Judaism within the walls of the classroom had some bearing on students' behavior. In the early 1930s, when teaching Yiddish literature in a Soviet Jewish school, Hirsh Reles "pretended" not to notice that a few students in his class refrained from taking notes on the Sabbath.[132] The teacher's acting as if he was not aware of the student's nonconformist behavior could encourage the observance of specific religious practices. In other words, deviance was not exclusively regulated by the degree of persecution or tolerance shown by the authorities toward nonconformist social behaviors. As was the case for most Soviet citizens, the behavior of the school children also depended on the social setting in which they operated.

To Circumcise, or Not to Circumcise?

On September 19, 1928, the construction worker Orman, employed in a Minsk state factory, addressed a letter to the Jewish section of the CPB. He complained because a local Soviet Jewish kindergarten refused to accept his son. The reason, he stated, was that his son (presumably born in 1922) had not been circumcised (as was noted in the Jewish section's report of the case, *"ego rebenok 'osobyi' vvidu nesovershenüa nad nim obriada obrezaniia"*).[133] At first, the possibility of such a case occurring in the late 1920s in the capital of a Soviet Republic might seem highly remote. As a Soviet institution, the kindergarten was, at least in theory, committed to conveying to the younger generation the ideals of Communism, which included among its core foundations an atheistic approach to the world and a passionate denigration of religious beliefs. However, viewing the worker's letter within the context of the widespread observance of this Jewish practice allows us to reconsider the nature of the case, therefore complicating our understanding of Jewish integration in Soviet society. During the 1920s and through the mid-1930s at least, circumcising one's son was the norm among Soviet Jews, not the exception. This norm could have led some Jews to view with disfavor children who had not been circumcised and could even have been shared by the personnel of a Soviet Jewish kindergarten. After all, this was probably the first time that a Jewish child who was not circumcised applied to attend that kindergarten.

The archives contain much evidence of Jewish Communist Party members who had their newborn sons circumcised. The observance of religious rituals was considered especially deviant when carried out by party members, who supposedly were professional revolutionaries well versed in Leninism and affiliated with the country's most sacred institution. As the vanguard of Soviet society, their adherence to party discipline had to be flawless, and their conformity to Soviet practice unconditional. While Jewish Communists rarely married with a religious ceremony and rarely if ever attended synagogue, many of them were still committed to the tradition of circumcision. As a member of the Minsk Construction Workers' party cell pointed out in 1927, "The performance of circumcisions among workers who are members of the Communist Party and are employed in the factories of the city of Minsk is so widespread that it has assumed a 'chronic character.' . . . [I]t has become an epidemic."[134] In most cases, the circumcision was performed by a *mohel* (a religious professional adept in the procedure and its ritual requirements); in other cases, especially among the local party leadership, as for example the chairman of the Minsk Metal Workers' Union, party members requested a doctor's certification of medical necessity and had the circumcision performed as a medical procedure.[135]

If a significant proportion of Jewish party members performed the ritual, we must assume that circumcision was even more common among those Jews, workers and nonworkers alike, who did not belong to the Communist Party. The commitment to the practice of circumcision on the part of Jewish Communists should not necessarily be seen as an indication of religious behavior. Circumcising one's newborn was rather perceived, at least by many Jewish Communists who had it privately performed, as the expression of ethnic identification and was the outgrowth of a specifically Jewish *mentalité* (or in the words of Jacques Le Goff, "what changes less in the historical evolution of the everyday man"),[136] which even Communists found difficult to renounce. As Jacob Katz explained in his study about the debate on circumcision in nineteenth-century Central Europe, the power of circumcision lies in "a ritual instinct in the human psyche [which] predisposes us to attribute more importance to once-in-a-lifetime rituals than to repetitive rituals. . . . It is this instinctual response," wrote Katz, "that assures the greater persistence of the practice of circumcision over those rituals performed daily or weekly or yearly."[137] Katz's anthropological explanation of circumcision becoming the indispensable marker of Jewish identity was true not only for many Jews in Central Europe in the second half of the nineteenth century, but also for most Soviet Jews in the interwar period.

In Minsk, the first public debate in a Communist setting about circumcision took place in mid-May 1924, when an investigative commission found three members of the Communist Party cell of the Construction Workers' Union guilty of circumcising their sons. While the Soviets never officially outlawed circumcision, there were numerous restrictions, which varied according to local ruling and were aimed primarily at the *mohelim*. In the Soviet understanding of the ritual, *mohelim* were not doctors and should not have been performing an unnecessary medical procedure supposedly detrimental to the infant's health.[138] The investigative commission was usually made up of three fellow party members, who would go to the home of the accused member after the birth of the baby to verify whether the newborn had been circumcised. Following the uncovering of the 1924 transgression, the guilty party members attempted to avoid the standard punishment for non-Communist behavior: their expulsion from the party. One Gurvitch stated that he found out about his son's circumcision only three or four weeks after it was carried out; as soon as he did and decided to inform the party cell, his wife implored him not to, promising that no circumcision would be carried out in the future. "In a few months we will have another baby," stated the party member to the party cell, "and I swear that there will be no *bris*." The same Gurvitch stressed his loyalty to Communism and emphasized his service as volunteer in the Red Army and as member of the local Communist underground movement before the revolution. One comrade, whose son had been circumcised, underlined his commitment to the Soviet value-system by stating, "I would more easily accept a death sentence than expulsion from the Party"; another asserted, "For me the verdict of exclusion from the party will be a huge blow, I'd more easily agree to divorce my wife."[139] Yet they did not deny that they had had their sons circumcised. There is no reason to doubt the sincere Communism of these party members, who sought to deviate, privately, from party norms in this one specific area.

Whereas Gurvitch was expelled from the party for one year, his two fellow comrades were advised to bring those responsible for carrying out the circumcision (namely, the *mohelim* who allegedly acted against the fathers' will) before the Minsk Jewish Court. In the meantime, the Construction Workers' party cell resolved to report the circumcision cases to the City's Executive Committee of the Communist Party: they expected the local party agency to petition higher All-Belorussian Party organs so that these would in turn issue a directive forbidding circumcision without the consent of both parents.[140] The Construction Workers' cell was evidently in search of an official party line on circumcision.[141]

The Case of Comrade Gorlin

At the end of 1924, a case of deviance in the party cell of the heavily Jewish Shveiprom clothing factory (renamed Minshvei in 1925, and then Oktyabr in 1930) set off another debate pertaining to Communists and circumcision.[142] Precisely because of the high proportion of Jews, the outcome of the debate was viewed as crucial to determine the accepted norm of behaviour vis-à-vis circumcision for Jewish workers, Communists and non-Communists alike. Very few issues concerning the lives and identity of Jewish workers emerge in the protocols of the factory's party cell. Besides questions related to the use of Yiddish in everyday life, the only "Jewish topic" that regularly appears in the minutes of the factory's party cell is the circumcision of children of Communists.

Comrade Gorlin informed the party cell that his wife's parents had "performed the ritual of circumcision during his and his wife's absence." After further investigation, the commission confirmed that Gorlin's wife was aware of her parents' initiative. One comrade argued that Gorlin should leave his wife; if he refused to, he should be expelled from the party. In the opinion of another comrade, Gorlin was not guilty and should not be deprived of his party membership: had it not been for the "bourgeois environment" surrounding his wife, the religious ritual would not have been carried out. It was the Communist Party member, not his wife or the milieu in which he lived, however, who was held responsible. By neglecting to educate his wife and prevent the circumcision from taking place, he had failed to behave as a true Bolshevik. After all, besides the substantial set of privileges to which the party card paved the way (such as job advancement, a new apartment, or vacations in resort areas) being a Communist also entailed a special calling and an absolute faith and devotion to the party's sacred cause.[143] Like many others at the time, Gorlin faced the painful tension between two incommensurate systems of belief, between the calling of a Communist and the calling of a Jew.

In the mid-1920s especially, Communists such as Gorlin were punished for having their sons circumcised mainly because their behavior represented a threat to the primacy of Communist norms in Soviet society. If the small caste of party members set the wrong example—in 1924, there were 847 Jewish Party members and candidates out of a population of approximately 50,000 Jews—their transgressive behavior would become the accepted social norm for non-Communists.[144] As the party cell resolution of January 9, 1925, stated, "The circumcision ritual discredits the prestige of the party in the eyes of nonparty workers . . . for carrying out such an act it is necessary to expel from the party." And Gorlin was accordingly expelled.[145]

But during the January 13, 1925, meeting, the party cell seemed to retrace its steps. There were protests on the part of several members, who argued that the resolution was too severe and that Gorlin, a party member since 1920, was not guilty. Another party-cell member emphasized that it was precisely because of his party experience and service as a volunteer in the Red Army that Gorlin should have prevented the circumcision from being carried out. Because of his weakness, argued another party member, Gorlin should at least retreat to party candidacy. In spite of the numerous protests and suggestions to reduce the punishment, the party cell confirmed the verdict: expulsion from the party.[146]

The closing chapter of the Gorlin affair took place on May 5, 1925, during the meeting of the Minshvei party cell, in front of 240 party members and candidates, and with the participation of higher party organs. In his opening statement, the secretary of the Central Control Commission (TsKK) Beilin (himself a Jew and most likely circumcised) explained, "Whoever joins the party in order to benefit from it; Whoever acts against what the party fights for; and whoever does not behave as a Communist and does not educate those around her/him; is not a party member and, consequently, not a Communist." The last two points, continued Beilin, applied to Gorlin, who was rightly expelled from the party because of religious practice. However, the party cell and the District Control Commission (OkKK) failed to consider that "Gorlin is a worker, and when he was mobilized by the Party to the front he did not refuse. His level of political consciousness is mediocre. . . . [In other words] we should not execute someone who is ill when he can still be saved. . . . Gorlin acted against the Party . . . , but we can still cure him, we must try." To the Central Control Commission's proposal to reinstate Gorlin in the party, several party-cell members reacted with surprise and pointed out, "Jewish workers still abide strictly by the tradition of circumcision, even when they do not attend synagogue or believe in God, . . . and a Communist who carried out a circumcision cannot be a model of behaviour for nonparty members . . . this act [i.e., circumcision] concerns not only Gorlin, but the party as a whole." In spite of the opposing view, the party cell resolved to reinstate Gorlin in the party, albeit with a warning, and to pay close attention to his work and education as a Communist.[147]

Backward Wives and Family Matters

In his short-story "Karl-Yankl," Isaac Babel lays out a brilliant satire of Jewish religious life during the NEP years. It takes place sometime in the 1920s, in the suburbs of Odessa, and depicts a family conspiracy against a good Communist father, who is duped by his wife and mother-in-law. While Ofsey Belotserkovsky is away on a business trip, his mother-in-law (with the approval of his wife) snatches the newborn grandson, takes him to the *mohel* Naftula, and unbeknownst to the father has the baby circumcised. Upon returning from his trip and discovering the women's evil scheme, the party-candidate Ofsey takes to court the mother-in-law and the *mohel*, in what becomes a show trial at the Odessa Petrovsky factory. He also names the baby Karl, in honor of Karl Marx, refusing the traditional Jewish name that the grandmother and mother opted for during the clandestine ceremony.[148] In this short-story Babel-the-narrator holds accountable for the circumcision-scheme the mother-in-law and wife only, while he portrays the Communist father as absolutely oblivious to the women's plot and wrongdoings. In doing so, the writer lampoons male Communist weakness and celebrates women's strength. In reality, however, family matters involving circumcision were much more complicated, and Communist men much more implicated in the *bris*-plots, than Babel's story seems to suggest.

When confronted with the failure to behave as true Communists, party men were usually willing to blame their wives and mothers, who allegedly associated with dangerous "bourgeois circles," in order to avoid expulsion from the party. Blaming one's wife as the exclusive source of "bourgeois behavior" became a standard reaction of a man who was a member of the party and was discovered breaking the rules of "party-mindedness." In November 1927, comrade Zorin warned the party cell to which he belonged about the likelihood of his wife planning to have their son circumcised (which almost certainly implies that the infant had already been circumcised). When a couple of weeks later, the investigative commission of the party cell confirmed that the infant had indeed been circumcised, Zorin was held responsible. As the party-cell resolution stated, by failing to convince his wife to renounce her "bourgeois beliefs," he had fallen short both "as a man and as a Communist."[149] When on November 19, 1927, party-member Funt was accused of circumcising his newborn son, he provided the following explanation. In the beginning, while he worked at a construction site not far from home and could easily check on his son, the wife agreed not to have the baby circumcised. But as soon as he was transferred to a second construction site, far from home, and could no longer keep an eye on his wife, her parents pressured her and the circumcision was carried out. Funt told the party cell that he would leave his wife at once, divorce her, and pay alimony. One comrade blamed Funt for not implementing the "revolution at home." Another party-cell member was proud to share with his comrades how successfully he had applied the revolutionary tenets to the home: if two years earlier his wife had their first-born son circumcised without his permission, when their second son was born his wife did not even hint at the possibility of carrying out a circumcision: "The truth is that wives can be easily bent in our direction."[150]

In both instances, the "man" is expected to forge the woman's behavior: while his conduct is tantamount to that of a good Communist, hers is closer to that of a bourgeois still anchored to the principles of the old world. In this Communist version of "paternalism," in which the husband is responsible for his wife's behavior, Jewish men, Communist and non-Communist alike, use their "backward wife" as a pretext to engage in religious practices. After all, wives were usually excluded from skilled or professional employment and had no careers to lose, whereas they, as members of the party could lose the privileges that party membership entailed and be dismissed from their jobs. Some party members were truly unaware of or opposed to their wife's initiative to carry out the circumcision, but were nevertheless held responsible and complained about male's accountability for the "bourgeois" actions performed by women. In March 1927, a member of the Construction Workers' party cell addressed the general meeting inquiring whether "a Party member [was] always guilty when his family observed religious rituals."[151] Overall, however, justifying one's behavior by blaming one's wife became very common. In February 1930, the Minsk Jewish daily *Oktyabr* sarcastically condemned this misuse of gender, commenting:

> If you meet on the street a worker who, on the eve of Passover, is . . . carrying a sack of *matsah*, you might think that he is religious and follows religious traditions. God forbid . . . he has nothing to do with that. It is she, the "cursed wife," who persists and wants only *matsah*. When someone carries out the barbaric ritual of circumcising a newborn son, the blame falls again on the wife, who put her foot down and wanted the baby to be Jewish.[152]

During the second part of the 1920s, most members of the Communist Party who had their sons circumcised, and whose cases became known to party officials, were ipso facto expelled from the party. On October 6, 1928, the party cell of the Minsk metal factory debated the case of comrade Yofin. After the investigative commission established that his son had indeed been circumcised, he resorted to the usual ploy of blaming his wife and her parents for supposedly performing the religious ritual without his approval, while he was out of town. Yofin might even have been the same Minsk worker who a few months before had sent an anonymous letter to *Oktyabr* with a warning to the Minsk *mohelim*, "I advise all the *mohelim* of Minsk not to circumcise

Figure 9. "My wife's aunt came and carried out the *bris*. Of course the father isn't too happy about this." *Oktyabr*, April 17, 1927, 4.

my son. If my son will be circumcised, I will hold responsible each and every *mohel* in Minsk."¹⁵³ Yofin could have used this letter as evidence of his "Communist" attempt to prevent the circumcision of his newborn son. Openly advertising one's objection to this "shameful practice" was a rather common practice among Communist fathers.¹⁵⁴ But in this case, at least, the party cell did not fall for the cunning scheme and resolved to exclude Yofin from party candidacy. Incidentally, his sister, a member of the Komsomol was also present at the circumcision ceremony.¹⁵⁵

The Complicated Lives of Jewish Communists

During the early 1930s, cases of Communists having their sons circumcised were hardly ever debated in local party cells. Not only was their number in progressive decline, but the practice itself was considered socially deviant regardless of the specific context in which it occurred. In other words, no matter who orchestrated the circumcision, expulsion from the party had become the standard punishment for party members whose sons had been circumcised. Debates became superfluous. When in 1933, the Oktyabr factory workers D. M. Dvorkin and E. S. Deifer, party members since 1931 and 1930, respectively, were expelled for having had their sons circumcised their behavior was simply deemed "a violation of party discipline" (*narushenie part-distsipliny*).[156] There was no ensuing debate.

With the fierce assault on religion that characterized Stalinism of the 1930s, keeping up with the practice of circumcision became more and more challenging for Soviet Jewish citizens. The social pressure against those who carried out the ritual intensified, while the number of active *mohelim*, or doctors willing to perform the procedure, gradually decreased. However, the propaganda bureau of the Executive Committee of the CPB still complained, in early 1932, about workers regularly performing the rituals of circumcision and baptism.[157] Warnings against *mohelim* to desist from circumcising Jewish children still appeared in the press in the second half of the 1930s. In mid-1936, on the eve of being sent on a military mission with the Red Army, Avreml Marshak admonished all potential *mohelim* not to "violate" his son in his absence. He was aware, he stated, of the intentions of his wife's relatives to have the baby circumcised and threatened to take the would-be *mohel* to court if the ritual was performed.[158]

In the unfortunate case of the newborn's accidental death, the *mohel* was brought to court, usually found guilty of performing an "unnecessary surgical treatment," and sentenced to prison. In March 1931, the Minsk *mohel* Yoyne Radunski was accused of circumcising a newborn baby unbeknown to the father (a twenty-three-year-old member of the Construction Workers' Union), thereby causing the infant's death by hemorrhage. The show trial against the "slaughterer of chicken and children," as he was referred to in the trial's official account, was held from March 21–24, 1931, in the large auditorium of the Jewish Workers' Club. During the trial the *mohel* admitted that the ritual was not carried out in full accordance with traditional Jewish law: it was performed without *metsitsah* (or the drawing of the blood at circumcision) and in the absence of a *minyan* (or prayer quorum of ten male adults required for religious services); "in our times," pointed out Radunski, "the *narod* [people] . . . is satisfied without this." By contrast, the prosecutor asserted the hollowness of the 1921 document that certified the *mohel*'s expertise in performing circumcisions and was signed by a Minsk doctor. He also emphasized the lack of hygiene and poor sanitary conditions in which the ceremony was carried out, accusing the *mohel* of storing his ritual instruments in the slaughterhouse in which he worked as a *shohet*.[159] In the final verdict, the Proletarian Tribunal blamed the infant's death on the "barbaric practice of circumcision" (and the backwardness of the twenty-year-old mother of the infant) and in full agreement with the official Soviet medical view, rejected circumcision as a harmful procedure that causes illness and death.[160] Radunski was sentenced to three years in prison.[161]

In spite of the growing demand to conform to Soviet behavior and thereby reject circumcision, most Jews—and among them a large segment of Jewish Communists—continued to look for ways to abide by this Jewish practice. Some even deferred their son's *bris* by a few years in order to circumvent the party's official line and avoid finger-pointing by the investigative commission of the local party cell.[162]

One final observation seems useful with regard to the coexistence between Jewish Communists and circumcision. The Bolshevik ideal of a revolutionary vanguard of young true believers who were fiercely committed to the creation of a new Socialist system and devoted to the cause of Communism often shapes our perception of party members. Although most party members might have matched this ideal, many did not. For some of them, the borderline between proper Communist behavior and deviant social practice was unclear or of little concern. Because Communist Party policy on member recruitment fluctuated during the interwar period, different groups of people with different aims and motivations aspired to become part of the new elite class in Soviet society and joined the party. Following Lenin's death in 1924, and throughout the late 1920s, Stalin launched heavy recruitment campaigns to strengthen his base in the party and reduce the influence of Communist veterans, or Old Bolsheviks. This mass intake of members saw the party expand from approximately 470,000 members and candidates in 1924 to several millions in 1933. For many, membership in the party became first and foremost a path to privileges usually denied to the average Soviet citizen. But party membership had its risks, particularly in the 1930s when reviews (*proverki*) and purges (*chistki*), during which the member's past was closely scrutinized, resulted in the expulsion of those "hostile elements" who failed to adhere to party discipline.

In 1930, during the review of party members and candidates of the Communist cell of the Minsk factory Elvoda, Lipa Livshits, who had served on the western front from 1919 to 1922, and had joined the party in 1924, was not only accused of being a Trotskyite. He was also found guilty of having kept for five years a *mezuzah* attached to the doorpost by the entrance to his home. When asked why he did not remove it, Livshits replied that he had not noticed it.[163] During the 1933 party review, Yankl Bliakher, a worker in the Telman Minsk shoe factory and party candidate since 1931, was expelled from the party for attending synagogue services. Born in 1870, Bliakher had joined the party at the unusually late age of sixty-one.[164] David Shapiro, a worker in the Kaganovich Minsk factory since 1930, had joined the party in 1932. Although he had served in the Red Army from 1919 to 1923, which was considered an asset, he had also worked as a *sofer*, or religious scribe, from 1926 to 1928, an occupation that was not exactly in tune with Soviet social norms and that ultimately cost him the expulsion from the party in 1933. What is interesting is not so much that a former *sofer* was expelled from the party, but rather that a Red Army soldier would become a *sofer* and, later, apply for party membership.[165] Whether the ambition for a career and social mobility in the Soviet system persuaded Shapiro to join the party, or whether he did so out of ideological conviction, is hard to establish. What seems likely, however, is that the former *sofer* did not reject all expressions of his Jewish religious identification.

Gender, Family Network, and the Jewish Body

Why were many Jewish Communists so committed to this one element of traditional Jewish identity? The practice of circumcision, it seems, was integral to the question of "being a Jew." In defiance of Jewish law, according to which one is Jewish even in the absence of circumcision, Jewish folk mentality considered circumcision to be the bedrock of Jewish ethnic identity.[166] In Soviet public settings away from the family, these Communists acknowledged the importance of the Marxist idea of the "merging of nations" to build Socialism, but in the private sphere of their home they could not fully renounce the deeply entrenched notion that only through circumcision would their son be truly Jewish. Even for Soviet Jews circumcision was, as Sander Gilman put it, the body marker that set the boundaries of Jewishness.[167] Unlike Ukrainian, Russian, and Belorussian Communists, who in the absence of baptism were no longer Christians but were still Ukrainians, Russians, and Belorussians, many Jewish Communists could not envision Jewishness without circumcision, as echoed in the Yiddish expression for circumcising one's son: *"yidishn dos kind,"* or to make Jewish the child. And the only way they could ensure this ethnic continuity was by relying on their wives and mothers, the alleged corrupting force on the Jewish street and the barrier against the sovietization of the Jewish home. Instead of enlightening their wives and mothers, Communist men joined with them, in secret, to circumvent the Soviet code of behavior for Jewish members of the Communist Party.

The practice of circumcision cannot be examined at length without taking into account two intertwined and largely unexplored themes in the study of everyday Soviet Jewish life in the interwar period—namely, gender and family networks.

If we compare the circumcision debates in interwar Soviet Minsk with the circumcision debates in Germany during the late nineteenth and early twentieth centuries, or with the well-known 1908 debate that erupted in the Warsaw Jewish community when the Hevrah Kadishah (a burial society) refused to bury an uncircumcised Jewish child, we notice a striking difference in the role played by women. In the German debate over circumcision, as well as in the Warsaw debate, women are completely absent, the only actors here being men, fathers, rabbis, German Jewish thinkers and reformers, and Yiddish writers and journalists.[168] In the Soviet context, however, circumcision becomes for the first time a women's domain and liability. Communist men, or men who held key positions in Soviet society, would publicly blame their wives and mothers for circumcising their sons while privately entrusting them with the responsibility of arranging this "new Soviet Jewish ritual," secretly performed by a doctor or by a *mohel*. Mothers and grandmothers thus came to replace fathers in this traditionally all-male Jewish covenant.

Although generational conflicts played a crucial role in the sovietization process, it seems that the importance of the family and close-to-kin network in Soviet Jewish life should be reconsidered and not reduced to "Jewish patricide."[169] As a rite of passage, the practice of circumcision (like baptism for Soviet Christians) was closely connected to the life of the family, the community, and deeply ingrained social customs.[170] In the case of Jewish Communists, living in large Jewish centers such as Minsk, family loyalty was a source of tension with their party allegiance. Although sons and daughters rebelled against their families and background, they still had to come to terms with their parents' views and traditions, particularly when coping with the everyday reality of living together in the same home, on the same street, in the same neighborhood, or even merely in the same city. This was much less the case in Moscow and Leningrad, which were centers of recent migration from the former Pale of Settlement, often by young people without their parents and relatives. As this case study of circumcision shows, family ties did shape the decisions and views of the younger Jewish generation of the 1920s and 1930s, influencing, to some extent, their level of obedience to party guidelines.

Conclusion

In every society, individuals are forced to adapt to the commonly accepted social norms—all the more so, of course, in an oppressive system like the one created by the Soviets, where the individual was expected to subscribe to the tenets of Soviet ideology and spiritually merge with the collective, converting his or her private sphere into a public one. While the patterns of deviance and complicity displayed by Soviet Jews were no different than those exhibited by the citizens of other modern states at the time, the Soviet Union raised the stakes on conformity to a much higher degree. It was extremely difficult, and it entailed a considerable amount of skills and luck, to survive in the Soviet system without participating in it (using bureaucratic agencies, offices, institutions) and without accepting, or at least acknowledging, the principles of Communist behavior. The rhythm of the lives of Soviet citizens (Jews and non-Jews alike), so profoundly marked by the familiarity of the religious experience, was suddenly altered, and behavior that had been perfectly normative in pre-Soviet times came to clash with the new Soviet worldview.

The study of religious practice in an urban setting provides a window into the fragmented lives of post-1917 Russian Jews, illuminating the intricacies of their acculturation into Soviet society and showing that religious identification was more common and multifaceted than is usually thought. Making a tabula rasa of the past and erasing centuries-long traditions was not so easy in a place like Minsk, where Jewish religious practice was deeply embedded in daily life. If the number of rabbis and Orthodox Jews involved in organizing religious and educational institutions in the city was comparatively small and in progressive decline, the number of Jews who participated in religious life, together with those who supported the institutions that made religious practice possible, was significant—especially given that Minsk was the capital of a Soviet Republic. The persistence of religious life in Soviet Minsk should not be seen as anomalous, but rather as representative (at least in most of its manifestations) of other cities in the former Pale of Settlement where Jews constituted a high proportion of the total population.

The lives that Jews came to lead involved participation in, circumvention of, and resistance to the terms of daily life that developed in Soviet Russia. The tendency to conform one's behavior to the norms, values, and practices accepted in Soviet society, which Stephen Kotkin has called "speaking Bolshevik,"[171] clashed, but often coexisted, with "acting Jewish" or conducting oneself according to Jewish customs, lifestyle, and religious practice. Within the context of the new system, the Jews of the Soviet Union were constrained to redefine their lives and reinvent an identity that was Soviet and Jewish, universal and particular, at the same time. Some were indeed eager to speak Bolshevik, as they heeded the authentic loyalty inspired in them by the Soviet state. Others could not avoid speaking Bolshevik, as they lived in a Soviet city, interacted with its residents, and worked in a local business. Most of the latter, and even many of the former, continued to act Jewishly, retaining some of Judaism's practices. But increasingly, these practices retreated to the private (or secretive) sphere of their lives.

Ironically, neither of the parties who took part in the 1922 strife over the former Talmud-Torah building noted at the beginning of this chapter (Jewish Communists versus rank-and-file Jews) relied on official religious institutions to express their Jewish identity. Although some Jews were impatient to escape the confines of Jewish religious practice, many others sought ways to maintain religious traditions in light of Soviet reality, either out of their own desire or because of their allegiance to preexisting social networks and family ties. The decline of rabbinic authority, which in all likelihood began in the late nineteenth century, intensified critically due to Bolshevik persecution and culminated in the 1930 arrest of the rabbis operating on Belorussian territory.[172] But the decline in traditional authority did not lead most Jews to abandon folk *yidishkayt*. As the Bolshevism of many became real, Jewish ties were both loosened and reconfigured, primarily in moving toward folk *yidishkayt*. In fact, the latter emerged with unusual strength precisely because of the weakness of official religious authority. The persistence of kosher meat production (often without rabbinic supervision) and circumcision (often by a medical doctor) are indicative of the evolution of Jewish practices from religious commandments to ethnic habits and the transformation of Jewish identity from a religious to an ethnic category.

6 Housewives, Mothers, and Workers

Roles and Representations of Jewish Women in Times of Revolution

> Where else in the world is it then possible for a neglected Jewish woman to receive an advanced education?[1]

THE STUDY OF the roles and representations of Jewish women in the cultural, social, and political settings of modern Eastern Europe has been confined to tsarist Russia and interwar Poland. This chapter recreates the composite picture of the lives of Soviet Jewish women, explaining their choices and beliefs under Bolshevik rule and balancing them against the experiences and voices of their gender counterpart.

The analysis of the "gender revolution" on the Jewish street reveals the endurance (and perhaps even intensification) of gender tensions, exposing the limits of the government's state-sponsored policy of equality of the sexes. While the revolution challenged patriarchal structures in fundamental ways and claimed to liberate women from the yoke of traditional society, it also enabled the perpetuation of certain conservative patterns of male behavior. It would seem, in fact, that despite the widely heralded political emancipation of women—the granting of legal equality on paper—their social emancipation largely failed. That is, in reality, Jewish women had limited influence on the principal and most powerful institutions in the Soviet public arena. This tension between political and social emancipation, between female activism and male conservatism, and between the different visions that men and women held of Jewish woman's path to sovietization, marked the gender discourse on the Jewish street and shaped the shifting roles that Jewish women came to play in the capital of the Belorussian Republic.

The tension between theory and practice (so inherent in the Bolshevik experiment) also played out in a particularly vivid way in the history of Jewish women under the Soviets. The clash between the theory of idealizing women as selfless warriors for the Socialist cause, and the practice of confining—or wishing to confine them—to the realm of the home, considerably affected their lives and experiences. Perhaps in no other Jewish community in the world at the time do we find such a fierce tension between a violent push for women's emancipation espoused by Soviet discourse and the conservative thrust to keep them out of the public sphere as we do in the case of Soviet Jewish women. The tension between theory and practice was exacerbated by the encounter between the Bolshevik experiment, or the most revolutionary and brutal attempt to implement social engineering from above, and Russian Jewry, a traditional and patriarchal Jewry when compared to other Jewish communities in Western and Central Europe at the time. While modernization of Jewish women took place in pre-revolutionary times, the Soviet regime's insistence on equality accelerated changes to a dizzying speed.

Besides effecting the lives of Jewish women, the tension between theory and practice regarding the "Jewish women's question" almost certainly increased the anxiety of Jewish men in connection with the rise of the modern woman. Male concern for the modernization and empowerment of Jewish women dated back to the Haskalah in the 1870s, but undoubtedly intensified during the Soviet period.[2] After all, Communist discourse egged on women to take power into their hands, as the Soviet state actively promoted gender equality. Under the Bolsheviks therefore male anxiety escalated, in some cases even turning Communist men against the principles of equality promoted by the party. Moreover, for the first time male anxiety about women's power became widespread to all social classes, including Jewish workers and artisans, who in the late nineteenth century did not feel threatened by the rise of a modern Jewish woman as did the Jewish middle class.

These gender tensions emerge in the three interrelated topics examined in this chapter: (1) The modus operandi of the Minsk Communist agencies responsible for drawing Jewish women into the revolution, and the strategies they envisioned to solve "the women's question" on the Jewish street. (2) Male reactions to the "Jewish women's question" and the fantasy image that male political activists who operated in the Jewish sphere conceived of Jewish women in public and private settings. (3) Jewish women's patterns of participation in the political, social, and cultural life of the city, and their involvement as "agents of revolution" in the building of the Soviet system.

Writing about Jewish women in the Soviet context is challenging not only due to the lack of preexistent scholarly work on the subject, but also because of the absence of institutions specifically created for and/or by Jewish women to address educational, economic, or social questions related to their lives. Institutions such as schools for Jewish girls or philanthropic associations run by Jewish women, which existed elsewhere in Eastern Europe, and which could serve as a starting point in evaluating women's integration into the political, economic, and cultural arena of the Belorussian capital, no longer existed under the Soviets. The Bolsheviks wiped out most separate spheres of public activity for Jewish women, such as the religious, cultural, and welfare societies established in late imperial Russia. Deemed as bourgeois institutions, these societies for Jewish women posed a threat to the unity of the Bolshevik cause, which indeed advocated fighting for the equality of sexes but not based on women's specific national, ethnic, or religious identity. However, in spite of the absence of Jewish women's institutions, not unlike any other mid- to large-sized city in the former Pale of Settlement, Minsk remains a most valuable source of information about Jewish women by virtue of its demographic nature. General Soviet agencies and organizations in which Jews, and particularly Jewish women, represented a large percentage—such as the Minsk branch of the Zhenotdel, or the Women's Department of the Communist Party—are an essential resource for the study of gender relations on the Jewish street and the positions that Jewish women occupied in the new revolutionary society.

The Women's Question on the Jewish Street

During the nineteenth century a growing preoccupation with the social condition of women emerged on the agenda of the Jewish intelligentsia. *Maskilic* writers, such as Y. L. Gordon, Joseph Perl, and Mendele Mocher Seforim, harshly condemned the submissive role to which the Jewish religion had confined women, both in public and private spaces.[3] In the 1850s and 1860s, the concern of the Haskalah movement for the plight of women resulted in efforts to make secular education available to them. *Maskilim* believed that a modern educational system for women would eventually free them from the overriding socioeconomic restraints imposed by the patriarchal religious society in which they lived and transform them into enlightened mothers responsible for the reformation of future generations of Jews. At the same time, however, enlightened Jewish men also feared the "dangers" of urban, middle-class Jewish women entering general secular educational institutions and straying from Judaism altogether. The main concern of most *maskilim* remained therefore to balance Jewish values with enlightened education, thereby guaranteeing that "Jewish daughters" remained Jewish enough while freeing themselves from medieval traditionalism.[4]

In a speech delivered in 1867 to mark the tenth anniversary of the founding of his private school for Jewish girls in Minsk, Chayim Funt spoke about the need to train the future modern Jewish mother, explaining that "she must be reborn; she must prepare herself for this modest, but great mission; she must renounce superstition, improve her taste, ennoble her understanding, attach her soul to general human need."[5] More than one hundred private Jewish schools for girls were established across the Pale of Settlement between 1844 and 1881.[6] With the encouragement of their parents, who found a curriculum composed of Russian, German, French, arithmetic, and religious courses attractive, many middle-class girls (indeed a small minority of Jewish girls) flocked to these new institutions.

By the time of the first revolution of 1905, Russian Jewish politics had produced a remarkable number of multifaceted movements and parties. Most of these—especially, but not exclusively, general Zionists—did not try to attract women to politics.

The un-receptiveness toward women and the "women's question" is reflected in the absence of Jewish women in the movements' rank-and-file and leadership, as well as in the content of the parties' programmatic platforms; these generally avoided clauses on women's political mobilization and gender social inequities. A notable exception to the tendency of neglecting the "fair sex" occurred in 1917, during the elections to the Constitutional Assembly, when Jewish parties across the political spectrum addressed women in order to attract them to the polls and win over their support. The left—Jewish and non-Jewish alike—helped disrupt patriarchal social traditions and liberate women from "family despotism," thus attracting a significant number of female members, who often joined the movement more out of commitment to their selfhood than to the general cause. Women made up one-third of the terrorist movement of the 1870s and 1880s, and by World War I they comprised 15 percent of the underground political movements of tsarist Russia. Reacting against their parents' political beliefs, and the very foundation of Jewish society (namely, their own role as women in the family), many Jewish women joined the Socialist Revolutionary Party, the SRs.[7] However, the radical leadership clearly stated that there was no separate women's question and that the emancipation of the proletariat would automatically solve gender discrimination.

The Bund, and to some degree the Poale-Zion, attracted a sizable female constituency, numerically more than any other Jewish or Russian Socialist Party did. In 1905, at the height of the Bund's influence among the Jewish public, Jewish women made up a third of the Bund's party membership.[8] Actively engaged in the class struggle on the Jewish street, some women even came to play a leading role in the high party echelons. Two women (out of a total of thirteen founding delegates) participated in the 1897 clandestine meeting in Vilna, which resulted in the establishment of the Bund. Henry Tobias mentions six women out of the forty-eight most important early Bundist leaders, and J. Sh. Hertz includes fifty-five women in his biographical profiles of the 320 most prominent Bundist leaders in the history of the party.[9] And in 1917, for the second time in the history of the Bund, a woman served on the party's Central Committee: the Minsk-born Malka Lifschitz, better known by her nom de guerre, Ester Frumkin.[10]

Despite the noteworthy presence of women in the Bund's leadership, and rank-and-file membership, hardly any Bundist activist openly addressed questions related to the status of women. The only exception was the grievance over low female wages and the competition between female and male workers. As Yelena Gelfand had stated as early as 1892, at an illegal celebration of May Day by Jewish workers in Vilna, "The women's question is not a separate issue, but part of the great Socialist question."[11]

The Bolshevik Revolution brought the "women's question" to the table making it a political priority for the Communist Party. After all, theorists of classic Socialism and Communism had concurred long before that women's liberation, along with the liberation of the proletariat, was necessary to create a more just and equal society. In a private letter, Marx paraphrased the words of the founding father of utopian Socialism Charles Fourier, saying that "social progress can be measured exactly by the social position of the fair sex (the ugly ones included)."[12] The new Soviet system intended to transform the lives of women, liberating them from the "dark forces" of religion, drawing them to the party and enticing them into playing an active role in the newly established Soviet institutions.[13] Two political agencies dealt with the status of Jewish women, envisioning for them a new role to play in Soviet society: the Evsektsiia and the Zhenotdel. Besides the pre-revolutionary Bund's meetings, most of which took place underground, this was the first time that Jewish women participated in a public political forum, debating questions related to the status of women in what had traditionally been a male-dominated and -oriented world.

Established in the second half of August 1920, the Zhenotdel CPB intended to eradicate women's illiteracy, to attract them to the social and political life of the new Soviet system, and to provide them with a firm knowledge of Communism. Equating their "ignorance" with danger to the cause, the Zhenotdel contended that only by virtue of Communist education could women fulfill the important role of caretakers of the younger generation, and ensure "a Communist . . . imprint on the children."[14] In standard bourgeois spirit women's education was justified by reference to their maternity. On the eve of March 8, 1922, on International Women's Day, the Zhenotdel CPB stated:

> Because of the conditions in which she lived under the bourgeois system, because of centuries without equal rights, . . . the female worker is more backward, ignorant, downtrodden. . . . Apathetic, backward women represent a great danger for the revolution, it is necessary . . . to raise the level of their consciousness . . . and turn them into active participants in the building of the Soviet Union.[15]

In accord with party guidelines, the Evsektsiia approached the "women's question" as a political priority, organizing meetings and concerts in Yiddish for Jewish women workers and wives of Jewish Red Army soldiers.[16] Women made their appearance in the Evsektsiia protocols immediately after its creation. As early as August 1920, a Jewish woman became responsible for carrying out propaganda among women: she coordinated the "women's pages" (*zhenskie stranichki*) in the Yiddish-language and Russian-language Communist periodicals published in the city and organized performances and political meetings for women.[17] In September 1920, the Evsektsiia organized four concert-meetings in the city, one of which was specifically devoted to the role of women in building the Soviet system.[18]

The Jewish section of the CPB collaborated closely with the Zhenotdel. In the summer of 1921, it claimed as one of its political priorities to "appoint an experienced secretary to work in the Zhenotdel."[19] The Jewish secretary of the Zhenotdel was in charge of organizing Jewish women workers and holding speeches in Yiddish at women's meetings. She worked primarily in the Minsk professional unions with a large percentage of Jewish workers.[20] Nominated by the Evsektsiia, one of the first Jewish secretaries to the Zhenotdel was former Bundist R. Meliakhovitskaia. She gave speeches in the Tobacco

Workers Union and city garment workshops and helped organize *ustnye gazety* (readings of newspapers for illiterate women) and Yiddish concerts.[21]

While acknowledging the importance of attracting Jewish women to the party, the Evsektsiia leadership encountered difficulties on the practical level. Criticizing Jewish activists for disregarding the "woman's question," in July 1921 it requested them to nominate instructors to coordinate propaganda in Yiddish in each factory with a majority of Jewish women.[22] The invitation fell on deaf ears and the Evsektsiia had to reiterate the order.[23] Meanwhile, the publication of the women's column in the Minsk Jewish daily was discontinued.[24] In May 1922, it was the turn of the Minsk Zhenotdel to complain about the absence of women's pages in *Veker* as well as in the Russian-language *Zvezda*. Not satisfied with the attention given to the "women's question," the Zhenotdel accused the editors of both newspapers, who were men, of disregarding party instructions.[25]

The Soviet political system created a new category for women interested in participating in the political arena. The so-called *delegatka*, or woman delegate, was elected by other women and coordinated propaganda on behalf of the Zhenotdel in the agency or factory in which she worked.[26] She held a card, or *delegatskaia kartochka*, an official party document that was supposed to be with her at all times. The *delegatka* was also expected to become a member in one of the two Central Workers' Clubs in Minsk, the Jewish club or the general one, the Profintern Club.[27] Delegates met on a regular basis to discuss topics related to women's everyday life, such as hygiene, children, marriage laws, unemployment, religion, nationality policy, and in the case of Jewish women, the significance of Yiddish-language schools.[28] They were also responsible for monitoring the social conditions of other women. In 1925, for instance, two delegates investigated a petition submitted to the Zhenotdel against a *melamed*. He was accused of mistreating his mother. As it turned out, he had never abused the mother. Rather, because of his occupation as a Hebrew teacher, he lived with the family, including his mother, in abject poverty. The sixty-three-year-old woman had turned to the delegates asking for guidance in obtaining social security.[29] Finally, delegates were expected to discuss women's questions in political brochures and wall-newspapers and to participate in the literary and political circles organized for women.[30]

Born in 1897 to a stove setter and a housewife with a small shop on the outskirts of the city, Dina Rubin had never had the opportunity to study or be politically active, spending most of her time at home taking care of her younger siblings. As she admitted, "The revolution of 1917 found me completely ignorant of political life." During the Polish occupation of Minsk she began to attend political meetings, and after joining the Red Army became "politically mature" (*politicheski razvita*). In 1924, the wives of the employees in the Finance Department, where her husband worked, elected Dina Zhenotdel delegate. She then became a member of the City Soviet, a correspondent in the local press, the director of a wall-newspaper, and the secretary of Minshvei factory committee.[31] Dina's status of delegate spurred her to take on new political and social responsibilities.

Like her, many Jewish women served prominently as delegates in party cells and agencies.[32] Because of the significant proportion of Jews in the workforce, and the higher level of literacy among Jewish women compared to their Belorussian counterpart, from the beginning Jewish women occupied most of the newly created positions for women.[33] In October 1924, two hundred women delegates participated in the Minsk District Committee meeting. Of these, eighty-nine were Jewish and thirty-four Belorussian (sixty-three Russian).[34] At the General City Women Delegates' Meeting, held on February 27, 1926, of the three hundred fifty-three delegates who participated, Jewish women were one hundred seventy, and Belorussian women one hundred twenty-five (there were also forty-one Russian women and eight Polish women).[35] These statistics are both a reflection of the Jewish demographics of the city as well as of the higher degree of urbanization, literacy, and tradition of political activism among Jewish women compared to Belorussian women. It is therefore not surprising that in the earlier stages of the Zhenotdel in Minsk, Jewish women exceeded the number of Belorussian women who engaged in party work.[36]

In some organizations the only women who participated in Zhenotdel initiatives were Jewish. At the general meeting of the Construction Workers' Union party cell, held in October 1924, comrade Grebenchik pointed out that "as far as work among women goes, there is one problem in our union. . . . [I]t is conducted only among Jewish women." Because of the absence of women of other nationalities in leadership positions, most women's meetings were held in Yiddish only.[37] In October of the following year, in an effort to attract non-Jewish women to propaganda work, bimonthly meetings were held in Yiddish and in Russian, on rotation. But Jewish women were still more active than Belorussian and Russian women: women's meetings had an average attendance of two hundred; of these, one hundred fifty were Jewish women. Of the eighteen Zhenotdel delegates elected in the Construction Workers' Union that year, fourteen were Jewish.[38] Despite the organization of Russian-language circles to reach out to Russian women, in December 1926, the union conducted propaganda work among women exclusively in Yiddish.[39] The head of the Minsk Zhenotdel justified the situation explaining that holding meetings in two languages (Yiddish and Russian) was impractical insofar as each speech had to be given twice, even when "there were only ten Russian [women present]."[40] In February 1927, the Construction Workers' party cell still criticized the lack of involvement in propaganda work of Belorussian and Russian women, emphasizing that only Jewish women attended women's meetings.[41] At the party-cell meeting of September 1927, three Zhenotdel delegates read their reports. Two out of three were in Yiddish.[42]

With the gradual implementation of the *korenizatsiia* campaign, a new language of propaganda emerged in women's activities, namely Belorussian. For 1927–28, the City District women's meeting anticipated to divide the delegates into three distinct groups that would operate in Belorussian, Russian, and Yiddish, respectively. General meetings, however, would be held in Russian, with the intention to shift them to Belorussian once the Jewish and Russian delegates became more familiar with the language. When the City District organizers of women's work met in December 1927 to debate the status of the Zhenotdel biweekly—*Belorussian Woman Worker and Peasant*—some argued that the journal should be published in Russian, and not in Belorussian, as most women (Jewish and Russian) did not understand the Belorussian language.[43] In compliance with the policies of *korenizatsiia*, however, the biweekly eventually shifted to Belorussian, and by the end of the 1920s most general women's conferences were no longer held in Yiddish.

In many ways, the Women's Department of the CPB acted as a Jewish institution. First, most of the women who played a key role in the agency since its inception were Jewish. On February 16, 1921, the secretary of the Zhenotdel was Vainer.[44] At the end of that same month, Sonia Kremer took on the chairmanship of the Women's Department. In May 1921, Kremer was replaced by Maria Reiser; Efroimskaia was appointed secretary, while Meliakhovitskaia, Chaia Kramnik, and Sara Braze became instructors, or responsible for educating women workers employed in city factories and Soviet organizations.[45] When looking through the protocols of the 1922 and 1923 meetings of the Central Committee of the Zhenotdel, it is difficult to find a non-Jewish name,[46] so much so that from a demographic vantage point, the Minsk Zhenotdel bore a stronger resemblance with the Evsektsiia and other Jewish agencies in the city than with general party organizations.

While it is hard to trace the cultural background of the Jewish women who became prominent in the Zhenotdel, it is possible to assume that many of them had been active in the Bund before the revolution. By attracting young Jewish women to its ranks, the Jewish party served as an important venue for the politicization of Jewish women, most of whom would have hardly considered so quickly and eagerly to participate in political and social life without their previous Bundist experience. In other words, the Bund served as a stepping stone into Soviet society and political work for Jewish women, perhaps even more than it did for Jewish men. After all, women active in Socialist politics were atypical and stood out from the masses of womankind by virtue of their commitment to Socialism, as well as their political activities. The high percentage of Jewish women active in the Zhenotdel persisted throughout the 1920s and up until 1930 when the party deemed the women's question solved and liquidated the department.[47]

Second, the Zhenotdel often voiced specifically Jewish concerns and interests. At the Zhenotdel meeting of the Minsk tobacco factory, held in August 1921, to argue for the struggle against clericalism Meliakhovitskaia referred to a trial against a Minsk rabbi. In a fusion of feminism and anti-Judaism, she stated that "the Holy Scriptures contain all kinds of . . . prohibitions for women. . . . But the trial showed that in a proletarian state there will no longer be any limitation for women. . . . [They] will be free . . . and . . . equal to men."[48] Following the Zhenotdel meeting of the Women Workers of the EPO Bakery, held in September 1921, comrade Gordon (a woman) read a few chapters from Sholem Aleichem's work *Fun Yarid* (From the market).[49] In 1922, to celebrate March 8, the Zhenotdel organized in collaboration with the Central Bureau of the CPB, the Komsomol, and the Soviet Trade Union of Belorussia, a delegates' meeting devoted to the historical importance of International Women's Day. This included a Yiddish concert.[50] On the occasion of the twentieth anniversary of the First Russian revolution of 1905, at the ceremonial delegates' meeting held in December 1925, one of the two speakers remembered 1905 by describing a pogrom. A worker in Bialystok at the time, she recalled the panic, the destruction, the dead children, and the burial of the victims.[51] These examples are indicative of how prominently Jewish themes loomed in the activities of the Zhenotdel in the 1920s, especially when compared to the absence of a specific Russian or Belorussian focus.

Third, the places in which the agency convened its general meetings were often Jewish or formerly Jewish, as in the case of the Choral Synagogue/House of Culture. In June 1924, the Second City Conference of Women Workers and Workers' Wives took place in the former synagogue and, among other things, discussed the activities of the Jewish section of the City Education Department.[52] In 1925, the Zhenotdel arranged the screening of a propaganda film on the use of chemical weapons in war, in the former synagogue;[53] on March 29, 1926, during Passover, Zhenotdel organizers held the Fourth Conference of Women Workers and Workers' Wives in the Jewish Club.[54] The Zhenotdel leadership convened general women conferences in Jewish places precisely because of their Jewish identity and the Jewishness of a large segment of the audience.

By the end of the NEP era, Communist work among women lost its momentum and became relegated to the margins of the party's political initiatives. Questions about women all but disappeared from Evsektsiia protocols. While articles related to Jewish women continued to appear in the Yiddish-language press, the number of women's columns declined steadily and appeared only on specific occasions. In June 1928, to celebrate the tenth anniversary of the establishment of a women's organization in the Union of the Belorussian Crafts Industry, the Evsektsiia planned to issue wall-newspapers in the women's workshops of Minsk and publish a woman's column in the Jewish daily.[55] This plan was never realized. At the general party meeting of the heavily Jewish factory Oktyabr, held on February 22–23, 1930, comrade Berchanskaia, a woman, probably Jewish, complained about the absence of party activity among women at a time when the number of women who participated in the life of the factory was growing. To her disappointment, the conclusions of the Control Committee of the party cell included almost no reference to future party work among women.[56] This might have been an indication of the imminent liquidation of the Zhenotdel in Minsk, a process initiated by the Secretariat of the Central Committee in Moscow in late 1929, primarily, but not exclusively, for lack of funds. Launched in 1929, Stalin's Great Turn confirmed the Bolsheviks' original intention to ban every form of separatism within the party that could impinge upon the united proletarian cause. At the end of 1930, the party closed down the Jewish section of the Communist Party as well as the Women's

Department of the Communist Party, deeming both agencies a useless threat to Communist harmony. And in the spirit of grandiose Soviet mythmaking Stalin declared the Jewish question solved and women's liberation achieved. For all intents and purposes, the abolishment of the Zhenotdel marked the end of political and educational work among women conducted by an official body devoted specifically to that goal. The alleged solution to the woman's question led to the virtual disappearance in post-1930 party documents of the category "woman," which had always been included in statistical data collected during the 1920s.

The most remarkable achievement of the Zhenotdel on the Jewish street of Minsk resulted in the creation of a new elite of Jewish women eager to partake in the building of the Socialist system and educate other women in the spirit of Communism and equality with men. Mostly untouched by politics in the past, they now learned the basics of political and cultural organization, monitoring factory conditions, fighting against female unemployment and prostitution, and teaching literacy classes. Moreover, Jewish women who became active in the Zhenotdel could act simultaneously as Communists, Jews, and women, interweaving these three identities in a new distinctive unity, harmonious and contentious at the same time. Finally, for the first time Jewish women were able to attain social mobility through the party and not through their fathers or husbands. For many Jewish women, becoming a delegate and joining the Women's Department was the first stage in their rise to high positions of responsibility and power in society. But female empowerment eventually met and collided with male empowerment, as Jewish men who found Bolshevism exhilarating also viewed Jewish women as dangerous competitors for power.

Imagining Soviet Jewish Women

—Sorke's been promoted to a better position.
—Certainly not by chance. She's probably sleeping with the party-cell secretary.
—What are you talking about? The cell's secretary is a woman.
—In that case, she's probably sleeping with the director of the factory.
—The director is also a woman.
—Then it must mean that your Sorke is a man.[57]

This anecdote about the blooming career of Sara—who is called by the endearing Yiddish diminutive of Sorke—appeared in the Jewish daily *Oktyabr* in July 1929. This was on the eve of the liquidation of the Zhenotdel, when the Bolshevik regime had "successfully settled the woman's question once and for all." On the one hand, this humorous sketch reflects men's expectations about the social inferiority of women, whose status could be altered and improved only through the "assistance" of their male superiors. On the other hand, it echoes the fear of the successful modern woman who, in the eyes of men, posed a threat to traditional gender roles, even in the progressive Soviet society that had supposedly put the word "end" to the woman's problem. In a

Yiddish-language collection of articles and short stories published by the Minsk Zhenotdel in the mid-1920s, for example, the anxiety about modern women is conveyed through the distress of a husband who found out that his wife became a women's delegate. Fearing that his wife's new public position would inevitably bring her to cheat on him with other men, Kershteyn abandoned her and informed her that he would return only if she gave up her new political responsibilities.[58] The new Soviet ideal of women as workers and members of the Communist leadership promoted by the party during the 1920s possibly increased the torment of many Jewish men over their wives' public careers, which ultimately broke down the equilibrium of the traditional gender hierarchy they were accustomed to. The anxiety over women's modernization might have been more intense among Jewish men than among their Belorussian, Ukrainian, or Russian counterpart. After all, Jewish women were more eager and better prepared to join the public sphere than non-Jewish women because of their higher level of literacy. A good number of Jewish women were literate in Yiddish, which was now considered a language of the public sphere. By contrast, Belorussian women were typically not literate in Belorussian or Russian. Finally, many Jewish women had relied on the Bund as a springboard for acculturation, modernization, and literacy, a resource that most Belorussian, Ukrainian, and even Russian women could not rely on; they were mostly peasants, a social group not known for political activism. So that whenever Jewish men looked around they typically saw Jewish women active in public and were both appalled and scared by that.

On March 8, 1923, the Minsk Party agencies organized lectures, meetings, and concerts to celebrate International Women's Day. During the program held in the Minsk Profintern Club, the Food Industry Workers' Union nominated Fruma Shteiman "hero of labor" (*geroina truda*). The congratulatory speech described her as a "devoted and productive worker." Employed in the tobacco industry for more than thirty-five years, Fruma had been arrested twice by the tsarist police because of her political activities and had served on the Executive Committee of the tobacco workers union from 1905 to 1918.[59] Her devotion to the trade union and the revolutionary cause, and the degree of her political awareness prompted this laudatory tribute. And while the speech gave absolute priority to Fruma's accomplishment as a worker and committed revolutionary, it made no mention of the private sphere of the home, more specifically her marital status and possible role of mother.

This idealization of Fruma's behavior was part of the attempt to create role models for Jewish women, expand their contribution to the building of Socialism, and boost their commitment to Communism. However, this ideal image strongly clashed with the widespread attitude that Communist men showed vis-à-vis the "women's question." Party men, Jews and non-Jews alike, viewed the existence of the Zhenotdel with scorn. Communists often referred to it as the "*bab-kom*" or "*tsentro-baba*,"[60] *baba* being a derogatory Russian term for woman. In 1926, at a meeting of Jewish women in Minsk, Shmuel Agursky, member of the Minsk Jewish Communist elite, praised the Women's

Department of the Communist Party and snidely concluded, "You see how much we Communist men have done for you—we even have an organ designed especially for women!"[61] Agursky's sexual remark was a joke at the expense of the Zhenotdel.

At the general meeting of the Construction Workers' party cell, held on October 21, 1924, comrade Vernik emphasized that the lack of interest on the part of Communist men significantly thwarted the attempt to mobilize women to political life. Constantly engaged in building the new Socialist order and attending workers' meetings, they did not encourage their wives to take part in the political life of the factory. Reporting on the Zhenotdel activities among construction workers, a woman delegate added that Communist husbands exploited their wives more than women married to nonparty men. Too busy fulfilling the task of child rearing and housework, the wives of Communists had no time to participate in the building of Socialism. A 1926 Zhenotdel meeting recorded complaints from housekeepers about their ten to twelve–hour-long working day. The grievance was voiced primarily by women married to Communist men who protested for the lack of spare time for themselves.[62] Another delegate reported instances of prominent trade union members who employed as "house-workers" underaged girls who had recently moved to Minsk from the provinces. The young women received a salary of three to five rubles a month, worked every day until midnight, had no leisure time (not even during the revolutionary holidays), and became the target of disreputable comments about their sexual behavior out of fear that they would bring home "infectious diseases from the square."[63] In other words, in a purportedly more enlightened and "revolutionary" household, in which the husband belonged to the Communist Party or was a well-known trade union member, women played the typically "bourgeois role" of raising children, knitting, sewing, and cooking for their husbands.

At times, the fantasy of exclusive male empowerment clashed with the reality of ambitious women who tried to counter the domestic utopia. Some women activists offered a feminist solution to the question of women's participation in public life. In the main Yiddish-language organ of the Sewing Industry Union, Kuntsevitskaia called for women's self-emancipation, encouraging female union members to quit their passive role in social life, escape domestic servitude, and show men that in addition to being good cooks, they could also serve as social activists.[64] Other women proposed something more concrete that would alter the traditional gender hierarchy at home. Noticing that of the four hundred women members of the Sewing Industry Union only fifty showed up at the union's meeting of December 1924, S. Vayner suggested that the husbands—"who typically hang out in the club every night, concealing from their wives the dates of upcoming women's assemblies—stay home at least once a week and give women the opportunity to attend the meeting."[65] Comrade Vilk criticized men who refused to help women in the house chores, especially in those cases in which wives, like their husbands, worked during the day: "Upon returning home from work, women go to the kitchen and men to political meetings." The only solution, stated comrade Vilk, was to introduce a fixed principle according to which women should be free to attend meetings at least twice a month.[66] In the words of another woman who, in the same Yiddish-language publication, blamed men for women's role in public life, "Whether they are at work, at a meeting, at the club, or in the factory, husbands are never home. . . . We must persuade them that women are equal . . . and arrange . . . for wives to attend meetings and for husbands to stay home with the children."[67]

Most men responded negatively to changes in traditional domestic female roles, especially in working-class families. The assumption was that while working and earning their share of family substance, working-class women would remain close to home or at least under male "supervision." Even more so in a Jewish setting where the model of men engaged in yeshiva studies and women serving as breadwinners and housewives loomed large, reflecting the hierarchy of Jewish traditional values. Studying and teaching classical rabbinic texts was more praiseworthy than baking and selling challas, cakes, and wine for the Sabbath, even though these female activities comprised the households' main income. In the early Soviet period, the awareness of a hierarchy of functions between men and women, enhanced by Jewish traditional values, marked the self-consciousness of many young Jewish men perhaps even more than it did Belorussian, Ukrainian, and Russian men.

While voicing their commitment to involve women in the social life of the factory, most party men retained toward female workers an ambivalent and mostly condescending attitude. Employers complained about women's "backwardness" but made sure to keep them in positions of social inferiority, as they usually allocated unskilled work to women and skilled work to men. At the same time, Communist leaders blamed women for not being part of the factory leadership and failing to take up the same administrative positions as men.[68] Condemning women's indifference, one comrade nagged about them as follows:

> Let's not fool ourselves. How many women actually read newspapers? Here [in Minsk] we publish *Oktyabr*, in Moscow *Der Emes*. How many women know about the existence of these two newspapers if not those who take them from their husbands to the butcher shop and wrap up meat with them? How many women show interest in evening classes and meetings? . . . Our government spends thousands of rubles every year to publish Yiddish books; have the majority of women ever read a Yiddish book? The truth is that as long as women will not educate themselves, read, and subscribe to newspapers they will remain backward.[69]

An article about the level of political awareness among women workers in the Minshvei factory substantiated this view, which might have even reflected the lack of Communist aspirations of many young women, but only to a degree. Many female employees, argued the author of the article, failed to engage in after-work lofty activities to support the building of Socialism. At the end of a day's work, instead of worrying about the class struggle or reading a newspaper, young women would usually dress up and promenade the streets of Minsk.[70]

Finally, even in cases when women and men shared the same knowledge of politics and level of literacy, women were typically precluded from promotion and successful careers. In the Yiddish poem "Kirpitshiki," or little bricks, a young destitute woman moves to pre-revolutionary Minsk, finds a job as a bricklayer in the city's brick factory, and meets her beloved Yankele. They work together in the same factory, join the workers' movement together, experience World War I, and fight for the October revolution. But as the ninth stanza unveils, it is Yankele alone who successfully climbs the social ladder and becomes director of the factory:

A sirene shrayt, der zavod banayt
Un, vi fryer, un lang nit getrakht
Hot men Yankelen, komsomolye mayn
Far a pred, a direktor gemakht.[71]

[The siren sounds, the factory resumes
And, like before, and without much thought
Yankele, my komsomolets
Was made into a director, a boss.]

Not only did the majority of Jewish men assume women's inferiority on the work place, but also many saw women as a dangerous counterrevolutionary force on the Jewish street, identifying them with one of the greatest threats to the success of the Bolshevik experiment: religious tradition. Because of their presumed backwardness, lack of interest in the party, and motherly responsibility for educating the next generation of Soviet Jews, women became the main target of antireligious propaganda on the Jewish street.[72] While the assault on religious beliefs and practices became a regular topic in Jewish women's meetings and in general women's meetings with a large percentage of Jewish participants, meetings that did not specifically address women rarely mentioned the danger of religion. Antireligious propaganda circles in Yiddish, which denounced first and foremost the observance of Jewish holidays and dietary laws, were usually organized for women only, and were rarely part of general cultural and political tasks (that is, for men).[73] In 1924, the Evsektsiia organized lectures about the upcoming Passover holiday as well as "Red Seders" or alternative political celebrations of Passover, for workers' wives only.[74] Not only did the propaganda effort not address men, but it also identified a priori women as a religious and nonproletarian element.[75] At a "Red Seder" held in 1925 in the Jewish Club, the speaker addressed the large audience of Jewish women who gathered for the "red celebration," praising those who "yesterday used their last piece of wood to kosher the dishes [for Passover] but today sit here with us at the conference," to build Socialism.[76]

As the mainstay of religious beliefs, Jewish women symbolized the principal obstacle for the implementation of Soviet ideals at home, among family members. Occasional public trials were organized in local clubs against wives who allegedly tried to corrupt the political beliefs of their husband workers, persuading them not to attend party meetings or participate in club's activities. In one instance, the prosecutor even accused a Jewish woman of beating up her son, the pioneer, and her daughter, the Komsomolka, because they rebuffed Jewish religious practices.[77] In a family vignette published in 1926, which takes place in the Minsk neighborhood of Komorovka, the young Leyke awaits the return of her husband Yankl from the front. Assuming her husband has not changed during the Civil War and is still religious, Leyke, encouraged by her mother Frume, resolves to wash Yankl's *tallit* so that he can wear it to synagogue. But Yankl returns home a triumphant Bolshevik: he instructs Leyke about the Zhenotdel activities and convinces her to send their seven-year-old son Khaymke to a Soviet school and not to heder. The grandfather Elye, who unbeknownst to his wife Frume buys nonkosher meat, admits to his son-in-law that Leyke "is still a calf and can be molded as you wish." However, his wife Frume cautions her nephew Khaymke against God's rage if he does not attend heder. The young boy brazenly replies that he will shoot God directly in the head with the gun his father gave him.[78] In this Communist fantasy those women who were not swayed by men toward the righteous path of Bolshevism usually made an effort to corrupt the revolutionary spirit of their sons, husbands, and fathers. Incidentally, the author of this short story was a woman, who seemingly internalized the common view of daughters-wives-mothers as latent counterrevolutionaries.

Of course, the image of women as bearers of the evil forces of religion and custodians of "bourgeois" traditions within the Jewish (and non-Jewish) family was based on some degree of reality. Jewish women, as well as Belorussian and Russian women, were generally more prone to abide by religious traditions because of their long-established focus on the home and their lower level of integration into the modern workforce. However, many Jewish women—more than their Belorussian and Russian counterparts—had become politically active, some rejected family life entirely and acted as the bearers of modernity rather than the mainstay of religious fanaticism. The fact that Soviet propaganda mentioned religious backwardness almost exclusively in the context of women's behavior deserves further elucidation. The similarity with the *maskilic* discourse of the nineteenth century is worth mentioning. As Eliyana Adler has suggested, while many *maskilim* supported the modernization and education of Jewish women, they also tended to exaggerate women's religiosity and doubt their ability to reform.[79] Similarly, while Communist men preached and encouraged the sovietization of their mothers, sisters, and daughters, they either doubted that the superstitious fairer sex was truly capable of adopting Communist values or purposely depicted Jewish women as "unenlightened elements" in society who could not be trusted with positions of responsibility and power. Female religious and political backwardness was therefore overstated. As the *maskilim* before them, Communist husbands could thereby always rely on the women's foil to explain their own shortcomings and rehabilitate themselves by blaming the other sex. By accusing their "bourgeois" wives, men could claim for themselves more power. After all, their gender made them inherently more trustworthy members of the new Bolshevik society than women.

To take a single but prominent example, Soviet organizations frequently conducted *proverki*, or verifications, to confirm the party-mindedness of Communists. The questions asked to male party members are revealing of the image of women's behavior as potentially religious and anti-Soviet. During the party meeting of the City Slaughterhouse held on October 24, 1924, the Communist cell judged comrade Katzenelson's political consciousness not only on the basis of his participation in social and cultural activities, such as club and theater, but also on the basis of his wife's behavior: "How does your wife relate to you? How does she relate to Communism? Is she religious? How do you regard your wife? Are you trying to involve her in public life?" These queries implied that the questioner assumed the woman/wife to be politically passive, ideologically dangerous, probably religious, and in general, opposed to her husband's allegiance to the party. Katzenelson replied following the party canon on women's liberation: "If I return home late from a meeting, [my wife] reacts properly. My wife is not religious. She cooks on the Sabbath. My wife and I are absolutely equal. At my request, my wife attends the meetings of the workers' wives."[80] It is noteworthy that similar questions about the religiosity and political involvement of a husband were usually not addressed to a woman who was member of the Communist Party. In other words, there was a tacit assumption that the husband of an "enlightened woman" had to necessarily be an "enlightened man." A woman's political consciousness, it was assumed, depended on her husband's level of commitment to the party. This double standard appears clearly in the following case.

On February 1, 1924, at the party-cell meeting of the Minsk Industry Sewing Workers, comrade Levit (a man) accused Kontorovich, a woman and member of the party since 1920, of being married in a Jewish religious ceremony. Kontorovich denied the accusations and defined the event as a "party among comrades" (*tovaricheskaia vecherinka*) and not as a wedding. At the following party-cell meetings, held on May 9 and June 19, 1924, Levit reiterated his accusations against Kontorovich and provided enough evidence to determine that she was indeed married with a Jewish religious ceremony, actually in the home of one of the Minsk rabbis. Levit's accusations were confirmed by a male party member and a female nonparty worker who attended the ceremony. The female worker who witnessed the event also stated, in passing, that Kontorovich's husband was very religious. While the party-cell members promptly connected Kontorovich's socially deviant behavior to her mediocre political knowledge and forced her to undergo verification of her political maturity through a set of questions, they never mentioned the possibility that her religious husband might have persuaded her to have a Jewish ceremony. Furthermore, to avoid eviction from the party, Kontorovich herself did not try to shift the responsibility for her actions on her husband and blame his religious beliefs for her deviant behavior.[81] By contrast—as the discussion about the ritual of circumcision has shown—this conduct had become standard practice among party men who willingly blamed their wives and mothers for their own deeds in order to shun expulsion from the party.

While the Jewish political establishment scorned the archetypal image of female backwardness, it also celebrated women's leading voices in the Jewish Cultural Revolution of the late 1920s. After all, if the most unenlightened element on the Jewish street managed to reject the old ways and joined the struggle against the previous order then every Jew still devoted to religious practice could do the same. Dated February 22, 1928, and entitled "Jewish Working Women against the *Yarmulke*," the first public petition addressed to the Minsk City Soviet to boycott the production of kosher meat in Minsk was read at a women's conference and signed by Jewish women delegates. The petition stated:

> The October revolution ... guided women toward a new way of life [*byt*]. But remains of the old mold, such as the rabbi and the *shohet*, are still trying to fool the working woman, forcing her to buy kosher meat.... We, working women ... are appalled by the fact that the Minsk City Soviet has not taken any measures against this evil. We ... declare that we do not need kosher meat and we ask the City Soviet to take the necessary steps to liberate our proletarian *byt* from the old mold as quickly as possible.[82]

The women delegates who signed this petition were members of an elite Soviet organization, and one can presume that their antireligious, antikosher sentiments were sincere. A member of the Evsektsiia may have suggested to the conference that it adopt the resolution, but this group of women would have eagerly agreed to such a suggestion. Indeed, activist Soviet Jewish women were ashamed of the widespread image of Jewish women as bearers of backwardness and superstition, and they were eager to dissociate themselves from it. To a certain extent, they may have accepted and internalized the negative image of their own group and compensated for their "guilt" with Communist zeal.

Encouraged to be part of the vanguard of the Cultural Revolution on the Jewish street, women were called on to participate in the campaign to collect gold, silver, iron, and copper, thus supporting the industrialization and collectivization campaign and fulfilling the First Five-Year Plan. The Soviet Union launched its gold campaign in 1930, five years before Mussolini urged the female citizens of fascist Italy to donate their golden wedding bands to the motherland in order to boost the country's economy.[83] In the early months of that year, the Minsk Jewish daily published several articles praising women who donated their Sabbath silver candlesticks and goblets to the revolution. So that in February 1930, the workers' wives of the Minsk shoemakers' collective bequeathed their religious objects and samovars to the Industrialization Fund, openly stating that they wished to serve as an example for the workers' wives of other factories in Minsk.[84] During the campaign, brigades of women and schoolchildren would go from house to house and collect religious objects to donate to the Socialist cause. The poet Sore Kahan celebrated Jewish women who supported the industrialization process by donating their jewelry and ceremonial objects to the party, and wrote: "Earrings and rings, candlesticks, samovars, the Kiddush-goblet and the fish pan, take them, remove them, comrades, may it be a contribution to brace our country."⁸⁵

During the 1920s and early 1930s, women's participation in the Bolshevik experiment and contribution to the Cultural Revolution, whether through petitions against the evil forces of Judaism or through donations of religious objects, was largely seen through the prism of conventional and old-fashioned notions of gender relations. Women were not portrayed as factory directors or party-cell secretaries, but as housewives who pledged they would no longer purchase kosher meat and offered their Kiddush goblets to the revolution, and as mothers who wished to see synagogues converted into nurseries to make room for their children.⁸⁶ The conservative approach to the role of Jewish women in Soviet society—clearly at odds with the assumption that the revolution forged new relations between men and women—appears in the Communist notion of female sexual habits as well.

In the 1920s, the sexual mores of Jewish (as well as non-Jewish) women inevitably changed. The early NEP years brought a new family legislation designed to destroy the old social order by liberating women. But the new laws that established equality for the sexes, providing for easy divorce and abortion, led to an explosion of free unions and in turn to a lack of security and an emotional crisis, which affected the personal lives of women especially.⁸⁷ In the words of one of the heroes in Alexandra Kollontai's short stories, "It suddenly dawned on me that if I hadn't had a husband, I would have been in the same position as her, with no job and nowhere to live! . . . [Her eyes] expressed the horror, the misery and the anguish of women without work and without a home, facing the inexorable enemy of unemployment."⁸⁸ Not only did 70 percent of the initial job cutbacks that occurred during the NEP period affect women,⁸⁹ but the thousands of women in "free unions" possessed none of the financial security and legal protection that might have rescued them with registered marriage.⁹⁰

The harsh conditions of the NEP years led to an escalation in prostitution. Young women who moved to the city from the surrounding *shtetlekh* in search of employment were recruited by agents and pimps posted at the railway station, who lured them into prostitution.⁹¹ But the yearning to experiment that distinguished the 1920s also set off a new desire to explore the realm of sexual morality, both for men and women. Experiments in "red love," particularly in the fashion of ménage a trois, became rather common at the time, especially in intellectual milieus. In this respect the correspondence between two Jewish literary critics is enlightening. When addressing Gurevitch (in Moscow) in 1926, Oyslender (from Minsk) informed his friend of a threesome between his wife (the Yiddish poet Mira Khenkina), a young girl studying in the Minsk Musical College, and himself. He mentioned the relationship in passing, with great ease, deeming it the outcome of common sexual behavior and expressing no judgment on the laxity of his wife and the young female student involved with the couple.⁹² But unlike the writers and critics of the time, party leaders drew a clear divide between acceptable sexual behavior for men and women.

In March 1926, the Construction Workers' party cell debated the following case. When a worker was informed by a party member that comrade Vasserman was living with his wife (the Russian verb living, *zhit*, is used here as a euphemism), the worker openly confronted Vasserman and accused him of acting immorally. The party member who made the allegations, however, defended himself asserting that he did not say that Vasserman did such a thing, but rather that he presumed Vasserman could do such a thing. While it is unclear whether Vasserman did in fact sleep with the worker's wife, the image of women that emerges from the document is in tune with the depth of traditional gender notions. In the ensuing discussion, party-cell members seemed to be much more concerned with the way in which the case would affect female union members than with Vasserman's behavior. As one comrade anxiously noted, "[This] may influence women. Rumours about this [case] are already circulating among them."[93] Women appear as susceptible and easily swayed into acting in a sexually improper fashion. Party-cell members feared female promiscuity, which would upset the traditional wife-husband relationship and disrupt the family. By contrast, party-cell members expressed no concern about the possible effect that the case might have on men's conduct. On the contrary, the message conveyed by the party cell was that men could freely experience love even outside the marital bond, and that just like Vasserman, they were not expected to conform to the traditional husband-wife relation.

Some photographic images of women activists on the Jewish street corroborate this conservative view of gender roles in times of revolution. Taken in the second part of the 1920s for the JDC, which sponsored a number of Jewish organizations in the city, the photographs of the Minsk Evpedtekhnikum provide a window on the notable differences between women and men with regard to clothing and roles. In all seventeen photographs, which reproduce students and teachers in the classroom, dormitory, and yard of the college, most female students are barefoot. However, the great majority of their male counterpart wears the black leather boots of the Bolshevik style of the day. In the photographs depicting groups of students, a number of women hold flowers. Two photographs represent women engaged in traditional female occupations, such as washing clothes, sewing, and ironing. By contrast, another photograph portrays men cutting wood, holding axes, and lifting bundles of hay into the carriage. The division of roles is conveyed most starkly in the photograph reproducing the students learning to shoot. On the background of a red flag with the Yiddish and Russian inscription "Jewish Pedagogical Training College of Minsk," male students hold rifles, aimed in the direction of the photographer. Women students, who represented three-quarters of the college's student body, are not holding rifles as to indicate that the symbol of revolutionary power belonged exclusively to men. Even in the new Communist Jewish institution for the creation of a vanguard of Red teachers, women were imagined playing a strikingly traditional role.[94]

The typology of photographic representations of women slightly changed in the mid and late-1930s. Photographs of modern and heroic Jewish women as powerful

Figure 10. Students of the Jewish Pedagogical Training College learning to shoot, Minsk, 1925. Courtesy of the American Jewish Joint Distribution Committee Archives (Collection 21/32 Russia).

Stakhanovites rewarded for exceptional diligence in increasing all records of production in their factory, or as courageous pilots who flew planes from Minsk to Moscow, emerged in the pages of the Minsk Jewish daily. Yet, the lasting power of traditional notions of femininity, together with the pronatalist policies advocated by Stalin as the country prepared for the anticipated aggression from Nazi Germany, led to the crystallization of the assumption that women had primary responsibility for child and family care. Photos like the one depicting Sore Patent holding her newborn son and surrounded by her husband Leybe and their eight children became the norm in the pages of *Oktyabr* during the second half of the 1930s.[95]

Bourgeois Domesticity or Revolutionary Agency?

As in any other modern society, the greatest challenge posed to Jewish women in the Soviet system was negotiating the role of active participants in the public arena, in particular the workplace, with the role of custodians of the hearth. Despite Communist theory, once they got married, most women, Jewish and non-Jewish alike, left their job and withdrew to the private sphere of the home. Even those who had served in the ranks of the Bund or other revolutionary parties, and were later employed in Communist agencies, usually gave up social and political life after their wedding or after bearing children. The same happened to women who tied the knot with prominent Communist leaders. Upon marrying Mikhail Gebelev, a top figure in interwar Minsk Party life and secretary of the underground Minsk District Committee under Nazi occupation, Chasia Gebeleva quit her job at the Bobruisk sawmill and became a housewife, as "it was necessary to set up for him normal work conditions."[96] A short story about Itke, who in spite of her six children does not renounce her commitment to public life but attends the Minsk City Soviet meetings bringing her infant Marxele, or Little Marx, with her and breastfeeding him in front of the presidium, sounds like exaggerated rhetoric when compared to the real status of married women.[97]

Even before the Bolshevik rise to power women usually gave up their jobs upon getting married. The author of a study about large-scale factories in turn-of the-century-Minsk, entitled "Jewish Workers on the Eve of the Workers' Movement" (Evreiskie rabochie na zare rabochego dvizheniia) and published in 1931, confirmed, "Jewish women never remained in the factory after they married . . . [which] meant that they considered their position in the factory . . . , and their social condition . . . as temporary."[98] In spite of their rhetorical efforts, the Bolsheviks did not reverse this trend. During his 1929 trip to the Soviet Union, Khanin noted how Soviet women worked in professions previously restricted to men. Young women studied apprenticeship as locksmiths, turners, carpenters. "They are trained in physically tiring jobs . . . with a saw and an axe . . . , with calloused hands covered in glue, and faces covered in grease, holding the heavy hammer." After three years, continued Khanin, these young women graduated from the professional school and became employed in a factory. But as soon as they got married and had children, they would quit their jobs.[99]

Mothers committed to public life in the city could rarely count on the support of social infrastructures to attend political conferences.[100] On October 14, 1923, at a women delegates' meeting in Minsk, comrade Zilberstein inquired whether the city clubs would provide women workers with child-care facilities. Rebecca Meliakhovitskaia, who was in charge of Yiddish-language propaganda in the Women's Department in Minsk, replied that women workers rarely attended the club anyway, as they were generally not used to participate in public life. She suggested instead that the Women's Department concentrate its efforts on single young women. While older women workers often had a family, "younger ones could be transformed, in due time, into staunch members of our Communist Party."[101] The women's meeting eventually discarded the suggestion to set up child-care facilities for mothers. This was clearly not a major concern for party institutions.

On September 29, 1927, the Komsomol cell of the almost exclusively Jewish Tailors' Union in Minsk, debated the behavior of a Communist woman who was also a mother. Comrade Shulman, it was noticed, had not attended party-cell meetings for more than one year and had not paid membership dues for the month of January. Shulman justified her conduct by explaining that she had stopped going to the meetings while she was pregnant. After the birth of her child, she was forced to discontinue her political activities due to the absence of a "housekeeper" who could take care of the newborn baby. One comrade reacted warning against the widespread phenomenon of young women who broke away from Communist work once they got married, noticing that those who were truly devoted to the party attended cell meetings anyway. Another comrade dismissed Shulman's conduct and noticed that she was "at risk of being forced out of the party." While Shulman was ultimately not expelled from the party—although she was "given a warning" and asked to pay her late dues—the party cell made no effort to come up with a solution that would make it possible for young mothers to be politically active.[102] While it is not particularly surprising to find out that in Soviet society—as in any other modern society—taking care of a family made it complicated for Jewish women to participate in cultural activities and enjoy leisure time, and that, for example, in 1926, the reading room of the Jewish Central Library in Minsk reported that with the exception of schoolgirls there were no women among its readers;[103] it is indeed remarkable to learn that Jewish women like comrade Shulman, who were members of the vanguard of Soviet society were left alone to face the difficult challenge of integrating their role of mothers and Communists, and that most times, in the absence of further assistance, ceased to participate actively in party life.[104]

* * *

What positions did Jewish women occupy in Soviet enterprises, such as factories and party organizations? What kind of careers did they preferably pursue, and in which professions did they excel the most? While the new economic policies adopted by the Soviets drove women into higher education and new occupational structures formerly dominated by men, female workers and activists rarely broke through the glass ceiling in the fields of higher economic management and politics. On the work-plant, for instance, positions of responsibility remained tightly closed to women, even when a high proportion of women workers belonged to the party. The absence of women in leadership positions might have resulted from the combination of two factors: on the one hand, the prejudice of factory managers (who were mostly men) against women seeking a career on the work-plant. On the other hand, the increase in workload for executive personnel members that meant that skilled workers and managers were expected to spend more time in the factory and less at home, something that women could not always handle.

An examination of the existing data on party membership reveals that the number of Jewish women who became members of the Communist Party did not grow significantly from 1921 to 1928 and certainly not as much as their male counterparts did at that time. In August 1921, 221 women in Minsk were members and candidates of the party. Of these, Jewish women represented the overwhelming majority, counting 160 (with only 34 Russian women, 13 Polish, and 7 Belorussian). More than one-third of the women (77) had formerly been members of the Bund.[105] Over the course of seven years, the number of Communist Jewish women increased by a little more than 200, that is, it doubled. On January 1, 1928, of the 1,542 Jewish members of the Communist Party, Jewish women were 328, that is, 11 percent of party members; of the 591 Jewish party candidates, women were 166 (they were 42 in 1921). Because the data from 1928 does not include the city only, but accounts for the whole district area of Minsk, the increase appears even more negligible.[106] It would seem, thus, that in spite of the alleged political emancipation brought about by the revolution, not many Jewish women had access to the principal and most powerful institution in the public arena, namely the party.[107]

Indeed, for some Jewish women pursuing a political career became the priority. In her autobiography, Rebecca Gimmelshtein portrays the unusual path to success of a Soviet Jewish woman in the early 1920s. Born in a *shtetl* in the Minsk *guberniia*, in a destitute family, Rebecca joined the Bund in 1904 and remained active in the Jewish party until 1920. When in 1919 her husband tried to dissuade her from working and being politically active, she left him and joined the western front as a special-mission agent. In 1921, upon completing the local institute of economics, Rebecca was hired in the statistics bureau of the Belorussian Council of National Economy in Minsk and served as the chair of its Communist Party cell. She later became the director of one of the largest stores in the newly established Minsk Central Workers' Cooperative.[108] What is noteworthy here, besides the exceptional career and female economic independence apart from marriage, is the outright sense of pride with which Rebecca stated that she abandoned her husband because he prevented her involvement in public life. She presumably did not remarry.

Jewish women who applied to join the Communist Party belonged to different social and political backgrounds and were driven by different motives. Some were former Bundists, some were not. Some came from religious homes, against which they had rebelled, while others grew up in a less traditional environment. Beginning in 1923, a woman by the name of Brener applied to join the party four consecutive times. All four times the application was rejected on the grounds of her Bundist past. More specifically, having served in the Bund's Central Committee, she could hardly be reeducated into a true Communist. In October 1925, following her fifth attempt, Brener's tenacity was finally rewarded, and she was accepted as a party candidate.[109] Born in 1894, the Minsk textile worker Chaia Mukaseia was expelled from the party during one of its earlier purging cycles, in 1921. She became a party candidate again in 1932, at the relatively late age of thirty-eight. But because of her Bundist background, in 1933 she was excluded from party candidacy for a second time.[110] Born in 1910, Berta Abramova was the daughter of a sexton in a local synagogue. She had completed secondary school in 1926 and had been working in the Minsk brush factory since 1927. In 1931, Abramova was accepted as a party candidate.[111]

In defiance of the religious milieu in which she lived, the young Rozavskaia had joined the Komsomol in 1925. While she was politically active and diligently attended party meetings, she lived with her religious father concealing from him the nature of her political involvement. When the Komsomol found out about this, in August

1927, a cell member reproached Rozavskaia and encouraged her to openly display "her Komsomol behavior" at home: being part of the Communist Youth Organization was a comprehensive way of life that could not be limited to meetings and membership dues.[112] Sonia Rozina, member of a poor family from Uzlian, a *shtetl* near Minsk, also had to struggle against her relatives' traditional background in order to become part of the Soviet political vanguard. After moving to Minsk, Sonia helped organize a Komsomol cell, becoming its secretary, and a school that met in the women's section of one of Minsk's synagogues, becoming its director. In 1922, following a violent clash with her family she enrolled in the Evpedtekhnikum, against her will: her uncle, in whose apartment in Minsk she lived, refused to have a *komsomolka* dwell in his home and kicked her out. Sonia moved to the college dormitory, worked with pioneers and homeless children, and eventually became a teacher in a Soviet Jewish school.[113]

Some Jewish women came to play a key role in promoting Communism on the Jewish street. A name that often appears in the Evsektsiia protocols and general party meetings' reports is that of Sara Mariasina, who during the 1920s became a successful Soviet Jewish woman. Born in 1890, Mariasina had been a member of the Bund prior to the revolution. In 1920, she joined the Communist Party and in 1921 became a member of the Minsk Evsektsiia and Jewish section of the People's Commissariat for Education. A well-educated woman, who besides Yiddish and Russian knew French and German, Mariasina had worked as a pedagogue before the revolution and had been the director of the local Sewing Professional School Shveiprom since 1916. A member of the Minsk City Soviet, she was active in the Zhenotdel and participated in the debates regarding the status of Jewish women and the use of Yiddish in the city factories with a high percentage of Jewish women workers. In 1925, she became director of the Cultural Department of the Union of Education Workers (Rabpros). At the end of 1925, at the age of thirty-five, she applied to law school at Belorussian State University. In 1929, while acting as a supervisor for Jewish culture in the District Education Department, Mariasina published a book on the new Soviet pedagogical system, entitled *The Old and New School*.[114] While Mariasina's success story as a Soviet and Jewish woman during the 1920s is exceptional, it is also indicative of the breadth of new opportunities available to Jewish women in the field of politics, education, and social life in a Soviet city.

Young Jewish men and women, often from underprivileged families in the *shtetlekh* of Belorussia, enrolled en masse in the new educational institutions established in Minsk. Women usually outnumbered Jewish men in Soviet learning institutions operating in Yiddish, which reflects how education remained a "female" realm even under the Soviets. The student body of the Jewish Pedagogical Training College was mostly female.[115] In 1925–26, out of 159 students, 109 were women.[116] The Evpedtekhnikum also served as a venue for spreading Communism among Jewish women, particularly among those who came from destitute families and grew up outside of the Belorussian capital. Once they moved to Minsk and enrolled in the college, they became exposed, for the first time, to Communist ideas, to a Socialist way of life, and to the principles of Soviet citizenship. In January 1925, Jewish women represented the majority of the institution's party-cell members: out of eighteen members, twelve were women.[117]

The life of M. Margon, a young woman who moved to Minsk to attend the Evpedtekhnikum, provides an example of Jewish women's social mobility through education in Soviet institutions. Margon was born in 1904 in a *shtetl* near Bobruisk. Her father was a blacksmith and her mother worked at home knitting stockings; she had three siblings, all of whom had studied in the heder (not herself) where they had become literate in Hebrew and Yiddish. At the age of twelve Margon was employed by a tailor as an apprentice. But once her father got sick, she was forced to engage in manual labor in order to support the family. In early 1922, she moved to Minsk to study in the Evpedtekhnikum. By 1927, Margon was completing her fourth year of studies and was a candidate in the Komsomol. As she wrote in her autobiography, during summer vacation she went back to the *shtetl* and worked in the local pioneer brigade unit.[118] Not only was Margon learning about Communism and bringing her knowledge back to the *shtetl*, thus fulfilling the college's primary objective; she also benefited from an education (and room and board) free of charge, something quite unlikely in pre-revolutionary years.

More women than men enrolled in the Jewish Department at Belorussian State University: in 1928–29, 102 female students (out of a total of 171 students) enrolled in the Jewish Department at BGU.[119] Jewish men, it seems, were more inclined to apply to the Belorussian Department. In fact, the Jewish Department, in which the primary language of instruction was Yiddish, did not guarantee its graduates an employment outside the Soviet Jewish educational, scholarly, and political institutions. This explains why in March 1932, there were only eight female first-year students in the Jewish section of Law School (and zero men), and fourteen female and two male second-year students in the Jewish section of that same school.[120] This enrollment pattern possibly reflects the deeply entrenched social expectation for men to achieve a successful career (more likely through Russian and/or Belorussian) and for women to be economically dependent on their husbands. The gender differentiation in Jewish education that existed in nineteenth-century Eastern Europe persisted under the Soviets, but in a different fashion. Girls from traditional middle-class Jewish families attended Russian-language public schools while their brothers studied in heders and yeshivas. Because girls' education did not matter much, parents did not pay attention to their attending Russian schools.[121] Similarly, Jewish girls from upwardly mobile working-class families in the Soviet Union were more likely to attend Yiddish institutions than their brothers—who usually enrolled in Belorussian or Russian schools—because the quality of their schooling as well as their employment mattered less.[122] In spite of the ongoing attempt to boost their prestige, Soviet Jewish institutions ultimately retained a lower status than their Russian and sometimes even Belorussian-language counterparts, thus enrolling women more easily than men.

In stark contrast with the role that Jewish women played in Jewish secondary and higher educational institutions, both as students and teachers, their proportion in Yiddish intellectual and literary circles was close to nothing. As in the case of party leadership, male preeminence remained intact among the Jewish cultural intelligentsia. While Soviet Jewish life made allowances for female economic power and social activism, it virtually foreclosed the possibility of an intellectual life for women. There were no women serving on the editorial board of the main Soviet Jewish newspapers issued in Minsk. In 1938, of the ten members on the editorial board of the literary journal *Shtern*, not one of them was a woman. Jewish women were also absent from the Minsk local group of young Yiddish writers and poets. At the All-Belorussian Conference of Jewish Komsomol Writers, held in the city in January 1932, there were no women participants.[123]

A careful look at the pages of the monthly *Shtern* reveals the minor share allotted to women's voices. During 1932, only two poems by female writers were published in the literary journal—one was by Sore Kahan, who at the time was the only woman member of the Jewish section of the Writers' Union of Belorussia.[124] Besides the two poems, *Shtern* published an article by the literary critic Rivka Rubin, who upon graduating from the Evpedtekhnikum and the Jewish Department at BGU, had moved to Moscow to join the Jewish literary establishment. Perhaps her distinguished status as a writer in the capital city of the USSR compensated for her low status as a woman and enabled her to get published in *Shtern*. But even though the name of Rivka Rubin appears quite regularly in the journal, the famed Jewish literary critics of Minsk remained men. The appraisals of Yasha Bronshteyn and Chatskl Dunets, who reviewed the work of Jewish writers in Minsk and elsewhere, usually pertained only to male writers' creativity and not to the works of female poets. Rivka Rubin herself rarely, if ever, reviewed the works of Jewish women writers.

Stalin's Women and the Myth of Equality

Jewish women workers actively participated in the Stakhanovite movement, the production movement named after the legendary achievements by Alexei Stakhanov who in 1935 exceeded his quota for digging coal in the Donets Basin by some 1,400 percent. The Stakhanovite movement, and its "shock workers" (or *Udarniki*) who through prizes and incentives exceeded their production quotas, inaugurated a new stage in Socialist competition and quickly spread through the factories of the Soviet Union. Comrade Levina became the hero of labor of the Stakhanovite movement in the Minsk brush factory. On December 11, 1935, the factory's party cell appraised the movement's status and pointed out that the number of Stakhanovite workers increased daily thanks to Levina: "[She] broke the world record.... Our Levina used to be such an insignificant person, nobody noticed her.... [Now thanks to her] the number of Stakhanovite workers grows by the hour."[125] Women workers, Jewish and non-Jewish alike, were drawn to the Stakhanovite movement particularly by the honor and privileges that the position entailed. Stakhanovite workers had access to better-quality food at a lower price, movie tickets, and improved living conditions.[126] In light of the rearrangement of apartment buildings and chronic shortage of living space in the city after the revolution, the promise of enhanced living conditions played a major part in luring women (as well as men) into the movement. If before World War I only one family lived in one apartment, under the Bolsheviks five to seven families lived in that same apartment. This rationalization of living space affected especially women, who generally took care of the home. The kitchen, where six to seven women were forced to cook together, would often become the theater of clashes over missing salt or oil.[127]

In early 1937, at the age of eighteen, Fanye Melnik became a Stakhanovite in the seam factory March 8. Raised under Soviet conditions, she never "experienced destitution, hunger or exploitation as the youth abroad." "I was one of the first in our factory to work with the Stakhanovite method," stated Fanye, and continued, "Each day I fill out my [production] plan by 150–160 percent; the Stakhanovite method taught me culture, timeliness, and discipline, and made me earn more." The extra money gave her the possibility to engage in those leisure activities that made a young woman in her late teens content: "Not only can I buy [new] clothes, but I can also go to the theater and movies."[128]

For some women, contributing to the Soviet industrialization endeavor and joining the ranks of the shock workers, was a major source of pride, enthusiasm, and optimism. In the fall of 1932, Alexander Pomerantz, a Communist Yiddish writer and political activist who had left Belorussia in 1921 to settle in America, met the young Yudes Grozovski. He met her at a literary evening in Minsk, while he was traveling in the USSR, through the Yiddish poet she was sentimentally involved with. Yudes spoke a good literary Yiddish, so much so that Pomerantz thought at first that she as well was a writer.[129] He soon found out that upon graduating from the Minsk Construction Technical Institute, Yudes began working as an engineer in key city buildings such as government offices, the Minsk electricity station, and the kitchen factory on Soviet Street. With a production of forty thousand meals per day, the latter became the first kitchen factory in Belorussia and the capital's main construction during the Second Five-Year Plan. Pomerantz was surprised that "a girl, and furthermore a Jewish girl, should erect buildings, be a foreman, a construction engineer."[130] Yudes, who saw the factory's chimney she was building as "her poem to the Five-Year Plan," combined harmoniously her ideological commitment to the system with her love for the Yiddish poet. As she wrote to him on the white margin of a photo depicting Lenin in his cabinet, "This picture of our great leader shall remind you of our great love . . . April 25, second year of the Second Five-Year Plan."[131]

While women were needed in the workforce in connection with the Five-Year Plans, they were also encouraged to have large families and view motherhood as a patriotic duty to increase the Soviet population. Stalin promoted family stability by constricting divorce laws, outlawing abortions, and increasing state funding for child-care facilities. Women generally supported the family policies of the 1930s, or at least favored them over the insecurity and chaos of the 1920s.[132] The number of divorces in the city of Minsk dropped from 173 in the month of June, 1936, to 11 in the month of July of that same year.[133] But the 1930s' mother beaming over a large family implied a less public role for women and the persistence of men in positions of power. While professing equality, the Soviet gender system valorized traditional women's deeds and gave priority to heroic masculinity.[134]

In September 1936, *Oktyabr* published two short articles about the workers Zilman and Kaplan who received a two thousand-ruble bonus from the state for the birth of their seventh child; Kaplan triumphantly even stated that he hoped "to have an eighth child by the end of next year."[135] While the name of Zilman's wife Nina is mentioned in passing, Kaplan's wife doesn't even make a cameo appearance in the paper's report, despite the childrearing and domestic work that alongside thousands of other Jewish and non-Jewish Soviet women she was expected to carry out. Another article about the ideal Soviet Jewish woman of the late 1930s, which describes a Minsk courtyard where Moshe Baranov lived with his eight children, juxtaposes two different female models. On the one hand, a woman with no children, employed as a bank clerk, who liked to stroll on the city streets wearing lipstick and holding a cigarette in her mouth. Whenever her husband tried to convince her to have a child, she would reply, "I am not so backward to end up sitting at home taking care of children. . . . [I]f he wants children he can go and find himself someone who will hang up . . . little shirts in the courtyard every day." On the other hand, Moshe's wife, Leyke Baranov, whose mythical motherly traits classify her as the ideal Stalinist woman, "was born to have children." "Quiet as a lamb, industrious, with the patience of a born pedagogue who never becomes angry, . . . you will never hear her shout, curse the children, she just loves their screeches . . . and when they all go to bed she sits by the table and . . . sows buttons."[136]

At the heyday of Stalin's conservatism and patriarchalism, Soviet women were thus expected to contribute to the building of Socialism primarily as mothers and wives and only marginally as workers and professionals. The shift back to the private sphere of the home led to the glorification of a new kind of "Soviet bourgeois domesticity."[137] So that when in 1936 the Minsk heavy industry tried to get workers' wives to be more active in the social life of the factories, it did not concern itself with teaching them Communism and party history and encouraging them to correspond in the wall-newspaper on the work-plant, as in the 1920s. In the second half of the 1930s, social life in the factories meant for women managing the factory's kitchen, supervising the kindergarten, and organizing embroidery circles. As Paulina Laskat, wife of the master craftsman in the Minsk Voroshilov factory, noted, "I am proud of my homeland and the role my family plays in building Socialism: my son Felix is an engineer who actively contributes to the Stakhanovite movement." She herself was active in social life (she ran the embroidery circle), read belle-lettre, often went to the theater and movies, owned a radio at home, and in the past eight years had been three times to a vacation resort, once together with her husband.[138]

The ideal of women as "vigilant flame-keepers" penetrated the public as well as private sphere. Even at home, in their "new" position of guardians of the hearth, Soviet Jewish women partook in the ongoing struggle to unmask and purge the "enemies of the people" that engulfed Minsk from 1936 to 1938. At times they debunked their husbands' actions and supported the accusations made by NKVD agents, mostly out of fear of retaliation against themselves and their families, but sometimes they stood up for their indicted husbands, as devoted wives. On August 3, 1937, B. E. Agurskaia, wife of prominent Communist Jewish activist Shmuel Agursky, wrote a letter to Stalin immediately following her husband's arrest, pleading for Agursky's life. In her appeal she referred to herself as a nonparty woman, as the wife of a Communist, and the mother of three small children: "Dear Josif Vissarionovich!" she wrote, "At this critical and difficult time in my life, I turn to you as a dear father, in the name of my children, asking you to save their father, a devoted member of the party and of our Motherland, from moral and physical destruction." She emphasized Agursky's twenty-year service in the party, his pioneering work in establishing Jewish Communist institutions, his proletarian origins, the numerous books on the history of the revolutionary movement he wrote in spite of his lack of formal education, and the role he played in exposing former Bundists, Poale-Zion leaders, Trotskyites, and Belorussian National Democrats, in Belorussia and elsewhere in the Soviet Union.

Besides the triumphant ode to her husband's life and work, behavior expected of a faithful Soviet wife and compassionate mother, Agurskaia did not stop short of expressing the roughness of a truly Bolshevik language. She wrote, "I never would have dared to turn to you [Stalin] for help if I suspected that the accusations brought against my husband were true. On the contrary, if I had the slightest doubt about his devotion to the Party of Lenin and Stalin, . . . I would be the first one to throw a stone at him." At the end of the letter, Agurskaia reaffirmed her identity of mother and wife: "Dear father Josif Vissarionovich, knowing how much you care about people, I turn to you on behalf of my three little ones . . . save the honor and life of their father, who fought arm in hand in the ranks of the Red Guards."[139] Petitioning—daringly—during the frightful years of the Great Terror, and at the risk of her own life, the great architect of the purges, the revolutionary wife and mother sought to fulfill her traditional role of supporter of her husband's cause and guardian of the peace of the home.[140]

Conclusion

This chapter has traced the ways in which the revolutionary changes introduced by the Bolshevik rise to power affected the lives of Jewish women. The campaign to solve the "women's question" on the Jewish street, launched in the early 1920s as a key component in the sovietization process of the Jews, was often led by former Bundist women who came to serve in the ranks of the Minsk Evsektsiia and Zhenotdel. For the first time after the collapse of the tsarist empire, the female activists who joined the ranks of these two political institutions acted in public political settings both qua Jews and qua women, at times even successfully merging these two identities with their commitment to Communism. But the Zhenotdel, which in Minsk took on some of the features of a Soviet Jewish institution, was not able to overcome the forces that regarded its work with resentment, or at least with indifference, and that believed women should carry on raising children, cooking, and housekeeping. Therefore, the attempt to transform women into "agents of revolution" and channels of sovietization in the factory often jarred with the way in which men imagined Jewish women. While some fathers, husbands, and brothers viewed women as passive "objects of revolution" and backward upholders of tradition who could be reforged in the revolutionary spirit only through male assistance, others frowned upon their mothers', wives', and sisters' commitment to public life mostly out of fear of the new progressive Jewish woman.

Moreover, the conviction that women were religious almost by nature, an assumption confirmed by the gendered nature of official antireligious campaigns, led Jewish men, party and nonparty members alike, to blame their wives for their own religious practice. A study of the representation of Jewish women in the context of Soviet society provides valuable insight into the social dimensions of gender in Soviet history, shedding light on the relationship between Jewish women and men in the first decades following the Bolshevik Revolution. While male sexism toward women is not surprising, the fact that members of the Communist Party—as well as nonparty members—were resisting sovietization through their own wives and mothers is indeed remarkable. By blaming them for their own behavior, or preventing them from being active in the public sphere, they were somehow defying the theory and tenets of the new system.

The conservative image of Jewish women, which seemingly prevailed throughout the interwar period, disregarding the assumption that the revolution forged new relations between men and women, was conceivably intensified by the provincial character of the city of Minsk. Here patriarchal and old-fashioned inclinations might have been more widespread than in other large Soviet cities. In other words, traditional assumptions about women and the role they should play in society may have been more resilient in the Belorussian capital than in a modern metropolis like Moscow. In Minsk, the demographic changes in the Jewish (and non-Jewish) population were mostly determined by the ongoing influx of new immigrants from surrounding *shtetlekh* and villages who had not exactly been exposed to the modernization trends of urban life. By contrast, the Jews (and non-Jews) who settled in Moscow were usually from small or medium-sized cities rather than *shtetlekh* and villages, and they consequently had already witnessed the porousness of conventional gender roles and gender boundaries.

For women (Jewish and non-Jewish alike) the revolution stood for dramatic upward mobility, professionalization, technical and medical education, and entry into all sectors of the urban economy. From 1926 to 1939 the percentage of literate females in the USSR rose from 42.7 to 81.6 percent, and the proportion of women in institutions of higher education rose from 31 percent in 1926 to 58 percent in 1940.[141]

Did the reticent attitude of Communist men toward Jewish women, that is, their veiled ideal of women-wives-mothers as home-actors rather than participants in the public arena, determine the actual role that Jewish women played in Soviet society? To some extent it did. A relatively small percentage of Jewish women held positions of power and responsibility in party organs, factory management, and Jewish cultural and literary institutions. In 1933, in the Minsk factory Oktyabr, in which the workers were almost exclusively Jewish, and where women represented 63 percent of the workforce, only 6 percent of women workers took up technical positions of inspectors, managers, and examiners of factory goods.[142] This low percentage was in spite of the fact that a relatively high proportion of women workers in the factory were also party members. Similarly, when the publisher *Der Emes* issued a series of twenty portraits of Jewish writers, in 1936, it did not include any portraits of female writers.[143] At the same time, however, the officially articulated ideal of gender equality had real impact. A large proportion of Jewish women who did not necessarily rise to the higher echelons of society or serve in Soviet decision-making bodies did contribute to the sovietization of the Jewish street, as educators and role models, as members of the Komsomol and Stakhanovites.

But of course, as Jewish women became more active in the workplace and public life, the tension between their role as guardians of the hearth and agents of revolution presumably grew. The unsympathetic attitude of party organizations and institutions vis-à-vis women-mothers, as well as male unease about female empowerment, deepened this tension.

7 Jewish Ordinary Life in the Midst of Extraordinary Purges

1934–1939

[A people] that was not a people before and that never would have become a people without the Lenin-Stalin nationality policy. This is the voice of the Jewish people.[1]

I didn't know where my notion of Jewishness came from, but I know it seeped through at home.[2]

BETWEEN 600,000 AND 2,000,000 Soviet citizens lost their lives in Stalin's terror campaign and witch hunt for "enemies, saboteurs, spies, and bourgeois-nationalists."[3] The political repression targeted first of all Communist Party members, government officials, and Red Army leaders who, accused of conspiring with capitalist countries against the Soviet Union, were executed by shooting or sent to labor camps. From 1936 to 1939, terror mushroomed across the capitals, towns, villages, and collective farms of the Soviet Union, in a system of institutionalized denunciations, in a climate of suspicion and spy mania. Those labeled "enemies of the people" by the NKVD were forced to write confessions naming their conspiratorial associates. They became "'plague-bearers,' . . . who . . . infected all around."[4] Whether fired, arrested, or killed, most members of the party leadership and the trade and industry management experienced the Terror, from the chairman of the Committee on Physical Education of the BSSR, accused of owning a luxurious apartment in Minsk and frequently getting drunk, to the supervisor for bread production in Belorussia, personally held accountable for the drop off in bread making and the swelling lines to buy bread across the city. In June 1937, the chairman of the Belorussian Supreme Soviet, A. N. Cherviakov, arrested on charges of "Right Opportunism," threw himself from the window of the fifth floor of the Minsk NKVD building during his interrogation.[5] Like several other Soviet leaders he chose suicide in a desperate attempt to protect perhaps his family or friends who could become enemies-by-association and be accused of counterrevolutionary actions against the motherland. The attack on the Belorussian political leadership, launched from Moscow, opened up a Pandora's box in Minsk, as terror encroached upon all walks of life. In 1937–38, Minsk's cultural, professional, and party elite was largely swept away.

Stalin's terror inevitably affected Jewish life in the city, as the most prominent leaders of Minsk's Jewish cultural organizations and academic institutions were purged. In a uniquely violent fashion—compared to other Soviet centers—leading figures on the Jewish street were killed and Yiddish-language institutions closed down. Accusations against imagined vestiges of "Bundism" resurfaced stubbornly in the form of fierce attacks in the Soviet Jewish schools and in city factories with a large Jewish management and workforce. The charge of "Bundism," as synonymous of "anti-Soviet counterrevolutionary activity" and "nationalism," became exceptionally common in Minsk, even exceeding charges of alleged Zionism.

But Soviet Jewish life in the late 1930s, so scantily researched, should not be associated with the brutality of the purges and let alone it should not be portrayed as the utter obliteration of Jewish life and identity. Purging the Jewish street from so-called bourgeois-nationalists and enemies of the people, while affecting severely the lives of Jews did not erase altogether ethnic self-identification among the great majority of the Jewish population of Minsk. The preservation of overwhelmingly Jewish neighborhoods throughout the city, where Yiddish continued to be spoken and heard, as well as the celebration of new Jewish heroes, such as the Jewish Stakhanovite, influenced the persistence and even revival of Jewish ethnic identity in the second half of the 1930s. Furthermore, and perhaps most importantly, the awareness of thriving anti-Semitism abroad—compared to the official intolerance against anti-Semitism at home—marked a new development in national pride and self-esteem among Soviet Jews in the latter part of the 1930s.

Ordinary Life in the 1930s

> Minsk is no longer the dull gloomy *shtetl* of the past with its small wooden sidewalks.... Minsk is now a city with a boisterous lively activity, with a vibrant cultural life at events and institutions, everywhere.[6]

In his satiric literary masterpiece *Zelmenyaner*, Moshe Kulbak described the sovietization of a Jewish family in the Belorussian capital. Narrated as a generational struggle between the old uncles and aunts and the young nephews and nieces, the adjustment to Soviet society entailed not only the acceptance of modernity, made of electricity and literacy, but also the systematic rejection of Judaism and Jewish traditions. The younger generation, spearheaded by Bere the Bolshevik, brought the revolution to the family's courtyard imposing its new practices upon a baffled older generation divested of its pre-revolutionary mores. This trend culminated in Bere's decision to call his son Marat after the leader of the French Revolution, and his refusal to have the newborn "barbarically" circumcised.[7] The younger generation was therefore stronger than the older one and ultimately succeeded in its sovietizing endeavor as the uncles and aunts gradually retired to the margins of the courtyard.

Figure 11. View of Lenin Street, from Freedom Square to Sovetskaia Street, 1930s. Courtesy of the Belorussian State Archives of Film and Photography (Collection 0–23478).

But Kulbak's novel also captured an important continuity factor crucial for the understanding of pre–World War II Soviet Jewish life, especially but not exclusively in the cities of the former Pale of Settlement: namely, the persistence of the ethnic neighborhood. While the traditions and practices that for centuries had guaranteed the preservation of Jewish identity increasingly faded away, most Jews still lived in the same neighborhoods among other Jews, thus upholding their ethnic identity. While leaving for Moscow and Leningrad became extremely trendy in the 1930s and a prerequisite for success, most Jews did not move there.[8] Some members of the Zelmenyaner dynasty moved to Vladivastok, but eventually returned to their courtyard in Minsk. Nearly all young Zelmenyaner stayed put and went on living in the same courtyard established by their founding father Reb Zelmele Khvost long before the revolution. Bere's cousin Sonye, who, ignoring the Jewish nuptial customs, married a Belorussian man, remained in the Zelmenyaner courtyard with her *goysh* husband. And even after moving to a new place in downtown Minsk, constantly returned to Zelmele's courtyard to hang out with family members. Kulbak furthermore accentuated the continuity across generations that flowed from their sharing the intimate common space of a single courtyard.[9] It seems as if Kulbak argued in the novel that so long as Jews lived in dense compact neighborhoods together, there would be a measure of continuity in their identity and way of life despite the changes brought about by sovietization.

In a place like Minsk, the geographic stability of the ethnic neighborhood represented a compelling challenge to the centripetal force of assimilation unleashed by the industrialization campaign of the 1930s. Miron Kagan, a native of Minsk who worked in the city as a telephone technician until 1939, when he was drafted into the Red Army, recalled, "I didn't feel that Minsk was a multinational city before the war, it was a Jewish city, where more than 85–90 percent of the population was Jewish. The concentration of Jews was so great that one didn't even feel the presence of other nationalities besides the Jews. This is what I felt."[10] The sheer number of Jews living in the city (approximately 71,000 in 1939, or 30 percent of the capital's population),[11] and their concentration in specific city neighborhoods, led Miron to misconceive and inflate the ratio of Jews vis-à-vis the non-Jewish city residents.

The Soviet Jewish neighborhood became an original mixture of Jewish historical spaces and new Soviet Jewish spaces. For example, a number of Jewish urban spaces were located in the Lower Market, or Old Town, as Nemiga was called before the revolution: The Peretz Jewish Library; the Evpedtekhnikum (former Talmud-Torah); the tailors' cooperative Proletarii, which, while not a Jewish institution, employed a majority of Jewish workers;[12] the Hirsh Lekert monument, which stood on the park in Freedom Square, adjacent to Nemiga; the former Foygl-shul, a synagogue requisitioned in 1929 and turned into a cultural institution for the Nemiga bread factory workers (also, largely Jewish);[13] one of the oldest Jewish cemeteries in the city; and the Soviet Jewish school no. 26, which, inaugurated in 1926 in the former apartment of a Minsk priest, was located in the heart of Yiddish-speaking Nemiga.[14] The proximity of these Jewish urban spaces, coupled with Jewish residential segregation, promoted ethnic self-identification among Jews, countering the speed of assimilation that was more rapid in other "non-Jewish" neighborhoods of the city. In spite of grandiose Soviet urban planning (which did not always materialize), Jewish neighborhoods such as this one survived in the city until World War II.[15]

* * *

With the erection of the Belorussian State University campus, with new dorms and classrooms; the massive Stalinist building Home of the Red Army, with the first swimming pool in Belorussia; the Kirov stadium, which seated eight thousand people for sporting events; the hippodrome for equestrian races; and the airport, with flights to and from Moscow, Minsk was turning into an authentic Soviet capital.[16] In mid-1937, the City Soviet approved a budget of two million rubles to rebuild the provincial city into a modern Soviet capital by 1941. In lieu of the narrow, irregular, and crimped streets of "Old Nemiga," the new plan envisioned building parks, hospitals, kindergartens, hotels, movie theaters, library buildings, and laundromats. The new real-estate developments would serve the growing population of the Belorussian capital.[17]

Like the urban population of any other Soviet city in the 1930s, the residents of Minsk faced chronic shortages in clothing, food, and housing. One Minsk resident complained about the shortage in children's shoes, which were nowhere to be found, not even in the children's department of the Glavnyi Universalnyi Magazin, GUM.[18] A young Yiddish poet, who had recently settled in Minsk from New York, complained that he had no place to write: his room was "cold, dark, small, dirty"; "I try not to come here [to work]," he wrote.[19] The State Jewish Theater, a central cultural institution in the Belorussian Republic, remained closed in late December 1936 because of the poor heating on stage.[20] Dining in one of the city cafeterias entailed standing in line for hours in order to receive food stubs and a table and, lastly, to chomp on a stale piece of *kugel*.[21] In a remarkable manifestation of continuity, local eateries offered Jewish ethnic foods, albeit of poor quality.

Nina Galperin, born in Minsk in 1923, recalled her father working from early in the morning until late at night, and occasionally not seeing him for several days in a row. In spite of the effort to fulfill his daily quotas, Nina's father rarely earned enough money to fully support the family and frequently turned to his own father for help; an older tailor, who because of his age had not been forced to join a cooperative, Nina's grandfather had a better income than most Soviet doctors and factory directors at the time, working on demand to supply the dearth of consumer goods for the city population.[22]

Public transportation was one of the miseries of urban life. The bus system connecting the city with the surrounding *shtetlekh* was so dysfunctional that in 1936 travel time to Lohoisk, a *shtetl* forty km from Minsk, almost equaled the two-day travel time by carriage before the revolution.[23] By 1938 Minsk had a total of twenty-six taxis stationed by the Central Train Station and the main city's square, indeed a luxurious means of transportation that only members of the political and cultural elite in the city could take advantage of.[24] While the electrification campaign of the 1920s had brought light to most neighborhoods in the Belorussian capital, some areas had no power from 6 p.m. in the evening. People would sit by a candle; youngsters would flee their dark homes for the Central Library, open until late at night, or hang out at a friend's place in the center of town, "where there usually was electricity, . . . and it was new, nice and heated in the winter."[25]

In the second part of the 1930s, Minsk residents spent their leisure time participating in long-distance bicycle races across the republic, or in the All-Belorussian Shvernik cross race, which every year saw a few thousand men and women running through the city.[26] To eat ice cream while strolling in the city parks became very fashionable at that time and affordable to most city residents.[27] Besides going to the movies, perhaps the foundation of Stalinist leisure culture,[28] and to the Minsk State Circus, inaugurated in the summer of 1936,[29] one of the newest attractions in the city was the traveling zoo from Moscow, with snakes, an elephant, a zebra, and lions. The show culminated with the feeding of the animals, at 8 p.m. in the evening. An announcement in the local press invited Minsk residents to sell their old horses to feed the zoo animals.[30]

Jewish Ordinary Life in the Midst of Extraordinary Purges | 181

In 1935, forty-nine-year-old Yona Akselrod, a Jewish tailor employed in the Oktyabr factory, lived on the second floor of Komunalka Street no. 25, in a two-room apartment with electricity, a radio, and access to a kitchen shared by two more families. He lived with his wife, twenty-year-old daughter and two sons, eleven and thirteen years old, respectively. Yona and his daughter, the two family breadwinners, earned together 335 rubles a month. They spent about 56 rubles for apartment-related expenses, 3.40 in union fees, 2.40 to access the radio system, and 75 rubles for meals in the factory and at school. Yona's wife spent approximately 70 rubles to purchase produce in the city cooperatives.[31] As most Minsk residents, Yona's family did not live in great comfort. While their income and living standards might have been somewhat above average, they still had to struggle to make ends meet. A nickel samovar, an essential item in every Soviet household at the time, cost approximately 130 rubles. Its purchase would have entailed some economic sacrifice on the part of the Akselrod family. By contrast, school enrollment and medical treatment were free of charge, and Yona's profession allowed the whole family to have access to clothing whenever in need, a luxury that other Soviet citizens had to part with given the chronic shortage of consumer goods in Soviet life. The factory management occasionally organized leisure activities for the approximately fifteen hundred workers, purchasing tickets for theater shows, concerts, and movies.[32] The workers could also participate in the factory's amatorial circles, such as the jazz orchestra, the choir, and the Yiddish theatrical circle.[33] Like most of his Belorussian and Russian acquaintances, Yona likely installed in his home a New Year's tree (or *yolka*) at the end of December.[34] For the entire month, *Oktyabr* published daily ads about the special toys and decorations of "Zeyde frost" (or "Old Man Frosty," as he was called in Yiddish and in Russian) that were sent to Minsk from Moscow and Leningrad. The ads also mentioned the availability of a store clerk to help customers set up the New Year's trees in their homes.[35]

Yona's everyday life conditions were very similar to those of any other Belorussian or Russian worker who lived in Minsk in the 1930s, but was not a party member, and who enjoyed the privileged but widespread status of "shock worker." However, there were some distinctively Jewish features in his life that he was likely to share only with other Jews in the city. First, Yona happened to speak Yiddish, which was probably the language used at the Akselrod residence during the 1930s. As a Jewish worker in pre-revolutionary times (he was thirty-one at the time of the 1917 revolution), he did not have access to education in Russian. Yona's sons, who because of their young age would have been more inclined to adopt Russian as their primary language, attended a Soviet Jewish school and thus knew Yiddish. In his spare time, Yona enjoyed reading the work of Yiddish writers Morris Vinchevski, Dovid Bergelson, and Izzy Kharik, and browsing through the pages of *Oktyabr*.[36] He either purchased the Yiddish daily by paying twenty-four rubles for the yearly subscription,[37] or borrowed a copy from the library or workers' club. Yona might have also bought *Hamlet* for four rubles and forty kopeks, *Romeo and Juliet* for three rubles

Figure 12. Belorussian State Jewish Theater, 1930s. Courtesy of YIVO Institute for Jewish Research (Collection R1 Minsk 49).

and twenty-five kopeks, or any other volume from the "Shakespeare in Yiddish" series, available in bookstores in Minsk.[38]

There were different "Jewish" events organized in the city in the 1930s that attracted mostly Jews and focused on Soviet Yiddish culture or Jewish life in the Soviet Union. Yona could have attended a literary evening celebrating the twentieth anniversary of Sholem Aleichem's death, at the Jewish Library in June 1936.[39] That same month, he could have visited the Sholem Aleichem exhibition at Belorussian State Library, featuring the writer's first published works in Yiddish, translations of his works in different languages (including Esperanto) and Gorky's letter to him.[40] As a devotee of Yiddish songs, Yona could have attended one of the several concerts held in the summer of 1936 by the Belorussian State Jewish Vocal Ensemble,

Jewish Ordinary Life in the Midst of Extraordinary Purges | 183

Figure 13. Detail of the Belorussian State Jewish Theater. Performance poster featuring Sholem Aleichem's *Motl Peysi dem Khazns* (Motl, the cantor's son). Courtesy of YIVO Institute for Jewish Research (Collection R1 Minsk 49).

directed by musical composer Liubian. A popular group of professional singers who performed in the Belorussian kolkhozy, clubs, *shtetlekh*, and radio, the ensemble was established in 1931 and acclaimed as a center for the best Yiddish musical culture in the USSR.[41] In December 1937, Yona could have seen a classical performance of the Jewish theater such as Goldfadn's operetta *Shulamis*, or simply spent time with acquaintances in the newly renovated building of Belgoset.[42] A year earlier the former synagogue had undergone thorough renovation to redecorate its interior, enlarge the stage, refurbish the lighting and furniture, and remove the "nationalistic Stars of David" from the windows and the *binah* where the cantor used to stand with his assistants or choir.[43] Moreover, in the absence of the Jewish club, which was closed down in the first half of the 1930s, a larger number of Jews chose the hall of the theater as a meeting point for social exchanges.[44]

Figure 14. From Avrom Goldfadn's play *The Witch*, staged by the Belorussian State Jewish Theater in 1939. Courtesy of the Belorussian State Archives of Film and Photography (2–1501).

Yona might have been part of the audience of *Iskateli Shchastia* or *Seekers of Happiness*, a film produced by Belgoskino about the utopian journey of a Jewish family to Birobidzhan and its successful adjustment to the challenges of rural life in the Jewish autonomous region. The movie was widely released in Minsk in the late 1930s. As a winter vacation activity in 1937, schoolchildren in Minsk were brought to the movie theater to see the four "best and favorite" films of the time: besides *Chapaev*, about the legendary Red Army commander, *Partinnyi bilet*, about a loyal and trustworthy party member, and *Karl Brunner*, about the tragedy of a German boy whose Communist parents were arrested by the Nazis, Minsk schoolchildren saw *Seekers of Happiness*.[45] While this is an indication of how popular the film was in the late 1930s, we should not forget that its overtly Jewish content attracted mostly a Jewish audience.[46]

Yona owned a radio. Since not all Minsk residents owned one (approximately fourteen thousand homes in the city had a radio receiver in 1936),[47] he most likely invited home, as was customary at the time, friends from work or from the neigborhood to listen to radio programs, including Yiddish radio programs. Of the Yiddish-language programs aired by the Yiddish-language editorial board of the Minsk radio station from mid-1936 to early 1938, Yona might have listened to the following ones: in May 1936, at 9:15 p.m., the radio broadcast a Sholem Aleichem evening dedicated to the twentieth anniversary of his death, with readings by Yiddish writers and actors of the

All-Belorussian Radio committee.[48] Throughout October and November of 1936, as part of the celebration of the nineteenth anniversary of the Bolshevik Revolution, the Minsk radio station broadcast Yiddish folksongs about the leaders of the revolution and readings of Yiddish literature.[49] On January 24, 1937, it broadcast an artistic evening in celebration of Kharik's newest poem, with speeches by Osherovitsh, Akselrod, Kulbak, Bronshteyn, and Kharik himself and songs performed by the Jewish Ensemble.[50] From February 1937 to March 1938, Yona and his friends probably listened to news reports in Yiddish about local election campaigns, to antireligious campaigns against the "clerical Passover days," and to literary programs devoted to the works of Yiddish poet Peretz Markish, to the hundredth anniversary of Pushkin's death, or to the Yiddish translations of Gorky's masterpieces.[51] Most of these programs were accompanied by music and songs performed by the Jewish Vocal Ensemble.[52] Some Minsk residents complained and demanded that the radio musical director increase the time allotted to Yiddish music: twelve minutes a day of Yiddish songs was not gratifying enough.[53] Radio broadcasts of folksongs, literary evenings, and political programs in Yiddish were a notable feature not only in Yona's life but for many Soviet Jews in the city. At the time this notable feature remained unthinkable for most of Jewish Eastern Europe—Poland in particular.

The Ethnic Community and its Heroes

There were scores of possibilities for young Jews to meet up and interact socially with other Jews in the second half of the 1930s. In the summer of 1936, the students of the Minsk Evpedtekhnikum got together with the students of the Vitebsk Evpedtekhnikum for a sporting contest, with races, high jump, and grenade pitching. The sporting event was followed by an evening party, with dancing, only for the students of the two institutions.[54] Yiddish-language schools served as vital spaces for the thriving of a Jewish ethnic identity during the 1930s. Jewish children would spend the day in the classroom together, interacting mostly in Yiddish with each other, and mostly with Jewish teachers. During intermission they would converse in Yiddish (or Russian) and play ball together. They'd participate in afterschool activities ranging from music, sports, and drama.[55] The friendship of four young Minsk Jews who attended the same school is depicted in the pages of *Oktyabr*. Graduates of Soviet Jewish school no. 12, they prepared for class together and went to the movies together. The school they shared for several years inspired their close friendship and the decision to pursue an academic career together. Not intimidated by the fact that they had studied chemistry and physics in Yiddish, they applied to the Minsk Politechnical Institute, where the language of instruction was Belorussian. While highlighting the alleged good quality of the Soviet Jewish schools' curriculum, which supposedly prepared its graduates for the elite institutions in the city, the article, inadvertently, suggests the degree of Jewish ethnic identity in the form of friendship fostered within the Communist confines of the Yiddish schools.[56]

The largely unchanged occupational pattern among the Jewish working class (mostly made of artisans) was another factor that promoted social contact among Jews and encouraged the emergence of an unconscious and "natural" Jewish identity. In spite of the industrialization drive and the absolute prominence given to heavy industry during the 1930s, most Jews not engaged in white-collar administrative and party-related positions were still employed in traditional Jewish professions. In 1936, Jews constituted 85 percent of tailors, 80 percent of cobblers, and 90 percent of leather workers in Belorussia, as even many younger Jews tended to join these professions while shunning the newly established heavy factories of the capital.[57] Because of their high proportion in the local garment industry, it was mostly Jews who in 1936 attended the summer resort for garment-worker Stakhanovites in Ratom, on the outskirts of Minsk. Here, even older Jews could draw on new Soviet spaces as outlets for "unintentional" Jewish identity. Besides leisure sporting activities and promenades in the woods, which were often accompanied by political activities, such as group readings of the most recent resolutions of the Central Committee of the CPB, the resort guests listened to music together and danced in couples.[58] There were regional amateurial contests for the garment workers of Belorussia, usually organized in the capital city of Minsk, which attracted Jews from Vitebsk, Gomel, Bobruisk, Mohilev, and Rogachev (Rahachow). Besides jazz, choir, and dance groups, Yiddish theater troupes played a central role in these artistic contests. In December 1936, ten Yiddish theater groups from different cities and *shtetlekh* in Belorussia convened in Minsk. The actors were usually so passionately devoted to their own amatorial troupe that they remained active in them for more than a decade. Pretending to be a retired actor of Belgoset, the amateur Rozenfeld led for years a theatrical group that performed his own dramas across the *shtetlekh* of Belorussia.[59]

The endurance of a Jewish ethnic identity within the Soviet context of the latter part of the 1930s was made possible not only by the frequent social interaction between Jews who engaged together in different leisure, educational, or political activities within diverse public settings. This endurance also depended, at least in part, on the positive content that official Soviet propaganda assigned to Soviet Jewish identity and on the creation of heroic role models for Soviet Jews.[60] In the absence of a more traditional and historical content, based on religion, on the bond with the Land of Israel, or on the allegiance to specific Jewish political movements, Soviet Jewish identity in the 1930s was nurtured by a new positive self-image conveyed in the literature, the press, and in everyday life. In the era of Nietzschean *übermenschlichen* Stakhanovites, the Jews had their own heroes—new physical models of Jewish masculinity—who took the place of the new villains, namely, the rabbis and the leaders of the Zionist and Bundist movements.

According to the official party narrative, the Stalinist era infused new life in the Jews, "emancipating" them from their past and transforming them into modern Soviet citizens. The songs included in the 1938 collection of Yiddish folksongs about the Red Army, put together by the folklore section of the Institute for History at the Belorussian Academy of Science, echoed this transformation, and celebrated the new ideal

Soviet Jew, as powerful, heroic, and patriotic. In one of the folksongs transcribed in Bobruisk by a twenty-six-year-old Red Army soldier, and included in the collection, both the fiancée and the mother encourage, rejoice, and take pride in the new Soviet Jewish heroes of the day:

> S'hot mayn khaverte in feld
> af der rakhves breyter
> mir gezogt: zolst zayn a held
> in armey der royter.
>
> Mayn zun iz a held
> Er rayt af a gutn ferd
> Az es vet zayn neytik
> vet er farhitn undzer frayer erd.⁶¹
>
> [My girl-friend in the field
> In the broad expanses
> Said to me: be a hero
> In the Red Army.
>
> My son is a hero
> He rides a good horse
> If need be
> He will protect our land and keep it free.]

This song is an example of authentic Soviet Jewish folklore, produced "from below," about the Soviet Jewish hero who defends the motherland and hastens the bright future of Communism. It indicates that the dissemination of official ideology from Minsk gave birth to popular culture in the hinterland that replicated its ideas and themes. The image of the heroic Jewish Red Army soldier, as an object of admiration, was embedded in many such songs.⁶²

In the age of industrialization, the image of a mighty Jewish hero was expounded in everyday life. N. F. Gikalo himself, secretary of the Central Executive Committee of the CPB, spoke of Jewish heroes in the Stalinist époque, celebrating their superhuman deeds as builders of the new civilization. "And the Jewish worker?" asked Gikalo in the summer of 1936, "Who does not remember how terrible his condition was under tsarism? ... [T]he Jewish poor ... who engaged in small crafts and peddling lived in the *shtetlekh* of the former Pale. Now 23 percent of the industrial working force of Belorussia is made up of Jewish workers, and [from their rows] have emerged the great Bolsheviks Skoblo and Rosenberg."⁶³ Hirshl Skoblo and S. Rosenberg, both workers in the Minsk shoe factory Kaganovich, were publicly celebrated among the founders of the Stakhanovite movement in Belorussia in speeches throughout the city factories. For setting new production records, and defying the rules of nature, they, together with others, received new apartments and bigger salaries to go to the theater and movies or send their wives to Moscow to buy new clothes.[64] Photos of these and other mighty heroes, together with epic depictions of their wide shoulders and heavy bodies, which set them dramatically apart from the stereotypical weak *shtetl* Jews, appeared regularly in the press.[65]

These heroes were obviously Jewish, their Jewishness being conveyed to the readers by their markedly Jewish names. The name of the four-time-record-winner and all-Belorussian and all-Union weight-lifting champion, who gave an exhibition of his might lifting eighty-six kilos with his right arm at the Kirov Stadium in front of thousands of schoolchildren in the summer of 1936, was Nahum Lapidus.[66] Unmistakably Jewish, his name appeared in the local press of the time. But these heroes were Jewish also by virtue of specific events that transpired in their life stories. In his speech at the plenum of the Minsk City Soviet, Hirshl Skoblo, the most authoritative Jewish Stakhanovite at the time, commented with awe on his experience as a delegate at the Extraordinary 8th Conference of Soviets, where he saw Stalin and stated, "As a Jew, I once had the right to live only in the suffocating Pale, and not in cities like Moscow and Leningrad.... [N]ow I am a free citizen, with rights.... [I] was in Moscow, the Moscow which I was once banned from."[67] Awarded a prize for achieving an all-Union production record, the young Chayka Gavrielova, a Stakhanovite in the Minsk printing factory Stalin, known in the city for her work performance, was a graduate of Soviet Jewish school no. 23;[68] and the typesetter in the same printing factory, Yasha Fridman, a party member since 1924, enjoyed reading Sholem Aleichem and singing Yiddish folksongs to his nephew.[69]

Besides the words of the local political elite and the depiction in the literature and press of great Jewish heroes, what encouraged, reassured, and gave a sense of ease to the ethnic identity of the Jewish inhabitants of the city was to see and hear about powerful local Jewish figures. In the late 1930s, one of the most prominent "Jewish Jews" who served as a role model for Jewish ethnic identity was Soviet Yiddish poet Izzy Kharik.[70] In the second half of the 1930s, literary evenings and cultural events celebrating Kharik and his work were organized in factories, middle schools, and institutions of higher learning, with wall-newspapers, concerts, and radio programs dedicated to him.[71] His poems were taped on gramophone records and performed in concerts by the Jewish Vocal Ensemble. The Kharik cult was so widespread that when his new poem "Af a fremder khasene" (At a strange wedding)—about the adventures of a Minsk jester, or *badkhn*—appeared in late 1936, young Jews across the city learned it by heart, in its musical version.[72] But Kharik played an important role even for those who did not associate in any way with the Jewish cultural milieu at the time. He served as a model for Soviet Jewish ethnic identity, primarily because of his visibility. A member of the Executive Committee of the CPB, Kharik would appear on the central triumphal balcony of the government complex in Minsk, next to Gikalo, Nikolai Matveevich Goloded (president of the Belorussian Council of People's Commissars), and

Cherviakov on festive occasions.[73] A delegate at the Twelfth All-Belorussian Conference, held in December 1936, it was Kharik who spoke from the grandstand in front of thousands of Minsk residents on behalf of Soviet nationality policy and the Jews. In a celebratory speech about the new Soviet Constitution of 1936, he stated, "that among the free peoples who debated the constitution the voice of one people was heard for the first time.... [A people] that was not a people before and that never would have become a people without the Lenin-Stalin nationality policy. This is the voice of the Jewish people."[74]

The presence of Jewish heroic figures and influential personalities, who publicly identified as Jews and served as positive ethnic role models, even for those unconcerned with Soviet Jewish culture, is in stark contrast with the absence of such heroes and personalities during the postwar Stalinist years. From the second half of the 1940s to 1953 (and thereafter), the systematic de-heroization and public vilification of the Jewish national group became the norm in Soviet society. In other words, the prewar Stalinist USSR and the late Stalinist USSR should not be confused with each other, as the position in society, as well as the representation and self-image of Soviet Jews were poles apart.

Purging the Jewish Street

In August 1936, the highest prosecutor of the USSR found the two eminent party leaders, Grigory Zinoviev and Lev Kamenev, guilty of organizing, in collaboration with Trotsky, acts of terror against the Soviet motherland. The members of the Trotskyite-Zinovievite block, or Left opposition, who allegedly plotted the murder of Leningrad party boss Kirov in 1934, were as "dangerous as snakes." "[There should be] no pity... for the enemies of the people," stated the central organ of the Communist Party.[75] The *Pravda* editorials, reissued in tens of different languages and newspapers and read in all the central and local party organizations across the country, gave the unmistakable signal from above to deal with the "enemies," setting into motion a destructive and seemingly unstoppable mechanism that would stifle Soviet society until early 1939. The signal from Moscow was instantly decoded in Minsk, as scores of party leaders, newspaper editors, factory managers, filmmakers, professors, and *komsomoltsy* were accused of being part of the Trotskyite clique, expelled from the party, and eventually shot or deported to labor camps.[76] On September 1, 1936, the director of Soviet Jewish school no. 28 welcomed the death sentence against Zinoviev, Kameniev, and their accomplices, stating the importance of inculcating in children the instinct "to destroy class-enemies ... and hatred and disgust against the spies."[77]

The Jewish (as well as non-Jewish) reaction to the Terror campaign ranged from incredulity, fear, cooperation with and trust in the secret police, and in rare cases, even resistance. The family of Asia Brasler, who at the time of the purges was seventeen, wasn't religious in any way. The language spoken at home was Yiddish. And Asia, together with her father, enjoyed going to the shows by the Jewish theater. When the

Belorussian political leadership was found guilty of counterrevolutionary acts of espionage on behalf of "fascist" Poland, Asia's reaction was of total disbelief. Together with her friends she used to cheer Goloded, Gikalo, and Cherviakov at public events and meetings; as their alleged actions against the party became known, she was incredulous and thought, "If they are enemies of the people, then who isn't?"[78] A few years younger, Nina Galperin shared Asia's views of the Belorussian leadership. A student in a Soviet Russian school, whose grandparents supported the system because it had put an end to pogroms, Nina recalled her relative lack of concern (due, perhaps, to her young age) and her trust in the NKVD's efforts to wipe out the enemies. She also spoke about her admiration for Gikalo and Cherviakov and her surprise when their alleged acts of espionage against the USSR were disclosed, "[How could it be that they] had done so much for Minsk and had suddenly become spies?"[79]

Mr. Brasler, Asia's father, a devoted Communist who had helped reorganize Minsk Jewish workers into cooperatives, and a committed Yiddishist active in an amateurial Yiddish theater group, continued to support the party as family friends disappeared. It was impossible, he argued, that people without sin were being arrested. And yet, as the purges picked up in momentum, like so many others who occupied leading positions in society, he came to realize that he too could be arrested any day. Ready to follow the NKVD agents in case they came for him, he packed his suitcase. Mr. Brasler was ultimately not arrested. But one night he was almost taken to the NKVD building, eerily located between Belgoset and the Minsk School of Music, as the agents mistakenly knocked on the Brasler's apartment door instead of the apartment of a neighboring family.[80]

Ruva Gelfand, a native of Borisov who moved to Minsk in 1919, had secretly studied Hebrew with a *melamed* and been a member of the Minsk underground Zionist youth group Ha-shomer ha-tsair.[81] His "counterrevolutionary" political activities led to his arrest and deportation in 1927. Upon returning to Minsk, when most Zionist underground groups had been wiped out, Ruva decided to "fit in." Together with his brother Leva (who in 1927 had fled to Moscow to avoid his brother's fate and returned to Minsk in the mid-1930s), Ruva strove to "proletarianize and adapt to the existing social order." But in 1938, during the second phase of the purges, when the "Right Trotskyite Block" led by Nikolai Bukharin, Genrikh Yagoda, and Alexey Rykov was uncovered, his past came back to haunt him. Eleven years after his first arrest, while he was a law student at Belorussian State University, Ruva was purged for counterrevolutionary activities and sent to a labor camp.[82]

In conformity with the "terror etiquette," Ruva's brother Leva, who in the meantime had become a chemical technician and a Komsomol member, was expected to publicly inform the party cell of the Communist youth organization about his brother's arrest. Failing to disclose the counterrevolutionary activities of a family member was a sufficient motive for expulsion from the party.[83] However, disclosing the culpability of a family member did not guarantee safety in any way. To the contrary, following the exposé and in full conformity with the "terror protocol," the Komsomol leadership insinuated Leva's complicity in his brother's counterrevolutionary activity: "Is it then possible . . . that you didn't know that your brother was an enemy of the people?" Leva couldn't hold his tongue and defiantly replied that "if all Communists were such enemies like Ruva, then we would already have built Communism."[84] It wasn't, however, this "obnoxious" reply that made him susceptible to arrest: the mere fact of being Ruva's brother put his life at risk. Ultimately, Leva avoided arrest by fleeing again to Moscow, a second time. To disappear in the maze of a distant metropolis was a common getaway for those Soviet citizens who were daring and fortunate enough to escape the purges.

During the Terror years, former members of pre-revolutionary "bourgeois" parties who had joined the Communist Party in 1921 or sometime thereafter, were automatically branded "enemies of the people" and almost certainly doomed. This process was facilitated by the fateful campaigns to replace party membership cards with new documents, carried out on the eve of the purges. The specific intention of these campaigns was to unmask the most treacherous enemies of the Soviet system, namely, those who had "hidden" from within the party, like party-member Elentuch, a student in the Gorky Pedagogical Institute of Minsk, who had allegedly been active in a Zionist organization until 1930.[85] But it was the Bundist legacy in particular that came back to haunt the city's inhabitants, especially (but not exclusively) those who used to have ties with the defunct (within the Soviet context) Jewish Labor Party. According to Communist Party member Mendl Marshak, the son of a worker in the Minsk kosher slaughterhouse and the director of the meat industry in Belorussia until World War II, not one of his former Bundist acquaintances from Minsk who had joined the Communist Party in 1921 survived the Terror.[86] To escape one's Bundist past became nearly impossible. It was to no avail that in 1937 comrade Kutman admitted in front of the party cell of the Minsk factory KIM her 1917–20 membership in the Bund, condemning the counterrevolutionary nature of the Jewish party, "so apparent in Poland today." She was still expelled from the party: "The KIM Party organization regards the words of Kutman . . . insufficient to enlighten the counterrevolutionary essence of the Bund, and its struggle against the Communist Party. . . . All this testifies to Kutman's dishonesty."[87]

Cyclical purges of former Bundists (*vykhodtsy iz Bunda*, or *bundovtsy*) who supposedly failed to acknowledge the anti-Bolshevik position of the Bundist organizations at the time of the revolution occurred throughout the city party cells several times during the mid-1930s.[88] This tendency, well rooted in the prominent historical role that the Jewish party played in Belorussia in general and in Minsk in particular, expanded during the Great Terror.[89] Gikalo himself singled out former Bundists as Trotskyites more than he did SRs, Mensheviks, or Zionists: "The campaign to replace party membership cards has shown that in most cases former Bundists who joined the CPB, later joined the Trotskyite faction . . . which means that most former Bundists . . . have essentially remained loyal to their previous views."[90] The secretary of the Central Executive Committee of the CPB uncompromisingly pointed his finger at the Bund, when he stated that "among the Trotskyites and Zinovievites expelled from the CPB, almost a half are former members of the Bund or other nationalist counterrevolutionary parties."[91] And in the summer of 1937, the newly appointed secretary of the Central Executive Committee of the CPB, V. F. Sharangovich, who replaced the purged Gikalo, egged on the scrupulous search for Bundists clarifying that "unmasking Bundist theories" was an urgent matter thus far not tackled scrupulously enough. Much more needed to be done.[92] And much more would indeed be done.

It was argued that the presence of former Bundists in the leaderships of the all-Belorussian and local organizations that promoted the resettlement of Jews on land caused the low turnout of Minsk Jews willing to move to Birobidzhan.[93] Former Bundists were unmasked on the editorial boards of *Zviazda* and *Rabochii*—the main organs of the CPB—and *Oktyabr*, where the frenzied hunt for Bundists was even more persevering because of the origin of the newspaper and the political past of Elye Osherovitsh, still the chief editor of the Jewish organ.[94] It was alleged that the wrongdoings of Trotskyites and Bundists in the Belorussian State Publishing House wasted more than twenty tons of paper and 100,000 rubles on counterrevolutionary literature.[95] In the textile factory Oktyabr, where the former chairman of the party organization Agulnik "remained a Bundist at heart," Bundism had disrupted production.[96] Traces of the Bundist "threat" were found in the tiny Jewish section of the library of the Minsk Club for the invalids, which held the Yiddish translation of Lenin's work with a bibliographical annotation encouraging the reader to examine none other than Ester Frumkin's study of Lenin, "full of Bundist chitchat."[97]

Despite the attempt to thoroughly sovietize him, Hirsh Lekert reemerged as a Bundist protagonist: the Polish-born writer A. Damesek was accused of celebrating Lekert as a Bundist hero in his literary work;[98] the Bundist play *Hirsh Lekert* was one of the "counterrevolutionary weapons" used by the artistic director of Belgoset;[99] and the former Bundist Halkin, director of the Belorussian State Film Studio, was responsible for producing the film *Hirsh Lekert*, "full of Bundist lies."[100] Lekert's monument was torn down.

During the Great Terror, "Bundism" became an empty, meaningless term. Similarly to "Trotskyism," it was randomly applied to anyone who had allegedly countered or deviated from the party line, regardless of his or her actual connection to the Bund or to Trotsky respectively. The fabrication of false accusations of "Bundism" or "Trotskyism" stemmed from the general political hysteria of the purges, as well as from the obligation that NKVD agents, who had to meet fixed quotas of arrests, give a legal basis for their detentions, deportations, and executions. It is therefore not surprising if allegations of "stubbornly idealizing the Bundist party" were applied to those Jews who had never had any connection to the Jewish labor movement, but who displayed "deviant" nationalist behavior. More than ever before charges of Jewish nationalism and Bundism were used interchangeably. However, attacks on former Zionists and Zionism as an expression of Jewish nationalism were occasional and sparse. In the late 1930s, Zionism was perceived almost exclusively as an evil ideology affecting the Middle East but not directly impinging on the Soviet Union: while it might occasionally penetrate Soviet territory through "spies from capitalist countries" such as Poland, it was assumed that its indigenous roots had been "deracinated and failed to corrupt Soviet citizens from within." As a rule, the charge of Bundism—and not of Zionism—could descend on those who abided by certain religious practices, or on those who, like the Jewish director of a wine cooperative in Minsk, exhibited Jewish chauvinism by calling Russian and Polish coworkers with the derogatory Yiddish term *"sheygets,"* or non-Jew.[101] The distinctive political and cultural heritage of Minsk, which led to the systematic harassment of former Bundists as well as Jews who were not former Bundists, but for a variety of specious reasons were charged of Bundism, affected in a specific way the local Jewish population perhaps more than the non-Jewish residents of the city.

The most paradoxical allegation of being a spokesman for Bundism was inflicted upon Shmuel Agursky. Director of the Institute for Jewish Proletarian Culture since 1934 and staff member of the historical section of the Belorussian Academy of Science, Agursky had lead the fierce attack against the Bund since the mid-1920s, making it his mission and career to debunk the revolutionary tenets of the Jewish party even before its collision with Lenin through a conspicuous number of books and articles. It was ironic (but in view of the Terror's logic perhaps inevitable) that the person who had been instrumental in boosting the indictments against Bundism in Minsk and elsewhere throughout the interwar period was in turn himself accused of idealizing the Bund and being the quintessential embodiment of Bundist duplicity.[102] He was arrested in the summer of 1937. A member of the Bund in the early years of the century—and an anarchist before the revolution—Agursky had possibly written too much about the Jewish party.

Purging the Jewish Cultural Sphere

What was so distinctictively Jewish about the purges in the Belorussian capital was the assault on the Jewish cultural leadership, much more intense, comprehensive, and efficient than in places like Moscow and Kiev. In its uniqueness, the 1936–38 terror campaign on the Jewish street of Minsk anticipated the postwar systematic liquidation of Soviet Yiddish culture, which, directly orchestrated by Stalin, reached its culmination in 1952.

The purging of the Jewish cultural sphere in Minsk began in mid-1937, as the leaders of the most prominent Jewish institutions in the city underwent systematic criticism in the pages of the local press. By the end of the summer of 1937, the artistic director and founder of Belgoset Mikhail Rafalskii, recipient of the prestigious title of National Artist of the BSSR (which included the prize of a car), was accused of having put on stage nationalistic plays that departed from the party line, of excluding Yiddish and Russian classics from the theater's repertoire and displaying dictatorial temper against the acting cast.[103] His bust removed from the theater's locale, Rafalskii was expelled from the party in July 1937 and branded an "enemy of the people."[104] Almost concomitantly to Rafalskii's dismissal, the literary critic Yasha Bronshteyn was suddenly exposed as a "Trotskyite-nationalist element."[105] Bronshteyn resorted to the preferred Bolshevik tactics of attack as the best defense and confronted the Jewish cultural leadership in Moscow, presenting himself (once again) as the leading voice of the Jewish proletarian establishment. He repeatedly challenged the Moscow-based Jewish elite (attacking Elye Folkovich, who commuted to Minsk to teach Yiddish in the Pedagogical Institute and who allegedly spoke to students about the legacy of the "nationalist" poet Nachman Bialik).[106] But as did most Terror victims, Bronshteyn acted in vain and was identified as an "enemy of the people."[107]

Moshe Kulbak, one of the greatest Yiddish writers of the twentieth century, also came under attack at this time. Employing the same desperate modus operandi of thousands of Soviet cultural and political figures he also attempted to avert the spiraling purge by pointing the finger at others.[108] His play *Boytre*, which had premiered in Moscow in the summer of 1936 and was first put on stage in Minsk in February of 1937, possibly became one of the grounds for Kulbak's arrest.[109] In the eyes of some Soviet critics, the folk story of Boytre, a legendary Jewish Robin Hood from Minsk, included some perilous expressions of anarchism and pessimism. As one critic put it, the play's protagonist appeared more like the Vilna Gaon's nephew than a Socialist hero.[110] Kulbak's literary work in the Yiddish original as well as in Belorussian translation was systematically purged from city libraries, bookstores, and personal collections. His most recent literary creation, a play about the Civil War in Belorussia entitled *Partisans*, which would have been included in Belgoset's upcoming season, was probably destroyed together with its author, in the fall of 1937.[111]

In the hope of circumventing NKVD officers and perhaps even taking up the positions of their purged senior colleagues, the younger (and less prominent) members of the Jewish section of the Writers' Union of Belorussia criticized their own work and blamed the most well-known writers for the political flaws on the Jewish street. Because they were not the cream of the crop, these younger poets were more likely to divert the upcoming purge by denouncing their own work through self-criticism (*samo-kritika*) and condemning the "counterrevolutionary" work of prominent figures like Izzy Kharik, for example. Born in 1910, Chayim Maltinsky, who publicly labeled his children's stories *Kinder* "horrible" and asked that it be removed from all school libraries in the city, escaped arrest and was only expelled from the party candidacy.[112] Kharik, by contrast, was too much of a high-up personality to preempt terror through self-criticism and denunciations. Together with the other leading voices on the Jewish street, he was engulfed in the terror trap.

The actions and words of Jewish cultural *vydvizhentsy*, or "up-climbers," undoubtedly hastened the terror process as accusations against top figures flocked from below.[113]

But the allegations by emerging cultural activists against elite figures only increased the purge tempo. Its process was essentially centralized. Terror on the Jewish street was orchestrated from Moscow and conducted locally with the accusers adding fuel to the engine. The purges of the Jewish cultural sphere should be viewed within the broader context of the growing distrust toward extraterritorial national minorities that initiated in the second part of the 1930s.[114] It is not coincidental that all the leading cultural personalities in Minsk were purged during the same months of 1937. Elye Osherovitsh, Moshe Kulbak, Izzy Kharik, Yasha Bronshteyn, Arn Yudlson, Lev Ziskind, Tsodek Dolgopolski,[115] and other prominent Jewish intellectuals were all arrested on September 11, tried and sentenced by the Military Collegium of the Higher Tribunal of the SSSR on October 28. Kulbak and Kharik,[116] as well as most members of the Jewish cultural intelligentsia, were executed the following day, on October 29.[117] They were not purged because they were Jewish, but rather because they formed the cultural leadership of the Jewish extraterritorial national minority. The mistrust toward the Jewish cultural elite was closely connected to the tendency to label diaspora nationalities as "enemy nations," targeting their members for arrest and execution solely because of their ethnic identity.[118] Between 1935 and 1938, Soviet ethnic-cleansing policies, which entailed the forcible relocation of certain Soviet nationalities away from a given territory, especially from a border region, affected primarily but not exclusively Poles, Germans, Finns, Estonians, Latvians, and Koreans.[119] While these peoples had "capitalist states" and could thus be regarded as potential enemies of the Soviet Union, the Jews did not. But the Jews had large communities in capitalist countries, in particular in neighboring "fascist" Poland and the United States. In other words, if the Terror did not specifically target the Jewish national minority per se, the process of undermining the languages and cultures, and categorizing as ominous the intellectual leaders of those ethnic minorities with no territorial concentration in the Soviet Union, significantly impinged on the Jewish cultural leadership and institutions of the Belorussian capital. Within this context, being a well-known Yiddish writer was not a trivial matter.

* * *

As prominent local Communist Party member Mr. Brasler packed his suitcase in preparation for his possible arrest, he made sure to destroy all the Yiddish books in his home library. He sensed that Soviet Jewish culture was being targeted by the Terror and felt that the presence of books by arrested Soviet Jewish writers (perhaps even Kulbak and Kharik), put his life, and that of his family, more at risk.[120] Soviet Jewish culture, which had flourished throughout the 1920s and 1930s, making Minsk one of the most important centers for Yiddish culture and scholarship in the Soviet Union (and perhaps in the world), was critically affected during the Terror. Visually this was symbolized by the removal of the city's name in Yiddish from the central station together with its Polish and Russian name (only the Belorussian name was retained).[121]

The absence of a cultural leadership left those who survived the purge perplexed. The writers and activists who came together to reorganize things in the early months of 1938, were at a loss and uncertain as to who would now take the lead of the Jewish publications in the city.[122] All but one of the members of the editorial board of the literary journal *Shtern* had been purged.[123] The worst blow to Soviet Jewish culture was the decree issued in July 1938 by the Central Executive Committee of the CPB that ordered the closing down of Soviet Jewish schools—namely, the strongest guarantee for a future for Yiddish in the Soviet Union. As of September 1, 1938, the entire network of Yiddish-language kindergartens, primary and secondary schools, and institutions of higher learning were reorganized mostly into Belorussian, and occasionally Russian-language institutions.[124] Linked to the rising tide of the purges, a similar decree like the one issued in Minsk and applied to every city and town in Belorussia was unique in the Soviet panorama. No other place in the Soviet Union suffered the same verdict. Why?

What follows is an attempt to assess the status of the Jewish schools in Minsk in the second half of the 1930s, and at the same time explain the four main factors that caused their demise. The official reason for closing down the schools—and as a result the Jewish academic and pedagogical institutions that trained its future instructors—was mentioned in the decree itself. The Central Committee of the CPB stated that its decision to "Belorussianize" the Jewish schools reflected the will of the Jewish population itself as parents and students had petitioned the authorities to switch over to Belorussian.[125] While there certainly might have been complaints from Jewish city residents whose children attended schools in Yiddish and as a consequence were disadvantaged in their knowledge of Russian or Belorussian, the shift toward a centralized and uniform national-cultural and linguistic landscape of the USSR in general and of the individual republics in particular should be held much more accountable than the officially stated reasons. The rejection of minority cultures in the Belorussian SSR appears therefore as the first key factor responsible for the liquidation of the Yiddish schools.

During the purges the growing focus on Belorussia and Belorussian overshadowed the extraterritorial national minorities' languages and cultures, primarily Yiddish and Polish. In stark contrast with previous years, not one word about the minorities' languages and cultures in Belorussia was included in the 1937 proceedings of the Sixteenth Assembly of the CPB. The section on the "national-cultural construction of the BSSR" only mentioned the Belorussian language, people, art, the percentage of Belorussian students and doctors in relation to the tsarist era, the number of books held in the Belorussian National Library (without any language classification), and the appearance of the Belorussian translation of Engels's work.[126] In 1937, it was not odd for the secretary of the Central Executive Committee of the CPB to complain about the undersized percentage of Belorussians in the industrial cadres, "as only 34 of the 104 directors of local enterprises are Belorussians . . . and in the food industry only 3 out of 101."[127] This new political trend (which given the large proportion of Jews in white-collar positions was just shy of anti-Semitism) produced a shift in the hierarchy of state languages and cultures established in the 1920s. It is noteworthy that beginning in early 1936, Yiddish was no longer compared to Belorussian in official statements and reports as it had been throughout the 1920s and early 1930s, when the two "jargons" of the two largest national groups in Minsk had been companions-in-arms for the struggle to achieve the status of literary, political, and cultural languages. The comparison in status was now between Yiddish and Polish, the languages of the two largest extraterritorial national minorities in Belorussia.[128]

The idealization of Russian as the main a all-Soviet language and Belorussian as the only all-republican language in the BSSR posed an imminent threat to the existence of national minority cultures and schools. In a radical adaptation of the *korenizatsiia* policies of the 1920s, which had been supportive of other diaspora languages and cultures (primarily Yiddish and Polish), in the late 1930s the indigenization campaign in Belorussia narrowed its focus exclusively to Belorussian, rejecting all minority cultures and languages in the republic.[129] Following in *Pravda*'s steps, which protested about the deplorable status of Russian being considered a foreign language in Soviet schools outside the RSFSR, the local press in Minsk complained about the poor knowledge of the all-Soviet language (Russian) and republic-wide language (Belorussian) in the Jewish and Polish schools.[130] Belorussian was not even taught in some Jewish schools in Minsk. While this phenomenon was largely ignored in the early 1930s, by 1937–38 within the context of the thrust for centralization that accompanied the Terror, it became intolerable.[131]

The admonition by all-Soviet and all-Belorussian organs against the poor knowledge of Russian and Belorussian among national minorities in the BSSR was partly legitimate. An eleven-year-old student in a Jewish (or Polish) school faced the exceptional challenge of studying, besides Yiddish or Polish, three more languages—Belorussian, Russian, and German. This inevitably weighed upon the student's knowledge of Russian and Belorussian. On the eve of the July decree, in Soviet Jewish school no. 8, of the two hundred forty-two students in fifth, sixth, and seventh grades, sixty-two failed in Russian, thirty-four failed the Belorussian oral examination, and forty-nine the written one.[132] How could the graduates of the Jewish schools successfully apply to institutions of higher learning when the entering exams were given in the fields of Belorussian and Russian language and literature?[133] Of the twenty-three students who in 1937 graduated from the Jewish section of the Literary Faculty in the Minsk Pedagogical Institute, only six passed the Russian-language exam.[134]

Underenrollment was another official rationale used to justify the liquidation of the Yiddish-language schools. As the new generation of young parents became increasingly acculturated to Russian, and increasingly identified with Belorussia, more and more of them shared the opinion that enrolling their children in a Belorussian or Russian school was a stronger guarantee for their having a successful career. Moreover, the comprehensive purge of the entire Yiddish-language literary and cultural elite in Minsk in September 1937 on charges of Bundism, Trotskyism, and espionage could not but make parents anxious that the status of the Yiddish language might be under official assault. This led to a significant decline in the enrollment figures of the Jewish schools. In mid-1938, Yiddish school no. 27 had no students enrolled in first and second grade, and school no. 7 only had fourteen students enrolled in first grade.[135]

But the decline in Yiddish-language school enrollment was not as catastrophic as the official July 1938 decree claimed. In fact, the second main factor that led to the demise of the schools was the relative success of Yiddish on the Jewish street at the time. There was still a sizeable social base for the schools in the late 1930s. According to the 1939 census, 49.8 percent of the Jews in Minsk declared Yiddish their mother tongue, making this the highest percentage of Jews in any medium-to-large Soviet city to do so.[136] Moreover, if a few Jewish schools in Minsk were indeed short of students in their first grades, not all ten institutions faced the same crisis. Evidence that Yiddish was still sufficiently popular as an instructional language is the enrollment in the Minsk Evpedtekhnikum. During the academic year 1936–37, the institution had so many applications that the director had to turn down one hundred and fifty of them.[137]

A number of Soviet citizens protested against the July 1938 decree and boldly appealed to the authorities to reverse the decision to liquidate the Jewish schools. The staff members of the Jewish daily newspaper, who argued that they received five hundred inquiries about the reasons for closing the schools, met with local authorities to ask them to reverse their decision. The third secretary of the Central Committee of the CPB Nadezhda Grekhova responded by accusing them of "Bundist inclinations."[138] There were also courageous complaints by ordinary Jews voicing their dissatisfaction with the decision. The Minsk resident Sh. Evenchik addressed a letter of protest to the Moscow *Der Emes*, stating that "this reform contradicts the wise Leninist-Stalinist policy by which each ethnic group has the right to build up its own culture as national in form and Socialist in content." The author of the complaint also remarked with a hint of sorrow, "If one walks along Liakhovka, Starozhevka, and Obuvnaia Streets, one meets thousands of Jewish children whose native language is Yiddish."[139] According to one source, even the Minsk Rabbi Yaakov Meir Kopelevich, together with a number of teachers and Jewish activists, petitioned the City Soviet. Emphasizing that Yiddish was the language spoken also by young Communists, they noted that "closing down the schools meant bringing Soviet Jewish culture to an end."[140] Finally, schoolchildren complained to their peers about being forced to transfer to other schools following the 1938 decree and voiced their frustration with studying in a different language.[141]

The protests and complaints that followed the liquidation of the Soviet Jewish schools are yet another indication of the considerable extent of popularity of the schools. In Ukraine, where no official decree forced the closing down of the Yiddish-language schools, the schools were left to wither away on their own. The enrollment figures in Kiev were presumably so low that the schools did not pose any threat to the supremacy of Ukrainian and Russian. By contrast, the relative success of Yiddish in the Belorussian capital, within the context of the Great Terror and the shift in policy toward minority cultures, rendered it a noteworthy threat—one that needed to be countered with administrative measures.

Minsk's geographic location was the third key factor in the purge of the Jewish cultural sphere. Unlike Kiev and Moscow, the Belorussian capital was close to the border with "fascist" Poland. In the Soviet geopolitical view of the world in the late 1930s, nearby Poland served as the main channel through which enemies and spies crossed into the USSR and planned acts of sabotage against the motherland.[142] More prone to fall into the hands of "the counterrevolutionary work of spies, Trotskyites, and nationalists of all kinds," the Belorussian capital was to be "scrupulously monitored," according to Soviet authorities. Stalin himself had singled out the border position of Belorussia as early as 1934, criticizing the Belorussian leadership for failing to prevent the "Polonization of Belorussian children."[143] The purges of the elites in the BSSR were more thorough than in any other republic and led to the downfall of 90 percent of the Belorussian intelligentsia.[144] "The difference of the Minsk Party organizations," stated a local party activist "lies in the fact that [the city] is located on the border with the capitalist West, and houses all the . . . central institutions and organizations of the BSSR."[145] In his June 1937 report, the secretary of the city committee of the CPB Khadasevich advised not to forget that "Minsk is located on the border with fascist countries, many of the spy groups that Japanese-German Trotskyite agents send on missions settle here in the border city of Minsk."[146] It was believed that the most susceptible to "bringing in spies" were the members of the extraterritorial minorities, primarily Poles and Jews.

While quantitatively negligible compared to the Jewish institutions in the city, the Polish institutions were hit perhaps more harshly than the Jewish ones. The two Soviet Polish schools in Minsk (no. 6 and no. 33) were closed down several months before the Jewish schools. The Polish section of the Writers' Union of Belorussia was branded a "nest of spies committed to Polonizing the BSSR" and liquidated in August 1937, as was the Polish newspaper *Orka* (Toil). Radio broadcasts in Polish were also eliminated.[147] The Jewish section of the Writers' Union, as well as the two major Soviet Jewish institutions in the city—the Jewish daily and the theater—continued to exist in Minsk until the German occupation of the city.[148]

The newly appointed First Secretary of the CPB, Panteleimon Ponomarenko, directly designated from Moscow, might have been particularly eager to show his vigilance in combating infiltration of spies and ideas from Poland. Since there were more than 3.5 million Jews in Poland, it was easy to identify Jewish institutions with the Polish threat. Ponomarenko wanted to satisfy the authorities in Moscow during his probation period as First Secretary. This meant liquidating the Jewish schools. After all, by the date of his appointment, June 18, 1938, the only ethnic schools still existing in Belorussia were the Jewish ones.[149]

The fourth and final key factor accountable for the brutality of the Terror on the Jewish street of the Belorussian capital was the persistent radicalism of Jewish political and cultural activists. Not only did many cultural figures in Minsk strive to abide literally to the party line; they also tried to anticipate its most extreme twists. This radicalization was voiced in the initial phases of the anti-Bundist campaign (in 1926 and in the early 1930s) as activists and contributors to *Oktyabr* turned to Moscow's *Der Emes* and, with an aura of superiority, indicted the central organ for failing to look for and unmask "Bundists" among its collaborators. Minsk, however—and this was stated with pride, or rather with a thrust for acknowledgment from the center—was the forerunner of the campaign.[150] Since the late 1920s, Bronshteyn had carried out an ongoing campaign to radicalize Soviet Yiddish literature, hunting for un-Marxist "bourgeois nationalist" literary works and authors past and present. Together with his colleague Chatskl Dunets (who in 1932 became also deputy minister of education in Belorussia) he had aimed at turning Minsk into a center of radical proletarian ideology in Soviet Yiddish literature. On the occasion of the fifth anniversary of the founding of the journal *Shtern*, Bronshteyn celebrated the new tradition in Jewish literary life created in Minsk based on the founding father of Russian Marxism, Georgi Plekhanov, and not on the "Yiddishist kitsch" of other centers in the USSR.[151]

The same happened in the field of history, as members of the Marxist Historical Society of Belorussia, and later of the Institute for Proletarian Jewish Culture in the Belorussian Academy of Science, struggled to radicalize the narrative of Jewish history and to reduce the number of topics that might be incorporated therein. The attack on historian Israel Sosis and the branding of his work as "nationalist and Bundist" was the expression of this tendency. The first to apply a Marxist reading to the Eastern European Jewish past based on the principles of class struggle and economic determinism, Sosis was nevertheless branded an "un-Marxist historian."[152] "Sosis is not a Marxist . . . because he lacks a class approach to the study of history," declared a member of the Historical Society in 1930.[153] Expelled from the party and publicly vilified in Minsk for his "idealization of the Bund and manifestations of Jewish chauvinism,"[154] in late 1931 Sosis relocated to Kiev where he worked in the local Jewish academic institutions at least until the mid-1930s. Sosis was Marxist enough for Jewish scholarship in Kiev, but not for Minsk.

In the mid-1930s this radicalism transmuted itself among some spokesmen of the cultural elite into an ideology of cultural self-liquidation. When the Jewish Lenin Club was closed in the first half of the 1930s—thereby rendering it the only larger city in the Soviet Union, with a major Jewish population, and no Jewish club—Yiddish writer Zelig Akselrod protested. He was promptly labeled a "nationalist," as if the absence of a Jewish club was an expression of internationalism.[155]

Minsk's Jewish radicalism had to do with the curious and perhaps even perverse phenomenon of a provincial city seeking to demonstrate its centrality within the broader Soviet landscape, struggling to de-provincialize itself, thereby showing off its importance and uniqueness.[156] In the context of the Soviet system, the only way to do that was to become more radical and produce, for example, the quintessentially proletarian Jewish culture. This tendency, which might very well be found in other provincial cities such as Gomel or Vitebsk, was enhanced in Minsk by the city's status of capital of a Soviet republic. By contrast, the tendency to excessively proletarianize Yiddish culture was not as pervasive in Moscow and Kiev, where the Jewish leadership never had to demonstrate that it belonged to a cultural or political center of Soviet Jewish (and non-Jewish) life. Unlike Minsk, these cities had always been established cultural and political centers.

When the purges kicked off, members of the Minsk Jewish elite, who were already predisposed to discover internal "enemies of the people," were eager to act and join the wave of accusations emanating from Moscow. In their eagerness to demonstrate their vigilence and loyalty to the party line, their actions turned out to be more self-destructive than elsewhere. They attacked the Jewish cultural institutions in which they had themselves been active, and their assaults contributed to the fatal blow against them.

The unique combination of these four factors—(1) the rejection of minority cultures and languages in the republic; (2) the relative success of the Yiddish experiment in Minsk; (3) the city's status of border capital; and (4) and the radicalism of the Jewish cultural and political leadership—produced the extraordinary sweep and intensity of terror on the Jewish street of Minsk.

Looking Toward "Fascist" Poland and Nazi Germany

> Di fashistn viln a milkhome-
> Zol zey aroys di neshome
> Di trotskistn tantsn nokh nokh zey-
> Zol zey zayn vind un vey
>
> Bolshevikes viln sholem zol zayn,
> A gezunt zol in zey arayn,
> Eyns, tsvey dray
> Geyt aroys fray![15]
>
> [The Fascists want war,
> May their souls expire,
> The Trotskyites are their lackeys,
> May they have endless woes
>
> Bolsheviks want there to be peace,
> May they be healthy,
> One, two, three,
> You are free.]
>
>   Yiddish Children's Counting Rhyme, 1937

In the context of the Great Terror, when so many Jewish cultural and political figures were accused of nationalism and counterrevolutionary activities, deported, and sentenced to death, it is surprising that the Minsk Jewish press focused at lenghth on overtly Jewish concerns. It would have been more prudent to avoid specifically Jewish topics, and thereby protect oneself from charges of Jewish nationalism. However, *Oktyabr* pursued an opposite tack. From 1936 to 1939, it recorded numerous, extensive reports about the legal discrimination and persecution endured by the Jews of Poland and Nazi Germany in the midst of rising political anti-Semitism. While the subject appeared in the general Soviet press, *Oktyabr* devoted more attention to it than *Pravda* or *Zviazda*. *Oktyabr* should therefore not be seen exclusively as a perfunctory instrument of the state propaganda machine, a Yiddish translation of the general press. If it had been the latter, it would not have devoted articles to pogroms in Poland—a topic of little interest to the general Soviet press. It would have limited itself to images of the decaying and threatening capitalist world surrounding the "peace-loving" Soviet Union, thus inculcating the general Manichean worldview of Soviet politics. *Oktyabr* expressed a specifically Jewish version of the general Soviet political line. Its harsh condemnation of Nazi and Polish persecution of Jews was an authentic Soviet Jewish expression, which was consonant with the general party line, but not identical to it. Within the constraints of the late 1930s, *Oktyabr* tended to focus on Jewish concerns and thereby expressed its nature as a Jewish newspaper.

Reading and/or hearing about the reports on Jewish suffering in Poland and Nazi Germany that appeared in the press must have reassured many Soviet Jews: whatever disturbing events were taking place in their motherland (most notably the purges), life for Jews was unquestionably better than what was occurring to Jews in capitalist Europe. The depictions of anti-Jewish persecution in Poland and Nazi Germany lacked the class-based interpretation of the events typical of a Communist publication and thereby encouraged a kind of comparison between the Jewish condition in the Soviet Union and elsewhere.

* * *

Since the 1920s and through the second part of the 1930s, the content of Soviet Jewish patriotism was grounded in a temporal focus of "better now than then." The temporal comparison emphasized the miseries of Jewish life before the Bolshevik Revolution (highlighting tsarist anti-Semitism, pogroms, the existence of the Pale of Settlement, the quotas for Jewish university students), and, by contrast, the infinite joys of Jewish life after 1917, characterized by the absence of anti-Jewish legislation. This kind of pro-Soviet patriotism grounded in the temporal focus was also expressed in Soviet Jewish folklore, in a sort of guided response to the party line from below. A folksong transcribed in 1937 celebrated the new Soviet Jewish people liberated from the tsarist yoke.

> Biter iz geven in shtot,
> Fun derfer hot men getribn
> Umetum in yedn ort
> Flegt men zayn batribn
>
> Az Nikolaike flegt pogromen
> Af zey blutike makhn,
> Flegt shteyn zhandarmen bay der zayt
> Kveln nor un lakhn.

Iz uf a shtern af der velt,
Un farshvundn iz di nakht
Farshvundn iz di nakht
Di fintsternish un kelt.

Rusn un yidn zaynen itst
Komandirn in eyn folk,
Gliklekh, ibergliklekh
Iz itst dos yidishe folk

Vi ale felker hobn mir
Itst di fulste rekht
Mir zaynen itst fray, fray,
Oys knekht! Oys knekht!¹⁵⁸

[Life in our city was bitter,
Jews were expelled from the villages
Everywhere and everywhere
Jews were despondent

When Little Nicholas used to
make bloody pogroms against them,
the gendarms used to stand at a side
Enjoy and laugh.

And then a star arose in the world,
and the night was gone
and the night was over
The darkness and the cold.

Russians and Jews are now together
the commanders of one people
Happy, overjoyed
is now the Jewish people

Like all peoples we have
full rights,
we are now free, free
Slaves no more! Slaves no more!]

In the latter part of the 1930s especially, the tsarist-Soviet dichotomy was complemented by a new comparison with a geographic focus on "better here than there." This focus distinguished between the social and legal discrimination against Jews in Poland and Germany and the countless successes of the Jews in Soviet territory. With few exceptions condemning anti-Semitism in Latvia, Italy, Romania, and other "fascist countries," the bulk of the articles in the local press focused on Poland because of its closeness to Minsk and on Nazi Germany because of the immediate ideological and political threat it posed to Soviet Russia. The awareness—or rather conviction—that life under the Soviets had overall significantly improved was testified most sharply by the geographic comparison with the status of nearby Polish and German Jews. The knowledge of intensifying anti-Semitism in Poland and Nazi Germany weighed against the absence of official anti-Semitism in the Soviet Union, influenced Jewish identity in the late 1930s and, most interestingly, led to the growth of the self-perception among Soviet Jews that they constituted the true vanguard of world Jewry. The notion that Soviet Jews—the first and only Socialist Jewry in the world—played a leading role vis-à-vis other Jewish communities of Europe had become quite common during the first decade of the Bolshevik experiment. During the 1930s, however, their pioneering status further expanded because of the rise of state-sponsored anti-Semitism in Europe.

The nature of the closeness between Minsk and Poland was geographic as well as emotional. Situated just across the border with Belorussia, the independent Polish state was very familiar to the Jewish population of Minsk as almost every Jewish resident had family or friends in Poland or had themselves moved to the Soviet Union from there. This intimacy was furthermore strengthened by the 1919–20 Polish occupation of the city, marked by pogroms against the Jewish population, which most certainly made Minsk Jews aware that they could have ended up under Polish rule instead of Soviet rule at the end of World War I. Articles featuring the rise of state anti-Semitism in neighboring Poland, following the death of Marshal Joseph Piłsudski and the shattering of his liberal vision of a multiethnic and multireligious Polish state, appeared throughout the local press, in Yiddish, Belorussian, and Russian, thus reaching a wide audience of readers. The articles in *Oktyabr* were either news translations from the Russian information bureau (also published in *Pravda*) and the Belorussian information bureau (also published in *Zviazda*) or original Yiddish accounts based on information collected from Jewish publications issued in Poland. From 1936–39, the reports about the rise of the right-wing National Democratic Movement in Poland and its effect on Polish Jewry portrayed state institutions as *Judenrein,* as Jewish doctors, lawyers, and professors were systematically laid off. "If you travel through Poland you will not find one Jew employed in a government office," remarked a Jewish worker who had moved to Soviet Minsk from Poland."[159] An *Oktyabr* editorial of mid-1937 focused on the geographic contrast "here-there," stating that "here in the Soviet Union Jewish engineers and doctors work wherever they wish and are employed in the biggest industrial complexes in the country. By contrast, the fascism of Poland [and Germany] . . . is taking society back to the middle ages with its barbaric nationalism."[160]

The Yiddish-language press was particularly concerned with the introduction of Jewish quotas and "ghetto benches" at Polish universities. Reminiscent of the anti-Jewish quotas imposed by Alexander III and Nicholas II in Russian universities, the Polish academic reality was in stark contrast with Soviet universities and the remarkable percentage of Jews in the Soviet student body. By 1937 the deans of virtually all universities in Poland had introduced "ghetto benches," forcing Jewish students to sit on separate benches on the left side of the lecture room. "In Soviet middle schools and institutions of higher learning there cannot be any difference between non-Jewish and Jewish students," stated in early 1937 the author of an article that appeared in *Oktyabr*, and continued

> [but] in Poland, where anti-Semitism and pogroms are on the rise, to be a Jew is essentially against the law.... [I]f you hit a Jew, steal from him, and even kill him you become a national hero.... Following the example of Warsaw, other universities organized "a day without Jews"; in Vilna twenty-four Jewish students [who entered the university on that day] were wounded.... Five hundred fifty Jewish students organized a hunger strike in protest.[161]

The growing legal and social discrimination against the Jews of Poland was accompanied by physical violence, with pogroms erupting throughout the country. Detailed reports on the pogroms—which at times included the names of the victims,[162] their occupation, the nature of the violence, and the outcome of the trial against the *pogromchiki*—were often accompanied by personal memoirs of those who had lived through pre-revolutionary pogroms.[163] Comparing "Red Minsk" to a "Polish Minsk," the author of an article in *Oktyabr* described the different situation in the two cities:

> While Jewish workers and artisans of the capital of Belorussia don't even know what national persecution means, as the doors to factories, schools and universities are open to them and their children,... in fascist Poland pogroms are being organized against the Jewish population.... The pogrom in Minsk-Mazowiecki stands out for its violence, with the burnings, the destruction of Jewish homes, and the thousands of Jews who were deprived of their property.... Just like under the tsar, the police was "neutral" and did nothing.[164]

Besides a few critical remarks against Zionists and rabbis who allegedly supported the fascists, and positive notes about Polish workers who did their best to defend the Jews during the pogroms, these reports usually fell short of sticking to a purely ideological and class-based discourse. They recorded in fact, with the same empathy, instances of attacks on Jewish businessmen and communal leaders in Poland.[165] For propaganda purposes, "capitalist" Jewish merchants and communal leaders should be condemned at least as much as the instigators of the pogroms. But the authors and editors of these press reports could not deny—and were perhaps not even interested in doing so—that the entire Jewish population in Poland, regardless of social class and political allegiance suffered during the pogroms.

The awareness of state anti-Semitism in Poland and the official prosecution of anti-Semites in neighboring Soviet Minsk played out in the comparison between instances of blood libels abroad and at home. On March 11, *Oktyabr* informed its readers about a blood libel that occurred in a *shtetl* in Poland. A Jewish couple was accused of killing a Polish girl to use her blood to bake *matsah* for Passover. The couple was arrested and found guilty.[166] Only ten days later, on March 21, 1937, a similar case erupted in the Belorussian capital, when two Belorussian workers accused the Jews of orchestrating the murder of a Minsk resident in order to use his blood for ritual purposes during Passover.[167] The two workers were promptly found guilty of spreading "counterrevolutionary anti-Semitic lies" and expelled from the workers' union. At the height of the purges, they were prosecuted in a public trial and sentenced to prison not for being members of a Trotskyite terror group, but for anti-Semitism. The Jews of Minsk who read about the Polish and Soviet blood libels in the press (or heard about them through word of mouth) could not avoid noticing the different reaction to the false accusation on the part of the Polish and Soviet legal systems, and perhaps even feel that the Soviet Union was at the time the only country in Europe that considered anti-Semitism a crime. Even within the context of the usual skepticism with which Soviet citizens approached official channels of information, the realization that the USSR dealt with anti-Semitism differently shaped the way in which Soviet Jews viewed themselves vis-à-vis the rest of world Jewry in the late 1930s.

The Jewish and Belorussian local press also discussed the rise of Hitler to power and the systematic persecution of German Jews. It captured the details of the main stages that led to the complete reversal of emancipation for those who had seemed to be the continent's most successful and integrated Jews in the early twentieth century. Though emotionally and geographically further removed from their border compared to Polish Jewry, the plight of German Jews inevitably attracted the attention of Soviet Jews. After all, German Jews were captives of the greatest ideological enemy of the Soviet Union at the time: Nazi Germany. Information about the economic boycott of Jewish businesses, the public burnings of books whose authors were Jewish, and the 1935 Nuremberg Laws, which outlawed marriages and sexual relations between Germans and Jews, regularly appeared in the local press,[168] and were often complemented by the anti-Semitic illustrations that appeared in German newspapers at the time.[169]

However, what is perhaps most striking in these reports—and missing from the non-Yiddish articles on German anti-Semitism—are displays of Jewish national pride and solidarity bearing the vision of a united Jewish people with an ancient and common history. Comparing the status of Soviet Jews with that of German Jews, a Minsk Jewish worker remarked:

> The USSR has solved the Jewish question long ago; thanks to the Lenin-Stalin nationality policy, we have no more Pale of Settlement, . . . no institutions of higher learning [are closed] to young Jewish students. . . . I am a Jew [e.a.]. The worst pages written with blood in the history of mankind are the pages of the history of my people [e.a.] made of pogroms and persecution. But the suffering is over for us [Soviet Jews]. . . . Fascism carries on after Pobedonostsev who ordered Nicholas II to kill one third of the Jews, to convert one third and to expel another third. . . . It is hard to

imagine that the official hymn of German fascism contains words such as "the hour of freedom will come when Jewish blood will gush from knives."[170]

Similar expressions of Jewish national pride and solidarity complicate our understanding of Jewish life in the late 1930s and counter the assumption that Stalin's Great Terror, the purging of Jewish intellectuals and the closing down of Yiddish institutions entailed the complete removal of all expressions of Jewish identity in the Soviet context. The sense of Jewish solidarity was expressed most starkly after Kristallnacht, the Night of the Broken Glass, on November 8–9, 1938, when the Nazi Party organized anti-Jewish riots throughout Germany, displaying a kind of public violence that had been witnessed before only in Eastern Europe in the form of pogroms.[171] In a poem published a few days after Kristallnacht, Yiddish writer Chayim Maltinsky voiced his rage for the suffering of German Jews—in particular those of Polish background who were expelled from the Third Reich—and announced a veiled promise of Jewish revenge against Germany.

> Child, woman and elderly man
> They lie in dirt without a roof or bread.
> And they have no warm clothing . . . , and no train.
> But they are beaten, they are lynched, they are murdered.
> Together with the glorious Russian people
> Together with the scores of peoples of the Soviet Union
> We [e.a.] will pay back the enemy for everything
> To take revenge is our destiny![172]

The perception of Jewish commonality articulated in this poem clearly goes beyond the geopolitical borders of the USSR. Echoing Maltinsky, another young member of the Jewish section of the Writers' Union of Belorussia, Motl Grubyan, responded to Kristallnacht addressing the question of Jewish solidarity. As the poet read in disbelief about the pogroms carried out in Germany, he wrote:

> The world has long forgotten about such malignancy, so grey
> A Jew is being chased, his home is dust and sadness . . . .
> You, my painful poem, escort my people [e.a.] out, and look
> Not in the forest, among tigers, are lives devoured,
> Not in shadowy corners, does the murderer satisfy his hunger
> But on the main streets of Berlin, where Goebbels the executioner stands.[173]

Voiced as the Terror was still ongoing, such expressions of Jewish solidarity counter our view of Soviet Jews as isolated from the rest of world Jewry. Less dictated from above, they also predated by a few years the 1942 establishment of the Jewish Anti-Fascist Committee, the organ headed by Itsik Feffer and Solomon Mikhoels, which, exploiting the idea of Jewish world solidarity, attempted to gather financial support for the Soviet war effort from American Jews.[174] An editorial that appeared in *Oktyabr* in late November 1938 powerfully denoted the empathy that Soviet Jews felt and were allowed to express for the suffering of fellow German Jews before World War II: "That glorious Jewry, which produced the famous names of Moses Mendelssohn, Heinrich Heine, Karl Marx, Albert Einstein, has been destroyed by the fascist cannibals, who exiled their children, requisitioned their property, and kicked out the best thinkers burning their work."[175] If throughout the 1920s and 1930s, Soviet Jews had been forced to sever all ties with other Jewries around the world—because the latter were "bourgeois," Zionist, or religious—now, for the first time in a long time, they could reconnect emotionally with them and even experience a renewal of Jewish identity.

Conclusion

> Then Minsk looked like the Jewish cities of Poland and Lithuania that are now under the clout of fascism and capitalism.... The former provincial Minsk, the former city of the Jewish Pale, is now a blooming free city for all workers.[176]

The knowledge of the upsurge in anti-Jewish violence in neighboring Poland and the systematic persecution of German Jews under Nazism helped shape Soviet Jewish identity in the late 1930s. Reports on anti-Jewish violence appeared in Yiddish as well as Russian and Belorussian, thus reaching those Jewish readers who steered clear of the Yiddish-language press. Information about anti-Jewish persecution became available in works of literature as well as in movies. In the summer of 1937, the Belorussian State Publishing House issued a Yiddish and Belorussian translation of *The Oppermanns*, the 1934 novel condemning surging anti-Semitism in Nazi Germany by well-known pro-Communist German-Jewish writer, Lion Feuchtwanger. Widely released throughout the movie theaters of the cities of the Soviet Union, at least three 1938 films featured in detail the increasing threat of anti-Semitism in Germany and specifically addressed the question of Jewish suffering under the Nazis. Many Minsk Jews most likely saw the film version of Feuchtwanger's novel, renamed *Semia Oppengeyma*, or *The family Oppenheym*, directed by Grigory Roshal; *Bolotnye soldaty*, or *Peat bog soldiers*, directed by Alexander Mecheret; and *Professor Mamlok*, about a prominent German Jewish surgeon who underwent anti-Jewish persecution, directed by Adolf Minkin and Herbert Rappaport.[177]

Those Jews who for a variety of reasons desisted from reading the Communist press learned about anti-Semitic attacks in Poland or in the streets of Berlin also through word of mouth. Soviet schools and local party cells debated cases of anti-Semitism, thus making young Jews aware of the harshness of anti-Jewish persecution abroad.[178] A specific Jewish twist emerged in the Yiddish-language press more often than not. After all, while anti-Semitism was just one aspect of Nazi brutality and not the most important one for the general Soviet press, for the Jewish press German anti-Semitism was given central attention. Encouraged by the openness with which party organs and government authorities addressed anti-Semitism and spoke about pogroms in Poland and killings (albeit not systematic) of Jews in Germany, the articles in Yiddish provided a stronger Jewish concern and preoccupation, a deeper and more detailed Jewish context of persecution as they referred back to the tsarist anti-Jewish legislation; provided the names and ages of the Jewish victims of violence almost like a *Yizkor*, or memorial, book; and relied on accounts from "bourgeois" Jewish newspapers like the Warsaw-based Zionist daily *Haynt* (Today). Occasionally the Soviet Jewish press even recorded instances of Jewish heroism abroad, as it documented—not short of Jewish national pride—the deeds of Jewish fighters in the battle against fascism in Spain:

> [T]he Jewish people has given its best sons for the struggle to free Spain . . . now covered in Jewish blood. . . . The commander Morris Skolko . . . a Jewish worker [from] Paris . . . together with eight more fighters, also Jews, defended the position against the attack of the Italians in Matoro and fell as heroes. . . . The Spanish worker will now be able to explain to his brethren what the sons of the Jewish people can do.[179]

In the context of the anti-Jewish policies adopted by Poland and Germany, the USSR appeared as the only country in Europe that still deemed anti-Semitism a crime. The knowledge of anti-Semitism abroad and the (official) lack thereof at home had a two-sided impact on the way in which Soviet Jews perceived themselves and other Jews. On the one hand, Soviet Jews came to feel empathy and concern for the persecuted Jews in Poland and Germany and experienced a renewed sense of national bond with the suffering Jews of "fascist" Poland and Nazi Germany. Soviet Jews had only partially been cut off from the rest of world Jewry and the ban on certain claims of Jewish identity was essentially incomplete. On the other hand, the Jews in the USSR looked at Polish and German Jews with a sense of superiority and confidence that, by virtue of their sovietness, they constituted the unquestionable forefront of world Jewry. The awareness of anti-Semitism abroad gave rise to a sense of pride in their own country, which in its struggle against anti-Semitism they felt was the best and most secure place for Jews in the world. After all, while for most Soviet citizens the threat of the "capitalist encirclement" was mainly rhetorical and had mere economic implications, for Jews fascism and Nazism had a real tangible upshot, as it had had for the Jews of Poland and Germany, marginalized from public life and victimized by violent pogroms.

The awareness that anti-Semitism was more acute in Poland than in the USSR grew within Polish Jewry itself during these years. A number of Jewish intellectuals and politicized youth responded to the sense of hopelessness and desperation that engulfed Polish Jewry by looking eastward. In spite of their ideological rejection of Communism, many Polish Jews came to place their hopes for the future in the Soviet Union, or at least in the adoption of a Soviet-type regime in Poland.[180] One of the main problems faced by left Zionist youth movements and Bundist youth groups in Poland in the late 1930s was defection to the banned Communist Party of Poland. The Yiddish intelligentsia in the Polish cities openly expressed pro-Soviet sympathies. A group of Yiddish poets from Warsaw, with a pro-Communist orientation, published their work in an anthology entitled *Life and Struggle: Collection of Yiddish Leftist Literature in Poland,* which appeared in Minsk in 1936. Some daring young Jews illegally crossed the border into Soviet Russia. After all, where could they look to if America and the Land of Israel were closed, and the tide of fascism was rising throughout Europe?[181]

It is paradoxical but true that Jews in Minsk probably knew more about the persecution of Jews in Nazi Germany, than did the Jews of Warsaw. Because of the close ties between the Polish military regime and the Germans, the Polish press, including the Yiddish press, was severely censored on matters related to Germany. On October 19, 1938, the Polish authorities closed down the most popular Yiddish daily in Warsaw, *Haynt,* in response to the publication of articles on the persecution of the Jews in Germany. Publication of *Haynt* resumed only in January 1939; in the interim period, it appeared as *Der tog* (The day), but underwent scrupulous censorship for any reference to the Jewish question in Germany.[182]

The USSR was virulently anti-Nazi in the 1930s, both for ideological and geopolitical reasons linked to the aggressiveness of Nazi Germany in its search for *Lebensraum,* or living space, in the east. This opposition to fascism and Nazi Germany enabled Soviet Jews to combine Soviet patriotism and Jewish identification with ease: in other words, they could hate fascism and Nazism for both reasons, as Soviet citizens and as Jews, as their Jewishness did not clash with the state's official line. From 1936 to 1939, Soviet Jews in Minsk were disturbed and troubled seeing their major intellectuals and writers arrested, their school system closed down, and their language demoted in status. Of course, they could not express these concerns in the press. The condition of Soviet Jewish culture and life deteriorated in the late 1930s, but many Soviet Jews in the depth of their heart felt reassured by the fact that they lived in a country that officially struggled against anti-Semitism, in the midst of fascist Europe. They revealed a remarkable, and very human, ability to compartmentalize between what the state was doing against them and what the state was doing on their behalf, and took comfort in the fact that the country in which they lived was the lesser of three evils.[183]

Conclusion

> The city which cannot be expunged from the mind is like an armature, a honey-comb in whose cells each of us can place the things he wants to remember: names of famous men, virtues, vegetables and mineral classifications, dates of battles, constellations, parts of speech. Between each idea and each point of the itinerary an affinity or a contrast can be established, serving as an immediate aid to memory. So the world's most learned men are those who have memorized Zora. But in vain I set out to visit the city: forced to remain motionless and always the same, in order to be more easily remembered, Zora has languished, disintegrated, disappeared. The earth has forgotten her.[1]

THIS BOOK HAS attempted to evaluate the development of Jewish collective and individual existence in a Soviet (Jewish) city during the interwar period. Soviet Jews did not emerge abruptly from a sudden rupture generated by the Bolshevik Revolution. In fact, many trends were at work before 1917 and were intensified by the revolution. A push for urbanization had set in since the 1890s and continued with incredible force during the 1920s and 1930s. Yiddish had made a modest appearance as a language of the Jewish public sphere at the beginning of the century and was further promoted by the Bolsheviks. Challenges to the role of religion, and the subsequent growth of a new ethnic-based identity among a number of Jews, emerged in the late decades of the nineteenth century, but grew drastically under Bolshevik pressure. Jewish women had searched for ways to "leave the home" and reject their traditional roles of guardians of the hearth long before the revolution. Younger generations had alternated patterns of Jewish cohesion with patterns of Jewish defection since the 1880s. Under the Soviets, they adjusted their views to comply with the Communist interpretation of reality and took on Bolshevism (with or without enthusiasm) as a vehicle to achieve social empowerment and advancement. Youth were the most susceptible and prone to the centripetal forces of assimilation, as they anxiously strove to belong to, and be accepted into, Soviet society. Often times, however, even young Jews maintained the habits, traditions, views, and language of the Jewish group, especially when living in compact Jewish demographic centers.

By the late 1930s, the social pressure to fully embrace the ideals of the Stalinist civilization, adopt Russian as an alternative to Yiddish, and intermarry with Belorussians or Russians took hold of young Jewish men and women with even greater intensity. Intermarriage grew exponentially in the Soviet Union from the 1920s to the 1930s. According to the 1926 Soviet census, 3.2 percent of Jewish men and women in Belorussia intermarried (5 percent in Ukraine, and 21 percent in Russia).[2] Approximately ten years later, in 1937, the rate of intermarriage increased three times over, reaching in Belorussia 10.5 percent for men and 14.8 percent for women (in Ukraine 16.4 percent for men and 14.9 percent for women; in Russia 42.3 percent for men and 36.8 percent for women).[3] Despite the staggering increase in intermarriage rates, the likelihood for Jews to intermarry in Belorussia (and therefore in Minsk) remained significantly lower than in Moscow and Leningrad, where in 1939 Jews made up 6 percent of the city population in both cities.[4]

This pressure to secularize, conform, and assimilate into the "Soviet people," boosted by the unrelenting propaganda and terror devices employed by the state, was unique to the Soviet Union. The second postrevolutionary generation of Soviet Jews experienced secularization, acculturation, and assimilation differently from the second generation of postindependence Polish Jews. Under Polish rule since World War I, the city of Grodno was located in what the Soviets called "Western Belorussia"—and as such would occupy and incorporate into the borders of the BSSR in 1939. Like Minsk, Grodno belonged to the Jewish cultural tradition of Lithuanian Jewish cities—its Jewish community dating back to the fourteenth century. While significantly smaller than the Belorussian capital, it shared with Minsk a comparable demographic profile and proportion of Jews vis-à-vis non-Jews: in 1931 Grodno counted 21,159 Jews, or 42.6 percent of the total city population; the rest of its residents were mostly Polish and Belorussian.[5]

Unlike Minsk Jewry, in the 1930s Grodno Jews experienced both popular and state-driven manifestations of anti-Semitism. These ranged from the profanation of the Jewish cemetery in the center of town, the 1935 pogrom, the institution of "ghetto benches" in the classroom, and the aggressive anti-Jewish economic measures (boycott of Jewish-owned stores) set off by the heightened general economic depression in the city.[6] The Jewish atmosphere in Grodno is hardly comparable to the one in Minsk at the time: among its buildings and institutions, in the early 1930s Grodno counted thirty-six synagogues and houses of prayer, several yeshivas, many Jewish schools in Hebrew, Yiddish, and Polish, Jewish sports clubs and libraries, and numerous Jewish publications in Hebrew, Yiddish, and Polish. Yet, the growing thrust toward secularization and the decline in religious observance among Grodno's younger generation of Jews shared some similarities with what was happening in the Belorussian capital.[7] In 1937, a group of scandalized Grodno rabbis addressed a letter to the local Jewish community complaining about the widespread practice of selling tickets for cultural events by the entrance to the main synagogue in the city on the holy Sabbath.[8] The loss of rabbinic authority and the concomitant shift toward a secular and mostly ethnic-based Jewish identity led to the rejection of traditional culture and fiery generational conflicts among many Polish Jews. However, if under Stalinism of the late 1930s Minsk Jews could replace the Jewish traditional option only by identifying with Communism, Grodno Jews had a variety of trade-off choices available, which ranged from Socialist-Zionism, Revisionism, and Bundism and included Communism. Furthermore, for most young Polish Jews the growing intensity of anti-Semitism impeded the integrationist choice, which remained the fundamental option embraced by the majority of Soviet Jews.

* * *

When did the Jewish institutions, attitudes, and ways of life described in this book come to an end? While the paradigms of Jewish life were severely wounded during the campaigns of political repression and persecution, overall they remained largely unchanged at the time of the Great Purges: the Jewish daily *Oktyabr*, the Belorussian State Jewish Theater, and the ethnic neighborhoods continued to exist, Yona still listened to Yiddish music and read recently published Yiddish books, and those who wished to could still obtain *matsah* for Passover.[9] More than ten synagogues and houses of prayer functioned in the capital of the Belorussian SSR on the eve of World War II.[10] In August 1937, a Jew (Alexei Mikhailovich Levitskii) was elected second secretary of the Central Committee of the CPB.

The Hitler-Stalin pact signed in the summer of 1939 by foreign ministers Vyacheslav Molotov and Joachim von Ribbentrop critically upset Jewish self-confidence and full identification with the Soviet Union. After more than a decade of systematic vilification of the Nazi arch-enemy, a general confusion grasped Soviet society as a whole. Some Red Army soldiers were so shocked that comments like "Why do our newspapers not scold Goebbels nowadays? Did he become a Bolshevik?" emerged often in the aftermath of the unexpected political turn.[11] Jews were taken aback more than others as the assumption that the Soviet Union represented the only country in Europe that officially combated anti-Semitism concerned all of them deeply and personally. While they ultimately adjusted to the swift change in the Soviet propaganda machine, the sudden dearth of anti-Nazi jargon in the press, and the abrupt removal from the movie theaters of antifascist films condemning anti-Semitism, many Jews grew anxious about the country's diplomatic turn. Just a few months before the signing of the pact, Minsk Jews had participated in a political rally greeting foreign minister Maxim Litvinov during his visit to the Belorussian capital. Some had even expressed "national" pride for the Jewishness of the Soviet diplomat who had publicly condemned German anti-Semitism and attacked Ribbentrop at the League of Nations.[12] Some Jews even protested openly against the pact, among them party members who were expelled from the party as a result of their grievance.[13]

And even though Stalin began a silent campaign to replace prominent Jews in the Commissariat for Foreign Affairs who, as Litvinov, were too visible for the new ally,[14] the treaty's impact on Jewish life should not be overstated. While *Oktyabr* was not allowed to record the economic and social destruction of the Jews in German-occupied Poland, nor write about the appalling conditions in the Warsaw ghetto, the newspaper carried on its publication undisturbed. In fact, no local Jewish institution was closed down following the pact, nor did any Jew in Minsk lose his or her job as a result of the alliance with Germany. A clear distinction was drawn between foreign policy and domestic policy. While the Hitler-Stalin pact represented a blow to the self-confidence of the Jews of Minsk, it did not directly harm Soviet Jewish life.

* * *

Unlike Jewish histories elsewhere in Europe, the Soviet Jewish "story," as a product of the voices and experiences of the densely populated cities and towns of the former Pale of Settlement, underwent a distinctive form of destruction, loss, and oblivion during and after World War II. The first and most brutal form of destruction, of course, was carried out by the Nazis and their local collaborators, who almost completely annihilated Minsk Jewry. The physical destruction of the vast majority of Minsk Jews (almost eighty thousand were killed between 1941 and 1943 within the boundaries of the city itself, most on the very site of the Minsk ghetto, the largest Jewish ghetto in the occupied USSR), produced an irreparable loss. The onslaught on the city and the destruction of its streets, houses, Jewish quarters, and institutions, wiped out by the German bombs launched during the offensive of the summer of 1941, further obliterated the memory of this community. Almost all buildings in the center of the city had been demolished, as well as the railway station, hundreds of industrial enterprises, most schools and institutes of higher education, including Belorussian State University, and 80 percent of the housing.[15] Unlike Vilna or Grodno, where the physical annihilation of the Jews was at least mediated by the preservation of most of their Jewish historic urban spaces, Minsk was razed to the ground. When Hersh Smoliar returned to Minsk after the war, he walked through the city in ruins, through its streets, searching for the buildings he had once known so well. He looked for the Writers' Union building on Sovetskaia Street in vain.[16] Some sixty years later, during the many months I spent in Minsk to conduct the bulk of the research on which this book in based, I also walked through the streets of the city in search of the places I had seen in prewar photos and read about in archival documents, press reports, and oral history accounts. But most of the places described in this book remained only in my imagination.

After the war, Soviet Jewry had little to no resemblance to what it had been before the Nazi invasion. Approximately twenty-five hundred Jews who had fled the Minsk ghetto before its liquidation to join the partisans' struggle against the Germans returned to the city in 1944 and 1945. A few thousand families from surrounding towns and *shtetlekh* who survived the Nazis also settled in Minsk.[17] Most survivors, however, preferred to move elsewhere in Soviet Russia and usually headed toward Moscow or Leningrad rather than go back to their destroyed hometowns.[18] A small number of Yiddish writers who survived the war returned to Minsk and nurtured the slight hope to see Yiddish culture revived in Belorussia. Encouraged by Belgoset's return to the city after evacuation, the resuming of radio programs in Yiddish, and the appearance of a yearly literary almanac in Minsk, three Jewish writers addressed the first secretary of the CPB, Panteleimon Ponomarenko, asking permission to reopen Yiddish schools in the BSSR. The first secretary turned down the appeal, dismissing it entirely as tainted by Bundism and Zionism.[19]

At the end of the 1940s, and following the assassination in Minsk of the well-known Moscow Jewish artist and chairman of the Jewish Anti-Fascist Committee, Solomon Mikhoels, local Jewish cultural figures experienced a new purge. Unlike the Terror campaign of the late 1930s, this one singled out Jews.[20] Soviet Jewish cultural institutions and personalities came under systematic attack. By 1948, the interwar capital of Yiddish no longer housed a Jewish section of the Writers' Union of Belorussia, Yiddish publications, or a State Jewish Theater (its building—the former synagogue—was transformed into the local Russian Theater, and its stage director Viktor Golovchiner accused of producing "harmful and antipatriotic plays").[21] According to the 1959 census, only approximately 14 percent of the total Jewish population of the city (thirty-eight thousand) declared Yiddish their native tongue. No Yiddish culture or literature existed in Minsk, and no Yiddish school or academic institution of any kind operated in the city.[22]

With the post–World War II reversal of the Bolshevik emancipation project, Soviet universalism and "brotherhood of peoples" largely rejected the Jews.[23] The new Cold War geopolitical order, in combination with the establishment of the state of Israel, led them to be considered the most unreliable and "foreign" ethnic group in the Soviet Union, whose patriotism could only be distrusted. Expressions of state anti-Semitism ranged from anti-Jewish quotas at universities and government posts to accusations of "cosmopolitanism" and arrests of students for allegedly organizing "Zionist cells."[24] Following the 1953 unmasking of the so-called Doctors' Plot, or the alleged conspiracy of Jewish medical assassins of Soviet leaders in Moscow, Jewish doctors were arrested in Minsk as well.[25]

In 1951, the Executive Committee of the Minsk City Council closed down the Jewish cemetery on Sukhaia Street and refused to allow any further burials there on the grounds of a lack of space.[26] According to one source, a number of black-marble stones used to build the postwar monument to Belorussian national writer Yakub Kolas were tombstones taken from this Jewish cemetery. Traces of the Hebrew inscriptions remained visible several years after the monument's inauguration in the early 1970s.[27] A group of Jews petitioned the Minsk City Council, asking it to fence off the territory of the cemetery in order to prevent pigs, goats, and cows from grazing there. Despite the petitioners' claim that "great revolutionary Jews who gave their life for the revolution" were buried there, the appeal fell on deaf ears.[28] In the mid-1970s, local authorities bulldozed an older Jewish cemetery, the ancient and historic one, to make way for a dance floor and a soccer field.[29] Only one synagogue functioned in Minsk from 1946 to the mid-1960s. Located on Nemiga Street and headed by the Kovno-born rabbi Yaakov-Yosef Berger until 1956,[30] this last synagogue in the Belorussian capital was closed down (and its building demolished to make room for an apartment building) in 1964.[31]

The atmosphere of anxiety persisted among Jews in the post-Stalin years. In the early 1960s, the campaign against so-called economic crimes overwhelmingly targeted Jews. Drawing on the anti-Semitic stereotype of Jews as money grubbers, in 1962, 54 percent of the eighty-four persons sentenced to death for economic offenses throughout the Soviet Union were Jews; in Ukraine, 90 percent of individuals sentenced to death were Jews.[32] In Minsk, Semion Briskin and his wife Celia were sentenced to death for supposedly engaging in speculation and selling gold on the black market. The three non-Jews convicted in the same trial received prison sentences ranging between six months and a year.[33] The money-grubbing Jew stereotype resurfaced in the context of the antireligious campaign of the early 1960s, specifically in the attacks on the "barbarian practice" of circumcision. When the *mohel* Aron Livshitz moved from Vilna to Minsk to perform circumcisions, he was accused of charging the enormous sum of five hundred rubles per circumcision.[34] The local newspaper *Minskaia Pravda* stated in 1961, "Money! That is the God of the Minsk Jewish religious community and their aides."[35] In stark contrast with the interwar period, anti-Semitism was encouraged by the Minsk authorities. In the absence of Jewish cultural institutions, and after 1964 of religious institutions, anti-Semitism became the single most important factor in sustaining Jewish identity in Minsk.

Postwar accounts of the city's history generally suppressed its Jewish character. Besides the epigrammatic mention that Jews were one of the groups that inhabited the city, the "Minsk" main entry to the 1954 *Great Soviet Encyclopedia* made no reference to its past Jewishness— to the fact that it was once called "the Jerusalem of Belorussia," that Yiddish had been an official state language before the war, or that the city's Jews had been exterminated by the Germans.[36] Tourist guidebooks of the Belorussian capital neglected to make the slightest allusion to the Jews of Minsk. The long and detailed historical overview included in a 1971 Minsk travel guide did not incorporate any reference to its past Jewish demographics. While it referred to the names of prominent Belorussian and Russian writers of the 1920s and 1930s, it failed to mention Jewish writers like Kharik and Kulbak, despite their posthumous rehabilitation in the late 1950s. The historical overview did not mention any of the Jewish cultural and academic institutions that had once existed in the city and did not care to remind tourists of the role that Yiddish had once played in the life of many of its Jewish residents. Throughout the entire guide, the only allusion to the Jews of Minsk was at the time of their destruction, when the authors admitted that "100,000 perished in the ghetto."[37]

This book is also intended to memorialize the community of Soviet Jews that existed in Minsk before World War II—their lifestyle, culture, identity, as well as the geography of the city in which they lived—a community that was first brutally erased from history and then knowingly removed from public memory.

Notes

Introduction

1. Solomon Grinberg. GAMO, f. 12, op. 1, d. 758, ll. 537, 537a.

2. On the legal status of Russian Jews, see Hans Rogger, *Jewish Policies and Right-Wing Politics in Imperial Russia* (Berkeley: University of California Press, 1986); and Michael Stanislawski, "Russian Jewry, the Russian State, and the Dynamics of Jewish Emancipation," in *Paths of Emancipation: Jews, States, and Citizenship*, edited by Pierre Birnbaum and Ira Katznelson (Princeton, NJ: Princeton University Press, 1995), 262–83.

3. In 1939 there were approximately 3,028,500 Jews living in the Soviet Union, or 1.8 percent of the total population. See Mordechai Altshuler, *Distribution of the Jewish Population of the USSR, 1939* (Hebrew University of Jerusalem, 1993), 9.

4. Benjamin Pinkus, *The Jews of the Soviet Union: The History of a National Minority* (Cambridge: Cambridge University Press, 1988), 83.

5. Arkadii Zeltser, "Jews in the Upper Ranks of the NKVD, 1934–1941," *Jews in Russia and Eastern Europe* 1, no. 52 (2004): 64–90; see 77.

6. Altshuler, *Distribution of the Jewish Population*, 11.

7. Mordechai Altshuler, *Soviet Jewry on the Eve of the Holocaust: A Social and Demographic Profile* (Jerusalem: The Center for Research of East European Jewry and Yad Vashem, 1998), 311–12. Overall, Jews held 19.1 percent of all white-collar positions in the BSSR in 1939.

8. See Simon Dubnow, *Kniga zhizni: vospominaniia i razmyshleniia dlia istorii moego vremeni* (St. Petersburg, 1998). On Isaac Babel's exam experience as *extern*, see "My Father's Dovecoat," in *The Complete Works of Isaac Babel* (New York: W. W. Norton, 2002).

9. GAMO, f. 12, op. 1, d. 758, ll. 537, 537a.

10. Both quotes are from Geoffrey Hosking, *The First Socialist Society: A History of the Soviet Union from Within* (Cambridge, MA: Harvard University Press, 1997), 70.

11. Ibid., 71.

12. Yuri Slezkine, *The Jewish Century* (Princeton, NJ: Princeton University Press, 2004), 254. See, in particular, chapters 3 and 4.

13. Carlo Ginzburg, *Il filo e le tracce: vero, falso, finto* (Milan: Feltrinelli, 2006), 258.

14. The importance of local studies in the writing of pre-revolutionary Russian Jewish history was first emphasized by Steven Zipperstein in his work on nineteenth-century Odessa; see Steven J. Zipperstein, *The Jews of Odessa: A Cultural History, 1794–1881* (Stanford, CA: Stanford University Press, 1986). On the Jews of St. Petersburg in late imperial Russia, see Benjamin Nathans, *Beyond the Pale: The Jewish Encounter with Late Imperial Russia* (Berkeley: University of California Press, 2002). On Jewish Kiev in the nineteenth century and Jewish Bialystok in the twentieth century, see Natan Meir, *Kiev: Jewish Metropolis, 1859–1914* (Bloomington: Indiana University Press, 2010); and Rebecca Kobrin, *Jewish Bialystok and Its Diaspora* (Bloomington: Indiana University Press, 2010). For regional approaches to the study of Soviet Jewry, see the innovative work of Arkadii Zeltser on the economic, cultural, and religious life of the Jews of Vitebsk and surrounding *shtetlekh* during the interwar period, *Evrei v sovetskoi provintsii: Vitebsk i mestechki, 1917–1941* (Moscow: Rosspen, 2006); and Mikhail Beizer on Leningrad, *Evrei Leningrada, 1917–1939: natsionalnaia zhizn i sovetizatsiia* (Moscow and Jerusalem: Gesharim, 1999).

15. In 1897, 47,562 Jews lived in Minsk, or 52.3 percent of the city population; in 1923, the Jews numbered 48,312 and made up for 43.6 percent of the city population; in 1926, they amounted to 53,686, or 41 percent. In 1939, 71,000 Jews lived in Minsk, or 30 percent of the total population. In June 1941, on the eve of the German invasion, with the influx of refugees from Poland, the Jewish city population had grown to 100,000. On the city's demographics, see "Minsk," in *Bolshaia Sovetskaia Entsiklopediia*, vol. 39 (Moscow, 1926), 465–68; Aron Rozin, "Ha-yishuv ha-yehudi be-Minsk bashanim 1917–1941," in *Minsk, ir va-em: korot, maasim, ishim, havai*, vol. 2, edited by Shlomo Even-Shoshan (Tel Aviv: Irgun yotsei Minsk u-venoteha be-Yisrael, 1985), 23 (hereafter *Minsk*); and Altshuler, *Distribution of the Jewish Population*, 38.

16. All the above population figures are from 1939. See Altshuler, *Distribution of the Jewish Population*, 20–23. See also Elina Chkolnikova, "The Transformation of the Shtetl in the USSR in the 1930s," *Jews in Russia and Eastern Europe* 1, no. 52 (2004): 91–129, see, in particular, 128.

17. Altshuler, *Soviet Jewry on the Eve of the Holocaust*, 36.

18. Ibid., 38. On the persistence of the Jewish neighborhood in Odessa and Kiev, see also 40–46.

19. For the Cold War legacy and the emphasis on Jewish suffering, even in serious works of scholarship, see, for example, Solomon M. Schwarz, *The Jews in the Soviet Union* (Syracuse, NY: Syracuse University Press, 1951); Solomon M. Schwarz, *Antisemitizm v sovetskom soiuze* (New York: Chekhov Publishing House, 1952); and Lionel Kochan, ed., *The Jews in Soviet Russia Since 1917* (Oxford, New York: Oxford University Press, 1978).

20. For this approach in the general field of Soviet history, see, for example, Yuri Slezkine, "The USSR as a Communal Apartment, or How a Socialist State Promoted Ethnic Particularism," in *Slavic Review* 53, no. 2 (summer 1994): 414–52; Stephen Kotkin, *Magnetic Mountain: Stalinism as Civilization* (Berkeley: University of California Press, 1995); Igal Halfin, *Terror in My Soul: Communist Autobiographies on Trial* (Cambridge, MA: Harvard University Press, 2003); and Jochen Hellbeck, *Revolution on My Mind: Writing a Diary Under Stalin* (Cambridge, MA: Harvard University Press, 2006). For examples of this approach in the field of Soviet Jewish history, see Jeffrey Veidlinger, *The Moscow State Yiddish Theater: Jewish Culture on the Soviet Stage* (Bloomington: Indiana University Press, 2000); David Shneer, *Yiddish and the Creation of Soviet Jewish Culture, 1918–1930* (Cambridge and New York: Cambridge University Press, 2004); and Anna Shternshis, *Soviet and Kosher: Jewish Popular Culture in the Soviet Union, 1923–1939* (Bloomington and Indianapolis: Indiana University Press, 2006).

21. See Zvi Y. Gitelman, *Jewish Nationality and Soviet Politics: The Jewish Sections of the CPSU 1917–1930* (Princeton, NJ: Princeton University Press, 1972); and Mordechai Altshuler, *Ha-Yevsektsya bi-Verit ha-Moatsot: ben leumiut le-komunizm* (Tel Aviv: Sifriyat poalim, 1981).

22. For the view of the Evsektsiia as a bureaucratic structure merely involved in destroying Jewish culture and life, see, for example, L. Zenzipper (Rafaeli), *Eser shnot redifot* (Tel Aviv: Akhdut, 1930); Jacob Maazeh, *Zikhronot*, 4 vols. (Tel Aviv: Yalkut, 1936); and Nahum Nir-Rafalkes, *Ershte yorn* (Tel Aviv: Y. L: Peretz farlag, 1960).

23. See Veidlinger, *Moscow State Yiddish Theater*; and Shneer, *Yiddish and the Creation of Soviet Jewish Culture*.

24. See Peter Kenez, *The Birth of the Propaganda State: Soviet Methods of Mass Mobilization, 1917–1929* (Cambridge: Cambridge University Press, 1985). On daily life in Soviet society and the rise of new Soviet social types, see, for example, Sheila Fitzpatrick, *Everyday Stalinism: Ordinary Life in Extraordinary Times, Soviet Russia in the 1930s* (New York: Oxford University Press, 1999); and Kotkin, *Magnetic Mountain*.

Chapter 1

1. Italo Calvino, *Invisible Cities* (New York: Harcourt Brace Jovanovich, 1974), 96–97.
2. Z. Rubashev, "Minsk," *Evreiskaia Entsiklopediia*, vol. XI, 86 (hereafter *EE*).
3. Mikhel Danilevich from Troki was the first Jew to settle in the city; he leased the city's custom duties in 1489 and paved the way for a small number of Jewish families to move to Minsk. "Minsk," *Kratkaia Evreiskaia Entsiklopediia*, vol. V, 358.
4. Rubashev, "Minsk," *EE*, vol. XI, 89.
5. See Ja. Shabad, "Minskaia guberniia," *EE*, vol. XI, 78.
6. Ibid.
7. A. Gunzburg, "Minsk," *EE*, vol. XI, 88.
8. For more on these debates, see John D. Klier, *Imperial Russia's Jewish Question, 1855–1881* (Cambridge: Cambridge University Press, 1995).
9. Ibid., in particular chapter 7.
10. "Minsk," *Kratkaia Evreiskaia Entsiklopediia*, vol. V, 358–59. See also Yakov Lestschinsky, *Dos yidishe folk in numern* (Berlin, 1922), 31; and Aron Rozin, "Ha-yishuv ha-yehudi be-Minsk, 1917–1941," in *Minsk*, 23.
11. In the Minsk *guberniia* Jews were more literate in Russian than non-Jews: 30.4 percent of Jewish men and 15.8 percent of Jewish women were able to read and write in Russian as opposed to 25.4 percent and 10.1 percent of non-Jewish men and women respectively. See Shabad, "Minskaia guberniia," 80.
12. Daniel Charny, *A Yortsendlik aza, 1914–1924* (New York: Tsiko Bikher farlag, 1943), 51.
13. Pauline Wengeroff, *Rememberings: The World of a Russian-Jewish Woman in the 19th Century* (Potomac: University Press of Maryland, 2000), 213, 221.
14. Ibid., 227–32.
15. OHD, (58) 6, Interview with Dr. Moshe Klutsh, April 13, 1969, 14.
16. Hillel Alexandrov, *Tsaytshrift*, vol. IV (Minsk, 1930), 222–24.
17. Quoted from *Voskhod* in Uri Finkel, "Minsker Yidisher dales amol," *Oktyabr*, July 15, 1936, no. 155, 3.
18. Gunzburg, "Minsk," 87. According to the 1897 census, in Vilna more than 3 percent of the total Jewish population (two thousand individuals) declared Russian their mother tongue; see "Vilna," in *EE*, vol. V, 591.
19. Wengeroff, *Rememberings*, 240.
20. See V. I. Kaliada, *Minsk uchora i sennia* (Minsk: Belarus, 1989).
21. Charny, *A Yortsendlik aza*, 55–56.
22. P. M. Shpilevskii, "Puteshchestvie po Polesiu i Belorusskomu kraiu: Minsk Belorusskii," *Sovremennik* 48. no. 11 (1854): 1.
23. Ibid., 2, 20.
24. Ibid., 28.
25. Ibid., 28–29.
26. Ibid., 16, 22–26.
27. Siani Leichter, "Toldot ha-kehilah ha-yehudit be-Minsk," *Minsk*, vol. I, 47.
28. Ibid., 22–26. On the struggle over the establishment of a Jewish state school, see Lev Levanda, "Daf me-toldot ha-hinukh yehudi be-Rusiyah," *Minsk*, vol. I, 120–26.
29. Wengeroff, *Rememberings*, 223.
30. OHD (58) 11, Interview with Leybush Rozenbaum, March 23, 1969, 3, 6–7.
31. Gunzburg, "Minsk," 87.
32. OHD (58) 19, Interview with Professor Shaul Liberman, June 24, 1971, folio 05545.
33. David Maggid, "Vilna," *EE*, vol. V, 572.

34. On Minsk rabbis and rabbinic institutions, see Ben-Zion Eisenstadt, *Rabanei Minsk vehakhameha: sefer ha-zikaron* (Vilna, 1898); and Meir Hailperin, "Ha-Gadol" mi-Minsk: R. Yerubam Yehudah Leyb Perlman, toldotav ve-korotav (Jerusalem and New York: Feldhaim, 1991).

35. Ben-Zion Gershuni, "Ha-yahadut ha-datit, mosdoteah ve-isheah," *Minsk*, 89–90.

36. Charny, *A Yortsendlik aza*, 51.

37. Shimon Yakov Gliksberg, "Hamesh shanim be-Minsk," *Minsk*, vol. 1, 484.

38. See Moshe Mishkinsky, "Regional Factors in the Formation of the Jewish Labor Movement in Czarist Russia," *YIVO Annual* 14 (1969): 27–52.

39. Isaiah Trunk, "Der onheyb fun der yidisher arbeter bavegung," vol. I, *Di geshikhte fun Bund* (New York, 1960), 56.

40. B. Katsenelson, "A. Liessin ve ha-opozitsiah be-Minsk," *Minsk*, vol. I, 263–64. See also A. Liessin, "Ha-opozitsiah be-Minsk be-tkufat yisudo shel ha-Bund," *Minsk*, 255–62.

41. Trunk, "Der onheyb fun der yidisher arbeter bavegung," 97.

42. Sh. Kazhdan, "Der Bund—biz dem finftn tsuzamenfor," in *Di geshikhte fun Bund*, edited by G. Aronson and J. S. Hertz, vol. 1 (New York, 1962), 200.

43. Sh. Hertz, "Di ershte ruslende revolutsye," *Di geshikhte fun Bund*, edited by G. Aronson and J. S. Hertz, vol. II (New York, 1962), 122.

44. Ibid., 119, 125.

45. See Alef Litvak, *Gezamlte shriftn* (New York: Arbeter Ring, 1945), 191–207.

46. On Syrkin in Minsk, see Mery Syrkin, "Avi, Nachman Syrkin," *Minsk*, vol. I, 386–87.

47. Nahum Kantorovich, "Poale-Zion 'nusah Minsk'," *Minsk*, vol. I, 408–13.

48. Daniel Persky, "Shimshon Rozenbaum," *Minsk*, vol. I, 348.

49. OHD (58) 15, Interview with Chanan Goldberg, July 7, 1970, 10–17.

50. Gitelman, *Jewish Nationality and Soviet Politics*, 80–81.

51. Rozin, "Ha-yishuv ha-yehudi," 9.

52. Ibid., 7–8.

53. Ibid., 7; and Grigory Aronson, "Minsk in der tsayt fun der daytshisher okupatsye," *Di Tsukunft*, 1938, 37.

54. A. Paleyes, "Zikhroynes vegn di ershte teg fun revolutsye in Minsk," *Dos fraye vort*, March 16, 1919, no. 13, 10–11.

55. See *Di Geshikhte fun Bund*, vol. 3, 139.

56. See V. Knorin, *1917 yor in Vaysrusland un afn mayrevfront*, Minsk, 1927.

57. OHD (58) 15, Interview with Chanan Goldberg, July 7, 1970, 12.

58. Rozin, "Ha-yishuv ha-yehudi," 9–10.

59. *Di Geshikhte fun Bund*, vol. 3, 109–10, 129.

60. Aronson, "Minsk in der tsayt," 29.

61. Ibid.

62. Ibid., 31.

63. See Moshe Levinson, "Hazanim ve-hazanut be-Minsk," *Minsk*, vol. I, 115.

64. Aronson, "Minsk in der tsayt," 31.

65. Quoted in Rozin, "Ha-yishuv ha-yehudi," 90.

66. Leyme Roznhoyz, "Di tsveyte oyser ordntlekhe konferents fun der yidisher s.d. arbeter partey Poale-Zion in der ratn Rusland," *Dos fraye vort*, February 3, 1919, no. 9, 2.

67. *Dos fraye vort*, March 25, 1919, no. 14, 31.

68. *Dos fraye vort*, March 16, 1919, no. 13, 15.

69. See I. M. Cherikover, "Bund," *EE*, vol. V, 94.

70. Rozin, "Ha-yishuv ha-yehudi," 13.

71. See ibid.

72. See Sh. Agursky, *Di Oktyabr-revolutsye in Vaysrusland: zamlbukh, artiklen un zikhroynes*, Minsk, 1927, 107–8.
73. See Aronson, "Minsk in der tsayt," 28–29.
74. Rozin, "Ha-yishuv ha-yehudi," 16.
75. *Farn folk*, March 2, 1920, no. 61, 1.
76. *Farn folk*, March 18, 1920, no. 64, 3.
77. *Farn folk*, May 21, 1920, no. 117, 3. Established in 1912 in Katowice as a world movement of Orthodox Jewry, in interwar Poland Agudat Israel functioned as a political party opposed to the Zionist movement.
78. NARB, f. 6, op. 1, d. 133, l. 26.
79. TsNANANB, f. 72, op. 1, d. 4, l. 67.
80. *Komune*, September 17, 1920, no. 26, 1.
81. Sara Rejzen, "Nu, oyb krig, to zol zayn krig," *Komune*, September 13, 1920, no. 24, 2.
82. Quoted in Rozin, "Ha-yishuv ha-yehudi," 95.
83. RGASPI, f. 445, op. 1, d. 9, ll. 25–26.
84. In 1921, seventy pogroms broke out in Belorussia resulting in five hundred fatalities and two hundred injured. See Yehuda Slutsky, *Bobruisk: sefer zikaron le-kehilat Bobruisk*, vol. I (Tel Aviv), 204. On the number of pogroms and fatalities in Ukraine in the years 1917–21, see Gitelman, *Jewish Nationality*, 162.
85. GARF, f. 1318, op. 1, d. 717, l. 10.
86. On the pogroms and their perpetrators in the early phases of the revolution, see Oleg Budnitskii, *Rossiiskie evrei mezhdu krasnymi i belymi (1917–1920)* (Moscow: Rosspen, 2005).
87. GARF, f. 1318, op. 1, d. 683, ll. 14, 18.

Chapter 2

1. GAMO, f. 322, op. 1, d. 30, l. 38.
2. GAMO, f. 322, op. 1, d. 30, l. 45.
3. *Der veker*, May 31, 1923, no. 125, 4.
4. NARB, f. 4, op. 1, d. 578, ll. 20–21.
5. On the establishment and goals of the Evsektsiia, see Gitelman, *Jewish Nationality and Soviet Politics*; and Altshuler, *Ha-Yevsektsyah bi-Verit ha-Moatsot*.
6. See Gitelman, *Jewish Nationality and Soviet Politics*, 250.
7. See RGASPI, f. 445, op. 1, d. 9, l. 87.
8. NARB, f. 42, op. 1, d. 72, l. 44.
9. On ORT activities in the USSR during the 1920s, see N. Khanin, *Soviet Rusland vi ikh hob ir gezen* (New York: Farlarg Veker, 1929), 34–35, 38–39.
10. NARB, f. 6, op. 1, d. 196, ll. 14, 18–19.
11. RGASPI, f. 445, op. 1, d. 64, ll. 10, 16. For JDC staff members in Minsk, see JDC Archives, Collection 21/32, file Minsk, List of Staff Members, June 1923.
12. JDC Archives, Collection 21/32, file 459, Letter from Edward Rosenblum (JDC Minsk) to Dr. Boris Bogen (JDC Moscow), October 25, 1923, 5.
13. JDC Archives, Collection 21/32, file 500, Letter by Boris Bogen, March 6, 1923.
14. Ibid.
15. GARF, f. 1065, op. 1, d. 367, l. 35.
16. See JDC Archives, Collection 21/32, file 478, Letter by Samarius Gourary to Dr. Hyman; and Letter by Rabbi Schneersohn to Adler, December 28, 1931.
17. JDC Archives, Collection 21/32, file 459, Letter from Rosenblum to Bogen, October 25, 1923, 6.

18. There were eighteen children's homes in Minsk in 1923, which provided shelter to approximately 1,536 children, most of them orphans. Six of these homes were Jewish (with 542 children); and twelve were Russian, Belorussian, and Polish (with a total of 994 children). JDC Archives, Collection 21/32, file 500, JDC Report on Minsk, June 13, 1923.
19. JDC Archives, Collection 21/32, file 4576.
20. See *Entsiklopediah shel ha-tsionut ha-datit: ishim, musagim, mifalim*, vol. I (Jerusalem: Mossad HaRav Kook, 1958), 224–25.
21. N. V. Brovkin, *Russia After Lenin: Politics, Culture and Society, 1921–1929* (London and New York: Routledge, 1998), 30–31.
22. GAMO, f. 6, op. 2, d. 1408, l. 62.
23. GAMO, f. 6, op. 2, d. 1408, l. 39.
24. See GAMO, f. 6, op. 2, d. 1429, ll. 28–35.
25. See JDC Archives, Collection 21/32, file 565, Statement of Industrial Activities of the JDC in Russia, August 1, 1930.
26. See Khanin, *Soviet Rusland*, 9, 11, 30–31, 51–53.
27. See, for example, Berl Nakhamkin, "A Rov zogt az men tor nit ganvenen," *Der veker*, June 1, 1925, no. 126, 3; and V. D., "Peklekh far zikh," *Oktyabr*, January 27, 1928, no. 23, 4.
28. JDC Archives, Collection 21/32, file 526, Report by Louis Fischer, 2–4.
29. GAMO, f. 12, op. 1, d. 475, l. 38.
30. NARB, f. 4, op. 1, d. 700, l. 119.
31. On the Evsektsiia's opposition to EMSO, see NARB, f. 4, op. 1, d. 430, ll. 97, 104–5.
32. See Z. V. Shibeko, *Minsk: stranitsy zhizni dorevolutsionnogo goroda* (Minsk: Polymija, 1990), 309.
33. See, for example, *Oktyabr*, May 19, 1928, no. 114, 4.
34. GAMO, f. 6, op. 1, d. 240, l. 32.
35. GAMO, f. 12, op. 1, d. 850, l. 28.
36. GAMO, f. 12, op. 1, d. 836, ll. 7–8, 23.
37. GAMO, f. 12, op 1, d. 561, ll. 29–30.
38. By March 1927, EMSO had 2,795 members. GAMO, f. 12, op. 1, d. 558, ll. 6–14, 28.
39. GAMO, f. 12, op. 1, d. 850, l. 35.
40. See GAMO, f. 12, op. 1, d. 850, l. 13, 19.
41. On EMSO's liquidation, see V. Rokhkind, "Ufdekn bizn sof di trotskistish-bundishe kontrabande," *Oktyabr*, July 26, 1937, no. 165, 3–4.
42. GARF, f. 1318, op. 1, d. 683, l. 8.
43. See Rozin, "Ha-yishuv ha-yehudi," 27–29.
44. GAMO, f. 12, op. 1, d. 758, l. 74.
45. Khone Shmeruk, "Ha-kibuts ha-yehudi ve-ha-hityashvut ha-haklait ha-yehudit be-Bielorusiah ha-sovetit, 1918–1932" (PhD dissertation, Hebrew University, 1961), 29–30.
46. See JDC Archives, Collection 21/32, file 459, Letter from Rosenblum to Bogen, October 25, 1923, 2; and "Minsk," *Bolshaia Sovetskaia Entsiklopediia*, vol. 39 (Moscow, 1926), 465–68.
47. See Rozin, "Ha-yishuv ha-yehudi," 27–29.
48. See, for example, *Der veker*, "Emigratsye," June 7, 1923, no. 131, 4.
49. *Der veker*, "Briv-kastn," June 12, 1923, no. 135, 4.
50. *Der veker*, "Briv-kastn," June 3, 1923, no. 128, 4.
51. See Aron Rozin, *Mayn veg aheym: zikhroynes fun an asir-tsiyon in Ratn Farband* (Jerusalem, 1981), 36–37, 122.
52. See NARB, f. 4, op. 1, d. 719, ll. 12–13.
53. GAMO, f. 12, op. 1, d. 367, ll. 2–7.
54. GAMO, f. 428, op. 1, d. 108, ll. 66–69.

55. In mid-1928, the city population counted 131,528 residents, including 55,778 (42.41 percent) Belorussians, 53,686 (40.82 percent) Jews, 12,617 (9.59 percent) Russians and 4,481 (3.40 percent) Poles; see GAMO, f. 12, op. 1, d. 837, l. 39.

56. "Militärgeographische Angaben über das Eropäische Rußland, Weißrußland," Generalstab des Heeres, Abteilung für Kriegskarten Vermessungswesen (Berlin, 1941), 140.

57. Yakov Basin, *Bolshevizm i evrei: Belorussia, 1920-e* (Minsk: Baraskin, 2008), 228.

58. NARB, f. 4, op. 1, d. 745, ll. 33–38.

59. See Rozin, "Ha-yishuv ha-yehudi," 31–34; and H. Alexandrov, "Yidishe bafelkerung in Minsk, 1897–1926," in *Tsaytshrift* (Minsk, 1930), 207, 217–18.

60. See NARB, f. 63, op. 1, d. 818 ll. 8–11, 55.

61. NARB, f. 63, op. 1, d. 750, ll. 70, 165.

62. See, for example, NARB, f. 4, op. 1, d. 745, l. 3.

63. NARB, f. 63, op. 1, d. 818, l. 55.

64. *Evrei v BSSR*, Minsk, 1929, 66–107.

65. NARB, f. 4, op. 1, d. 692, l. 48.

66. GAMO, f. 12, op. 1, d. 562, l. 25.

67. OHD (58) 17, Interview with Mendl Marshak, March 29, 1970, First Session, 4–7.

68. YIVO, RG 315, file 85, Letters from H. Leyvik to his wife, 1914–27.

69. Khanin, *Soviet Rusland*, 9, 11, 30–31.

70. OHD (58) 11, Interview with L. Rozenbaum, March 23, 1969, 23–25.

71. *Der veker*, June 12, 1923, no. 135, 4.

72. Isroel Fuks, "Der yidisher melukhisher-teater," *Oktyabr*, January 12, 1928, no. 10, 3.

73. Zonenshteyn, "Der teater farn arbeter-tsushoyer," *Oktyabr*, January 20, 1928, no. 17, 4.

74. Shuster, "Minsker Peretz Bibliotek: a shtim fun a lezer," *Oktyabr*, January 20, 1928, no. 17, 4.

75. *Oktyabr*, "In Yidishin opteyl fun muzey," January 1, 1926, no. 3, 4.

76. *Oktyabr*, "Muzey oyshtelungen," January 8, 1928, no. 7, 4.

77. GAMO, f. 12, op. 1, d. 758, l. 539.

78. Khanin, *Soviet Rusland*, 202–4.

79. Ibid., 213–16.

80. Ibid., 235.

81. NARB, f. 205, op. 1, d. 261, ll. 16–47.

82. NARB, f. 205, op. 1, d. 372, ll. 1–2, 51, 111.

83. OHD (58) 15, Interview with Ch. Goldberg, January 7, 1970, 10. Appointed instructor of Hebrew at Minsk University in 1921, Merlis died the day of his arrest in 1925 and was replaced by Jewish poet and scholar Yehiel Ravrebe.

84. Zalmen Rejzen, *Leksikon fun der yidisher literatur, prese, un filologye*, vol. I (Vilna: Kletskin, 1928–30), 104–6.

85. OHD (58) 11, Interview with L. Rozenbaum, March 23, 1969, 28–32.

86. NARB, f. 4, op. 1, d. 578, ll. 1–2.

87. GAMO, f. 12, op. 1, d. 1, l. 108.

88. Rozin, *Mayn veg aheym*, 106.

89. Central Zionist Archives, F30 Zenzipper Collection, file 82, 1.

90. Central Zionist Archives, F30 Zenzipper Collection, file 85, 1–4.

91. OHD (58) 11, Interview with L. Rozenbaum, March 23, 1969, First Session, 32. See also Sh. Even-Shoshan, "Mesimah she-nikhzevah," *Minsk*, vol. II, 256–58.

92. GAMO, f. 428, op. 1, d. 108, ll. 124–25.

93. NARB, f. 4, op. 1, d. 577, l. 58.

94. Rozin, *Mayn veg aheym*, 49–50.

95. NARB, f. 42, op. 1, d. 1141, ll. 5–7, 9.

96. NARB, f. 42, op. 1, d. 1142, l. 10.
97. NARB, f. 42, op. 1, d. 1614, l. 45.
98. JDC Archives, Collection 21/32, file 472, Aide-mémoire on Religious Education, July 3, 1926, 3.
99. In Moscow there were fifty Hebrew classes, with 250 students and twenty teachers; in Kiev, fifty classes, with 250 students and twenty-five teachers. See JDC Archives, Collection 21/32, file 475, Budget for Tarbut schools in Russia, 1928/1929; and Letter by Tarbut Teachers to Cyrus Adler, 1928.
100. Central Zionist Archives, F30 Zenzipper Collection, file 78, 1–9.
101. Central Zionist Archives, F30 Zenzipper Collection, file 121/1, Anketa n. 34.
102. OHD, (217) 150, Interview with Lev Gelfand, August 30, 1994, 3.
103. See GAMO, f. 12, op. 1, d. 166, l. 23.
104. See Yad Vashem, Collection 0.3, file 3760, Witness Account of Zhitnitskii S. Marc, March 1974, 1–4.
105. GAMO, f. 428, op. 1, d. 297, ll. 141–43.
106. Until its liquidation, the Poale-Zion's Central Committee met in a room, which sat up to forty people, located in the center of Minsk; see Rozin, *Mayn veg aheym*, 100.
107. GAMO, f. 428, op. 1, d. 164, l. 119.
108. GAMO, f. 12, op. 1, d. 851, ll. 77–78.
109. Rozin, *Mayn veg aheym*, 57.
110. Ibid., 61–62.
111. JDC Archives, Collection 21/32, file 4576, Interview with Sh. Ninburg December 20, 1986, 4.
112. GAMO, f. 428, op. 1, d. 107, ll. 19–27.
113. *Oktyabr*, "In redaktsye fun Oktyabr," January 8, 1928, no. 7, 4.
114. Rozin, *Mayn veg aheym*, 30–34.
115. Ibid., 130–31, 133.
116. Ibid., 96.
117. Ibid., 97.
118. Quoted in Gitelman, *Jewish Nationality and Soviet Politics*, 291.
119. I. J. Singer, *Nay-Rusland: bilder fun a rayze* (Vilna: Kletskin, 1928), 28.

Chapter 3

1. Ester Frumkin, member of the Central Committee of the Bund, Minsk, February 1921. Quoted in Gitelman, *Jewish Nationality and Soviet Politics*, 209.
2. Rakhmiel Vaynshteyn, member of the Central Committee of the Bund, Minsk, February 1921. Quoted in ibid., 212–13.
3. The Bund to its members, Minsk, March 1921. Quoted in ibid., 214.
4. See B. Brutskus, *Professionalnyi sostav evreiskogo naseleniia Rossii* (St. Petersburg, 1908), 35.
5. On a Belorussian worker who joined the Bund in 1902 see, for example, NARB, f. 4, op. 1, d. 660, l. 9, 10–17.
6. See David E. Fishman, "From Shtadlanut to Mass-Parties: Jewish Political Movements in Lithuania," in *History of Lithuanian Jews*, edited by Darius Staliunas (Vilnius: Institute of History, forthcoming).
7. See Tobias, *Jewish Bund in Russia*, 37–38; and G. Aronson and J. S. Hertz, eds., *Di geshikhte fun Bund*, vol. 1 (New York, 1960), 109.
8. Liov Mutskin, "Merhats ha-damim be-Minsk be-1905," *Minsk*, vol. I, 457–62.
9. The two most rigorous studies of the Evsektsiia, its activities and challenges remain those of Gitelman and Altshuler. Both consider continuities in the political tactics retained by former

Bundists who joined the ranks of the Evsektsiia. See Gitelman, *Jewish Nationality and Soviet Politics*; and Altshuler, *Ha-Yevsektsyah bi-Verit ha-Moatsot*.

10. Former Bundists exploited their new position of power by pursuing the pre-revolutionary *Kulturkampf* against Zionists, their arch-enemies on the Jewish street, and therefore expedited the regime's decision to liquidate cultural activities in Hebrew. See Gitelman, *Jewish Nationality and Soviet Politics*, in particular 217–30, 266–91.

11. See Gitelman, *Jewish Nationality and Soviet Politics*, 286–91.

12. *Geshikhte fun Bund*, vol. 2, 144.

13. Boris K. Markiianov, *Borba Kommunisticheskoi partii Belorussii za ukreplenie edinstva svoikh riadov v 1921–1925 gg.* (Minsk, 1961), 22.

14. Quoted in Gitelman, *Century of Ambivalence*, 73.

15. Ivan S. Lubachko, *Belorussia Under Soviet Rule, 1917–1957* (Lexington: University Press of Kentucky, 1972), 6–7. In 1897, 71 percent of the population was illiterate; in 1905, 63 percent.

16. Ibid., 7–8. On the Belorussian national movement, see Per Anders Rudling, "The Battle Over Belorussia: The Rise and Fall of the Belarusian National Movement, 1906–1931" (PhD dissertation, University of Alberta, 2009), in particular chapters 1 and 2.

17. Ibid., 15, 28.

18. Ibid., 60.

19. GAMO, f. 6, op. 2, d. 1403, ll. 14, 17.

20. NARB, f. 4, op. 1, d. 225, l. 19.

21. RGASPI, f. 445, op. 1, d. 9, ll. 1–2.

22. GARF, f. 1318, op. 1, d. 683, l. 76.

23. RGASPI, f. 445, op. 1, d. 9, ll. 2, 63.

24. See, for example, GARF, f. 1318, op. 1, d. 683, ll. 24, 41.

25. RGASPI, f. 445, op. 1, d. 9, l. 2.

26. RGASPI, f. 445, op. 1, d. 9, l. 19.

27. RGASPI, f. 445, op. 1, d. 9, ll. 82–83.

28. RGASPI, f. 445, op. 1, d. 9, ll. 92, 93.

29. NARB, f. 4, op. 1, d. 226, l. 47.

30. RGASPI, f. 445, op. 1, d. 9, ll. 18, 20, 24–26, 31–32.

31. The Communist Bund, or Kombund, aligned itself with the Communist Party and favored a more pro-Bolshevik position. See Gitelman, *Jewish Nationality and Politics*, 174–77, 196–97.

32. Ibid., 206.

33. On Lenin's position on the Bund's claim for national rights for the Jewish proletariat and his view of the Jewish question, see V. I. Lenin, *Critical Remarks on the National Question: The Right of Nations to Self-Determination* (Moscow: Progress Publishers, 1968), 15–21; and Yohanan Petrovsky-Shtern, *Lenin's Jewish Question* (New Haven, CT: Yale University Press, 2010).

34. NARB, f. 4, op. 1, d. 430, ll. 4, 6, 8, 30–33. See also *Di geshikhte fun Bund*, vol. III, 38.

35. NARB, f. 4, op. 1, d. 225, l. 1.

36. Yankl Levin, *Kleyn-Bund: fun yene yorn* (Minsk, 1924).

37. NARB, f. 4, op. 1, d. 227, ll. 46–52. In 1923, all members of the Jewish section of the Minsk Komsomol were former Bundists. See NARB, f. 4, op. 1, d. 815, l. 1.

38. NARB, f. 4, op. 1, d. 227, l. 71.

39. NARB, f. 4, op. 1, d. 430, l. 33.

40. RGASPI, f. 445, op. 1, d. 64, ll. 48, 50, 53.

41. NARB, f. 4, op. 1, d. 578, l. 29.

42. NARB, f. 4, op. 1, d. 577, l. 46.

43. NARB, f. 4, op. 1, d. 225, l. 34. The Evsektsiia depended on the general party organization for financial matters as well. While the Evsektsiia operated in Yiddish, and party meetings' reports and

circulars were drafted in Yiddish, the originals were also translated into Russian and passed on to the Central Bureau of the CPB.

44. GAMO, f. 162, op. 1, d. 360a, l. 162.

45. Isak Aginsky, "Materyaln tsu der geshikhte fun nodl-fareyn in Vaysrusland," *Di royte nodl* 2, no. 8 (1925): 25–26.

46. Rozin,"Ha-yishuv ha-yehudi," 17.

47. A member of the Gomel Yugend-Bund, Yankl Levin was elected member of the Bund's Central Committee in 1919. See Yaakov Shatsky and Sh. Niger, eds., *Leksikon fun der nayer Yidisher literatur* (New York, 1956), vol. V, 274–75.

48. Elye Osherovitsh joined the Bund in the early 1900s and remained active in the Jewish party until 1918; he was elected member of the Central Committee of the CPB more than once. See *Leksikon fun der nayer Yidisher literatur*, vol. I, 194.

49. Born in Horodok, Vitebsk *guberniia*, Ber Orshansky had been active in the Vilna Bund since 1909. See Zalmen Rejzen, *Leksikon fun der yidisher literatur, prese, un filologye*, vol. I (Vilna: Kletskin, 1928–29), 172–73.

50. NARB, f. 4, op. 1, d. 577, ll. 18–19.

51. See Hertz, *Doyres Bundistn*, 321–34.

52. RGASPI, f. 445, op. 1, d. 9, l. 1. There were three Jewish clubs in Minsk in mid-1921: the Grosser Club, the Poale-Zionist Club Ber Borochov, and the Yugend-Bund Club Z. Pishanski.

53. NARB, f. 4, op. 1, d. 225, l. 41.

54. See Sh. Dimanshteyn, "Di yidishe komisariatn," in *Di Oktyabr revolutsye in Vaysrusland: zamlbukh, artiklen un zikhroynes*, edited by Sh. Agursky (Minsk, 1927), 285–91.

55. NARB, f. 4, op. 5, d. 409, ll. 45–47.

56. NARB, f. 4, op. 1, d. 430, l. 35.

57. NARB, f. 4, op. 1, d. 578, ll. 4–5.

58. NARB, f. 4, op. 1, d. 578, ll. 10–11.

59. RGASPI, f. 445, op. 1, d. 64, ll. 48, 50. The club maintained the same director even after its renaming; see GAMO, f. 12, op. 1, d. 376, ll. 24–25.

60. NARB, f. 4, op. 1, d. 580, ll. 55–56.

61. On the number of Yiddish, Hebrew, and Russian books in different city institutions at the end of 1921, see NARB, f. 42, op. 1, d. 1141, ll. 5–7, 9.

62. GAMO, f. 12, op. 1, d. 166, ll. 40–41.

63. GAMO, f. 12, op. 1, d. 166, ll. 12–13.

64. For a photograph of the former hotel's building in the 1930s, see V. I. Kaliada, *Minsk uchora i sennia*, 56. The club was relocated here in the early 1920s.

65. On the Jewish Workers' University, see NARB, f. 4, op. 1, d. 803, l. 9.

66. NARB, f. 42, op. 1, d. 1625, l. 20.

67. GAMO, f. 12, op. 1, d. 562, l. 16. Based on a resolution passed in December 1927, club members had to be eighteen years old, members of a professional union, and be recommended by their party cell. See GAMO, f. 12, op. 1, d. 836, l. 57.

68. NARB, f. 4, op. 5, d. 409, ll. 45–47.

69. "Di yidishe bildung arbet in Vaysrusland," *Af di vegn tsu der nayer shul*, January, 1924, 95; and "Di arbet fun der Ts.A.B.B. in Vaysrusland," *Af di vegn tsu der nayer shul*, December, 1924, 25.

70. *Geshikhte fun Bund*, vol. III, 212, 134. Among the first newspaper collaborators were: Max Weinreich, Arn Vaynshteyn, Avram Yuditski, Noyakh Lurye, A. Litvak, Ester Frumkin, B. Slutsky, Sore Fuks, Avrom Kirzhnits, and Dr. Itshak Teumim (who presided over the Minsk Bundist organization). See also Elias Schulman, "Yidishe kultur-tetikayt in Minsk, 1917–1941," *Hesed le-Avraham: sefer ha-yovel le-Avraham Golomb, tsu zayn akhtsikstn geboyrn-tog*, edited by M. Shtarkman (Los Angeles, 1970), 784–85.

71. See *Doyres Bundistn*, vol. I, 317.
72. See Agursky, "Fun Shtern biz Oktyabr," *Oktyabr*, November 7, 1925, no. 1, 2. On the fate of the newspaper in 1919 and 1920, see Agursky, "Di Yidishe arbeter fun yidishn komissariat in Vaysrusland," in *Di Oktyabr revolutsye in Vaysrusland*, 309.
73. NARB, f. 4, op. 1, d. 578, l. 11.
74. NARB, f. 4, op. 1, d. 577, ll. 28, 33.
75. NARB, f. 4, op. 1, d. 577, l. 26.
76. NARB, f. 4, op. 1, d. 580, l. 27, 44–45. On the circulation of *Veker*, see also GAMO, f. 12, op. 1, d. 374, ll. 3–9, 28, 33–37.
77. GAMO, f. 1260, op. 1, d. 1, l. 18. On the circulation of *Der Emes*, see David Shneer, *Yiddish and the Creation of Soviet Jewish Culture*, 250, n. 110.
78. For suggestions on how to improve the daily's content and circulation, see NARB, f. 4, op. 1, d. 692, ll. 184–87.
79. Meyer Pishkin, "Ikh zukh," *Oktyabr*, January 7, 1926, nos. 24, 4.
80. *Oktyabr*, February 18, 1928, no. 50, 4.
81. NARB, f. 4, op. 1, d. 585, ll. 31–33.
82. See *Di geshikhte fun Bund*, vol. III, 135.
83. Moshe Shulman, "Fun Veker tsu Oktyabr," *Oktyabr*, November 7, 1925, nos. 1, 2–3.
84. On Hirsh Lekert's role in the Bund and his becoming a legendary hero postmortem, see J. S. Hertz, *Hirsh Lekert* (New York: Undzer Tsayt, 1952); and *Geshikhte fun Bund*, vol. 1, 231.
85. Ibid., 34–35, 41–42.
86. See, for example, GAMO, f. 12, op. 1, d. 361, l. 74.
87. NARB, f. 42, op. 1, d. 1967, l. 16.
88. NARB, f. 1340, op. 1, d. 11, l. 36.
89. NARB, f. 4, op. 1, d. 580, l. 25.
90. NARB, f. 4, op. 1, d. 498, l. 3. This reference is to the floggings that occurred in Minsk a few weeks after the assassination attempt on Von Wahl. See Hertz, *Hirsh Lekert*, 67–68; and Ester Frumkin, *Hirsh Lekert* (Moscow, 1922), 27–28.
91. Some Minsk residents complained that a monument to Lekert replaced the monument to Tsar Alexander II. See NARB, f. 4, op. 1, d. 578, ll. 20–21.
92. For a description of the monument in 1929, see Khanin, *Soviet Rusland*, 21.
93. GAMO, f. 37, op. 1, d. 224, l. 107–8.
94. GAMO, f. 1260, op. 1, d. 1, l. 17.
95. On Bundist continuities, see, for example, Reytshuk, "Tsu di yidishe leder-arbeter fun Vaysrusland," *Di garber un bershter shtime*, June 1924, no. 1, 2.
96. M. Rafes, *Girsh Lekert (Rasskaz o tsarskikh rosgakh)* (Minsk, 1922).
97. NARB, f. 4, op. 1, d. 578, ll. 20–21, 23–25.
98. NARB, f. 4, op. 1, d. 508, l. 169.
99. NARB, f. 4, op. 1, d. 804, ll. 5, 15–26.
100. NARB, f. 4, op. 1, d. 580, l. 31.
101. See, for example, NARB, f. 42, op. 1, d. 1625, ll. 53–54.
102. Frumkin, *Hirsh Lekert*, 8–9. See also 35, 37.
103. Khanin, *Soviet Rusland*, 21. On Lekert's statue, see Leon Dennen, *Where the Ghetto Ends: Jews in Soviet Russia* (New York, 1934), 145; Yakov Basin, *Bolshevizm i evrei: Belorussia, 1920-e*, Baraksin (Minsk, 2008), 229; and Yakov Basin, "Delo Girsha Lekkerta (1902) i ego interpretatsiia v filme Belgoskino *Ego prevoskhoditelstvo*, 1927," *Belarus y XX stagoddzi* no. 3 (2004): 34–45. On Brazer's work, see Irina Voronovich, "Sudba mastera," *Mishpocha* no. 25 (2010): 52–56.
104. NARB, f. 4, op. 1, d. 508, l. 224.
105. *Vsia Belarussiia, spravochnaia kniga, 1924*, 51.

106. *Oktyabr*, June 11, 1936, no. 128, 4. See also Styrne, ed., *Usia BSSR, Karotkaia adrasna-davedachnaia kniga* (Minsk, 1935), 93–95.
107. NARB, f. 4, op. 1, d. 804, ll. 18–19.
108. See Shternshis, *Soviet and Kosher*, 80, 110.
109. Interview with Nina Rogov, New York City, January 30, 2005.
110. K. Hodoshevitsh, Sh. Yofe, and M. Mogilnitski, *Undzer royte heym: arbet-bukh af gezelshaftkentenish farn 4tn lernyor* (Moscow, Kharkov, and Minsk, 1931), 56–58. According to the Bundist account of the events, the Vilna *rabiner* (*kazennyi ravin*) Nemzer approached Lekert at the gallows encouraging him to repent for his sin. This scene also became the subject of the 1926 painting "Last Moments in Hirsh Lekert's Life," by artist Yaakov Kruger, who was living in Minsk at the time. See Basin, *Bolshevizm i evrei*, 230, 245.
111. Hirsh Reles, *Di yidishe-sovetishe shrayber fun Vaysrusland* (Minsk, 2004), 55–62.
112. On the film, cast, and director, see Basin, *Bolshevizm i evrei*, 228, 231.
113. "Beginning on Tuesday, March 20, Belgoskino will feature the great artistic film *Zayn ekselents*. Tickets may be purchased everyday from 3 to 11 p.m. at the movie theater." See *Oktyabr*, March 18, 1928, no. 66, 4.
114. NARB, f. 63, op. 2, d. 462, ll. 85–86.
115. BGAMLI, f. 81, op. 1, d. 61, ll. 28, 30–31, 37.
116. Aron Kushnirov, *Hirsh Lekert* (Kharkov, 1930).
117. Avraham Greenbaum, "The Belorussian State Jewish Theater in the Interwar Period," *Jews in Eastern Europe* 2, no. 42 (fall 2000): 66–67.
118. See Hertz, *Hirsh Lekert*, 113. See, in particular, Kushnirov, *Hirsh Lekert*, 17, 30, 68, 92–94.
119. Moshe Rafalskii, *Oktyabr*, February 19, 1928, no. 43, 3.
120. "An inhalt-raykhe vanttsaytung: VEYMT," *Oktyabr*, October 27, 1936, no. 239, 3. For a positive appraisal of the play, see Gurevitch, "10 yor fun Yidishn Melukhe-Teater fun Vaysrusland," *Der Yunger Leninets*, February 16, 1932, no. 8, 4.
121. Fishman, *Rise of Modern Yiddish Culture*, 70–71.
122. See, for example, RGASPI, f. 445, op. 1, d. 9, ll. 64, 80–84.
123. RGASPI, f. 445, op. 1, d. 64, l. 1.
124. See Mark Von Hagen, *Soldiers in the Proletarian Dictatorship: The Red Army and the Soviet Socialist State, 1917–1930* (Ithaca, NY: Cornell University Press, 1990).
125. GAMO, f. 2884, op. 1, d. 184, ll. 56–57.
126. NARB, f. 4, op. 1, d. 158, ll. 68–69.
127. GAMO, f. 37, op. 1, d. 1198, ll. 13–14.
128. See GARF, f. 1318, op. 1, d. 683, l. 23.
129. GAMO, f. 12, op. 1, d. 837, l. 39.
130. See, for example, Smoliar, *Fun ineveynik*, 116, 160–62.
131. Ibid., 304.
132. Shneer, *Yiddish and the Creation of Soviet Jewish Culture*, 21.
133. GARF, f. 1318, op. 1, d. 683, ll. 29, 30b, 32–33.
134. RGASPI, f. 445, op. 1, d. 64, ll. 48, 50, 53.
135. NARB, f. 4, op. 1, d. 578, l. 29.
136. NARB, f. 4, op. 1, d. 430, ll. 32, 48.
137. Smoliar, *Sovetishe yidn hinter geto-tsoymen*, 22.
138. RGASPI, f. 445, op. 1, d. 64, l. 17. On Belgoset, see Anna Gershtein, "Notes on the Jewish State Theater of Belorussia," in *Jews in Eastern Europe* 2, no. 27 (fall 1995): 27–42; and Altshuler, ed. *Ha-teatron ha-yehudi bi-Verit ha-Moatsot* (Jerusalem, 1996), in particular 133–201.
139. NARB, f. 42, op. 1, d. 1615, l. 37.
140. Rozin, *Mayn veg aheym*, 70–71.

141. Under Rafalskii's direction, the troupe Undzer vinkl performed in Minsk in 1920 to "bring art to the Jewish street." See "Teater un kunst," *Komune*, August 28, 1920, no. 11, 2.

142. NARB, f. 42, op. 1, d. 1615, ll. 17–26.

143. NARB, f. 42, op. 1, d. 1615, ll. 36–38.

144. See, for example, Rafalskii, "Der Teater bay zey un ba undz," *Shtern*, 1932, nos. 10/11, 183–94; and Orshansky, "Der kamf far a proletarishn yidishn teater," *Shtern*, 1931, nos. 8–9, 129–30; nos. 10–11, 101–15.

145. See Veidlinger, *Moscow State Yiddish Theater*, 53, 147.

146. RGASPI, f. 445, op. 1, d. 64, ll. 64–68.

147. Matthew Lenoe, *Agitation, Propaganda and the Stalinization of the Soviet Press, 1922–1930*, Carl Beck Papers in Russian and East European Studies, no. 1305 (Pittsburgh, PA: University of Pittsburgh, 1998), 10.

148. See NARB, f. 1340, op. 1, d. 32, ll. 175–89.

149. Goset was almost relocated to Belorussia twice, in 1925 and then again in 1926; see Veidlinger, *Moscow State Yiddish Theater*, 68–71.

150. GARF, f. 406, op. 25, d. 474, ll. 8–10. See also Shneer, *Yiddish and the Creation of Soviet Jewish Culture*, 130–31.

151. On Birobidzhan, see Robert Weinberg, *Stalin's Forgotten Zion: Birobidzhan and the Making of a Soviet Jewish Homeland, 1928–1966* (Berkeley: University of California Press, 2002).

152. See Altshuler, *Ha-Yevsektsya*, in particular 234–41.

153. On the Belorussian *shtetl*, see, for example, I. Osherovitsh, ed., *Di shtetlekh fun V.S.S.R. in rekonstruktivn peryod* (Minsk, 1932).

154. On local patriotism and the tendency to publish only works from Belorussia, see Shneer, *Yiddish and the Creation of Soviet Jewish Culture*, 161.

155. GAMO, f. 12, op. 1, d. 164, ll. 40–41.

156. Smoliar, *Fun ineveynik*, 307, 309.

157. NARB, f. 4, op. 1, d.1, l. 337.

158. NARB, f. 4, op. 5, d. 409, ll. 67, 77.

159. NARB, f. 4, op. 1, d. 804, ll. 62–63.

160. GAMO, f. 12, op. 1, d. 982, ll. 2–3.

161. See GAMO, f. 1260, op. 1, d. 4, l. 49.

162. NARB, f. 4, op. 5, d. 409, ll. 1–6.

163. NARB, f. 4, op. 5, d. 409, ll. 64–65.

164. NARB, f. 4, op. 5, d. 409, l. 77.

165. NARB, f. 4, op. 5, d. 409, ll. 63–65, 88, 111–12.

166. NARB, f. 4, op. 5, d. 409, l. 113.

167. NARB, f. 4, op. 5, d. 409, l. 46.

168. NARB, f. 4, op. 5, d. 409, ll. 39, 42.

169. Khanin, *Soviet Rusland*, 226–36.

170. See, for example, GAMO, f. 1260, op. 1, d. 9, ll. 87, 89.

171. See, for example, NARB, f. 4, op. 5, d. 409, ll. 57a, 86–87.

172. GAMO, f. 1260, op. 1, d. 7, l. 80.

173. GAMO, f. 164, op. 1, d. 71, ll. 1–189.

174. The first to uncover the counterrevolutionary nature of the Bund was Agursky, who made it his mission to unmask the national-bourgeois allegiance of former Bundists. See Gitelman, *Jewish Nationality and Soviet Politics*, 121.

175. NARB, f. 1340, op. 1, d. 32, ll. 18–19, 175–89.

176. Sh. Levin, "Oktyabr oder Veker (nit keyn diskusye kholile)," *Oktyabr*, November 7, 1925, no. 1, 5.

177. Smoliar, *Fun ineveynik*, 172–73, 179.
178. On the dissolution of the Evsektsiia, see, for example, Gitelman, *Jewish Nationality and Soviet Politics*, 475–81; and Smoliar, *Fun ineveynik*, 427.
179. On the anti-Bundist campaigns of the 1930s, see Altshuler, *Ha-Yevsektsya*, 242; and Gitelman, *Jewish Nationality and Soviet Politics*, 458–64.

Chapter 4

1. Leybovitsh, "Vegn ariberfirn di fareyn-arbet af yidish," *Di royte nodl* 2, no. 8 (1925):27.
2. See Greenbaum, *Jewish Scholarship and Scholarly Institutions*, 6.
3. For the text of the declaration of independence of the Belorussian Republic, see *Prakticheskoe razreshenie natsionalnogo voprosa v Belorusskoi SSR* (Minsk, 1927), 120–23.
4. Ibid., 134–35.
5. On the Soviet nationality policy and *korenizatsiia* campaign, see Tedd Martin, *The Affirmative Action Empire: Nations and Nationalism in the Soviet Union, 1923–1939* (Ithaca, NY: Cornell University Press, 2001). For an assessment of the Belorussianization campaign in the 1920s, see Arkadii Zeltser, "Belorusizatsiia 1920-x gg.: dostizheniia i neudachi," in *Evrei Belarusi: istoriia i kultura* III–IV (Minsk, 1998): 60–93; see 60–92.
6. See Klier, *Imperial Russia's Jewish Question 1855–1881*, 152–53.
7. On the Belorussian national movement, see Rudling, "Battle over Belarus"; and Beth Baird Yocum, "Constructing a Socialist Tower of Babel: Nationality Policy in Soviet Belorussia, 1921–1933" (PhD dissertation, Brandeis University, 2003).
8. Rudling, "Battle over Belarus," 315.
9. Hirsch, *Empire of Nations*, 149–50; see, also, 151–55.
10. *Prakticheskoe razreshenie*, 132–33.
11. GAMO, f. 428, op. 1, d. 297, ll. 141–43.
12. NARB, f. 4, op. 1, d. 669, ll. 5, 38. The same 1924 resolution also instructed to issue orders from local and central agencies in the four state languages, namely, Belorussian, Russian, Yiddish, and Polish.
13. See Gitelman, *Jewish Nationality and Soviet Politics*, 400–401; and Altshuler, *Ha-Yevsektsya bi-Verit ha-Moatsot*, 169.
14. By 1926, most union wall-newspapers in the city continued to appear in Russian and refused to shift to Belorussian. See NARB, f. 4, op. 16, d. 47, ll. 16–19.
15. GAMO, f. 37, op. 1, d. 1228, ll. 54–72.
16. Ibid.
17. NARB, f. 4, op. 1, d. 669, ll. 5, 38.
18. It should be noticed that a few Jewish writers opted for Belorussian as the language of their literary creativity; among them, Shmuel Nokhem Plavnik, who wrote as Zmiatrok Biadulia. See Viacheslav Selemenev and Arkadii Zeltser, "The Jewish Intelligentsia and the Liquidation of Yiddish Schools in Belorussia, 1938," *Jews in Eastern Europe* 3, no. 43 (2000): 81, n 10.
19. GAMO, f. 1260, op. 1, d. 3, ll. 38, 78.
20. NARB, f. 42, op. 1, d. 1892, l. 12.
21. NARB, f. 42, op. 1, d. 1844, l. 28.
22. OHD (58) 20, Interview with Dr. Nina Shalit-Galperin, July 12, 1970, 6.
23. GAMO, f. 162, op. 1, d. 291, ll. 2–12.
24. See, for example, NARB, f. 63, op. 2, d. 233, ll. 4–7.
25. OHD (58) 17, Interview with Mendl Marshak, March 29, 1970, First Session, 7–8; and OHD (58) 20, Interview with Dr. Nina Shalit-Galperin, July 12, 1970, 8.

26. GAMO, f. 1260, op. 1, d. 3, ll. 37–41.
27. NARB, f. 4, op. 1, d. 55, ll. 118–119.
28. NARB, f. 6, op. 1, d. 196, ll. 20–27.
29. Singer, *Nay-Rusland*, 25.
30. Mikhl Surits, *Soviet-rusland in 1931, ayndrikn fun a rayze* (Warsaw, 1932), 16, 312.
31. A resolution to broadcast a radio-newspaper in Yiddish once a week was passed in mid-1926. NARB, f. 42, op. 1, d. 1803, l. 12.
32. A number of films produced by Belgoskino were shown with Yiddish intertitles. See Osherovitsh, "Mobilizirn di visnshaft tsu dinst fun 2–tn finfyor," *Afn visnshaftlekhn front*, nos. 1–2 (Minsk, 1932), 4.
33. NARB, f. 6, op. 1, d. 1432, ll. 26, 38.
34. See, for example, GAMO, f. 12, op. 2, d. 1453, ll. 32, 77–78.
35. See, for example, GAMO, f. 12, op. 1, d. 758, ll. 138–139, 225, 238, 756–57.
36. GAMO, f. 12, op. 1, d. 562, l. 1, 9.
37. GAMO, f. 12, op. 1, d. 562, l. 1.
38. GAMO, f. 591, op. 1, d. 13, ll. 44–45.
39. I. Zaretski, "Amaratses," *Oktyabr*, July 11, 1937, no. 153, 4.
40. GAMO, f. 12, op. 1, d. 562, ll. 1, 16, 53, 54.
41. GAMO, f. 320, op. 1, d. 249, l. 43.
42. RGALI, f. 2270, op. 1, d. 294 and d. 158. On May 20, 1926, Oyslender wrote, "One more appearance at the theater (... this time I speak in Yiddish for a Belorussian audience—oh, how lucky! But we must!)."
43. On the court's growing popularity, see GAMO, f. 3, op. 1, d. 172, l. 38.
44. Singer, *Nay-Rusland*, 33.
45. GAMO, f. 12, op. 1, d. 561, ll. 15, 32–33.
46. Singer, *Nay-Rusland*, 32. On mixing Russian and Yiddish in the Odessa Jewish courtroom, see Surits, *Soviet-rusland*, 35–37; on Moscow, see ibid., 80–86.
47. OHD (58) 15, Interview with Chanan Goldberg, January 7, 1970, 22.
48. For more on Yung-Skoyt, see NARB, f. 42, op. 1, d. 1140, ll. 21–25.
49. In August 1921, the club counted 150 active members, most of whom were children under thirteen. NARB, f. 42, op. 1, d. 1140, ll. 26–27.
50. NARB, f. 42, op. 1, d. 1132, ll. 39–42. The Evsektsiia closed down the club in 1922 because of "Zionist elements"; see NARB, f. 4, op. 1, d. 580, l. 56.
51. The Central Jewish Kindergarten, also known as Evreiskii detskii gorodok or Minsker kinder-shtetl, was established in 1922 on the initiative of a group of Minsk women. See NARB, f. 42, op. 1, d. 1597, ll. 25–33.
52. The Minsk Jewish Agricultural Educational Farm was established in 1921 and reorganized on the basis of the Jewish farm school "Eydelman," founded in 1900. Its goal was to create a new leadership of Jewish agronomists. On the farm, see NARB, f. 42, op. 3, d. 290, ll. 1, 3, 8, 12–33, 43–44.
53. NARB, f. 4, op. 1, d. 816, l. 71.
54. GAMO, f. 12, op. 1, d. 562, ll. 1, 54.
55. NARB, f. 42, op. 1, d. 1632, ll. 57–58, 60.
56. GAMO, f. 12, op. 1, d. 170, ll. 82–83.
57. See GAMO, f. 12, op. 1, d. 562, l. 53.
58. NARB, f. 42, op. 1, d. 1634, ll. 17–18.
59. Interview with Anna Gershtein, Minsk, March 16, 2004.
60. RGASPI, f. 445, op. 1, d. 64, l. 10.
61. Yiddish schools introduced the study of Russian in their curriculum in June 1921. NARB, f. 42, op. 1, d. 72, ll. 4, 7, 9–12, 19–22, 25–26.

62. See, for example, NARB, f. 42, op. 1, d. 1966, ll. 1–2, 5, 17.
63. GAMO, f. 12, op. 1, d. 851, l. 37.
64. GAMO, f. 12, op. 1, d. 851, l. 77. See also *Shriftn fun Vaysrusishn universitet*, Minsk, 1929, 158.
65. GAMO, f. 164, op. 5, d. 176, ll. 15–28.
66. Ester Rosental-Shnayderman, *Af vegn un umvegn: zikhroynes, gesheenishn, perzenlekhkaytn*, vol. I (Tel Aviv: Farlag Peretz, 1974), 354.
67. See Ezra Mendelsohn, "Jewish Politics in Interwar Poland: An Overview," in *The Jews of Poland Between Two World Wars*, edited by Yisrael Gutman (Hanover, NH: Brandeis University Press, 1989), 19.
68. "Fun redaktsye," *Tsaytshrift*, I, 1926, v.
69. "Fun di bashlusn fun der III-er sesye fun tsentraln oysfir-komitet fun der VSSR," in *Tsaytshrift*, I, 1926, vi.
70. One such example was the scholarly journal *Evreiskaia Starina* (Jewish antiquities), founded by Dubnow in 1908 and issued in the USSR until 1930.
71. I. Tsinberg, "Novye raboty po evreiskoi etnografii i iazykovedeniu," *Evreiskaia Starina*, XII, 1928, 341.
72. I. Tsinberg, "Novye raboty po evreiskomu iazykovedeniu, literature i etnografii," *Evreiskaia Starina*, XIII, 1930, 145–63.
73. Zalmen Rejzen, *Leksikon fun der nayer yidisher literatur*, 1914, 303–5.
74. Rejzen, *Leksikon fun der yidisher literatur*, vol. I, 945–48. See also NARB, f. 205, op. 3, d. 1204, ll. 5–7, 40–41.
75. Rejzen, *Leksikon fun der yidisher literatur*, 51–53. See also NARB, f. 205, op. 1, d. 5947, ll. 1, 3–4.
76. RGALI, f. 2270, op. 1, d. 72, Letter from Gurshtein to Oyslender, May 4, 1925. On Moscow as a center of Jewish cultural life, see Gennady Estraikh, "Evreiskaia literaturnaia zhizn v poslerevolutsionnoi Moskve," *Arkhiv Evreiskoi Istorii*, vol. II, 2005, 187–212.
77. "Fun redaktsye," *Tsaytshrift*, I, 1926, II. Gurshtein also voiced his concern over the primitive state of Yiddish printing in Minsk. See RGALI, f. 2270, op. 1, d. 72, Letter from Gurshtein to Oyslender, May 4, 1925.
78. NARB, f. 42, op. 1, d. 1610, ll. 5–6.
79. NARB, f. 42, op. 1, d. 1610, l. 102.
80. NARB, f. 42, op. 1, d. 1610, ll. 105, 106.
81. NARB, f. 42, op. 1, d. 1612, l. 105.
82. NARB, f. 42, op. 3, d. 291, l. 5.
83. NARB, f. 42, op. 3, d. 291, l. 112.
84. NARB, f. 42, op. 3, d. 291, ll. 13–14, 103.
85. NARB, f. 42, op. 3, d. 291, l. 41.
86. NARB, f. 42, op. 3, d. 291, l. 23.
87. NARB, f. 42, op. 3, d. 291, ll. 25–26.
88. NARB, f. 42, op. 3, d. 291, ll. 33, 37.
89. Ber Orshansky, "Di Yidishe opteylung fun Invayskult," *Af di vegn tsu der nayer shul*, nos. 7–8, 1927, 66.
90. NARB, f. 42, op. 1, d. 1438, l. 6.
91. NARB, f. 42, op. 1, d. 1437, ll. 53–69.
92. NARB, f. 42, op. 1, d. 1437, ll. 40, 50.
93. NARB, f. 42, op. 1, d. 1437, ll. 26, 56, 620b, 63, 630b.
94. NARB, f. 4, op. 1, d. 578, ll. 10–11.
95. See NARB, f. 42, op. 1, d. 1468, ll. 12, 64.
96. GAMO, f. 37, op. 1, d. 227, ll. 103–5.
97. NARB, f. 4, op. 5, d. 409, ll. 86–87.

98. NARB, f. 42, op. 1, d. 1468, ll. 56–57.
99. NARB, f. 4, op. 1, d. 430, ll. 38, 48.
100. RGASPI, f. 445, op. 1, d. 64, l. 76.
101. RGASPI, f. 445, op. 1, d. 64, l. 38.
102. NARB, f. 42, op. 1, d. 1611, l. 24. The commission tried (unsuccessfully) to appoint Tevye Heilikman and Yulii Gessen to teach Jewish history in Minsk.
103. NARB, f. 42, op. 1, d. 1625, l. 102.
104. GAMO, f. 12, op. 1, d. 1, ll. 31, 45–46.
105. NARB, f. 42, op. 1, d. 1642, l. 3.
106. See NARB, f. 205, op. 3, d. 127, l. 3.
107. Professor Nikolskii, who was not Jewish but spoke excellent Yiddish, had a keen interest in Jewish folklore. At BGU he taught courses on ancient Jewish history. On Nikolskii's work collecting Jewish folklore in and around Minsk, see OHD (58) 11, Interview with Leybush Rozenbaum, March 23, 1969, 20–26.
108. GAMO, f. 12, op. 1, d. 851, l. 77.
109. GAMO, f. 164, op. 5, d. 176, ll. 77–78.
110. NARB, f. 205, op. 1, d. 261, ll. 16, 47, 68. Overall 187 students were enrolled in the Jewish Department in 1928–29. See NARB, f. 205, op. 1, d. 306, ll. 1–2, 3–4, 6–7, 9–13, 15–19, 25–38.
111. NARB, f. 42, op. 3, d. 325, ll. 14a, b, c. In 1927, nine of the thirty-four graduates from the Pedagogical Faculty graduated from the Jewish Department. In 1929, the number of graduates in Jewish studies grew to twenty-eight. See NARB, f. 205, op. 1, d. 924, l. 28.
112. NARB, f. 205, op. 3, d. 86, ll. 4, 6.
113. NARB, f. 205, op. 3, d. 1738, ll. 2–3. The proportion of Jewish instructors in Minsk was noteworthy. In 1927, 1,532 Jewish teachers were employed in city institutions (901 Belorussians, 142 Russians, and 134 Poles). See NARB, f. 4, op. 1, d. 750, ll. 5, 51.
114. NARB, f. 205, op. 3, d. 7120, ll. 2–3. Some well-known postgraduate students in the Jewish Department at BGU included the literary critic Yasha Bronshteyn and the linguist Leizer Vilenkin. On the graduate program in the Jewish Department at BGU, see also NARB, f. 205, op. 3, d. 6006, l. 60.
115. A Jewish studies program continued to exist at BGU until 1938. In 1935, a two-year Pedagogical Institute, with a Jewish, Russian, and Polish section, was established in the Institute for National Minorities, part of the Belorussian Academy of Sciences.
116. "Naye 15 literatur-lerer far der yidisher shul," *Oktyabr*, July 5, 1936, no. 147, 3.
117. V. Shats, "Der folkombild firt nit on," *Oktyabr*, April 26, 1937, no. 93, 3.
118. NARB, f. 42, op. 1, d. 1642, ll. 11–14.
119. TsNANANB, f. 67, op. 1, d. 8, l. 10.
120. On the Polish section of Inbelkut, see TsNANANB, f. 67, op. 1, d. 8, l. 69.
121. GAMO, f. 12, op. 1, d. 1, l. 31, 45–46. With the goal of assembling a bibliography of all Jewish publications issued in the USSR, as well as a scientific catalog of Jewish publications issued from the sixteenth century onward, a bibliographic section was added to the Jewish Department in 1927. Its inventory included memoirs from the 1905 revolution; correspondence by Sholem Aleichem and Y. L. Peretz; the Belorussian-Yiddish, Yiddish-Belorussian dictionary; excerpts from the Minsk *Pinkas*; eighteenth-century rabbinical responsa; photographs of synagogues and ritual objects; and Yiddish jokes. See YIVO, RG 3, f. 3223, ll. 110366–77.
122. On the Historical Commission, see Ber Orshansky, "Di Yidishe opteylung fun Invayskult," 67.
123. On the Literary Commission, see ibid., 70.
124. On the Language Commission, see ibid., 71–72.
125. TsNANANB, f. 67, op. 1, d. 4, l. 226. On the creation of a Belorussian military terminology, see also Rudling, "Battle over Belarus," 284–86.

126. Central Zionist Archive, J122 Collection Sefer Minsk (not cataloged); Letter from Inbelkult to Yehuda L. Kahan, New York, July 22, 1925; and Letter from Inbelkult to Yehuda Joffe, New York, September 9, 1925.

127. TsNANANB, f. 67, op. 1, d. 18, ll. 7–10.

128. See "Fun redaktsye," *Tsaytshrift*, I, 1926, v.

129. Singer, *Nay-Rusland*, 35. Dubnow was in Berlin at the time.

130. *Afn visnshaftlekhn front, biuleten fun Yidsektor*, no. 1, 1932, 167.

131. The first two issues of the journal were published by the Jewish division of the Academy of Science of the BSSR. The third issue—as well as the following ones, until 1935—were published by the Institute for Proletarian Jewish Culture of the Academy of Science of the BSSR. See *Afn visnshaftlekhn front, biuleten fun Yidsektor*, nos. 1–2, Minsk, 1932; and *Afn visnshaftlekhn front, biuleten fun Institut far Yidisher proletarisher kultur*, nos. 3–4, Minsk, 1933.

132. Born in 1896, in the *shtetl* of Smorgon, Kulbak moved to Minsk in 1918. A year later he relocated to Vilna, where he became one of the most celebrated poets in the city. In 1928, he returned to Minsk (where his parents lived) and joined the Soviet Jewish literary intelligentsia. In 1937, a few months before Kulbak's arrest, the Belorussian State Publishing House issued his translation of Gogol's *Revizor*, or *The Government Inspector*; see "Naye bikher," *Oktyabr*, April 4, 1937, no. 75, 4.

133. *Afn visnshaftlekhn front*, no. 1, 160.

134. See "Lingvistishe zamlung no. 3," *Oktyabr*, May 26, 1936, no. 116, 4.

135. H., "A visnshaftlekhe arbet vegn kahal als gever fun eksploitatsye," *Oktyabr*, June 3, 1937, no. 123, 3.

136. See L. Dushman, "Materyaln tsu der geshikhte fun Yidishn teater in Vaysrusland biz der Oktyabr revolutsye," *Afn visnshaftlekhn front*, no. 7, 1935, 162–94.

137. Quoted in Gitelman, *Jewish Nationality and Soviet Politics*, 397.

138. The Minsk literary group published a collection of poems dedicated to the victims of the White Terror. See *Kep: lider-zamlung, gevidmet di korbones funem vaysn teror* (Minsk, 1926).

139. NARB, f. 63, op. 2, d. 276, ll. 29–30.

140. NARB, f. 42, op. 1, d. 1600, l. 4.

141. NARB, f. 42, op. 1, d. 1600, ll. 47–48, 56–58.

142. YIVO, Pomeranz Collection, RG 500, box 1, ff. 16–28.

143. Sh. Eynhorn, "Mishlei-am be-yidish be-Minsk," in *Minsk*, vol. 1, 639. *Boytre* was first published in the literary journal *Shtern* in 1936 (nos. 7, 9, 11). For the play's original text with the author's proofreading, see BGAMLI, f. 182, op. 1, d. 1, *Boytre*.

144. The one exception in Kulbak's work, which predates his Soviet years, is the epic poem on Belorussia entitled *Raysn* and published in Vilna in 1922.

145. Introduction to I. Kharik and Y. Bronshteyn, eds., *Sovetishe Vaysrusland: literarishe zamlung* (Minsk, 1935).

146. NARB, f. 4, op. 1, d. 816, l. 6.

147. See S. Dubnow, "Ob izuchenii istorii russkikh evreev i uchrezhdenii istoricheskogo obshchestva" (Voskhod, 1891).

148. NARB, f. 42, op. 3, d. 289, l. 4.

149. NARB, f. 42, op. 1, d. 1614, ll. 4, 9. Favoring the study of Jewish Socialism did not however entail dismissing the *Pinkasim* as valuable historical sources. For one, Israel Sosis, who corresponded with Rabbi Yehoshua Tsimbalist requesting to view the *Pinkasim* under his tutelage, believed that community records were crucial for historical research. See NARB, f. 42, op. 1, d. 1642, l. 16.

150. I. Sosis, "Tsu der sotsyaler geshikhte fun yidn in Lite un Vaysrusland," *Tsaytshrift*, I, 1926, 1–4; see in particular 1.

151. I. Sosis, "Tsu der antviklung fun der yidisher historyografye," *Shriftn fun Vaysrusishn melukhe-universitet*, I, 1929, 8.

152. Ibid., 12. On the perception of Belorussia as a region with a history, an identity, and a culture that predated the establishment of the Soviet Union, see, for example, I. Sosis, "Der yidisher seym in Lite un Vaysrusland in zayn gezetsgeberisher tetikayt (1623–1761), loyt zayne protokoln," *Tsaytshrift*, II–III, 1928, 76–79.

153. M. Veinger, *Forsht yidishe dialektn! Program farn materyalnklayber* (Minsk, 1925).

154. H. Alexandrov, *Forsht ayer shtetl!* (Minsk, 1928), 9.

155. See H. Alexandrov and I. Roznhoyz, *Undzer kant: bashraybungen fun der Vaysrusisher Sotsyalistisher Sovetn Republik* (Minsk, 1929), v. I, 3–4, 25.

156. L. Dushman, "Materyaln tsu der geshikhte fun Yidishn teater in Vaysrusland," 162–94.

157. One of the most vicious attacks by the Minsk Jewish scholars was launched against the YIVO Institute in Vilna as early as 1930. Some prominent scholars, including Israel Sosis and Max Erik (professor of Yiddish literature in Minsk since 1928), took part in this highly propagandistic enterprise, which reflected the general growing ideological pressure on Soviet intellectual life. See *Fashizirter Yidishizm un zayn visnshaft* (Minsk, 1930).

158. Zlatkin, "Minsker alshtotishe arbeter-konferents," *Oktyabr*, May 28, 1936, no. 118, 4.

159. Moshe Lewin, "Society, State and Ideology During the First Five-Year Plan," in *Cultural Revolution in Russia, 1928–1931*, edited by Sheila Fitzpatrick (Bloomington: Indiana University Press, 1984), 41–77.

160. On the influence of the *shtetl* on Soviet Jewish life, see Altshuler, *Soviet Jewry on the Eve of the Holocaust*, 45–46.

161. GAMO, f. 164, op. 1, d. 428, ll. 23–26; and Interview with Nina Rogov, March 13, 2007, New York City.

162. See Schwarz, *Jews in the Soviet Union*, 136.

163. GAMO, f. 12, op. 1, d. 851, l. 4. In 1927–28, 3,859 Jewish students attended Yiddish-language schools, and 2,816 attended Russian or Belorussian schools. In 1928–29, the number of students enrolled in Yiddish-language schools increased to 4,042, while the number of Jewish students in Russian and Belorussian schools decreased to 2,718. See GAMO, f. 320, op. 1, d. 599, l. 18.

164. In 1926, 83 percent of Minsk Jews declared Yiddish their mother tongue; see *Yidn in BSSR*, 11.

165. Altshuler, *Soviet Jewry on the Eve of the Holocaust*, 277.

166. Ts. D., "Notitsn vegn tsirk," *Oktyabr*, July 4, 1937, no. 147, 4.

167. GAMO, f. 164, op. 1, d. 395, ll. 26–30, 42–45. In October 1938, the presidium of the Academy of Science of Belorussia endorsed the publication of a Yiddish-Russian dictionary (not a Yiddish-Belorussian one). See TsNANANB, f. 1, op. 1, d. 62, l. 60.

168. L. Frid, "Nit azoy darf men handln mit natsmindishe literatur," *Oktyabr*, September 21, 1936, no. 234, 3.

169. "Vegn der arbet funem yidishn kinder-gortn," *Oktyabr*, May 11, 1936, no. 104, 3–4.

Chapter 5

1. François Furet and Jacques Le Goff, "Histoire et ethnologie," in *Méthodologie de l'histoire et des sciences humaines*, vol. 2 of *Mélanges en l'honneur de Fernand Braudel* (Toulouse, 1973), 237.

2. NARB, f. 42, op. 1, d. 1437, ll. 53–69.

3. On the Minsk Talmud-Torah, see Elias Schulman, "Yidishe kultur-tetikayt in Minsk, 1917–1941," 782.

4. See GAMO, f. 37, op. 1, d. 224, ll. 97, 99.

5. Quoted in Salo Baron, *The Russian Jew Under Tsar and Soviets* (New York: Macmillan, 1964), 246.

6. NARB, f. 521, op. 1, d. 1, ll. 1–5.

7. NARB, f. 6, op. 1, d. 196, l. 33.

8. NARB, f. 521, op. 1, d. 1, ll. 1–5, 10, 13, 15–18, 21–23.
9. See GAMO, f. 9, op. 1, d. 18, l. 17.
10. NARB, f. 4, op. 1, d. 3, ll. 192–193.
11. GAMO, f. 9, op. 1, d. 18, ll. 6–7, 11–12.
12. See GAMO, f. 591, op. 1, d. 13, l. 19.
13. GAMO, f. 591, op. 1, d. 14, l. 82. There were eighty-three synagogues, houses of prayer, and *minyonim* in Minsk before the revolution; see Ben-Zion Gershuni, "Ha-yahadut ha-datit, mosdoteah ve-isheah," in *Minsk*, vol. 1, 89–90.
14. NARB, f. 261, op. 1, d. 13, l. 4. That same year, there were ninety-nine Jewish religious associations and buildings in use in Mohilev, ninety-nine in Bobruisk, and seventy-seven in Vitebsk.
15. I thank Mikhail Kalnitskii for sharing with me his vast knowledge about Kiev.
16. Zeltser, *Evrei v sovetskoi provintsii*, 257; 426.
17. See GAMO, f. 48, op. 1, d. 44, ll. 6, 18, 22, 24.
18. GAMO, f. 9, op. 1, d. 33, ll. 9, 10, 11.
19. GAMO, f. 48, op. 1, d. 47, ll. 10, 18, 26.
20. GAMO, f. 12, op. 1, d. 1016, ll. 53, 67, 70, 72.
21. GAMO, f. 48, op. 1, d. 40, ll. 10, 11–22.
22. GAMO, f. 12, op. 1, d. 1016, ll. 104–5.
23. Zalman, "1,000 arbeter-familyes fodern farmakhn dem Nemiger mikve-besmedresh," *Oktyabr*, March 3, 1930, no. 52, 2.
24. For petitions to take over synagogues, see GAMO, f. 12, op. 1, d. 1016, ll. 104–5.
25. See, for example, Surits, *Soviet-rusland in 1931*, 316.
26. Apikoyres, "Der starodoroger iz vider do," *Oktyabr*, February 7, 1928, no. 32, 4.
27. GAMO, f. 12, op. 1, d. 1158, ll. 11–22.
28. GAMO, f. 48, op. 1, d. 52, ll. 28–29.
29. GAMO, f. 48, op. 1, d. 63, ll. 1, 10, 16.
30. GAMO, f. 12, op. 1, d. 1016, ll. 104–5.
31. GAMO, f. 12, op. 1, d. 367, ll. 2–7.
32. For petitions to close down synagogues (or to retain them as religious spaces) in 1933 in and around Minsk, see NARB, f. 12, op. 1, d. 4, ll. 1, 3, 16–21, 50, 95–97, 102.
33. NARB, f. 261, op. 1, d. 14, l. 33.
34. NARB, f. 261, op. 1, d. 14, ll. 20–26.
35. NARB, f. 12, op. 1, d. 4, ll. 95–97.
36. See "Barikht fortrog fun kh. Khadasevich vegn der arbet fun Minsker Shtotkom KPbV," *Oktyabr*, June 3, 1937, no. 122, 2.
37. NARB, f. 6, op. 1, d. 133, l. 13.
38. NARB, f. 4, op. 1, d. 578, ll. 22–25.
39. NARB, f. 6, op. 1, d. 133, l. 17.
40. GAMO, f. 162, op. 1, d. 356, ll. 226, 229.
41. NARB, f. 6, op. 1, d. 196, ll. 8–13.
42. In 1924, 30 officially registered rabbis lived in Minsk. See GAMO, f. 591, op. 1, d. 14, l. 82.
43. GAMO, f. 48, op. 1, d. 51, ll. 4, 8.
44. On the *korobka*, see Isaac Levitats, *The Jewish Community in Russia, 1772–1884* (New York: Columbia University Press, 1943), vol. 1, 52–57; and Isaac Levitats, *The Jewish Community in Russia, 1844–1917* (Jerusalem: Posner & Son, 1981), vol. 2, 23–31.
45. Kh. Ber, "Der protses fun shokhtim-trest in Minsk," *Der Emes*, March 6, 1925, no. 54, 3.
46. On the Soviet *korobka* in Vitebsk and surrounding *shtetlekh*, see Zeltser, *Evrei v sovetskoi provintsii*, 246–47.
47. Brovkin, *Russia After Lenin*, 30–31.

48. Interview with Gita Gluskina, June 18, 2004, Ramat Gan, Israel.
49. See NARB, f. 4, op. 1, d. 586, l. 32.
50. On Rabbi Tsimbalist, see *Rabi Yehoshua me-Horodna zatsal: more tsedek ve-rosh metivtah, kovets le-zikhro* (Jerusalem, 1949).
51. A. A. Gershuni, *Yahadut be-rusiyah ha-sovyetit: le-korot redifot ha-dat* (Jerusalem, 1961), 140–42. On the fate of Lithuanian yeshivas in the Soviet Union, and specifically the Shoavei Mayim yeshiva in Minsk, see Ben-Tsion Klibansky, "Ha-yeshivot ha-litaiot be-mizrah Eropah ben shtei milhamot ha-olam" (PhD dissertation, Tel Aviv University, 2009), 116–19 in particular.
52. For a list of Minsk yeshivas and heders, and number of students see JDC Archives, Collection 21/32, file 476, "Report of the Accomplishments of the Rabbinical Board in Russia during 5688."
53. See Moshe-Zvi Neriyah, "Al ha-yeshiva be-Minsk ve-mashehu al ha-hayim ha-datiim," in *Minsk*, vol. 2, 159–67; and Asher Kershteyn, "Im gdolei ha-Torah be-Minsk," in *Minsk*, 152–58.
54. GAMO, f. 12, op. 1, d. 1016, ll. 25–30.
55. See, for example, GAMO, f. 320, op. 1, d. 600, ll. 3–6, 10–12.
56. JDC Archives, Collection 21/32, file 476, "Report of the Accomplishments of the Rabbinical Board," 3. For more on the Council of Rabbis of the USSR, see David E. Fishman, "To Our Brethren Abroad: Letters and Reports by Soviet Rabbis, 1925–1930," *Jews in Russia and Eastern Europe* 1–2, nos. 54–55 (2005): 108–79.
57. "Report of the Accomplishments of the Rabbinical Board," 12. With 250 members, the Tifereth Bachurim in Vitebsk was the largest in the Soviet Union.
58. *Rabi Yehoshua me-Horodna*, 36–37.
59. JDC Archives, Collection 21/32, file 473, "Survey of the Religious and Cultural Work Accomplished with the Funds offered by the JDC in the USSR," 3.
60. JDC Archives, Collection 21/32, file 472, "Aide-mémoire about Religious Education in Russia," 3. On JDC relief assistance to yeshiva students in Minsk, see YIVO Archives, RG 358, file 12, l. 057, Letter of March 6, 1923, from Boris Bogen to JDC in New York.
61. *Di Rabonim in dinst fun finants-kapital* (Moscow, Kharkov, and Minsk, 1930), 26–27.
62. GAMO, f. 428, op. 1, d. 164, ll. 80–81, 93, 119–23, 137.
63. Underground heders still operated in Minsk in 1935. See Rozin, *Mayn veg aheym*, 76. On the adult Torah study group that existed in Minsk until World War II, see Gershuni, *Yahadut be-rusiyah*, 142.
64. See *Di Rabonim in dinst fun finants-kapital*, 26–29.
65. Kh. Ber, "Der protses fun shokhtim-trest in Minsk," *Der Emes*, March 5, 1925, no. 53, 3.
66. Kh. Ber, "Der protses fun shokhtim-trest in Minsk," *Der Emes*, March 11, 1925, no. 58, 2. On similar conflicts between rabbis and *shohtim* in Vitebsk, see Zeltser, *Evrei v sovetskoi provintsii*, 250–51.
67. According to the custom, the rabbi is the person who inspects the knife (*halef*) of the ritual slaughterers and provides them with a written authorization attesting their qualification as *shohtim*. As a result, even if Droykin followed the remaining rules of *shehitah*, but did not operate under rabbinical supervision, his meat was technically not kosher.
68. JDC Archives, Collection 21/32, file 475, S. Gourary, "Denkschrift über die Materielle Lage des Rabbinerstandes in Russland," December 5, 1928.
69. Zelig Kalmanovitch, "Yidishe bildlekh fun rusland," *Letste nayes*, March 24, 1925, 2; and Zelig Kalmanovitch, "Yidishe tipn in ratn-rusland," *Letste nayes*, April 7, 1925, 3.
70. M. Shimshelievitsh, *Minsker shokhtim-trest* (Minsk, 1925).
71. Kalmanovitch, "Yidishe bildlekh fun rusland," 2.
72. Kh. Ber, "Der protses fun shokhtim-trest in Minsk," *Der Emes*, March 3, 1925, no. 51, 3.
73. Ibid.
74. Kh. Ber, "Der protses fun shokhtim-trest in Minsk. Haynt iz der yom ha-din," *Der Emes*, March 10, 1925, no. 57, 2.

75. "Der psak-din," *Der Emes*, March 11, 1925, no. 58, 2.

76. JDC Archives, Collection 21/32, file 474, Letter from Haffkine to Dr. Cyrus Adler, November 3, 1927, 8.

77. GAMO, f. 12, op. 1, d. 539, ll. 22–24.

78. Abe, "Zol nemen a sof tsu der shvartser khutspe!" *Oktyabr*, February 4, 1928, no. 30, 3. See also *Di Rabonim in dinst fun finants-kapital*, 27.

79. GAMO, f. 12, op. 1, d. 1016, l. 37. For a similar case in Germany, see Robin Judd, "The Politics of Beef: Animal Advocacy and the Kosher Butchering Debates in Germany," *Jewish Social Studies* 10, no. 1 (fall 2003): 126–27.

80. "Gots-straptshes in Minsker shekht-hoyz," *Oktyabr*, February 25, 1928, no. 48, 3.

81. Kh. Ber, "Der protses fun shokhtim-trest in Minsk," 3.

82. GAMO, f. 12, op. 1, d. 1016, l. 37.

83. "An ofener briv dem Minsker rov Gluskin," *Oktyabr*, February 5, 1928, no. 31, 4.

84. GAMO, f. 12, op. 1, d. 1016, ll. 37, 43–44.

85. On Jewish women in food riots, see, for example, Paula E. Hyman, "Immigrant Women and Consumer Protest: The New York City Kosher Meat Boycott of 1902," *American Jewish History*, vol. XX (September 1980): 91–105.

86. GAMO, f. 12, op. 1, d. 1016, ll. 34–35.

87. GAMO, f. 12, op. 1, d. 1016, l. 74.

88. G. Naumov, "A koshere artel," *Oktyabr*, April 18, 1928, no. 90, 4.

89. GAMO, f. 12, op. 1, d. 1016, l. 48.

90. On Jews (and *shohtim*) employed in the Minsk Slaughterhouse, see GAMO, f. 37, op. 1, d. 1188, ll. 1076–107, 117–19.

91. See GAMO, f. 12, op. 1, d. 1016, l. 113.

92. On plans to establish kosher kitchens and a plant for the production of preserved kosher meats in the Urals, see JDC Archives, Collection 21/32, file 476, "Interview with Rabbi Schneerson and Rabbi Gourary, October 9, 1929," 2, 5.

93. See JDC Archives, Collection 21/32, file 477, "Memorandum to Dr. Rosen on Behalf of the Rabbis of Russia, August 20, 1930," 2.

94. Klibansky, "Ha-yeshivot ha-litaiot," 119.

95. According to one source, the Shoavei Mayim yeshiva was closed down after Rabbi Tsimbalist's departure for Palestine, in 1933. See *Rabi Yehoshua*, 7.

96. A. A. Gershuni, *Yehudim ve-yahadut bi-Verit ha-Moatsot: yahadut Rusiyah me-tkufat Stalin ve-ad ha-zman ha-aharon* (Jerusalem, 1970), vol. 2, 86.

97. Shifres, "Shoykhet Rapoport," *Oktyabr*, March 30, 1934, no. 72, 3.

98. A. D., "Di klerikal-sadistishe fizyonomye fun reb Yankev-Tevye Rapoport," *Oktyabr*, April 2, 1934, no. 75, 3.

99. On Rapoport, see Gershuni, *Yehudim ve-yahadut*, 88–91; and Rozin, *Mayn veg aheym*, 38, 43–45.

100. *Farn proletarishn gerikht: protses ibern fargvaltiker-farbrekher dem shoykhet Rapoport* (Minsk, 1934), 100.

101. On sexual anxieties and Jewish butchers in fin-de-siècle Germany, see Judd, "Politics of Beef," 125.

102. See "Gerikht ibern farbrekher-sadist-shoykhet reb Yankev-Tevye Rapoport," *Oktyabr*, April 1, 1934, no. 73, 4.

103. *Farn proletarishn gerikht*, 65–66, 101–2.

104. "Urteyl," *Oktyabr*, April 7, 1934, no. 78, 3.

105. David L. Hoffmann, *Peasant Metropolis: Social Identities in Moscow, 1929-1941* (Ithaca, NY: Cornell University Press, 1994).

106. On kosher butchering in the 1930s, see Gershuni, *Yehudim ve-yahadut*, 86–87.
107. GAMO, f. 320, op. 1, d. 239, ll. 1–2, 11–12.
108. NARB, f. 205, op. 1, d. 890, ll. 33–36.
109. GAMO, f. 320, op. 1, d. 592, l. 1.
110. GAMO, f. 320, op. 1, d. 588, ll. 1–5, 9.
111. Magilnitski, "Arbetn vos vayter alts beser," *Oktyabr*, March 1, 1937, no. 48, 3.
112. NARB, f. 205, op. 1, d. 229, ll. 24–31, 38–40.
113. GAMO, f. 320, op. 1, d. 239, l. 6.
114. On Soviet Jewish schools in the Minsk District that closed on Rosh Hashanah and Yom Kippur, see GAMO, f. 12, op. 1, d. 367, ll. 2–7.
115. GAMO, f. 320, op. 1, d. 575, ll. 1, 3–4, 6, 8, 10, 11, 13.
116. GAMO, f. 320, op. 1, d. 553, ll. 1, 3–5.
117. On school attendance in Minsk during Yom Kippur and Rosh Hashanah in 1929, see GAMO, f. 320, op. 1, d. 546, ll. 3–5, 10–12; and GAMO, f. 320, op. 1, d. 600, ll. 3–6, 10, 12, 14.
118. GAMO, f. 320, op. 1, d. 249, l. 98.
119. GAMO, f. 320, op. 1, d. 249, l. 100.
120. Ibid.
121. GAMO, f. 320, op. 1, d. 575, ll. 1, 10, 11, 13.
122. GAMO, f. 320, op. 1, d. 546, l. 11.
123. B. Sh., "Ernster zikh nemen far der antireligyezer arbet," *Oktyabr*, March 14, 1937, no. 58, 3.
124. GAMO, f. 320, op. 1, d. 592, l. 1.
125. GAMO, f. 320, op. 1, d. 588, l. 9.
126. GAMO, f. 320, op. 1, d. 249, ll. 77–78, 81–82.
127. GAMO, f. 320, op. 1, d. 399, ll. 3–20.
128. GAMO, f. 320, op. 1, d. 599, l. 28.
129. GAMO, f. 320, op. 1, d. 239, ll. 1–2, 11–12.
130. GAMO, f. 12, op. 1, d. 851, ll. 29–33.
131. GAMO, f. 320, op. 1, d. 558, ll. 8–9.
132. Interview with Hirsh Reles, March 9, 2004, Minsk.
133. NARB, f. 63, op. 2, d. 462, ll. 24–25, 72.
134. GAMO, f. 37, op. 1, d. 229, ll. 417–18.
135. GAMO, f. 37, op. 1, d. 229, ll. 408–10.
136. Le Goff, "Histoire et ethnologie," 237.
137. Quoted in Elizabeth Wyner Mark, ed., *The Covenant of Circumcision: New Perspectives on an Ancient Jewish Rite* (Hanover, NH: Brandeis University Press, 2003), xx.
138. Joshua Rothenberg, *The Jewish Religion in the Soviet Union* (New York: Ktav Publishing House, 1971), 142–43.
139. NARB, f. 37, op. 1, d. 228, ll. 37–38.
140. NARB, f. 37, op. 1, d. 228, l. 38.
141. In 1924, 60 percent of the members of the Construction Workers' Union were Jewish; GAMO, f. 12, op. 1, d. 166, l. 11.
142. See GAMO, f. 1260, op. 1, d. 3, ll. 37–41.
143. Kotkin, *Magnetic Mountain*, 295.
144. GAMO, f. 12, op. 1, d. 166, ll. 11–12.
145. GAMO, f. 1260, op. 1, d. 2, ll. 54–56, 64.
146. GAMO, f. 1260, op. 1, d. 3, ll. 75–76.
147. GAMO, f. 1260, op. 1, d. 3, ll. 99–101.
148. "Karl-Yankl," in *Complete Works of Isaac Babel*, 619–27.
149. GAMO, f. 37, op. 1, d. 308, ll. 16–17.

150. GAMO, f. 37, op. 1, d. 229, ll. 216–217, 408–10, 417–18.
151. GAMO, f. 37, op. 1, d. 229, ll. 313–17, 473–81.
152. Sh. Levin, "Undzere 'opgeshtanene' froyen," *Oktyabr*, February 28, 1930, no. 49, 2.
153. "A briv in redaktsye," *Oktyabr*, January 15, 1928, no. 13, 4.
154. See, for example, Rothenberg, *Jewish Religion*, 147; and Zeltser, *Evrei sovetskoi provintsii*, 274.
155. GAMO, f. 37, op. 1, d. 1335, ll. 5–6.
156. GAMO, f. 164, op. 5, d. 89, ll. 231–34.
157. NARB, f. 261, op. 1, d. 14, l. 33.
158. *Oktyabr*, May 18, 1936, no. 110, 4.
159. "Di klerikaln-shediker farn proletarishn gerikht," *Oktyabr*, March 22, 1931, no. 66, 3.
160. On Soviet attacks on circumcision, see L. I. Kilimnik, ed., *Kommunisticheskaia vlast protiv religii Moiseia: Dokumenty 1920–1937 i 1945–1953 gg.* (Vinnitsa: "Xrani i pomni," 2005), 146–51; and G. Ia. Kiselev, *O kreshchenii i obrezanii* (Moscow: Ogiz, 1937), 24–30.
161. "Di klerikaln-shediker farn proletarishn gerikht," *Oktyabr*, March 25, 1931, no. 68, 3.
162. See Gershuni, *Yehudim ve-yahadut*, 93–95; and David L. Mekler, *Mentsh un mashin in Sovyetn-land: faktn, bilder, ayndrukn fun a rayze iber Sovyet Rusland* (Warsaw, 1936), 297–98.
163. GAMO, f. 1257, op. 1, d. 21, ll. 32–35.
164. GAMO, f. 164, op. 5, d. 94, ll. 17–30.
165. GAMO, f. 164, op. 5, d. 92, ll. 143, 175.
166. In Jewish folk mentality, a noncircumcised Jew was not considered Jewish. See, for example, D. Dalhinever, "Der goyele," in *Akhter mart: zamlbukh*, edited by Y. Rubentchik (Minsk, 1926), 39–42.
167. Sander Gilman, *The Jew's Body* (New York: Routledge, 1991), 123, 155.
168. Robin Judd, "Circumcision and Modern Jewish Life: A German Case Study, 1843–1914," in *The Covenant of Circumcision: New Perspectives on an Ancient Jewish Rite*, edited by Elizabeth Wyner Mark (Hanover, NH: Brandeis University Press, 2003); and Gershon Bacon, "Kefiya datit, hofesh bitui ve-zehut modernit be-Polin: Y.L. Peretz, Shalom Asch ve-shaaruryat ha-mila be-Varsha, 1908," in *Mi-Vilna le-Yerushalaym*, edited by David Assaf et al. (Jerusalem: Magnes, 2002), 167–85.
169. Slezkine, *Jewish Century*, 254.
170. On baptism, see Christel Lane, *Christian Religion in the Soviet Union: A Sociological Study* (Albany: State University of New York Press, 1978), in particular 59–62; Gerald Buss, *The Bear's Hug: Christian Belief and the Soviet State, 1917–1986* (Grand Rapids, MI: W. B. Eerdmans, 1987), 28; and NARB, f. 261, op. 1, d. 27, l. 19.
171. Kotkin, *Magnetic Mountain*, in particular chapter 5.
172. On the persecution and arrest of the Minsk rabbis in 1930, see Gershuni, *Yahadut be-Rusiya*, 70–71; "Tsu ale gloybike yidn," *Oktyabr*, February 27, 1930, no. 48, 3; JDC Archives, Collection 21/32, file 447, "Memorandum on Requests Conveyed to Dr. Rosen on Behalf of Rabbis in Russia, 1930," 1.

Chapter 6

1. P. I. Glushets, twenty-nine years old. P. I. Glushets, "Ikh bin an inzhenier," *Oktyabr*, March 8, 1937, no. 53, 2.
2. On gender and male anxiety in the literature of the Haskalah, see Olga Litvak, *Conscription and the Search for Modern Russian Jewry* (Bloomington: Indiana University Press, 2006), in particular chapter 3.
3. On Y. L. Gordon, see Michael Stanislawski, *For Whom Do I Toil? Judah Leib Gordon and the Crisis of Russian Jewry* (New York, 1988). On Joseph Perl and Jewish women, see Nancy Sinkoff, "The Maskil, the Convert, and the *Agunah*: Joseph Perl as a Historian of Jewish Divorce Law," *AJS Review* 27, no. 2 (November 2003): 281–99. On the Haskalah's criticism of traditional family relations, see

David Biale, *Eros and the Jews: From Biblical Israel to Contemporary America* (Berkeley: University of California Press, 1997); on women in Haskalah writings, see Tova Cohen, *Ha-ahat ahuvah ve-ha-ahat senuah: ben metsiut le-bidayon beteurei ha-ishah besifrut ha-haskalah* (Jerusalem, 2002); on women's reading habits, see Iris Parush, *Nashim korot: Yitronah shel shuliyut ba-hevrah ha-yehudit be-mizrah eropah ba-meah ha-tesha-esreh* (Tel Aviv, 2001).

    4. For many *maskilim*, "women were both the problem and the solution to the preservation of Judaism." See Litvak, *Conscription and the Search*, 93–98.

    5. Eliyana R. Adler, "Women's Education in the Pages of the Russian Jewish Press," *Polin* 18 (2005): 123.

    6. Ibid., 126.

    7. Amy Knight, "Female Terrorists in the Russian Socialist Revolutionary Party," *Russian Review* 38, no. 2 (April 1979): 139–59; in particular 141–42.

    8. Paula Hyman, *Gender and Assimilation in Modern Jewish History: The Roles and Representation of Women* (Seattle: University of Washington Press, 1995), 78.

    9. Ibid.

    10. The first woman to serve on the Bund's Central Committee was Tsivia Hurvitsh, in 1899. See Tobias, *Jewish Bund in Russia*, 90.

    11. Quoted in Shepherd, *Price Below Rubies*, 146–47.

    12. Quoted in *Socialist Women, European Socialist Feminism*, 8.

    13. On the birth of the women's movement in Russia, see Richard Stites, *The Women's Liberation Movement in Russia: Feminism, Nihilism, and Bolshevism, 1860–1930* (Princeton NJ: Princeton University Press, 1978). On gender politics in Soviet Russia, see Elizabeth Wood, *The Baba and the Comrade: Gender and Politics in Revolutionary Russia* (Bloomington: Indiana University Press, 1997).

    14. NARB, f. 4, op. 1, d. 569, l. 3.

    15. NARB, f. 4, op. 1, d. 570, l. 43.

    16. See, for example, NARB, f. 4, op. 1, d. 225, l. 22.

    17. RGASPI, f. 445, op. 1, d. 9, l. 1.

    18. RGASPI, f. 445, op. 1, d. 9, l. 3.

    19. NARB, f. 4, op. 1, d. 225, l. 9.

    20. NARB, f. 4, op. 1, d. 103, l. 88.

    21. RGASPI, f. 445, op. 1, d. 64, l. 161.

    22. RGASPI, f. 445, op. 1, d. 64, ll. 38, 139.

    23. RGASPI, f. 445, op. 1, d. 64, l. 9.

    24. RGASPI, f. 445, op. 1, d. 64, ll. 38, 139.

    25. NARB, f. 4, op. 1, d. 569, ll. 9–10. In 1924, the Minsk Zhenotdel issued its own biweekly called *Belorusskaia rabotnitsa i selianka*, and later renamed *Rabotnitsa i kolkhoznitsa Belarusi*.

    26. See, for example, NARB, f. 4, op. 1, d. 578, ll. 13–15.

    27. NARB, f. 4, op. 1, d. 692, l. 87.

    28. GAMO, f. 162, op. 1, d. 201, l. 7.

    29. GAMO, f. 162, op. 1, d. 356, ll. 226, 229.

    30. See GAMO, f. 162, op. 1, d. 227, ll. 1, 13.

    31. GAMO, f. 12, op. 1, d. 758, l. 238.

    32. NARB, f. 4, op. 1, d. 578, l. 44.

    33. See, for example, NARB, f. 4, op. 1, d. 103, ll. 69, 70–73, 117.

    34. See NARB, f. 37, op. 1, d. 228, l. 90.

    35. GAMO, f. 12, op. 1, d. 321, ll. 2–4.

    36. GAMO, f. 12, op. 1, d. 1123, ll. 1, 10.

    37. GAMO, f. 37, op. 1, d. 228, ll. 90, 95–98.

    38. On Jewish members of the Construction Workers' Union, see GAMO, f. 12, op. 1, d. 359, l. 10.

39. See GAMO, f. 37, op. 1, d. 229, ll. 50–52, 202, 242–44.
40. GAMO, f. 591, op. 1, d. 22, ll. 25–26, 34–36.
41. GAMO, f. 37, op. 1, d. 229, l. 289.
42. GAMO, f. 37, op. 1, d. 229, ll. 384–85.
43. GAMO, f. 12, op. 1, d. 828, ll. 79–81.
44. NARB, f. 4, op. 1, d. 219, l. 2.
45. NARB, f. 4, op. 1, d. 171, ll. 1. In 1922, there were four members in the Central Committee of the Minsk Zhenotdel: the chairperson, the secretary, the instructor responsible for the district, and the instructor responsible for propaganda work in Yiddish. On the structure of the Moscow Zhenotdel, see Stites, *Women's Liberation Movement in Russia*, 334–35.
46. See NARB, f. 4, op. 1, d. 568, ll. 1–3, 10.
47. On the dissolution of the Zhenotdel, see Stites, *Women's Liberation Movement in Russia*, 341–45.
48. See NARB, f. 4, op. 1, d. 417, l. 101.
49. NARB, f. 4, op. 1, d. 417, ll. 28, 35.
50. NARB, f. 4, op. 1, d. 570, l. 17.
51. GAMO, f. 12, op. 1, d. 321, ll. 45–46.
52. GAMO, f. 591, op. 1, d. 13, l. 19.
53. NARB, f. 4, op. 9, d. 14, l. 252.
54. GAMO, f. 12, op. 1, d. 376, ll. 24–25.
55. GAMO, f. 12, op. 1, d. 1010, l. 13.
56. GAMO, f. 1260, op. 1, d. 9, ll. 87–89. In 1928, fifty-five of the sixty-four delegates elected in the Minshvei party-cell meeting were Jewish (and six Belorussian); see GAMO, f. 12, op. 1, d. 1006, ll. 74–75, 83.
57. "A beyzer tsung," *Oktyabr*, July 27, 1929, no. 169, 4.
58. Yankl Peshes, "Itke fun biuro," in *Akhter mart: zamlbukh*, edited by Y. Rubentchik (Minsk, 1926), 36. On the image of progressive women in Yiddish popular songs of the 1920s and 1930s, see Shternshis, *Soviet and Kosher*, in particular 136–40.
59. NARB, f. 4, op. 1, d. 799, l. 2.
60. See Wendy Z. Goldman, *Women, the State and Revolution: Soviet Family Policy and Social Life, 1917–1936* (Cambridge: Cambridge University Press, 1993), 111.
61. Quoted in Gitelman, *Jewish Nationality and Soviet Politics*, 135.
62. GAMO, f. 12, op. 1, d. 537, ll. 1–5.
63. M. Sandomirski, "Hoyzarbeterns zaynen nit keyn dinstn!" *Oktyabr*, January 7, 1926, no. 57, 3.
64. Kuntsevitskaia, "Tsu undzere froyen," *Di royte nodl*, July 1924, no. 1, 13.
65. S. V., "Di froy af undzere farzamlungen," *Di royte nodl*, December 1924, no. 6, 14.
66. Vilk, "Fun redaktsye," *Di royte nodl*, January 1925, no. 7, 11–12.
67. V. Rokhkind, "A bisl vegn dem lebn fun der arbeters froy," *Di royte nodl*, January 1925, no. 7, 11.
68. See GAMO, f. 1260, op. 1, d. 9, ll. 25, 31–36.
69. Kh. Ber, "Di froy darf vern glaykhbarekhtikt," *Akhter mart: zamlbukh*, edited by Y. Rubentchik (Minsk, 1926), 4.
70. Brener, "Di froy-arbetern in kesl fun melukhe verkshtat," *Di royte nodl*, September–October 1924, nos. 3–4, 11.
71. *Kirpitshiki*, in *Akhter mart: zamlbukh*, edited by Y. Rubentchik (Minsk, 1926), 52–53.
72. See, for example, *Alvaysruslendishe konferents fun yidishe kultur un bildungs tuer* (Minsk, 1931), 32.
73. On antireligious propaganda in Yiddish addressed to women only, see GAMO, f. 37, op. 1, d. 229, ll. 473–81.
74. On "Red Seders" and "Red Haggadahs," see Shternshis, *Soviet and Kosher*, 27–35.

75. GAMO, f. 12, op. 1, d. 1, l. 52.
76. GAMO, f. 12, op. 1, d. 321, ll. 56–58, 65.
77. GAMO, f. 12, op. 1, d. 170, l. 15.
78. Henye Slobodskaia, "Der ershter trot," *Akhter mart: zamlbukh*, edited by Y. Rubentchik (Minsk, 1926), 61–71.
79. Adler, "Women's Education in the Russian Jewish Press," 126.
80. GAMO, f. 37, op. 1, d. 1188, ll. 105–7.
81. GAMO, f. 1260, op. 1, d. 9, ll. 39, 58, 72.
82. GAMO, f. 12, op. 1, d. 1016, ll. 43–44.
83. See, for example, Petra Terhoeven, *Oro alla patria: donne, guerra e propaganda nella giornata della fede fascista* (Bologna: Il Mulino, 2006).
84. See "Bentsh-laykhter far der industryalizatsye," *Oktyabr*, February 27, 1930, no. 48, 3.
85. Sore Kahan, "Tsum 8tn Mart," *Oktyabr*, March 8, 1930, no. 56, 4.
86. See, for example, GAMO, f. 48, op. 1, d. 63, l. 21.
87. See, for example, Rokhl Brokhes, "Der gerikht," *Oktyabr*, June 9, 1936, no. 126, 3.
88. Alexandra Kollontai, "Sisters," in *Love of Worker Bees* (Chicago: Cassandra Editions, 1992), 220–22.
89. Stites, "Women and the Revolutionary Process in Russia," in *Becoming Visible: Women in European history*, edited by Renate Bridenthal, Klaudia Koonz, and Susan Stuard (Boston: Houghton Mifflin, 1987), 429.
90. See Goldman, *Women, the State, and Revolution*, in particular chapter 5.
91. See, for example, Yankl Peshes, "Itke fun biuro," *Akhter mart: zamlbukh*, edited by Y. Rubentchik (Minsk, 1926), 33–35.
92. See RGALI, f. 2270, op. 1, d. 72. l. 6.
93. GAMO, f. 37, op. 1, d. 229, ll. 38–39.
94. JDC Archives, Collection 21/32, file 519, 1–20.
95. *Oktyabr*, June 6, 1936, no. 124, 2.
96. Yad Vashem Archives, M. 41, file no. 5, Gebeleva Chasia Beniaminovna on Mikhail Gebelev, July 12, 1981.
97. Peshes, "Itke fun biuro," 35–36.
98. See NARB, f. 4935, op. 1, d. 29, ll. 1, 8–11, 13, 30–32, 41.
99. Khanin, *Soviet Rusland: vi ikh hob ir gezen*, 88–89.
100. The majority of women workers delegates were not married. In the City District (with sixty Jewish women workers and twenty-nine Jewish workers' wives) only thirty-three out of a total of one hundred twenty-two women workers were married; GAMO, f. 591, op. 1, d. 22, l. 33.
101. NARB, f. 4, op. 1, d. 692, ll. 87, 161.
102. GAMO, f. 2884, op. 1, d. 240, ll. 29–30. On women in the Komsomol in the 1920s, see also Anne E. Gorsuch, "A Woman Is Not a Man: The Culture of Gender and Generation in Soviet Russia, 1921–1928," *Slavic Review* 55, no. 3 (fall 1996): 636–60.
103. GAMO, f. 12, op. 1, d. 361, l. 29.
104. See, also, GAMO, f. 1260, op. 1, d. 4, l. 70.
105. The Jewish percentage is even more striking when considering only party members. Of the 160 women who joined the Communist Party, 118 were Jewish, 23 Russian, 9 Polish, and 4 Belorussian (75 of the Jewish Party members had been members of the Bund); NARB, f. 4, op. 1, d. 421, l. 95.
106. Including both members and candidates, Jews were 2,133 (1,639 men and 494 women); GAMO, f. 12, op. 1, d. 982, ll. 1–2.
107. See Yankl Rubentchik, "Der tsvishnfelkerlekher komunistisher froyentog," *Akhter mart: zamlbukh*, edited by Y. Rubentchik (Minsk, 1926), 18.
108. GAMO, f. 162, op. 1, d. 360a, l. 162.

109. GAMO, f. 37, op. 1, d. 1197, ll. 10–12.
110. GAMO, f. 164, op. 5, d. 89, l. 61.
111. GAMO, f. 164, op. 5, d. 87, ll. 18–58.
112. GAMO, f. 2884, op. 1, d. 240, ll. 29–30.
113. GAMO, f. 12, op. 1, d. 758, ll. 756–57.
114. On Sara Mariasina, see NARB, f. 205, op. 3, d. 5262, ll. 3, 5; and Mariasina, *Di alte un di naye shul (a bikhl farn masn-leyener)* (Minsk, 1929).
115. NARB, f. 42, op. 1, d. 1437, ll. 3, 57a, 61.
116. NARB, f. 42, op. 1, d. 1468, ll. 56–57. In 1925–26, 92 women (out of a total of 130 students) were JDC stipend recipients; 101 (out of a total of 143 students) lived in the college dormitory.
117. GAMO, f. 37, op. 1, d. 227, ll. 16, 63–64.
118. GAMO, f. 4782, op. 1, d. 27, ll. 47–48.
119. NARB, f. 205, op. 1, d. 363, l. 7.
120. NARB, f. 205, op. 1, d. 531, ll. 6, 19.
121. See Shaul Shtampfer, "Gender Differentiation and the Education of the Jewish Woman in Nineteenth-Century Eastern Europe," *Polin* 7 (1992): 63–85.
122. It seems that the use of Yiddish in autobiographical writings was also gendered as more Jewish women than men used Yiddish when corresponding with party agencies. For autobiographies in Yiddish, see GAMO, f. 12, op. 1, d. 758, ll. 79, 81–83, 137–39, 145, 225, 238, 537a–b, 667, 756–57.
123. "Ershte Alvaysruslendishe baratung fun di yidishe komyugishe shrayber," *Shtern*, 1932, nos. 1–2, 112–13.
124. Sore Kahan, "Dermonung," *Shtern*, 1932, nos. 7–8, 31–34.
125. GAMO, f. 164, op. 1, d. 268, ll. 1–18.
126. On the Stakhanovite movement, see Lewis H. Siegelbaum, *Stakhanovism and the Politics of Productivity in the USSR, 1935–1941* (Cambridge: Cambridge University Press, 1988).
127. Khanin, *Soviet Rusland*, 91–93.
128. Fanye Melnik, "Di sotsyalistishe fabrik hot mikh dertsoygn," *Oktyabr*, January 4, 1937, no. 3, 6.
129. Alexander Pomerantz, *A meydl fun Minsk* (New York, 1942), 4.
130. Ibid., 5.
131. Ibid., 6.
132. On Jewish women's support for Stalin's family laws, see, for example, L., "Undzere froyen lebn in di gliklekhste badingungen," *Oktyabr*, May 28, 1936, no. 118, 2. On family and divorce laws in the 1930s, see W. Goldman, "Women, Abortion, and the State, 1917–1936," in *Russia's Women: Accommodation, Resistance, Transformation*, edited by Barbara Evans Clements (Berkeley: University of California Press, 1991).
133. "In Minsk iz shtark gefaln di tsol getn," *Oktyabr*, August 5, 1936, no. 172, 4.
134. On the tension between Soviet women as heroes and the priority that the Soviet system gave to heroic masculinity, see Karen Petrone, *Life Has Become More Joyous, Comrades: Celebrations in the Time of Stalin* (Bloomington and Indianapolis: Indiana University Press, 2000), in particular 71–75.
135. See Yasilevski, "Bakumen 2,000 rubl melukhe hilf," *Oktyabr*, September 14, 1936, no. 204, 4; and Kaplan, "Zol gezunt zayn der khaver Stalin far zayn hilf," *Oktyabr*, September 20, 1936, no. 209, 4.
136. N. Gordon, "A groyse gezind," *Oktyabr*, October 9, 1936, no. 224, 3.
137. On the shift toward a more conservative approach to women in Soviet society during the 1930s, see Goldman, *Women, the State and Revolution*, in particular chapter 8.
138. H. Helterman, "Di froyen vern arayngetsoygn in gezelshaftlekher arbet," *Oktyabr*, May 10, 1936, no. 103, 2.
139. GAMO, f. 164, op. 2, d. 42, ll. 17–31.
140. According to Avraham Greenbaum, Agursky was released from prison during the purges. If this was the case—indeed exceptional under the circumstances—then it might have been prompted

by his wife's intercession. Whether he was released at the time, he eventually died in a gulag in Pavlodar, in August 1947. See TsNANANB, f. 2, d. 3660, personal files, Shmuel Agursky, l. 2.

141. Stites, "Women and the Revolutionary Process in Russia," in *Becoming Visible*, 430.
142. See GAMO, f. 164, op. 5, d. 89, ll. 84–87, 230.
143. "Portretn fun di yidishe shrayber," *Oktyabr*, July 24, 1936, no. 163, 4.

Chapter 7

1. Izzy Kharik, *Oktyabr*, December 8, 1936, no. 271, 6.
2. OHD (58) 7, Interview with Asia Brasler, April 8, 1969, 2.
3. On the origins of the Great Terror, its phases and number of victims, see, for example, Robert Conquest, *The Great Terror: A Reassessment* (New York, Oxford University Press, 1990); J. Arch Getty and Oleg Naumov, *The Road to Terror: Stalin and the Self-Destruction of the Bolsheviks* (New Haven, CT: Yale University Press, 1999); Oleg Khlevniuk, *Politbiuro. Mekhanizmy politicheskoi vlasti v 1930-e gody* (Moscow: Rosspen, 1996); and Hiroaki Kuromiya, *The Voices of the Dead: Stalin's Great Terror in the 1930s* (New Haven, CT: Yale University Press, 2008).
4. Fitzpatrick, *Everyday Stalinism*, 205.
5. *Oktyabr*, June 17, 1937, no. 134, 2.
6. N. Semin, "Minsk, di shtot vos vakst," *Iberboy*, no. 5, May 2, 1934, 30–31.
7. Moshe Kulbak, *Zelmenyaner*, vol. 1, Minsk, 1931, 118–19.
8. On the number of Jews who, on the eve of World War II, lived outside the historic Pale of Settlement, see Slezkine, *Jewish Century*, 217; and Altshuler, *Soviet Jewry on the Eve of the Holocaust*, 15, 224–35.
9. Kulbak's novel, which has no clearly stated chronological boundaries, ends with the demolition of the courtyard, as the small Zelmenyaner wooden houses make place to the new modern factory that will be built in its lieu. See Kulbak, *Zelmenyaner*, vol. 2, Minsk, 1935, 221–26.
10. OHD (217) 93, Interview with Miron Kagan, July 24, 1993, 5.
11. Altshuler, *Soviet Jewry on the Eve of the Holocaust*, 277.
12. Styrne, *Usia BSSR*, 85.
13. "Foygl-shul—dem broyt zavod," *Oktyabr*, July 28, 1929, no. 170, 4.
14. Rubin, "Vi undzer shul iz gevaksn," *Oktyabr*, May 28, 1936, no. 118, 3.
15. See, for example, Arkadii Kapilov, *Zamkovaia 2/7: povesti i rasskazy* (Minsk, 1995).
16. *Oktyabr*, July 22, 1936, no. 161, 4.
17. S. Furye, "Der generaler plan fun rekonstruirn Minsk," *Oktyabr*, May 26, 1937, no. 116, 4.
18. Sh. Z., "Vegn a kindershn shikhl," *Oktyabr*, October 12, 1936, no. 227, 4.
19. See Pomerantz, *Di sovetishe harugei-malkes*, 404.
20. *Oktyabr*, December 26, 1936, no. 286, 8.
21. "Di arbet in di kikhn muz ibergeboyt vern," *Oktyabr*, July 23, 1936, no. 162, 4.
22. OHD (58) 20, Interview with Dr. Nina Shalit-Galperin, July 12, 1970, 3–4.
23. Manes, "Untervegns," *Oktyabr*, August 10, 1936, no. 176, 5.
24. *Oktyabr*, March 26, 1938, no. 69, 4.
25. OHD (58) 20, Interview with Dr. Nina Shalit-Galperin, July 12, 1970, 6–7.
26. *Oktyabr*, May 18, 1936, no. 110, 4.
27. *Oktyabr*, July 11, 1936, no. 152, 2.
28. On entertainment in Soviet life in the 1930s, see Fitzpatrick, *Everyday Stalinism*, 93–95.
29. S. Furye, "Di ershte program fun melukhe-tsirk," *Oktyabr*, July 10, 1936, no. 151, 4.
30. *Oktyabr*, May 9, 1936, no. 102, 4.
31. M. O., "An ovnt in hoyz fun a minsker yidisher arbeter," *Fraynd*, January 6, 1935, 4.

32. Ibid.

33. Zelikov, "Kinstlerishe zelbsttetikayt," *Oktyabr*, October 4, 1936, no. 220, 4.

34. While New Year's tree decorations became normative among most Soviet Jews after 1935, setting up a tree at home was already in vogue at the end of the nineteenth century among some acculturated Russian Jewish families of high social status.

35. *Oktyabr*, December 9, 1936, no. 272, 8.

36. M. O. "An ovnt in hoyz fun a minsker yidisher arbeter," 4.

37. *Oktyabr*, May 9, 1936, no. 102, 4.

38. *Oktyabr*, November 26, 1936, no. 262, 8.

39. *Oktyabr*, May 12, 1936, no. 105, 4.

40. T., "Di Sholem Aleykhem oyshtelung in der melukhe bibliotek fun VSSR," *Oktyabr*, June 1, 1936, no. 20, 4.

41. *Oktyabr*, May 16, 1936, no. 108, 4.

42. *Oktyabr*, "Tsu di hoykhn fun der sotsialistisher kunst," November 3, 1936, no. 245, 1.

43. M. Zimerov, "A prekhtike teater gebayde," *Oktyabr*, November 3, 1936, no. 245, 4.

44. See H. Ts., "Di barikht-farzamlung fun di Yidishe Sovetishe shrayber in Vaysrusland," *Oktyabr*, June 2, 1937, no. 121, 3–4.

45. I. Masarski, "Groyse meglekhkaytn," *Oktyabr*, February 5, 1937, no. 29, 3.

46. For a different assessment of how widespread the film was at the time, see Shternshis, *Soviet and Kosher*, 170. On *Iskateli shchastia*, see also J. Hoberman, *The Red Atlantis: Communist Culture in the Absence of Communism* (Philadelphia, PA: Temple University Press, 1998), 84–85, 282 n 42; and M. Chernenko, *Krasnaia zvezda, zheltaia zvezda* (Vinnitsa, 2001).

47. M-e, "Bay di radio-rupors," *Oktyabr*, November 26, 1936, no. 262, 7.

48. *Oktyabr*, May 16, 1936, no. 108, 4.

49. "Tsu di oktyabr fayerungen: yidishe radio-ibergebungen," *Oktyabr*, October 20, 1936, no. 233, 8.

50. S. F., "A radio-ovnt gevidmet Izy Khariks naye poeme," *Oktyabr*, January 24, 1937, no. 19, 4.

51. See, for example, *Oktyabr*, "Haynt durkh radio," November 21, 1937, no. 258, 4.

52. See, for example, *Oktyabr*, January 18, 1937, no. 15, 4. On the Minsk Yiddish radio programs, see also M. Surits, *Der Moment*, April 14, 1935, no. 89, 5.

53. M., "An ovnt gevidmet der yidisher sovetisher kultur," *Oktyabr*, December 9, 1936, no. 272, 5.

54. Chayim Kopman, "Fizkultur farmestungen tsvishn Minsker un Vitebsker yidpedtekhnikumen," *Oktyabr*, June 9, 1936, no. 126, 4.

55. Sh. Buz, "Mir hobn gehekhert di grametnkayt," *Oktyabr*, May 23, 1936, no. 114, 3.

56. F. Rozin, "Fir khaveyrim," *Oktyabr*, June 25, 1936, no. 139, 2.

57. Rozin, *Mayn veg aheym*, 138–39.

58. Mendelson, "A tog inem Ratomker opru-hoyz," *Oktyabr*, June 15, 1936, no. 131, 3.

59. M. L., "Beser zikh farnemen mit di dramatishe krayzn," *Oktyabr*, December 30, 1936, no. 289, 4. On Yiddish amateurial groups, see Shternshis, *Soviet and Kosher*, in particular chapter 3.

60. On the influence of Soviet nationality policies on the identities of national minorities, see Yuri Slezkine, "The USSR as a Communal Apartment, or How a Socialist State Promoted Ethnic Particularism," *Slavic Review* 53, no. 2 (summer 1994): 414–52.

61. TsNANANB, f. 72, op. 1, d. 2, *Yidishe folkslider*, 12–13.

62. On Soviet Yiddish folklore, see Shternshis, *Soviet and Kosher*, in particular chapter 4.

63. "Undzer groyser folks-yontev," *Oktyabr*, July 11, 1936, no. 152, 1.

64. I. Medresh, "Shmuel der toker," *Oktyabr*, May 11, 1936, no. 104, 2.

65. See, for example, *Oktyabr*, September 18, 1936, no. 208, 3. On the rhetorical construction of the new Soviet hero under Stalinism, see Lilya Kaganovsky, *How the Soviet Man Was (Un)Made: Cultural Fantasy and Male Subjectivity Under Stalin* (Pittsburgh, PA: University of Pittsburgh Press, 2008).

66. "Der fizkultur-yontev fun di shiler un pionern," *Oktyabr*, June 26, 1936, no. 140, 4.
67. Sh. R., "Barikht funem delegat funem oyserordntlekhn 8tn sovetn-tsuzamenfor Hirhsl Skoblo," *Oktyabr*, December 16, 1936, no. 278, 2.
68. Leyzer Katsovitsh, "Chayke Gavrielova," *Oktyabr*, June 17, 1936, no. 133, 3.
69. P. Shenker, "Mentshn fun der Stalinishe epokhe," *Oktyabr*, June 26, 1936, no. 140, 3.
70. On Kharik's literary career, see Shneer, *Yiddish and the Creation of Soviet Jewish Culture*, in particular chapter 6.
71. See, for example, "A radio ovnt gevidmet Izy Khariks naye poeme," *Oktyabr*, January 24, 1937, no. 19, 4.
72. Interview with Hirsh Reles, February 15, 2004, Minsk.
73. F. S., "Afn alfolkishn miting gevidmet dem 16tn yortog zint VSSR hot zikh bafrayt," *Oktyabr*, July 12, 1936, no. 153, 4.
74. "Rede fun kh. Izy Kharik," *Oktyabr*, December 8, 1936, no. 271, 6.
75. "Di sonim fun folk zaynen gekhapt bam hant," *Oktyabr*, August 16, 1936, no. 181, 1.
76. L. Frid, "Ernste signal," *Oktyabr*, August 16, 1936, no. 181, 2.
77. N. I. Stelman, "Tsum nayem lernyor," *Oktyabr*, September 1, 1936, no. 193, 2.
78. OHD (58) 7, Interview with Asia Brasler, April 8, 1969, 2–3.
79. OHD (58) 20, Interview with Dr. Nina Shalit-Galperin, July 12, 1970, 6–8.
80. OHD (58) 7, Interview with Asia Brasler, April 8, 1969, 3.
81. OHD (217) 150, Interview with Lev Gelfand, August 30, 1994, 2–3.
82. Ibid.
83. See, for example, K. N., "Oysgeshlosn di tsveypenemdik Bliumkine fun partey," *Oktyabr*, August 14, 1936, no. 179, 2.
84. OHD (217) 150, Interview with Lev Gelfand, August 30, 1994, 5.
85. Katzenelson, "Partey bildung: a vertfuler onheyb," *Oktyabr*, June 5, 1936, no. 123, 2.
86. OHD (58) 17, Interview with Mendl Marshak, April 5, 1970 (Second session), 78.
87. GAMO, f. 164P, op. 1, d. 310, ll. 1–2, 3–5.
88. On purges of Bundists in local party cells in 1933 and 1935, see, for example, GAMO, f. 164P, op. 1, d. 309, ll. 1–13.
89. See, for example, NARB, f. 4, op. 14, d. 132, ll. 4, 32, 214, 230.
90. "Hekhern di revolutsyonere vakhzamkayt!" *Oktyabr*, August 8, 1936, no. 174, 1.
91. N. Gikalo, "Di tsveypenemendikayt iz der metod fun klasn-soyne," *Oktyabr*, October 11, 1936, no. 226, 1.
92. V. F. Sharangovich, "Barikht funem Tsentral Komitet fun KPbV," *Oktyabr*, June 20, 1937, no. 136, 2.
93. R-d, "Opreynikn di gezerd-organizatsyes fun klasn-fayntlekhe trotskistish-bundishe element," *Oktyabr*, November 16, 1937, no. 254, 4.
94. See NARB, f. 1340, op. 1, d. 32, ll. 18–19, 175–89.
95. "An ernste lektsye," *Oktyabr*, July 30, 1936, no. 167, 2.
96. Katzenelson, "Der trotskist Agulnik oysgeshlosn fun partey," *Oktyabr*, August 12, 1936, no. 178, 3.
97. M. Liberman, "Trotskistishe literatur af di bikher politses," *Oktyabr*, September 5, 1936, no. 197, 2.
98. Maltinsky and Grubian "Trotskistish-bundishe kontrabande," *Oktyabr*, June 11, 1937, no. 129, 3.
99. "Rezolutsye fun der algemeyner farzamlung fun Melukhisher Yidisher Teater," *Oktyabr*, June 15, 1937, no. 132, 3.
100. H. Ts., "Afn aktiv fun Vaysmelukhe kino," *Oktyabr*, June 23, 1937, no. 143, 3.
101. M. Liberman, "Farshtarkn dem kamf kegn dem yidishn shovinizm," *Oktyabr*, October 11, 1936, no. 226, 2.
102. Rokhkind, "Ufdekn bizn sof di trotskistish-bundishe kontraband," 3–4. On Agursky's lifelong commitment to uncover the Bund's counterrevolutionary essence, see NARB, f. 1340, op. 1, d. 32, ll. 175–78.

103. "Oystseykhenung farn grinder fun Minsker yidishn melukhe teater," *Fraynd*, January 6, 1935.

104. "Rafalskii oysgeshlosn fun partey," *Oktyabr*, July 30, 1937, no. 168, 2. See also Rozin, *Mayn veg aheym*, 70–73.

105. M. Liberman, "Af der farzamlung fun di sovetishe shrayber fun VSSR," *Oktyabr*, March 29, 1937, no. 70, 3.

106. See, for example, Y. Bronshteyn, "Natsyonalistishe kontrabande unter der fon fun kultur-yerushe," *Oktyabr*, April 9, 1937, no. 79, 3.

107. N. Kabakov, "Di trotskistishe diversye in der Yidisher sovetisher literatur," *Oktyabr*, June 30, 1937, no. 144, 2–3.

108. See H. Ts., "Di barikht-farzamlung fun di Yidishe sovetishe shrayber in Vaysrusland," 3–4.

109. Veidlinger, *Moscow State Yiddish Theater*, 160, 183.

110. M. L., "Far hekherer kvalitet un politisher aktuelkayt," *Oktyabr*, March 30, 1937, no. 71, 2.

111. Ibid., 4.

112. Maltinsky, "A shedlekh bikhl," *Oktyabr*, July 23, 1937, no. 163, 4.

113. On *vydvizhentsy* and the purges, see Fitzpatrick, *Accusatory Practices*, 107–10.

114. Martin, *Affirmative Action Empire*, in particular chapters 8 and 9.

115. See Reles, *Di yidishe-sovetishe shrayber*, 59–60.

116. TsNANANB, f. 2, op. 1, d. 3682, ll. 2–3, Personal File of Moshe Kulbak. The date of death recorded in this file—possibly pushed forward to give the impression that Kulbak had died of natural causes in the Gulag—is fabricated.

117. The date of Kharik's death was also fabricated and recorded as December 5, 1938; see TsNANANB, f. 2, op. 1, d. 3676, ll. 2, 11. On Bronshteyn, see TsNANANB, f. 2, op. 1, d. 3662, l. 2, Personal File of Yasha Bronshteyn. On purging the Jewish street in Minsk, see also Pomerantz, *Di sovetishe harugei-malkhes*, 149, 211, 482, 484.

118. Martin, *Affirmative Action Empire*, 311.

119. Ibid.

120. OHD (58) 7, Interview with Asia Brasler, April 8, 1969, 3.

121. BGAKffD, archive number I—1956, Minsk Train Station, 1936.

122. "A bagegenish mit di yidishe shrayber," *Oktyabr*, February 15, 1938, no. 37, 4.

123. Pomerantz, *Di sovetishe harugei-malkhes*, 436.

124. NARB, f. 4P, op. 3, d. 575, l. 287. Based on the decree, the Evpedtekhnikum and the Jewish sections of the Minsk Teachers' Institute, the Minsk Pedagogical Institute, and Belorussian State University were to be reorganized into Belorussian-language institutions as well.

125. Ibid.

126. V. F. Sharangovich, "Barikht funem tsentral komitet fun KPb fun Vaysrusland," *Oktyabr*, June 17, 1937, no. 134, 2.

127. Ibid.

128. See, for example, N. K., "Avekshteln di politishe agitatsye af der gehoriker hoykh," *Oktyabr*, January 12, 1936, no. 10, 2.

129. Martin, *Affirmative Action Empire*, 328–29.

130. In 1937, the BSSR had 6,323 Belorussian schools, 196 Jewish schools, 178 Russian schools, 107 Polish schools, 24 Ukrainian schools, 12 Latvian schools, and 9 Lithuanian schools. "Beser onfirn mit der yidisher sovetisher shul," *Oktyabr*, March 6, 1937, no. 52, 1.

131. "Natsyonalistishe farkriplungen in di shuln fun Vaysrusland," *Oktyabr*, April 11, 1937, no. 81, 3.

132. I. Khaymovich, "Aynike shul-fragn," *Oktyabr*, April 20, 1938, no. 90, 3.

133. See, for example, *Oktyabr*, July 29, 1936, no. 166, 4.

134. M. Sandlier, "Vegn der yidsektsye funem pedagogishn institut," *Oktyabr*, August 3, 1937, no. 171, 4.

Notes to Pages 198–206 | 249

135. I. Khaymovich, "Aynike shul-fragn," *Oktyabr*, April 20, 1938, no. 90, 3.
136. Altshuler, *Soviet Jewry on the Eve of the Holocaust*, 277.
137. B. Okun, "In kamf far likvidirn dem 'grunt-feler'," *Oktyabr*, July 5, 1936, no. 147, 3.
138. On petitions protesting the decree, see Zeltser and Selimenev, "Jewish Intelligentsia and the Liquidation of Yiddish Schools," 81, 89–90.
139. Zeltser and Selimenev, "Liquidation of Yiddish Schools," 110–11. For a letter addressed by a Yiddish writer to Stalin protesting the liquidation of the schools, see Reles, *Di yidishe-sovetishe shrayber*, 121.
140. OHD (58) 17, Interview with Mendl Marshak, March 29, 1970, 25–26; and second session of the interview, April 5, 1970, 78–79.
141. OHD (58) 20, Interview with Dr. Nina Shalit-Galperin, July 12, 1970, 2.
142. Conquest, *Great Terror*, 339. On the geographic factor as accountable for the purges in Minsk, see also Rozin, *Mayn veg aheym*, 19.
143. Martin, *Affirmative Action Empire*, 364–65.
144. See Rudling, "Battle over Belarus," in particular chapter 8.
145. "Hekher di revolutsyonere vakhzamkayt!" *Oktyabr*, August 8, 1936, no. 174, 1.
146. "Barikht fortrog fun kh. Khadasevich vegn der arbet fun Minsker shtotkom KPbV," *Oktyabr*, June 3, 1937, 122, 2.
147. Zeltser and Selimenev, "Liquidation of Yiddish Schools," 74, n. 2.
148. "In farvaltung funem shrayber fareyn in Vaysrusland," *Oktyabr*, August 9, 1937, no. 176, 3. On the Polish "enemy nation" in Belorussia, see Martin, *Affirmative Action Empire*, 328–29, 364–65.
149. Zeltser and Selimenev, "Liquidation of Yiddish Schools," 75–78.
150. See NARB, f. 1340, op. 1, d. 32, ll. 178–80.
151. See Krutikov, "Yasha Bronshteyn and His Struggle," 176–77.
152. For Sosis's Marxist reading of Eastern European Jewish history, see, for example, Sosis, *Geshikhte fun Yidishe gezelshaftlekhe shtrebungen in Rusland in 19tn y"h* (Minsk, 1930).
153. See NARB, f. 4935, op. 1, d. 5, ll. 1–54.
154. See GAMO, f. 164, op. 1, d. 71, l. 173, *Materialy da spravazdachy Menskaga garadtskoga komitetu KPBb*.
155. See H. Ts., "Di barikht-farzamlung fun di Yidishe Sovetishe shrayber in Vaysrusland," 3–4. The Jewish club does not appear in the 1935 address book of the city of Minsk. See Styrne, *Usia BSSR*, 29.
156. On attempts to de-provincialize Jewish institutions and overtake Moscow, see, for example, Ize Levin, "Der ershter spektakl nokhn langn iberays," *Oktyabr*, November 15, 1936, no. 254, 5; and Smoliar, *Fun ineveynik*, 436.
157. TsNANANB, f. 72, op. 1, d. 2, *Yidishe folkslider*, 22.
158. TsNANANB, f. 72, op. 1, d. 2, *Yidishe folkslider*, 17–18.
159. "Es bahandeln di arbeter fun der ney-fabrik Oktyabr," *Oktyabr*, July 4, 1936, no. 146, 2.
160. Lin, "In land fun fashistisher mentshn-freserai," *Oktyabr*, May 17, 1937, no. 109, 4.
161. Sem, "Di pogromen in Vilner universitet," *Oktyabr*, February 27, 1937, no. 47, 3.
162. "Vegn pogrom in Poylishn shtetl Tshizshev," *Oktyabr*, January 14, 1936, no. 11, 2.
163. Moyshe Teyf, "Der ershter tog fun mayn kindhayt," *Oktyabr*, July 14, 1936, no. 154, 3.
164. I. Shnayder, "Minsk-Mazovetsk," *Oktyabr*, June 15, 1936, no. 131, 3.
165. Sem, "Pogromen in Vilne," *Oktyabr*, December 10, 1936, no. 273, 6.
166. Sem, "Mitlelter," *Oktyabr*, March 11, 1937, no. 56, 3.
167. Levin, "Af der Minsker shukh-fabrik fun individuele bashtelungen arudeven konterevolutsyonere elementn," *Oktyabr*, March 21, 1937, no. 64, 4.
168. See, for example, "Khayshe antisemitizm in Daytshland," *Oktyabr*, September 21, 1936, no. 234, 6.

169. See, for example, *Oktyabr*, November 23, 1938, 267, 1.

170. "A gliklekh folk," *Oktyabr*, June 18, 1936, no. 134, 1. For references to Jewish history and Jewish pride, see also Moyshe Teyf, "Durkh heysn eybikn gerangl," *Oktyabr*, July 6, 1936, no. 148, 2.

171. On Kristallnacht, see also "Yidishe pogromen in Daytshland," *Oktyabr*, November 11, 1938, no. 257, 1.

172. Chayim Maltinsky, "Helish hot haynt zikh mayn sine tsebrent," *Oktyabr*, November 21, 1938, no. 265, 2.

173. Motl Grubyan, "Der blutiker shoyder," *Oktyabr*, November 24, 1938, no. 268, 3.

174. On the Jewish Anti-Fascist Committee, see Shimon Redlich, *War, Holocaust and Stalinism: A Documented Study of the Jewish Anti-Fascist Committee in the US* (Luxembourg: Harwood Academic Publishers, 1995).

175. "Fssr—der laykht turem far ale unterdrikte," *Oktyabr*, November 28, 1938, no. 271, 1.

176. L. Dushman, "Minsk biz der Oktyabr revolutsye," *Oktyabr*, December 31, 1936, no. 257, 4–5.

177. I thank Olga Ghershenson for sharing with me her vast knowledge of Soviet films.

178. See, for example, N. Stelman, "A yor fun produktiver arbet," *Oktyabr*, June 25, 1936, no. 139, 3.

179. "Di yidn zaynen heroyshe kemfer in der folks-armey fun Shpanye," *Oktyabr*, July 20, 1937, no. 160, 4.

180. See, for example, Shmuel Spector, ed., *Lost Jewish Worlds: The Communities of Grodno, Lida, Olkieniki, Vishav* (Jerusalem: Yad Vashem, 1996), 80.

181. See Emanuel Melzer, *No Way Out: The Politics of Polish Jewry, 1935–1939* (Cincinnati, OH: Hebrew Union College Press, 1997). On the opposition to anti-Semitism by the Communist Party of Poland (KPP), see 25, 36. On the growing proportion of Jewish membership in the Communist Party of Poland, see Joseph Marcus, *Social and Political History of the Jews of Poland, 1919–1939* (Berlin: Mouton Publishers, 1983), 290.

182. E. Melzer, "Relations Between Poland and Germany and the Impact on the Jewish Problem in Poland, 1935–1938," *Yad Vashem Studies* 12 (1977): 208.

183. Besides a few references to the economic decline and unemployment in America and its effects on the relatives of Jews living in Minsk, there is little mention in the Jewish press of a "fourth American evil." See, for example, Shenker, "Sheyne Zaltsman␣shraybt a briv dem khaver Goloder," *Oktyabr*, March 8, 1937, no. 53, 3.

Conclusion

1. Italo Calvino, *Invisible Cities* (New York: Harcourt Brace Jovanovich, 1974), 15–16.

2. Yuri Larin, *Evrei i antisemitizm v SSSR* (Moscow, Leningrad, 1929), 304.

3. See Altshuler, *Soviet Jews on the Eve of the Holocaust*, 74.

4. Altshuler, *Distribution of the Jewish Population*, 28, 30.

5. Spector, *Lost Jewish Worlds*, 18.

6. Olga Sobolevskaia and Vladimir Gancharov, *Evrei Grodnenshchiny: zhizn do katastrofy* (Donetsk: Nordpress, 2005), 120–22.

7. Spector, *Lost Jewish Worlds*, 59–65.

8. Sobolevskaia and Gancharov, *Evrei Grodnenshchiny*, 233.

9. On the eve of World War II, Rachel Shmailovits, who was born in Minsk in 1933, described her home as a traditional one. Her grandfather was a *shohet* and a *mohel*; her brother secretly studied Hebrew; and the food at home was kosher. During Passover, family members gathered at her home to celebrate a traditional Seder. See Dr. Rachel Shmailovits, "Yaldut ba-geto," *Minsk*, vol. II, 408.

10. Leonid Smilovitski, "Jewish Religious Life in Minsk, 1944–1953," *Jews in Eastern Europe*, 2, no. 30 (fall 1996): 6, in particular n. 10.

11. Quoted in Amir Weiner, "Saving Private Ivan: From What? Why? How?" *Kritika, Explorations in Russian and Eurasian History* 1, no. 2 (2000): 312.

12. OHD (58) 17, Interview with Mendl Marshak, April 5, 1970, Second Session, 85–86.

13. Ibid., 86. According to Marshak several Minsk Jews who publicly protested against the Soviet-Nazi pact were expelled from the party.

14. On the origin of state anti-Semitism under Stalin, see Gennady Kostyrchenko, "The Genesis of Establishment Anti-Semitism in the USSR: The Black Years, 1948–1953," in *Revolution, Repression and Revival: The Soviet Jewish Experience*, edited by Zvi Gitelman and Yaacov Roi (Lanham, MD: Rowman and Littlefield Publishers, 2007), 179–92.

15. Smilovitski, "Jewish Religious Life in Minsk," 5.

16. Smoliar, *Sovetishe yidn hinter geto tsoymen* (Tel Aviv: Farlag Y. L. Peretz, 1985), 22.

17. Smilovitski, "Jewish Religious Life in Minsk," 6.

18. See, for example, Reles, *Di yidishe-sovetishe shrayber fun Vaysrusland* (Minsk, 2004), 60, 83, 101, 163.

19. Ibid., 52. On Ponomarenko's opposition to Judaism, see also Altshuler, *Yahadut ba-makhbesh ha-Sovieti: ben dat le-zehut yehudit bi-Verit ha-Moatsot, 1941–1964* (Jerusalem: The Zalman Shazar Center for Jewish History, 2007), 49.

20. Ibid., 70, 159.

21. Benjamin Pinkus, *The Soviet Government and the Jews, 1948–1967: A Documented Study* (Cambridge: Cambridge University Press, 1984), 150.

22. By 1959, a little over 7 percent of the population of Minsk was Jewish; approximately 14 percent of Jews declared Yiddish their native or second language. See M. Altshuler, *Soviet Jewry Since the Second World War: Population and Social Structure* (New York; Westport, CT; and London: Greenwood Press, 1987), 88, 205. In 1970, the Jewish population of Minsk amounted to a little over 5 percent of the total city population; see Pinkus, *Soviet Government and the Jews*, 473, n. 48.

23. On the rise of anti-Semitism as a postwar phenomenon of rejection of Jewish particularity, see Amir Weiner, *Making Sense of War: The Second World War and the Fate of the Bolshevik Revolution* (Princeton, NJ: Princeton University Press, 2001), in particular chapter 6. On anti-Semitism as a widespread political and social phenomenon in post–World War II Stalinist Russia, see Kostyrchenko, ed., *Gosudarstvennyi antisemitizm v SSSR ot nachala do kulminatsii, 1938–1953* (Moscow: Masterik, 2005).

24. Pinkus, *Soviet Government*, 330. See also Leonard Schroeter, *The Last Exodus* (New York: Universe Books, 1974), 275.

25. Jewish Telegraphic Agency (JTA), "Drive Against Jewish Doctors Started in Soviet Belorussia," January 26, 1953.

26. Ibid., 13.

27. OHD (58) 17, Interview with Mendl Marshak, March 29, 1970, First Session, 28.

28. Ibid., 27.

29. JTA, "Minsk Cemetery Desecrated," June 29, 1976.

30. Smilovitski, "Jewish Religious Life in Minsk," 7. For more on the synagogue and its rabbi, see Altshuler, *Yahadut ba-makhbesh*, 205–7, 382–84, 472.

31. JTA, "Last Synagogue in Minsk Demolished," June 19, 1964.

32. Yaacov Roi, "Economic Trials," *The YIVO Encyclopedia of Jews in Eastern Europe*, vol. 1 (New Haven, CT: Yale University Press, 2008), 454.

33. JTA, "Soviet Jew and Wife Sentenced to Death for 'Economic Crimes,'" February 5, 1965.

34. Altshuler, *Yahadut ha-makhbesh*, 317, n. 34.

35. Quoted in William Korey, *The Soviet Cage: Anti-Semitism in Russia* (New York: Viking Press, 1973), 80.

36. *Bolshaia Sovetskaia Entsiklopediia*, vol. 27 (Moscow, 1926–47), 545–48.

37. *Minsk, Spadarozhnik turysta* (Belarus: Minsk, 1971).

Selected Bibliography

Archival Collections

Natsionalnyi arkhiv Respubliki Belarus (NARB), Minsk

Fond 4 Central Committee of the Communist Party of Belorussia.
Fond 6 Central Executive Committee, BSSR.
Fond 42 Narkompros BSSR.
Fond 63 VSNKh BSSR, 1919–1932.
Fond 205 Belorussian State University (BGU).
Fond 207 Jewish Workers' University, 1925–1926.
Fond 255 Society for Rural Settlement of Toiling Jews, Belorussian Branch, 1925–1934.
Fond 261 Association of Militant Atheists of the BSSR, 1926–1934.
Fond 701 Commission for National Minorities Policy of the Central Executive Committee of the BSSR, 1925–1931.
Fond R-782 People's Commissariat for the Affairs of National Minorities in Belorussia, 1921–1922.
Fond 1340 Collection of Documents of Party Organizations of Newspapers and Periodicals, 1926–1935.

Gosudarstvennyi arkhiv Minskoi oblasti (GAMO), Minsk

Fond 6 Executive Committee of the Minsk Councils of Workers, Peasants and Red Army Deputies.
Fond 9 Executive Committees of the Councils of Workers, Peasants and Red Army Deputies, 1918–1924.
Fond 12 Minsk District Committee of the KP(b)B.
Fond 37 Minsk Municipal District Committee KP(b)B, 1920–1932.
Fond 48 Administrative Department, Executive Committee of the Minsk Area, 1922–1930.
Fond 162 Records of the Local Offices of the Communist Party of Belorussia, Minsk Province, 1921–1930.
Fond 164 Records of the Local Offices of the Communist Party of Belorussia, City of Minsk, 1929–1941.
Fond 320 Inspector of Public Education of the Minsk District Council, 1923–1930.
Fond 322 Inspector of Public Education of the Minsk Municipal Council, 1917–1931.
Fond 423 Jewish Chamber of the People's Court in Minsk, 1926–1934.
Fond 428 Records of Komsomol Organizations, Minsk Province, 1921–1930.
Fond 591 Records of the Local Offices of the Communist Party of Belorussia, Minsk Province and City, 1922–1925.
Fond 1257 Primary Organizations of the KP(b)B, City of Minsk, 1921–1934.
Fond 1260 Primary Organizations of the KP(b)B.
Fond 1865 Executive Committee of the District Council of Workers, Peasants, and Red Army Deputies, 1924–1936.

Fond 2884 Records of the City Komsomol Organization of Minsk.

Tsentralnyi Nauchnyi Arkhiv Natsionalnoi Akademii Nauk Belarusi (TsNANANB), Minsk

Fond 1 Presidium of the Academy of Sciences of the BSSR.
Fond 2 Personal Files of Employees of the Academy of Sciences of Belarus.
Fond 3 Institute of History, Academy of Sciences of the BSSR.
Fond 67 Institute of Belorussian Culture.
Fond 72 Institute of National Minorities, Academy of Sciences BSSR.

Belorusskii gosudarstvennyi arkhiv-muzei literatury i iskusstva (BGAMLI), Minsk

Fond 81 Belorussian Republic Division of the All-Soviet Administration for the Protection of Author's Rights, 1917–1935.
Fond 182 Kulbak, Moisei Solomonovich. Papers, 1924–1936.
Fond 222 Belorussian State Jewish Theatre.
Fond 225 Maladniak All-Belorussian Society of Poets and Writers, 1924–1925.

Belorusskii gosudarstvennyi arkhiv kinofotofonodokumentov (BGAKffD), Minsk

Rossiiskii gosudarstvennyi arkhiv literatury i iskusstva (RGALI), Moscow

Fond 2270, Gurshteyn, Aron Sheftelevich. Papers, 1900–1957.
Fond 2536, Khenkina Mirra Solomonovna. Papers, 1907–1967.

Gosudarstvennyi arkhiv Rossiiskoi Federatsii (GARF), Moscow

Fond A—296 Department of Education of national minorities of the USSR, 1918–1934.
Fond 1318 Narkomnats RSFSR, 1917–1924.
Fond A—1575 Administration of Social Upbringing and Political Education of Children in the Narkompros of the USSR, 1921–1930.
Fond A—2306 People's Commissariat of Education of the RSFSR, 1917–1988.
Fond 2551 Narkompros.
Fond R—9498 Society for Rural Settlements of Jewish Toilers in the USSR, 1925–1938.

Rossiiskii gosudarstvennyi arkhiv sotsialno-politicheskoi istorii (RGASPI), Moscow

Fond 445 Central Bureau of the Jewish Sections of the Communist Party, 1918–1930.
Fond 529 YU. Communist University of National Minorities of the Western Regions, 1921–1937.

YIVO Institute for Jewish Research, New York City

RG 3, Yiddish Literature and Language. 1802–1941.
RG 205, Marmor, Kalman. Papers. 1880s–1950s.

RG 315, Leivik, H. Papers, 1914–1959.
RG 358, Rosen, Joseph. Papers, 1921–1938.
RG 500, Pomerantz, Alexander. Papers. 1920s–1960s.

Central Zionist Archives (CZA,) Jerusalem

F30 Russia (A. Rafaeli-Zenzipper Collection), 1890–1971.
J122 Collection, Sefer Minsk (Even-Shoshan project—not cataloged).

Yad Vashem Archives, Jerusalem

Collections 0.3, 0.33, M 41 (Individual testimonies).

Oral History Division, Hebrew University, Institute for Contemporary Jewry, Jerusalem

OHD Collections 42, 51, 58, 131, 223 (Interviews conducted by David Cohen on Interwar Minsk Jewry).

Joint Distribution Committee Archives, New York City

JDC Collection 21/32 Russia.

Newspapers and Periodicals

In Minsk

Afn visnshaftlekhn front
Der Veker
Di royte nodl
Di shul un kultur fun Ratn-Vaysrusland
Dos fraye vort
Farn folk
Komune
Oktyabr
Rabochii
Shriftn fun Vaysrusishn melukhe-universitet
Shtern
Tsaytshrift
Undzer komune
Yunger arbeter
Yunger Leninets
Zviazda

In Kiev, Moscow, St. Petersburg (Petrograd, Leningrad), Vilna, or Warsaw

Af di vegn tsu der nayer shul
Der Emes
Der froyen-tog
Di garber un bershter shtime

Evreiskaia Starina
Evreiskii Krestianin
Fraynd
Haynt
Iberboy
Jewish Telegraphic Agency Daily Bulletin
Moment
Pravda
Shtern
Tribuna evreiskoi sovetskoi obshchestvennosti
Voskhod

Memoirs

Chanin, N. *Soviet rusland: vi ikh hob ir gezen*. New York: Farlag Veker, 1929.
Charny, D. *A yortsendlik aza, 1914–1924*. New York: Tsiko Bikher farlag, 1943.
Maazeh, J. *Zikhronot*. 4 vols. Tel Aviv: Yalkut, 1936.
Medem, V. *Fun mayn lebn*. 2 vols. New York, 1923.
Nir-Rafalkes, N. *Ershte yorn*. Tel Aviv: Y. L: Peretz farlag, 1960.
Reles, H. *Di yidish-sovetish shrayber fun Vaysrusland: memuarn*. Minsk, 2004.
Rozental-Shnayderman, E. *Af vegn un umvegn: zikhroynes, geshenishn, perzenlekhkaytn*. 3 vols. Tel Aviv: 1972, 1978, 1982.
Rozin, A. *Mayn veg aheym: memuarn fun an asir-tsiyon in Ratn-Farband*. Jerusalem, 1981.
Singer, I. J. *Nay-Rusland: bilder fun a rayze*. Vilna: Kletskin, 1928.
Smoliar, H. *Fun ineveynik: zikhroynes vegn der "Yevsektsye."* Tel Aviv: Farlag Peretz, 1978.
Wengeroff, P. *Rememberings: The World of a Russian-Jewish Woman in the 19th Century*. Ed. Bernard J. Cooperman. Potomac: University Press of Maryland, 2000.
Zenzipper (Rafaeli), L. *Eser shanot redifot*. Tel Aviv: Akhdut, 1930.

Oral Interviews

Gershtein, Anna. Minsk, March 2004.
Gluskina, Gita. Ramat Gan, June 2004.
Reles, Hirsh. Minsk, February–April 2004.
Rogov, Nina. New York, March 2007.

Primary Sources

Agliad. Minsk, 1926.
Agursky, Sh. *Kegn Bund*. Minsk, 1933.
———, ed. *Di Oktyabr-revolutsye in Vaysrusland: zamlbukh, artiklen un zikhroynes*. Minsk, 1927.
———. *Di yidishe komissariatn un di yidishe komunistishe sektsyes (protokoln, rezolutsyes, un dokumentn, 1918–1921)*. Minsk, 1928.
Akselrod, Z. *Ordentregerish Vaysrusland: Literarishe zamlbukh*. 1939.
Alexandrov, H. *Forsht ayer shtetl!* Minsk, 1928.
Alexandrov, H., and I. Roznhoyz. *Undzer kant: bashraybungen fun der Vaysrusisher Sotsyalistisher Sovetn-Republik*. Minsk, 1929.

Almanak tsum XV yorteg fun der Oktyabr revolutsye. Minsk, 1932.
Aronson, G. *Di yidishe problem in sovetish rusland.* New York, 1944.
———. "Minsk in der tsayt fun der daytshisher okupatsye." *Di Tsukunft* 1. 1938: 27–41.
Bakst, Y., and Y. Grinberg. *Arbets-kinder: khrestomatye un arbets-bukh farn dritn lernyor.* Moscow, 1928.
Di bashtimung fun Ts.K.K.P.V. vegn der onfang un mitl shul. Minsk, 1931.
Di froy un ir zoyg kind. Minsk, 1926.
Di rabonim in dinst fun finants-kapital. Moscow, Kharkov, and Minsk, 1930.
Di rezolutsyes fun der Alvaysruslendishe konferents fun yidishe kultur un bildung tuer. Minsk, 1931.
Di yidishe horepashne froy in der sotsyalistisher iberboyung. Kharkov, 1931.
Dimanshtein, S., ed. *Yidn in FSSR, zamlbukh.* Moscow, 1935.
Dobrushin, Y. M. *Kinder teater.* Minsk, 1931.
Dubnow, S. *Kniga zhizni: vospominaniia i razmyshleniia dlia istorii moego vremeni.* St. Petersburg, 1998.
———. "Ob izuchenii istorii russkikh evreev i uchrezhdenii istoricheskogo obshchestva." *Voskhod* 4, no. 9 (April–September 1891): 1–91.
Eisenstadt, B. T. *Rabanei Minsk ve-hakhameha: sefer ha-zikaron.* Vilna, 1898.
Ekster, I., ed. *Di froy: zamlung.* Kiev, 1924.
Ershter Alvaysrusisher tsuzamenfor fun "GEZERD." Minsk, 1929.
Farn proletarishn gerikht, protses ibern fargvaltiker-farbrekher dem shoykhet Rapoport. Minsk, 1934.
Fashizirter yidishizm un zayn visnshaft. Minsk, 1930.
Frumkin, E. *Doloi ravinov.* Moscow, 1923.
———. *Hirsh Lekert.* Moscow, 1922.
Fun kinder-veltl. Minsk, 1928.
Kahan, S. *Di ershte premye: a monolog fun an elterer froy.* Minsk 1938.
Kantor, Y. *Natsionalnoe stroitelstvo sredi evreev v SSSR.* Moscow, 1923.
Kharik, I., and I. Bronshteyn, eds. *Sovetishe Vaysrusland: literarishe zamlung.* Minsk, 1935.
Kilimnik, L. I., ed. *Kommunisticheskaia vlast protiv religii Moiseia: Dokumenty 1920–1937 i 1945–1953 gg.* Vinnitsa: "Xrani i pomni," 2005.
Kinder teater. Moscow, Kharkov, and Minsk, 1931.
Kiselev, G. Ia. *O kreshchenii i obrezanii.* Moscow: Ogiz, 1937.
Klitenik, S. *Di kultur arbet tsvishn di yidishe arbetndike inem ratn farband.* Moscow, 1931.
Knorin, V. *1917 yor in Vaysrusland un afn mayrevfront.* Minsk, 1927.
Kostyrchenko, G., ed. *Gosudarstvennyi antisemitizm v SSSR ot nachala do kulminatsii, 1938–1953.* Moscow: Masterik, 2005.
Krol, L. *Di arbetnde froy un ir onteyl in der kooperatsye.* Minsk, 1926.
Larin, Y. *Evrei i antisemitizm SSSR.* Moscow and Leningrad, 1929.
Lestschinsky, Y. *Dos yidishe folk in numern.* Berlin, 1922.
Levin, Y. *Kleyn-Bund: fun yene yorn.* Minsk, 1924.
Literarishe khrestomatye. Minsk, 1926.
Literatur in shul. Moscow, Kharkov, and Minsk, 1930.
Litvak, A. *Gezamlte shriftn.* New York, 1945.
Mariasina, S. *Di alte un di naye shul (a bikhl farn masn-leyener).* Minsk, 1929.
Mekler, D. L. *Mentsh un mashin in Sovyetn-land: faktn, bilder, ayndrukn fun a rayze iber Sovyet Rusland.* Warsaw, 1936.
"Militärgeographische Angaben über das Eropäische Rußland, Weißrußland." Generalstab des Heeres, Abteilung für Kriegskarten Vermessungswesen. Berlin, 1941.

Minsker literarishe grupe "Yunger Arbeter." *Kep: lider-zamlung, gevidmet di korbones funem vaysn teror.* Minsk, 1926.
Osherovitsh, I., ed. *Di shtetlekh fun V.S.S.R. in rekonstruktivn peryod.* Minsk, 1932.
Otchet Minskoi Khoralnoi sinagogi za 1908/1909. Minsk, 1910.
Oyslender, N., Y. Bakst, and G. Fridland. *Arbet un kamf: literarishe khrestomatye: hilf-bukh farn 4tn 5tn un 6tn lernyor.* Moscow, 1926.
Pomerantz, A. J. S. *A meydl fun Minsk.* New York, 1942.
———. *Di sovetishe harugei-malkhes tsu zeyer tsentn yortsayt: vegn dem tragishn goyrl fun di yidishe shrayber.* Buenos Aires, 1962.
Prakticheskoe razreshenie natsionalnogo voprosa v Belorusskoi SSR. Minsk, 1927.
Program af shprakh un literatur. Moscow, Kharkov, and Minsk, 1931.
Program far gezelshaftkentenish in di yidishe zibnyorike shuln. Minsk, 1928.
Program fun der yidisher shprakh un literatur. Moscow, Kharkov, and Minsk, 1930.
Program fun yidish un literatur far der zibnyoriker shul. Minsk, 1927.
Rabi Yehoshua me-Horodna zatsal: more tsedek ve-rosh metivtah, kovets le-zikhro. Jerusalem, 1949.
Rabinovitsh, I., ed. *Froyen: literarishe zamlung.* Moscow, 1928.
Rosenshtein, Kh. D. (Even-Shoshan). *Ketuvim: maamarim, reshimot, divrei sifrut.* Jerusalem, 1973.
Rozshanski, Sh., ed. *Dovid Hofshteyn, Izzy Kharik, Itsik Fefer. Oysgeklibene shriftn: lider mit nigunim tsu 7 lider.* Buenos Aires, 1962.
Rubentchik, Y., ed. *Akhter mart: zamlbukh.* Minsk, 1926.
Rubin, R. *Yidishe froyen: fartseykhenungen.* Moscow, 1943.
Shimshelievitsh, M. *Minsker shokhtim-trest.* Minsk, 1925.
Sosis, I. *Geshikhte fun Yidishe gezelshaftlekhe shtrebungen in Rusland in 19tn y"h.* Minsk, 1930.
Styrne, V. ed. *Usia BSSR: Karotkaia adrasna-davedachnaia kniga.* Minsk, 1935.
Subbotin, A. P. *V cherte osedlosti. Otryvki iz ekonomicheskikh issledovanii v zapadno i iugo-zapadno Rossii za leto 1887.* St. Petersburg, 1888.
Surits, M. *Soviet-rusland in 1931, ayndrikn fun a rayze.* Warsaw, 1932.
Tsum XV yortog fun der Oktyabr revolutsye, sotsyal-ekonomishe zamlbukh. Minsk, 1932.
Vaysrusland. Ershter Alvaysruslendisher tsuzamenfor fun yidishe poyerim. Minsk, 1925.
Vaysrusland. Komisariat far sotsyaler farzorgung. Eytses far muters. Minsk, 1919.
Veinger, M. *Forsht yidishe dialektn! Program farn materyalnklayber.* Minsk, 1925.
Vsia Belarussiia, spravochnaia kniga, 1924. Minsk, 1924.
Yabrov, G. *Di yidishe literatur in frages, ufgabes un temes.* Minsk, 1928, 1929.
———. *Praktishe gramatik.* Minsk, 1926.
Yidisher pedagogisher tekhnikum. Tsu di Lenin-teg in shul. Minsk, 1925.
Yidn in BSSR: statistishe materyaln. Minsk, 1929.
Yidn in FSSR atlas fun kartogramen un diagramen. Moscow, Kharkov, and Minsk, 1930.
Zamlung fun pionierishe dertseylungen. Minsk, 1927.

Secondary Sources

Adler, E. *In Her Hands: The Education of Jewish Girls in Tsarist Russia.* Wayne State University Press, 2010.
———. "Women's Education in the Pages of the Russian Jewish Press." *Polin* 18 (2005): 121–32.

Altshuler, M. *Distribution of the Jewish Population of the USSR 1939*. Centre for Research and Documentation of East European Jewry, the Hebrew University of Jerusalem, 1993.
——, ed. *Ha-teatron ha-yehudi bi-Verit ha-Moatsot*. Jerusalem, 1996.
——. *Ha-Yevsektsya bi-Verit ha-Moatsot: ben leumiut le-komunizm, 1918–1930*. Tel Aviv: Sifriyat poalim, 1981.
——. *Soviet Jewry on the Eve of the Holocaust: A Social and Demographic Profile*. Jerusalem: The Center for Research of East European Jewry, the Hebrew University of Jerusalem, 1998.
——. *Soviet Jewry Since the Second World War: Population and Social Structure*. New York; Westport, CT; and London: Greenwood Press, 1987.
——. *Yahadut ba-makhbesh ha-Sovieti: ben dat le-zehut yehudit bi-Verit ha-Moatsot, 1941–1964*. The Zalman Shazar Center for Jewish History. Jerusalem, 2007.
Aronson, G., and J. S. Hertz, eds. *Di geshikhte fun Bund*. 4 vols. New York, 1962.
Assaf, D. et al., eds. *Mi-Vilna le-Yerushalaym: mehkarim be-toldotehem ve-be-tarbutam shel yehudei mizrah eropa mugashim le-professor Shmuel Werses*. Jerusalem: Magnes, 2002.
Babel, I. *The Complete Works of Isaac Babel*. New York: W. W. Norton, 2002.
Bacon, G. "Kefiya datit, hofesh bitui ve-zehut modernit be-Polin: Y.L. Peretz, Shalom Asch ve-shaaruryat ha-mila be-Varsha, 1908." In *Mi-Vilna le-Yerushalaym*, edited by David Assaf et al. Jerusalem: Magnes, 2002.
Balin, C. B. *To Reveal Our Hearts: Jewish Women Writers in Tsarist Russia*. Cincinnati, OH: Hebrew Union College Press, 2000.
Baron, S. W. *The Russian Jew Under Tsars and Soviets*. New York: Macmillan, 1964.
Bartal, I. *Jews of Eastern Europe, 1772–1881*. Philadelphia: University of Pennsylvania Press, 2005.
Basin, Y. *Bolshevizm i evrei: Belorussia, 1920–e*. Minsk: Baraskin, 2008.
——. "Delo Girsha Lekkerta (1902) i ego interpretatsiia v filme Belgoskino *Ego prevoskhoditelstvo*, 1927." *Belarus y XX stagoddzi* no. 3 (2004): 34–45.
Beizer, M. *Evrei Leningrada, 1917–1939: natsionalnaia zhizn i sovetizatsiia*. Moscow and Jerusalem: Gesharim, 1999.
Bemporad, E. "Behavior Unbecoming a Communist: Jewish Religious Practice in Soviet Minsk." *Jewish Social Studies* 14, no. 2 (2008): 1–31.
——. "Da letteratura del popolo a storia del popolo: Simon Dubnov e l'origine della storiografia russo-ebraica." *Annali di storia dell'esegesi* 18, no. 2 (2001): 533–57.
Biale, D. *Eros and the Jews: From Biblical Israel to Contemporary America*. Berkeley: University of California Press, 1997.
Birnbaum P., and I. Katznelson, eds. *Paths of Emancipation: Jews, States, and Citizenship*. Princeton, NJ: Princeton University Press, 1995.
Bolshaia Sovetskaia Entsiklopediia. Vols. 1–65. Moscow, 1926–47.
Boym, S. *Common Places: Mythologies of Everyday Life in Russia*. Cambridge, MA: Harvard University Press, 1994.
Brovkin, N. V. *Russia After Lenin: Politics, Culture and Society, 1921–1929*. London and New York: Routledge, 1998.
Brutskus, B. *Professionalnyi sostav evreiskogo naseleniia Rossii*. St. Petersburg, 1908.
Budnitskii, O. *Rossiiskie evrei mezhdu krasnymi i belymi (1917–1920)*. Moscow: Rosspen, 2005.
Buslova, K. P., ed. *Iz istorii borby za rasprostranenie marksizma v Belorussii (1893–1917 gg.)*. Minsk, 1958.

Buss, G. *The Bear's Hug: Christian Belief and the Soviet State, 1917–1986*. Grand Rapids, MI: W. B. Eerdmans, 1987.
Chernenko, M. *Krasnaia zvezda, zheltaia zvezda*. Vinnitsa, 2001.
Chkolnikova, E. "The Transformation of the Shtetl in the USSR in the 1930s." *Jews in Russia and Eastern Europe* 1, no. 52 (2004): 91–129.
Clark, K. *Petersburg: Crucible of Cultural Revolution*. Cambridge, MA: Harvard University Press, 1995.
Cohen, T. *Ha-ahat ahuvah ve-ha-ahat senuah: ben metsiut lebidyon beteurei ha-ishah be-sifrut ha-haskalah*. Jerusalem, 2002.
Conquest, R. *The Great Terror: A Reassessment*. New York: Oxford University Press, 1990.
David-Fox, M. *Revolution of the Mind: Higher Learning Among the Bolsheviks, 1918–1929*. Ithaca, NY: Cornell University Press, 1997.
Dennen, L. *Where the Ghetto Ends: Jews in Soviet Russia*. New York, 1934.
Dönninghaus, V. *Minderheiten in Bedrängnis: Sowjetische Politik gegenüber Deutschen, Polen und andere Diaspora-Nationalitäten 1917-1938*. Munich: R. Oldenburg, 2009.
Entsiklopediah shel ha-tsionut ha-datit: ishim, musagim, mifalim. Vol. I. Jerusalem: Mossad HaRav Kook, 1958.
Estraikh, G. "Evreiskaia literaturnaia zhizn v poslerevolutsionnoi Moskve." *Arkhiv Evreiskoi Istorii*, vol. II, 2005.
———. *In Harness: Yiddish Writers' Romance With Communism*. Syracuse, NY: Syracuse University Press, 2005.
———. *Soviet Yiddish: Language Planning and Linguistic Development*. New York: Clarendon Press, 1999.
Evans Clements, B., B. Alpern Engel, and C. D. Worobec, eds. *Russia's Women: Accommodation, Resistance, Transformation*. Berkeley: University of California Press, 1991.
Even-Shoshan, Sh., ed. *Minsk, ir va-em: korot, maasim, ishim, havai*. 2 vols. Tel Aviv: Irgun yotsei Minsk u-venoteha be-Yisrael, 1975, 1985.
Evrei Belarusi. Istoriia i Kultura. Vols. 3–4. Minsk, 1998.
Evreiskaia Entsiklopediia: svod znanii o evreistve i ego kulture v proshlom i nastoiashem. 16 vols. St. Petersburg: Brokgauz-Efron, 1906–13.
Fishman, D. E. "From Shtadlanut to Mass-Parties: Jewish Political Movements in Lithuania." In *History of Lithuanian Jews*, edited by Darius Staliunas. Vilnius: Institute of History, forthcoming.
———. "Preserving Tradition in the Land of Revolution: The Religious Leadership of Soviet Jewry, 1917–1930." In *The Use of Tradition: Jewish Continuity in the Modern Era*, edited by Jack Wertheimer. New York: The Jewish Theological Seminary of America, 1992.
———. *The Rise of Modern Yiddish Culture*. Pittsburgh, PA: University of Pittsburgh Press, 2005.
———. "To Our Brethren Abroad: Letters and reports by Soviet Rabbis, 1925–1930." *Jews in Russia and Eastern Europe* 1–2, nos. 54–55 (2005): 108–79.
Fitzpatrick, Sh. *Accusatory Practices: Denunciation in Modern European History, 1789–1989*. Chicago: University of Chicago Press Journals, 1997.
———. *The Cultural Front: Power and Culture in Revolutionary Russia*. Ithaca, NY: Cornell University Press, 1992.
———. *Everyday Stalinism: Ordinary Life in Extraordinary Times, Soviet Russia in the 1930s*. New York: Oxford University Press, 1999.

Freeze, Ch., P. Hyman, and A. Polonsky, eds. *Jewish Women in Eastern Europe, Polin: Studies in Polish Jewry.* Vol. 18. Oxford and Portland: Littman Library of Jewish Civilization, 2005.
Friedlander, S. "Martin Broszat and the Historization of National Socialism." In *History, Memory, and the Extermination of the Jews of Europe,* 90–95. Bloomington: Indiana University Press, 1993.
Furet, F., and J. Le Goff. *Méthodologie de l'histoire et des sciences humaines.* Vol. 2 of *Mélanges en l'honneur de Fernand Braudel.* Toulouse, 1973.
Gerasimova, I. P. "K istorii evreiskogo otdela Instituta belorusskoi kultury (Inbelkulta) i evreiskogo sektora Belorusskoi Akademii nauk v 20–30xx godakh." *Vestnik evreiskogo universiteta v Moskve* 12, no. 2 (1996): 144–67.
Gershtein, A. "Notes on the Jewish State Theater of Belorussia." *Jews in Eastern Europe* 2, no. 27 (fall 1995): 27–42.
Gershuni A. A., *Yahadut be-Rusiyah ha-sovyetit: le-korot redifot ha-dat.* Jerusalem, 1961.
———. *Yehudim ve-yahadut bi-Verit ha-Moatsot: yahadut Rusiyah me-tkufah Stalin ve-ad hazman ha-aharon.* Jerusalem: Feldheim, 1970.
Getty, J. A., and O. Naumov. *Origins of the Great Purges: The Soviet Communist Party Reconsidered, 1933–1938.* Cambridge: Cambridge University Press, 1985.
———. *The Road to Terror: Stalin and the Self-Destruction of the Bolsheviks.* New Haven, CT: Yale University Press, 1999.
Gillerman, Sh. *Germans into Jews: Remaking the Jewish Social Body in the Weimar Republic.* Stanford, CA: Stanford University Press, 2009.
Gilman, S. *The Jew's Body.* New York: Routledge, 1991.
Ginzburg, C. *Il filo e le tracce: vero, falso, finto.* Milan: Feltrinelli, 2006.
Gitelman, Z. *A Century of Ambivalence: The Jews of Russia and the Soviet Union, 1881 to the Present.* Bloomington: Indiana University Press, 2001.
———. *Jewish Nationality and Soviet Politics: The Jewish Sections of the CPSU, 1917–1930.* Princeton, NJ: Princeton University Press, 1972.
Gitelman, Z., and Y. Roi, eds. *Revolution, Repression and Revival: The Soviet Jewish Experience.* Lanham, MD: Rowman and Littlefield Publishers, 2007.
Gleason, A., P. Kenez, and R. Stites, eds. *Bolshevik Culture: Experiment and Order in the Russian Revolution.* Bloomington: Indiana University Press, 1985.
Goldberg Ruthchild, R. "Ester Frumkin: Jewish Woman Radical in Early Soviet Russia." In *Di froyen: Women and Yiddish.* National Council of Jewish Women New York Section, 1997.
Goldman, W. "Women, Abortion, and the State, 1917–1936." In *Russia's Women: Accommodation, Resistance, Transformation,* edited by Barbara Evans Clements. Berkeley: University of California Press, 1991.
———. *Women at the Gates: Gender and Industry in Stalin's Russia.* Cambridge: Cambridge University Press, 2002.
———. *Women, the State and Revolution: Soviet Family Policy and Social Life, 1917–1936.* Cambridge: Cambridge University Press, 1993.
Gorsuch, A. E. "A Woman Is Not a Man: The Culture of Gender and Generation in Soviet Russia, 1921–1928." *Slavic Review* 55, no. 3 (fall 1996): 636–60.
Greenbaum, A. A. "The Belorussian State Jewish Theater in the Interwar Period." *Jews in Russia and Eastern Europe* 42 (2001): 56–75.
———. *Jewish Scholarship and Scholarly Institutions in Soviet Russia, 1918–1953.* Jerusalem: Hebrew University of Jerusalem, 1978.

Hailperin, M. *"Ha-Gadol" mi-Minsk: R. Yerubam Yehudah Leyb Perlman, toldotav ve-korotav.* Jerusalem, New York: Feldheim, 1991.

Halevy, Z. *Jewish Schools Under Czarism and Communism: A Struggle for Cultural Identity.* New York, 1976.

Halfin, I. *Terror in My Soul: Communist Autobiographies on Trial.* Cambridge, MA: Harvard University Press, 2003.

Hellbeck, J. *Revolution on My Mind: Writing a Diary Under Stalin.* Cambridge, MA: Harvard University Press, 2006.

Hertz, J. S., ed. *Doyres Bundistn.* Vol. I. New York: Undzer Tsayt, 1956.

———. *Hirsh Lekert.* New York: Undzer Tsayt, 1952.

Hirsch, F. *Empire of Nations: Ethnographic Knowledge and the Making of the Soviet Union.* Ithaca, NY, and London: Cornell University Press, 2005.

———. "Toward an Empire of Nations: Border-Making and the Formation of Soviet National Identities." *Russian Review* 59, no. 2 (April 2000): 201–26.

Hoberman, J. *The Red Atlantis: Communist Culture in the Absence of Communism.* Philadelphia, PA: Temple University Press, 1998.

Hoffman, D. *Peasant Metropolis: Social Identities in Moscow, 1929–1941.* Ithaca, NY: Cornell University Press, 1994.

Hosking, G. *The First Socialist Society: A History of the Soviet Union from Within.* Cambridge, MA: Harvard University Press, 1997.

Hyman, P. *Gender and Assimilation in Modern Jewish History: The Roles and Representations of Women.* Seattle: University of Washington Press, 1995.

———. "Immigrant Women and Consumer Protest: The New York Kosher Meat Boycott of 1902." *American Jewish History* 70, no. 1 (September 1980): 91–105.

Judd, R. "Circumcision and Modern Jewish Life: A German Case Study, 1843–1914." In *The Covenant of Circumcision: New Perspectives on an Ancient Jewish Rite,* edited by Elizabeth Wyner Mark. Hanover, NH: Brandeis University Press, 2003.

———. "The Politics of Beef: Animal Advocacy and the Kosher Butchering Debates in Germany." *Jewish Social Studies* 10, no. 1 (fall 2003): 126–27.

Kaganovsky, L. *How the Soviet Man Was (Un)Made: Cultural Fantasy and Male Subjectivity Under Stalin.* Pittsburgh, PA: University of Pittsburgh Press, 2008.

Kaliada, V. I. *Minsk uchora i sennia.* Minsk: Belarus, 1989.

Kapilov, A. *Zamkovaia 2/7: povesti i rasskazy.* Minsk, 1995.

Katz, D. *Lithuanian Jewish Culture.* Baltos Lankos, Lithuania, 2004.

Kenez, P. *The Birth of the Propaganda State: Soviet Methods of Mass Mobilization, 1917–1929.* Cambridge: Cambridge University Press, 1985.

Khlevniuk, O. *Politbiuro. Mekhanizmy politicheskoi vlasti v 1930–e gody.* Moscow: Rosspen, 1996.

Klibansky, B. T. Ha-yeshivot ha-litaiot be-mizrah Eropah ben shtei milhamot ha-olam. PhD dissertation, Tel Aviv University, 2009.

Klier, J. D. *Imperial Russia's Jewish Question, 1855–1881.* Cambridge: Cambridge University Press, 1995.

Knight, A. "Female Terrorists in the Russian Socialist Revolutionary Party." *Russian Review* 38, no. 2 (April 1979): 139–59.

Kobrin, R. *Jewish Bialystok and Its Diaspora.* Bloomington: Indiana University Press, 2010.

Kochan, L., ed. *The Jews in Soviet Russia Since 1917.* London and New York: Oxford University Press, 1970.

Kollontai, A. "Sisters." In *Love of Worker Bees.* Chicago: Cassandra Editions, 1992.

Korey, W. *The Soviet Cage: Anti-Semitism in Russia*. New York: Viking Press, 1973.
Kostyrchenko, G. "The Genesis of Establishment Anti-Semitism in the USSR: The Black Years, 1948–1953." In *Revolution, Repression and Revival: The Soviet Jewish Experience*, edited by Zvi Gitelman and Yaacov Roi. Lanham, MD: Rowman and Littlefield Publishers, 2007.
Kotkin, S. *Magnetic Mountain: Stalinism as a Civilization*. Berkeley: University of California Press, 1995.
Kratkaia Evreiskaia Entsiklopediia. 7 vols. Jerusalem: Keter, 1976.
Krutikov, M., and V. Selemenev. "Yasha Bronshteyn and His Struggle for Control over Soviet Yiddish Literature." *Jews in Russia and Eastern Europe* 50 (2003): 175–90.
Kulbak, M. *Zelmenyaner*. Vol. 1, Minsk, 1931; Vol. 2, Minsk, 1935.
Kuromiya, H. *The Voices of the Dead: Stalin's Great Terror in the 1930s*. New Haven, CT: Yale University Press, 2008.
Kushnirov, A. *Hirsh Lekert*. Kharkov, 1930.
Lane, C. *Christian Religion in the Soviet Union: A Sociological Study*. Albany: State University of New York Press, 1978.
Le Foll, C. "The 'Belorussianisation' of the Jewish Population During the Interwar Period: Discourses and Achievements in Political and Cultural Spheres." *East European Jewish Affairs* 38, no. 1 (2008): 65–88.
Lenin, V. I. *Critical Remarks on the National Question: The Right of Nations to Self-Determination*. Moscow: Progress Publishers, 1968.
Lenoe, M. *Agitation, Propaganda, and the Stalinization of the Soviet Press, 1922–1930*. Carl Beck Papers in Russian and East European Studies, no. 1305. Pittsburgh, PA: Pittsburgh University Press, 1998.
Levitats, I. *The Jewish Community in Russia, 1772–1884*. Vol. 1. New York: Columbia University Press, 1943.
———. *The Jewish Community in Russia, 1844–1917*. Vol. 2. Jerusalem: Posner & Son, 1981.
Lewin, M. *The Making of the Soviet System*. London: Methuen, 1985.
———. "Society, State and Ideology During the First Five-Year Plan." In *Cultural Revolution in Russia, 1928–1931*, edited by Sheila Fitzpatrick. Bloomington: Indiana University Press, 1984: 41–77.
Likhodedov, V. *Sinagogi/Synagogues*. Minsk: Riftur, 2007.
Litvak, O. *Conscription and the Search for Modern Russian Jewry*. Bloomington: Indiana University Press, 2006.
Litvin, A. *Yidishe neshomes*. Vol. III. New York, 1917.
Lubachko, I. *Belorussia Under Soviet Rule, 1917–1957*. Lexington: University Press of Kentucky, 1972.
Marcus, J. *Social and Political History of the Jews of Poland, 1919–1939*. Berlin: Mouton Publishers, 1983.
Markiianov, B. K. *Borba kommunisticheskoi partii Belorussii za ukreplenie edinstva svoikh riadov v 1921–1925 gg.* Minsk, 1961.
Martin, T. *The Affirmative Action Empire: Nations and Nationalism in the Soviet Union, 1923–1939*. Ithaca, NY: Cornell University Press, 2001.
Mayzel, N. *Dos yidishe shafn un der yidisher shrayber in Sovetnfarband*. New York, 1959.
Meir, N. *Kiev: Jewish Metropolis, 1859–1914*. Bloomington: Indiana University Press, 2010.
Melzer, E. *No Way Out: The Politics of Polish Jewry, 1935–1939*. Cincinnati, OH: Hebrew Union College Press, 1997.

———. "Relations Between Poland and Germany and the Impact on the Jewish Problem in Poland, 1935–1938." *Yad Vashem Studies* 12 (1977): 193–229.
Mendelsohn, E. *Class Struggle in the Pale: The Formative Years of the Jewish Workers Movement in Tsarist Russia*. Cambridge: Cambridge University Press, 1970.
Mendelsohn, E., Y. Gutman, J. Reinharz, and Kh. Shmeruk, eds. *The Jews of Poland Between Two World Wars*. Boston: Brandeis University Press, 1989.
Minsk, Spadarozhnik turysta. Minsk, Belarus, 1971.
Mishkinsky, M. "Regional Factors in the Formation of the Jewish Labor Movement in Czarist Russia." *YIVO Annual* 14 (1969): 27–52.
Motokoff, G., and S. A. Sack. *Where Once We Walked: A Guide to Jewish Communities Destroyed in the Holocaust*. Teaneck, NJ: Avotaynu, 1991.
Naiman, E. *Sex in Public: The Incarnation of Early Soviet Ideology*. Princeton, NJ: Princeton University Press, 1997.
Nathans, B. *Beyond the Pale: The Jewish Encounter with Late Imperial Russia*. Berkeley: University of California Press, 2002.
Parush, I. *Nashim korot: Yitronah shel shuliyut ba-hevrah ha-yehudit be-mizrah eropah ba-meah ha-tesha-esreh*. Tel Aviv, 2001.
Petrone, K. *Life Has Become More Joyous, Comrades: Celebrations in the Time of Stalin*. Bloomington and Indianapolis: Indiana University Press, 2000.
Petrovsky-Shtern, Y. *Lenin's Jewish Question*. New Haven, CT: Yale University Press, 2010.
Pinkus, B. *The Jews of the Soviet Union: The History of a National Minority*. Cambridge: Cambridge University Press, 1988.
———. *The Soviet Government and the Jews, 1948–1967: A Documented Study*. Cambridge: Cambridge University Press, 1984.
Pipes, R. *The Russian Revolution*. New York: Vintage, 1990.
Rabinowitch, A., and R. Stites, eds. *Russia in the Era of NEP: Explorations in Soviet Society and Culture*. Bloomington: Indiana University Press, 1991.
Rafes, M. *Girsh Lekert (Rasskaz o tsarskikh rosgakh)*. Minsk, 1922.
Redlich, Sh. *War, Holocaust and Stalinism: A Documented Study of the Jewish Anti-Fascist Committee in the US*. Luxembourg: Harwood Academic Publishers, 1995.
Rejzen, Z. *Leksikon fun der nayer yidisher literatur*. 1914.
———. *Leksikon fun der yidisher literatur, prese, un filologye*. 4 vols. Vilna: Kletskin, 1928–30.
Robin, R. *L'Amour du Yiddish: Écriture juive et sentiment de la langue (1830–1930)*. Paris: Éditions du Sorbier, 1984.
Rogger, H. *Jewish Policies and Right-Wing Politics in Imperial Russia*. Berkeley: University of California Press, 1986.
Roi, Y. "Economic Trials." *The YIVO Encyclopedia of Jews in Eastern Europe*. Vol. 1. New Haven, CT: Yale University Press, 2008.
Roi, Y., and A. Beker, eds. *Jewish Culture and Identity in the Soviet Union*. New York: New York University Press, 1991.
Rothenberg, J. *The Jewish Religion in the Soviet Union*. New York: Ktav Publishing House, 1971.
Rubentchik, Y., ed. *Akhter mart: zamlbukh*. Minsk, 1926.
Rudling, P. A. The Battle over Belorussia: The Rise and Fall of the Belarusian National Movement, 1906–1931. PhD Dissertation, University of Alberta, 2009.
Shatsky, Y., and Sh. Niger. *Leksikon fun der nayer Yidisher literatur*. New York, 1956.
Schroeter, L. *The Last Exodus*. New York: Universe Books, 1974.
Schulman, E. *A History of Jewish Education in the Soviet Union*. New York, 1971.

———. "Yidishe kultur-tetikayt in Minsk, 1917–1941." In *Hesed le-Avraham: sefer ha-yovel le-Avraham Golomb, tsu zayn akhtsikstn geboyrn-tog*, ed. M. Shtarkman, 784–85. Los Angeles, 1970.
Schwarz, S. M. *Antisemitizm v sovetskom soiuze*. New York: Chekhov Publishing House, 1952.
———. *Di sovetish-yidishe literatur*. New York: Tsiko, 1971.
———. *The Jews in the Soviet Union*. Syracuse, NY: Syracuse University Press, 1951.
Shapiro, L. *The Origins of the Communist Autocracy*. Cambridge, MA: Harvard University Press, 1977.
Shibeko, Z. V. *Minsk: stranitsy zhizni dorevolutsionnogo goroda*. Minsk: Polimia, 1990.
Shmeruk, Kh. Ha-kibuts ha-yehudi ve-ha-hityashvut ha-haklait ha-yehudit be-Bielorusiah ha-sovetit, 1918–1932. Hebrew University, PhD dissertation, 1961.
Shneer, D. *Yiddish and the Creation of Soviet Jewish Culture, 1918–1930*. Cambridge and New York: Cambridge University Press, 2004.
Shpilevskii, P. M. "Puteshchestvie po Polesiu i Belorusskomu kraiu: Minsk Belorusskii." *Sovremennik* 48, no. 11: 1–33.
Shtampfer, Sh. "Gender Differentiation and Education of the Jewish Woman in Nineteenth-Century Eastern Europe." *Polin* 7 (1992): 63–87. Oxford and Portland: Littman Library of Jewish Civilization.
Shtarkman, M., ed. *Hesed le-Avraham: sefer ha-yovel le-Avraham Golomb, tsu zayn akhtsikstn geboyrn-tog*. Los Angeles, 1970.
Shternshis, A. *Soviet and Kosher: Jewish Popular Culture in the Soviet Union, 1923–1939*. Bloomington: Indiana University Press, 2006.
Sicher, E. *Jews in Russian Literature After the October Revolution: Writers and Artists Between Hope and Apostasy*. Cambridge: Cambridge University Press, 1995.
Siegelbaum, L. H. *Stakhanovism and the Politics of Productivity in the USSR, 1935–1941*. Cambridge: Cambridge University Press, 1988.
Simon, G. *Nationalism and Policy Toward the Nationalities in the Soviet Union: From Totalitarian Dictatorship to Post-Stalinist Society*. Boulder, CO; San Francisco; and Oxford: Westview Press, 1991.
Sinkoff, N. "The Maskil, the Convert, and the *Agunah*: Joseph Perl as a Historian of Jewish Divorce Law." *AJS Review* 27, no. 2 (November 2003): 281–99.
Skir, A. *Evreiskaia dukhovnaia kultura v Belarusi: Istoriko-literaturnyi ocherk*. Minsk: Mastatskaia literatura, 1995.
Slezkine, Y. *Arctic Mirrors: Russia and the Small Peoples of the North*. Ithaca, NY: Cornell University Press, 1994.
———. *The Jewish Century*. Princeton, NJ: Princeton University Press, 2004.
———. "The USSR as a Communal Apartment, or How a Socialist State Promoted Ethnic Particularism." *Slavic Review* 53, no. 2 (summer 1994): 414–52.
Sloin, A. "Speculators, Swindlers and Other Jews: Regulating Trade in Revolutionary White Russia." *East Euripean Jewish Affairs* 40, no. 2 (2010): 103–125.
Slutsky, Y. *Bobruisk: sefer zikaron le-kehilat Bobruisk*. Vol. I. Tel Aviv.
Smilovitski, L. *Evrei Belarusi: iz nashei obshei istorii, 1905–1953*. Minsk: Arti-Feks, 1999.
———. "Jewish Religious Life in Minsk, 1944–1953." *Jews in Eastern Europe* 2, no. 30 (fall 1996): 5–17.
Smoliar, H. *Sovetishe yidn hinter geto tsoymen*. Tel Aviv: Farlag Y. L. Peretz, 1985.
Sobolevskaia, O., and V. Gancharov. *Evrei Grodnenshchiny: zhizn do katastrofy*. Donetsk: Nordpress, 2005.

Spector, Sh., ed. *Lost Jewish Worlds: The Communities of Grodno, Lida, Olkieniki, Vishav.* Jerusalem: Yad Vashem, 1996.

Stanislawski, M. *For Whom Do I Toil? Judah Leib Gordon and the Crisis of Russian Jewry.* New York: Oxford University Press, 1988.

———. "Russian Jewry, the Russian State, and the Dynamics of Jewish Emancipation." In *Paths of Emancipation: Jews, States, and Citizenship,* edited by Pierre Birnbaum and Ira Katznelson, 262–83. Princeton, NJ: Princeton University Press, 1995.

Stites, R. *Revolutionary Dreams: Utopian Vision and Experimental Life in the Russian Revolution.* New York: Oxford University Press, 1989.

———. "Women and the Revolutionary Process in Russia." In *Becoming Visible: Women in European History,* edited by Renate Bridenthal, Klaudia Koonz, and Susan Stuard, 451–71. Boston: Houghton Mifflin, 1987.

———. *The Women's Liberation Movement in Russia: Feminism, Nihilims, and Bolshevism, 1860–1930.* Princeton, NJ: Princeton University Press, 1978.

Terhoeven, P. *Oro alla patria: Donne, guerra e propaganda nella giornata della fede fascista.* Bologna: Il Mulino, 2006.

Tobias, H. *Jewish Bund in Russia from Its Origin to 1905.* Stanford, CA: Stanford University Press, 1972.

Traverso, E. *Il totalitarismo: storia di un dibatto.* Bruno Mondadori, 2002.

Vakar, N. *Belorussia: The Making of a Nation.* Cambridge, MA: Harvard University Press, 1956.

Veidlinger, J. *Jewish Public Culture in the Late Russian Empire.* Bloomington: Indiana University Press, 2009.

———. *The Moscow State Yiddish Theater: Jewish Culture on the Soviet Stage.* Bloomington: Indiana University Press, 2000.

Von Hagen, M. *Soldiers in the Proletarian Dictatorship: The Red Army and the Soviet Socialist State, 1917–1930.* Ithaca, NY: Cornell University Press, 1990.

Voronovich, I. "Sudba mastera." *Mishpocha* no. 25 (2010): 52–56.

Weinberg, R. *Stalin's Forgotten Zion: Birobidzhan and the Making of a Soviet Jewish Homeland, 1928–1966.* Berkeley: University of California Press, 2002.

Weiner, A. *Making Sense of War: The Second World War and the Fate of the Bolshevik Revolution.* Princeton, NJ: Princeton University Press, 2001.

———. "Saving Private Ivan: From What? Why? How?" *Kritika, Explorations in Russian and Eurasian History* 1, no. 2 (2000): 305–36.

Wood, E. *The Baba and the Comrade: Gender and Politics in Revolutionary Russia.* Bloomington: Indiana University Press, 1997.

Wyner Mark, E., ed. *The Covenant of Circumcision: New Perspectives on an Ancient Jewish Rite.* Hanover, NH: Brandeis University Press, 2003.

Yalen, D. "Documenting the New 'Red Kasrilevke': Shtetl Ethnography as Revolutionary Narrative." *East European Jewish Affairs* 37, no. 3 (2007): 353–75.

Yocum, B. B. Constructing a Socialist Tower of Babel: Nationality Policy in Soviet Belorussia, 1921–1933. PhD dissertation, Brandeis University, 2003.

Yoffe, E.G. *Po dostovernym istochnikam: Evrei v istorii gorodov Belarusi.* Minsk, 2001.

YIVO Encyclopedia of Jews in Eastern Europe. New Haven, CT: Yale University Press, 2008.

Zeltser, A. "Belorusizatsiia 1920-x gg.: dostizheniia i neudachi." In *Evrei Belarusi: istoriia i kultura* III–IV (Minsk, 1998): 60–93.

———. *Evrei v sovetskoi provintsii: Vitebsk i mestechki, 1917–1941.* Moscow: Rosspen, 2006.

———. "Jews in the Upper Ranks of the NKVD, 1934–1941." *Jews in Russia and Eastern Europe* 1, no. 52 (2004): 64–90.
Zeltser, A., and V. Selimenev. "The Jewish Intelligentsia and the Liquidation of Yiddish Schools in Belorussia, 1938." *Jews in Russia and Eastern Europe* 43 (2001): 78–97.
———. "The Liquidation of Yiddish Schools in Belorussia and Jewish Reaction." *Jews in Russia and Eastern Europe* (41) 2001: 74–111.
Zinger, V. *Di yidishe bafelkerung in SSSR*. Moscow 1930.
Zipperstein, S. J. *Imagining Russian Jewry: Memory, History, Identity*. Seattle and London: University of Washington Press, 1999.
———. *The Jews of Odessa: A Cultural History, 1794–1881*. Stanford, CA: Stanford University Press, 1986.

Index

Agursky, Shmuel, 193: *Afn visnshaftlekhn front* (On the scholarly front), 103; arrest in 1937, 193; idealization of the Bund, 79; new "Beilis trial", 125; *Veker* (The alarm) 61; wife's plea to Stalin, 173; Women's Department of the Communist Party, 155–56
Akselrod, Yona: everyday life, 181–85
Akselrod, Zelig: nationalist label, 200
Aleichem, Sholem, 64–65, 69: celebrations of, 64–65, 89–90, 182, 184; interpretations of work, 46; *Kasrilevke*, 41
All-Belorussian Radio committee, 184–85
All-Belorussian Union of Poets and Writers, 104
All-Union Association of Proletarian Writers, 104
anti-Jewish violence: Polish occupation of Minsk, 28; reports, 208–9
anti-Semitism: Poland, 204–6, 209–10; violence reports, 208–209
Arbeter bletl (The worker's leaflet), 22
Arbeter Ring (Workmen's circle), 22
Artisans' House of Prayer, 114
Atlas of Yiddish Dialects, 101

Babel, Isaac, "Karl-Yankl," 137–39
Basok, Zalman Y., arrest of, 34
Belarus National Republic, 25
Belgoset (Belorussian State Jewish Theater), 73–74, 104, 182–83: Damesek, A., 192; *Hirsh Lekert*, 68–69; Kulbak, Moshe, 194; Minsk, return to, 215; Moscow stages and, 74; Rafalskii, Mikhail, 193; Rapoport case, 129
Belorusizatsiia, 82: Yidishizatsiia, 84
Belorussia: Historical Commission of Belorussia, 105–6; Marxism, 53; Yiddish as state language, 82
Belorussia, 104
Belorussian: All-republican language, 197; language, 84–89; nationalists, Polish Minsk residents, 25; state language, 84
Belorussian Academy of Science, 102–3
Belorussian Republic, Minsk as hub, 71–72
Belorussian Social-Democratic Party, 83
Belorussian State Jewish Theater. *See* Belgoset
Belorussian State University, 44–45, 99–100; Gorky Belorussian Higher Pedagogical Institute, 100; Hebrew language, 45; Jewish Department, 73; Jewish Department women enrollment, 169–70; Zionist youth groups, 45–46
Belorussianization, 82: Bronshteyn, Yasha, 105; Jewish Pedagogical College hiring, 85; Jewish scholarly output, 108; Kharik, Izzy, 105; literary themes and, 103–4; resistance, 84; resistance, warnings against, 86; Russian and 98; workplace resistance, 85; Yiddishization and, 84, 92
Belorussian-Jewish identity, 106–7; creation, 103–9
blood libels, 205–6
Bolshevik regime, Minsk reestablishment, 29–30
Bolshevik Revolution: Minsk borders, 21; Rejzen, Sore, 29; Ukraine, 30
Bolsheviks: Belorussian Council, 25; Minsk, 5; Zionism and, 26
Bolshevization, *Der Veker* and, 62
books: Hebrew language, 46–47; printing, 20–21; Zionist, 47
bourgeois institutions, sovietization and, 32–33
Boytre (Kulbak), 105
Brasler, Asia, family, 189–90
Breinin, Reuben, religious practice, 113
Bronislaw Grosser Library, 58
Bronislaw Grosser Workers' Club. *See* Grosser Club
Bronshteyn, Yasha, 194: Bolshevik Revolution anniversary celebration, 185; Institute for Proletarian Jewish Culture, 103; purges and, 195; Soviet Yiddish literature, 200; *Sovetishe Vaysrusland*, 105; Trotskyite accusation, 194
BSSR (Belorussian Soviet Socialist Republic), 2
Bund, preservation of name, 58–59
the Bund: allegiances, 51–53; Bronislaw Grosser Workers' Club, 57; Bundist institutions, 58–60; cultural strategies and, 69–76; *Der Veker* and, 61–62; Evsektsiia and, 52; founding celebration, 56; Frumkin, Ester, 53; Jewish labor movement and, 52; Jewish separateness, 58; Left Bundists, 57; library relocation, 59; Mensheviks and, 52; merge with CPB, 32, 55–56; neutralist position on national question, 58; political strategies and, 69–76; Right Bundists, 57; size in early twentieth century, 52; women in, 148; Yiddish language and culture, 69–70
Bundism accusations, 78; Agursky, Shmuel, 193; Great Terror, 177, 191–93

269

Index

Central Jewish Workers' Club, 58–60. *See also* Grosser Club
Cheka, 4
Cherviakov, A.N., 176
circumcision observance, 113; accidental death of newborn, 140; Babel, Isaac ("Karl-Yankl"), 137–39; Comrade Gorlin, 135–37; deferring, 140; family and, 142–43; gender roles, 142; Jewish Communists, 133–34, 137–39, 139–42; Jewish identity and, 142–43; Katz, Jacob, 134; restrictions, 134–35; school admittance and, 133
Commission for the Requisition of Church Treasures of the Minsk Region, 114
Communism: proverki (verifications), 160; women's education, 149; women's liberation, 148–49
Communist Jewish elite, ancien régime Jews and, 113
Communist Party. *See also* CPB (Communist Party of Belorussia): Bund, name preservation, 58–59; Bund merge, 32; Elvoda factory review of party members, 141; growth under Stalin, 141; Jewish members, 3; women's membership, 166–69
Communist schools, 130–33
Comrade Gorlin case, 135–37
confiscation of property, synagogues, 114–16, 117
counterrevolutionaries, 77–79; *Hirsh Lekert*, 192; women as, 159
courtrooms, Yiddish and, 90
CPB (Communist Party of Belorussia): Bund merge, 55–56; Evsektsiia as administrative body, 56; Grinberg, Solomon, CPB application, 3; liquidation of political parties and factions, 55; Minsk Bundist leadership and, 53–54; Women's Department, 151–53
Cultural Revolution, 51; religion, 117; women, 161–62
cultural sphere purge, 193–96
cultural strategies, Bundist effect, 69–76

Der Emes (The truth), 61; *Der Veker* controversy, 75–76
Der minsker arbeter (The Minsk worker) 22
Der Shtern (The star) 61
Der Veker, 24–25, 57, 58–59, 61–62. *See also* Oktyabr (October): the Bund and, 61–62; *Der Emes* controversy, 75–76; name change, 63–64
Der yid (The Jew), 24
Der yunger arbeter (The young worker), 25
Der Yunger Leninets (The young Leninist) 63–64
Der Yunger Veker, 63–64
Di Tsukunft, 22
Dimanshteyn, Semion, Bund (the name question), 58–59

domestic life, women and, 164–66
Dos yidishe vort (The Jewish word) 24–25

education. *See also* scholarship; schools; universities: heder and yeshiva banning, 119–23; Jewish students, 3; Red Teachers, 98; Rosental-Shnayderman, Ester, 94–95; women, 147, 149; Yiddish and, 91–98
Ego prevoskhoditelstvo, 68
Elvoda factory review of party members, 141
emancipation of Jews, 3
emancipation of women: male anxiety, 146; self-emancipation, 156; theory and practice tension, 145–46
EMSO (Evreiskoe Meditsinskoe Sanitarnoe Obshchestvo): attacks on, 36; lishchentsy, 35–36; Soviet influence, 37
enemies of the people (Great Terror), 176, 191
ethnic neighborhood stability, 179
Evpedtekhnikum (Jewish Pedagogical Training College), 112: gender roles and, 163, 168–69; *Shlos gas*, 112; sporting contests, 185; synagogue takeovers, 119; Yiddish as instructional language, 198
Evsektsiia: Bundists and, 52; as CPB administrative body, 56; *Der Shtern*, 61; Jewish self rule, 56; Minsk takeover, 53–57; particularity and universalism, 6–7; propaganda against Jews, 56; sovietization and, 32; women and, 149–50
exclusion of Jews, prior to Bolsheviks, 2

fascism, 201–4; anti-Jewish violence reports, 208–9
financial support for Jews, American relatives, 34–35
folksongs, Soviet Jews, 202–3
folksongs of Stalinist era, 186–87
For the Proletarian Court, 129
Frumkin, Ester, 53; Lekert, Hirsh, and, 67; Lifschitz, Malka, 148

garment workers, 186
Gelfand, Ruva, 47; Great Terror, 190–91
gender equality. *See also* women: abortion and, 162; divorce, 162; free unions, 162; hierarchy of functions between men and women, 157; male anxiety, 146, 154–56; wages, 148; women activists photographs, 163–64; women married to Communist men, 156–57; workplace attitudes, 158
General City Women Delegates' Meeting, 151
geocultural character of Minsk, 19–21
German Jews: Hitler's rise and, 206–7; Soviet Jews' empathy for, 208
Germans, Minsk occupation, 25–26

Germany, Belorussian Council, 25
"ghetto benches" in Polish universities, 204–5
Gimmelshteyn, Rebecca, 56–57, 167
Ginzberg, Aryeh Leib b. Asher, 20
Ginzburg House of Prayer, 114
Gluskin, Menachem Mendel, 121
Gluskin trust trial, 123–24
gold campaign, 161–62
Goldberg, Chanan, 23–24: on Yiddish, 90–91, 94
Gorky Belorussian Higher Pedagogical Institute, 100
Granovsky, Alexander, 74
Great Minsk Choral Synagogue, 114–15
Great Terror: Brasler, Asia, family, 189–90; Bronshteyn, Yasha, 194; Bundism, 177, 191–93; Cherviakov, A.N., suicide, 176; enemies of the people, 176, 191; Gelfand, Ruva, 190–91; Jewish cultural sphere, 193–96; Jewish national pride displays, 206–8; Jewish radicalism, 199–201; Jewish reactions, 189–90; Kharik, Izzy, 194; Kulbak, Moshe, 194; Minsk's geographic location, 199; Polish institutions, 199–200; Rafalskii, Mikhail, 193–94; school closings, 196, 197–99; Sosis, Israel, 200; "terror etiquette," 190–91; Trotskyite accusations, 189; Zionism, 193
Grinberg, Solomon, CPB application, 3
Grosser, Bronislaw, 58
Grosser Club, 57, 58–59; Bundist management, 59–60; growth, 60; name preservation, 59
Grubyan, Motl, 207

Ha-poel He-haluts, 23
Hebrew language. *See also* Yiddish: Belorussian State University, 45; books, 46–47
heder, banning, 119–23
He-haver, 46
Heilprin, Yehiel, 20
Hirsh Lekert, 66
Hirsh Lekert stage production, 68–69; as counterrevolutionary weapon, 192
Historical Commission of Belorussia, 105–6
Hitler, Adolf, German Jews and, 206–7
Hovovei Zion, 23
Hurwitz, Chayim Dov, 45–46

Inbelkult: *Belorussia* (literary collection), 104; Jewish studies, 100–102; Language Commission, 107; *Research Yiddish Dialects!*, 107; *Research Your Shtetl!*, 107
industrialization, Minsk and, 16
Institute for Belorussian Culture. *See* Inbelkult
Institute for Jewish Culture, Minsk *versus* Moscow, 73

Institute for Proletarian Jewish Culture, 103
International Women's Day 1923, 155
Iskateli Shchastia, 184

JDC (Joint Distribution Committee): assistance, 33–34; lishchentsy, 34–35; Minsk university, 33; shoe distribution, 33
Jewish Anti-Fascist Committee, 207–8
Jewish cemetery: as goat grazing field, 31–32; use, 41; bulldozing, 215
Jewish Communists, circumcision and, 133–34, 139–42
Jewish community: conversion to Russian Orthodoxy, 15–16; history in Minsk, 14–15
Jewish Department of Belorussian State Museum, 42
Jewish Department of Belorussian State University, women enrollment, 169–70
Jewish heros: Kharik, Izzy, 188–89; Lapidus, Nahum, 188; Skoblo, Hirshl, 187; Stalinist era, 186–88
Jewish holidays, adherence, 113
Jewish identity: circumcision and, 142–43; late 1930s, 186–87; rebellion against, 4
Jewish institutions, Bolshevik shut down, 31–32
Jewish labor movement, 52
Jewish Labor Party Bund, establishment, 22
Jewish Medical and Sanitary Society, 35–36
Jewish National Fund, 23
Jewish particularity: delegitimization, 4; interwar period, 6–7
Jewish Pedagogical Training College. *See* Evpedtekhnikum
Jewish political organizations, 4
Jewish question, early twentieth century, 21–22
Jewish quotas, 3, 204–5
Jewish radicalism, Vilna, 22
Jewish Socialist parties, Minsk, 26–27
Jewish Sports Club Hamer, Yiddish and, 91
Jewish women, role models, 155–56
Jewish women's question, 146. *See also* women's question

Kaplan, Avraham, 27–28
Kaplan, Eliezer, 24
"Karl-Yankl" (Babel), 137–39
kashrut laws: korobka and, 121; maintenance, 120–21
kassy, 52
Katz, Jacob, on circumcision, 134
Khanin, Nokhem, 34–35; on Minsk, 41–43
Kharik, Izzy, 188–89; celebration of newest poem, 185; Great Terror, 194; idealization of the Bund,

79; purges and, 194–95; postwar accounts of city history, 216; *Sovetishe Vaysrusland*, 105
Kibbuts Niddehei Israel, 23
korenizatsiia, 82; regional idiosyncrasies, 83–84; women and, 151–52; Yiddishization, 92
korobka, 121; collapse, 128; underground religious education institutions, 121–23
kosher meat production, 113. *See also* kashrut laws; arrests, 128; chicken, 128; chicken consumption decline, 129; increase in, 125–26; industry tradition, 127; postwar accounts of city history, 216; Rapoport trial, 128–29; Red Army, 126
Kristallnacht, 207
Kronstadt Rebellion, 4
Kulbak, Moshe: Great Terror, 194–95; Institute for Proletarian Jewish Culture, 103; Kharik celebration, 185; *Zelmenyaner*, 105, 177–78
Kurlovskii shooting, 52
Kushnirov, Aron, *Hirsh Lekert* stage production, 68–69

Labor Zionism, Minsk and, 26
language. *See also* Yiddish: Belorussian, 82–86, 197; Belorussian and Yiddish, 82–89; Bolsheviks and, 95–96; courts of law, 82; korenizatsiia and, 82–83; Goldberg, Chanan on, 90–91; legal equality, 82; NKVD and Belorussian, 84–86; propaganda and, 81–82; Russian, 82, 85–86, 197; Russian versus Yiddish, 89–90; schools, 92–94, 197; social events, 91
late 1930s. *See* Stalinist era
LBSSR (Lithuanian-Belorussian Soviet Socialist Republic), 26
Left Bundists, 57
leisure time activities in republic, 180
Lekert, Hirsh, 64–65; biography rewrite, 65; as Bundist protagonist, 192; *Ego prevoskhoditelstvo*, 68; Frumkin, Ester, and, 67; memorialization, 65–68; monument destruction, 69; *Zayn Exelents*, 68
Lenin, Vladimir: purge of the Russian land, 4; War Communism, 4
Levin, Yankl, 57: Bundist-Communist dualism, 79; Grosser Club and, 59; leaving Minsk, 77
Leyvik, H., impressions of Minsk, 40–41
Liberman, Saul, on Minsk, 19
Liessin, Abraham, 22
Life and Struggle: Collection of Yiddish Leftist Literature in Poland, 210
Lifshitz, Malka (Ester Frumkin), 148
Lilienthal, Max, 17
lishchentsy, 34–35; medical services, 35–36; religious functionaries and, 121

literature, Yiddish, 93–94
Lithuania, division of political entities, 21
Litvak, Alef, 73
litvish tradition, 20
living standards, Great Terror, 181–83

mail, languages, 89
Malkin, Dov Ber, 23–24
Maltinsky, Chayim, 207
Marxism, Belorussia, 53
Maskilim, women's education, 147
Medem, Vladimir, 58
medical services: attacks on, 36; lishchentsy, 35–36
Mensheviks, Bund and
merging of nations, Jews embracing, 4
Minsk: Belorussian Republic hub, 71–72; Bolshevik regime reestablishment, 29–30; borders and Bolshevik Revolution, 21; Commission for the Separation of Church and State, 117; comparison to Vilna, 15, 20–21; demographics, 17, 19; description, 13–14; ethnic neighborhood stability, 179; Evsektsiia takeover, 53–57; geocultural character, 19–21; geopolitical status change in twentieth century, 21; German occupation, 25–26; Historical Commission of Belorussia, 105–6; historical orientation, 71–72; incorporation into Russian empire, 13; Jewish community history, 14–15; Jewish holidays, 28; Jewish population changes, 37–39; Jewish Socialist parties, 26–27; Jewish university students, 43–45; Khanin, Nokhem, 41–43; Labor Zionism, 26; language, 13–15; Leyvik, H., 40–43; Liberman, Saul, 19; litvish tradition, 20; Nemiga, 112; Pale of Settlement, 19–20; Poland and, 204–205; Polish Minsk *versus* Red Minsk, 205; Polish occupation, 27–28; rebuild as Soviet capital, 179–80; revolution and, 24–25; Russian Jewry supervision, 14–15; shortages, 179–80; Shpilevskii's description, 16–18; Socialism and, 22; tension with Moscow, 71–73; transformation of, 1–2; traveling zoo, 180; uniqueness, 5–6; universities and colleges, 99–100; urbanization and, 16; vocations of Jews, 16; Yiddish as state language, 82; Zionist organizations post-revolution, 46
Minsk Bund Committee, 22; Communists and, 53–54
Minsk Central Train Station, 87–88
Minsk State Circus, 180
Minsk university, JDC and, 33
Moscow: Bronshteyn, Yasha, 194; Communist Party Central Bureau, 32; cultural reference point, 21; Doctors' Plot, 215; gender issues, 174;

Great Terror, 195; Gurshtein, Sh.A. complaint, 96–97; *Hirsh Lekert*, 66–69; history study, 105; intermarriage, 212; Jewish center, building, 76–77; Jewish political leadership, 57; korenizatsiia, 83–84; kosher meat production, 127; Minsk relationship changes, 50; Nazi survivors, 214; Nemiga Jews, 125; newspapers, 61–63, 75; one-party system, 54; relocation to, 38–39; tension with Minsk, 71–73; theater, 73–75; underground educational system, 122; urbanization and, 16–17; women workers, 157; Yiddish, 82; Yiddish culture, 200–201
Moscow State Yiddish Theater, 73–74
motherhood as patriotic duty, 171–72

national identification, Yiddish and, 82
nationalist school, Yiddish and, 69–70
Nazi Germany: anti-Semitism and, 201–2; fascism and, 201–4; German Jews and, 206–7; Kristallnacht, 207; USSR anti-Nazi, 210
Nemiga, 112; "Beilis trial", 125; kosher meat production, 127; Minsk description, 41–42; Old Town, 179–80; Shivah Kruim synagogue, 116–17; strife of 1922, 112–14; Talmud-Torah seizure, 112–13
NEP (New Economic Policy), 51; prostitution, 162; women's liberation, 162
newspapers: *Arbeter bletl*, 22; centralization/regionalism tension, 75–76; *Der Emes*, 61; *Der minsker arbeter*, 22; *Der Shtern*, 61; *Der Veker*, 61–62; *Der yunger arbeter*, 25; *Di Tsukunft*, 22; *Oktyabr*, 63–64; *Pravda* (The truth), 4; Yiddish, 89–90; *Zvezda* (The star) 125; *Zviazda*, 192
NKVD (People's Commissariat of Internal Affairs), 3: Cherviakov, A.N, suicide, 176; false accusations, 192; forced confessions, 176; Galperin, Nina, 190; linguistic Belorussianization, 84–85; Mr. Brasler, 190; women and accusations against husbands, 173

Oktyabr: campaigning for subscription, restrictions, 89; blood libel story, 205–6; Bundists exposed, 192; circumcision issues, 138–39; *Der Veker* renaming, 63–64; German Jews, sympathy for, 208; Great Terror, 201; idealization of the Bund, 79; kosher meat and, 126–27; persecution reports, 201–2; Polish occupation, 204–6; Roznhoyz, Leyme, 129; Sorke, 154–55; women workers, 157; Zeyde frost, 181
Oktyabr textile factory, 135: employees expelled for circumcising, 139–40; women workers, 175
On the History of Russian Jews and the Establishment of a Historical Society (Dubnow), 106

Orshansky, Ber, 57
Osherovitsh, Elye, 57; attacks on *Der Veker*, 75; Bundism, 192; Kharik celebration, 185; *Der Veker* and, 61–62; purges, 195; on territorialization, 103
Oyslender, Nahum, 96–97

Pale of Settlement, 1–2: archives and historical documents, 106; Belorussian Soviet Socialist Republic hub, 5; girls schools, private, 147; educational institutions, 96; everyday life, 113; Jerusalem of Raysn, Minsk as, 50; Jewish geography and, 72; Minsk location, 19–20; Minsk-Moscow tension, 72; Nazis, 214; newspaper relocation, 75; religious life, persistence, 143; Social Democrats, 2; Soviet Jewish patriotism, 202; Soviet Jews compared to German Jews, 206; women's institutions, 147; *Zelmenyaner* (Kulbak), 178
Paole-Zion, 47–48: establishment, 23; events, 26; Goldberg, Chanan, 23; Minsker Tolk, 23; Polish troops' advance, 27; Russian Constituent Assembly, 24; Zionist organization disbanding, 32
patriotic duty of motherhood, 171–72
patriotism, temporal comparison, 202–3
Pedagogical Training College, 98–99
People's Commissariat of Internal Affairs. *See* NKVD
Perelman, Jeroham Judah Leib, 20
Peretz Jewish Library (Jewish Central Library), 46–47: Jewish employment, 179; women as readers, 166
photographs of women activists, 163–64
pioneering status Soviet Jews, 204
pogroms, 205–6
Poland: anti-Semitism, 204–6, 209–10; anti-Semitism and, 201–2; fascism and, 201–4; Minsk and, 204–5; pogroms, 205–6
Poles: Belorussian nationalists, 25; Great Terror, 199–200
Polish Minsk *versus* Red Minsk, 205
Polish occupation of Minsk, 27–28
political development, Yiddish and, 70
political strategies, Bundist effect, 69–76
politics: awareness among women, 157; woman delegate, 150; women in, 148
population, 177–80, 215: Grodno, 212; Jews in Minsk, changes, 5–6, 19, 37–39; Jews in Soviet Union, 2
printing industry, 20–21
propaganda, Yiddish, 81
propaganda against Jews: Bund liquidation and, 56; women and, 158
prostitution, NEP and, 162
proverki, 160

Provisional Government, Zionist groups, 24–25
purges. *See also* Great Terror: enemies of the people, 176; former Bundists, 191–92; Jewish cultural sphere, 193–201; Trotskyite accusations, 189

Rabinovitsh-Charny, Michael, 22
rada (Belorussian), 25
radicalism, Great Terror and, 199–201
radio programs, 184–85
Rafalskii, Mikhail, 193–94
Rafes, Moshe, *Hirsh Lekert,* 66
Rapoport, Yankev-Tevye: rape allegations, 128–29; shohtim trial, 124
rebellion against Jewish identity, 4
Red Army: Jews holding command posts, 3; kosher meat consumption, 126; Yiddish and, 71
Red Minsk *versus* Polish Minsk, 205
Red Teachers, 98
regional studies, 107
Rejzen, Sore, Bolshevik revolution, 29
religion: antireligious propaganda, 158; Commission for the Separation of Church and State, 117; Cultural Revolution, 117; verification of party-mindedness, 160; women as custodians of tradition, 159–60; worshipper demographics, 118–19
religious buildings. *See also* synagogues: Artisans' House of Prayer, 114; conversion, 114–19; Ginzburg House of Prayer, 114; Great Minsk Choral Synagogue, 114; religious society registration, 115–16; ritual baths, 117; separating from Soviet, 116–17; Shivah Kruim Synagogue, 114; Shoemakers' House of Prayer, 114; synagogues, 114; Talmud-Torah seizure, 112–13
religious education: heder ban and, 119–23; resurgence, 122; underground institutions, 121–23
religious practice, 113; lishchentsy and, 121; Union of Congregants of Synagogues and Houses of Prayer, 120
religious society registration, 115–16
restrictions on Jews, prior to Bolsheviks, 2
Right Bundists, 57
ritual baths, building confiscation protest, 117
role models for Jewish women, 155–56
Rosental-Shnayderman, Ester, Yiddish culture, 94–95
Rozenbaum, Semyon, 23
Rozin, Aron, 38; Zionism, 48–49
RSDP (Russian Socialist Democratic Party), founding congress, 22
Russian, All-Soviet language, 197

Russian Constituent Assembly, Zionist groups, 24
Russian language, Yiddish and, 70
Russian Orthodoxy, conversion to, 15–16

Sabbath school attendance, 131
scholarship: Pedagogical Training College, 98; regional studies, 107; Yiddish and, 95–98
schools: acceptance of circumcised boys, 133; anti-Passover measure, 131–32; Communist, 130–33; Great Terror, 196, 197–99; Jewish girls, 146–47; Jewish teachers, 132–33; language study, 197; religious identity, 131–33; Sabbath attendance, 131; Soviet Jewish schools, 130–31
scientific atheism, 130
Seforim, Mendele Mocher: Belorussian State Museum, 42; celebrations for, 64–65; *Di takse,* 125; women's issues, 147; Jewish heroes, 69
separatist tendencies, Yiddish and, 70–71
sexual mores of Jewish women change, 162–63
Shivah Kruim Synagogue, 114; demolition, 116–17
Shoemakers' House of Prayer, 114
shohtim trial, 123–25
shortages, Great Terror, 179–80
Shpilevskii's description of Minsk, 16–17; Jewishness of Minsk, 17, 19
shtetl: Belorussian, 105; theater and, 74–75
Skoblo, Hirshl, Jewish freedom under Stalin, 188
sliianie, 70
Smoliar, Hersh, 73: return to Minsk, 214
Socialism: Jewish Socialist parties in Minsk, 26–27; Jewish support, 21–22; Minsk and, 22; women's contribution, 172–73; women's liberation, 148–49
Socialist-Zionism, 23
Sosis, Israel, 99, 200; territorialization of scholarship, 106–7
Sovetishe Vaysrusland, 105
Soviet bureaucracy, Minsk and Moscow, 72–73
Soviet Jewish folklore, 202–3
Soviet Jewish neighborhoods, 179
Soviet Jewish schools, 130–33
Soviet Jews: empathy for German Jews, 208; pioneering status, 204
sovietization: bookstores, 31; bourgeois institutions, 32–33; Evsektsiia and, 32; Jewish institutions, 31–32; *Zelmenyaner* (Kulbak), 177–78
sports, Yiddish and Russian, 91
SSRB (Soviet Socialist Republic of Belarus), 26
Stakhanovite movement, women and, 170–71
Stalinist era. *See also* Great Terror: Communist Party growth under, 141; ethnic neighborhood stability, 179; family stability, 171–72; Jewish event

organization, 182–83; Jewish freedom, Hirshl Skoblo on, 188; Jewish heroes, 186–88; Jewish identity, 186–87; Jewish working class, 186; Kharik, Izzy, 188–89; leisure time activities in republic, 180; living standards, 181–83; Minsk rebuild, 179–80; public transportation, 180; radio programs, 184–85; shortages, 179–80; Soviet Jewish neighborhoods, 179; transformation of Jews, 186–87; Yiddish, 181–82; Yiddish folksongs, 186–87; youth activities, 185; *Zelmenyaner* (Kulbak), 177–78

students: Belorussian State University, 44–45; Jewish, 3; Jewish in Minsk, 43–45

synagogues. *See also* religious buildings: confiscation of property, 114–15; conversion, 118–19; protest, 117; Great Minsk Choral Synagogue, 114–15; as social center, 118; worshipper demographics, 118–19

Syrkin, Nachman, 23

Talmud-Torah seizure, 112–13
teachers, Jewish, surveillance of, 132–33
Terror campaign. *See* Great Terror
theater: Belgoset, 74; Belorussian State Jewish Theater, 73–74, 182–83; Granovsky, Alexander, 74; Moscow State Yiddish Theater, 73–74; shtetl and, 74–75
Trotskyite accusations, 189
Tsimbalist, Yehoshua, 122, 128
Tsinberg, Israel, 96

Ukraine: Bolshevik Revolution, 30; nationalism, 83; Yiddish, 82–83
Ukrainianization (Ukrainizatsiia), 82
underground religious education institutions: korobka and, 121–123; yeshivas, 122–123
underground Zionist groups, Belorussian State University, 45–46
Union of Congregants of Synagogues and Houses of Prayer, religious practice support, 120
universities: Belorussian Academy of Science, 102–3; Belorussian State University, 44–45; ghetto benches, 204–5; Gorky Belorussian Higher Pedagogical Institute, 100; Inbelkult, 100–102; Institute for Proletarian Jewish Culture, 103; Jewish students, 3; Jewish students in Minsk, 43–45; Minsk, 99–100
upward mobility of Jews, 3
urbanization: master plan demolitions, 116–17; Minsk and, 16

Vasserman case, 163

Vaynshteyn, Arn: Bundist accusations, 54; career celebration, 56; minister of social affairs, 27; Municipal Duma, 25; Yiddish, 70
Vilna, 19–22; Belorussian Social-Democratic Party founding, 83; Bundist organization, 64; compared to Minsk, 15; *Der Veker*, 61; Hirsh Lekert, 65–69; Jewish labor movement, 52; Jewish radicalism, 22; May Day celebration, 148; Minsk turning toward Moscow, 50; religion in, 113; universities, 205; Yiddish, 96; YIVO Institute for Jewish Research, 101
vocations of Jews, Minsk, 16
VSNKh (Supreme Soviet of the National Economy of Belorussia), 39

War Communism, 4
Wengeroff, Chonon Afanasii, 15–16
Wengeroff, Pauline, 15–16
women. *See also* emancipation of women; gender equality: activists' photographs, 163–64; the Bund, 148; careers, 158; Communist husbands, 156–57; Communist Party membership, 166–69; as counterrevolutionaries, 159; Cultural Revolution, 161–62; delegates, 150; domestic life, 164–66; education, 147; Evsektsiia and, 149–50; as flame-keepers, 173; General City Women Delegates' Meeting, 151; gold campaign, 161–62; ideal Soviet Jewish woman, 172; illiteracy, 149; Jewish Department of Belorussian State University, 169–70; korenizatsiia campaign, 151–52; marriage and job forfeiture, 165–66; motherhood as patriotic duty, 171–72; political awareness, 157; public activity, 146–47; receptiveness, 148; scripture's limitations *versus* proletarian state, 152–53; self-emancipation, 156–57; sexual mores changes, 162–63; Socialism, contributions to, 172–73; Soviet ideals at home, 158–59; Stakhanovite movement, 170–71; verification of party-mindedness, 160; wages, 148; Zhenotdel and, 149–54
women's liberation: Communism and, 148–49; Socialism and, 148–49
women's question, 146. *See also* Jewish women's question; women in politics, 148
working class in Stalinist era, 186, 187–88
workplace attitudes and gender equality, 158

yeshivas, 20; banning, 119–23; Blumkes kloyz, 20; underground educational system, 122–23
Yiddish: anti-Jewish violence reports, 208; *Atlas of Yiddish Dialects*, 101; Belorussian and, 84–89; Belorussian-Jewish identity, 103–9; the Bund

and, 69–70; commitment to, 70–71; courtrooms, 90; cultural sphere purge, 195–96; folksongs of Stalinist era, 186–87; Great Terror and, 181–82; Great Terror school closings, 197–99; Inbelkult Jewish studies, 100–102; Jewish education, 91–98; Jewish scholarship, 96–97; Jewish Sports Club Hamer, 91; korenizatsiia, 92; *Life and Struggle: Collection of Yiddish Leftist Literature in Poland*, 210; literary works territorialization, 104–5; literature, 93–94; Minsk Central Train Station, 87–88; national identification and, 82; neutralist school, 69–70; newspapers, 89–90; as official language, 81; Pedagogical Training College, 98; political development and, 70; propaganda, 81; radio programs, 184–85; Red Army and, 71; Rosental-Shnayderman, Ester, 94–95; separatist tendencies and, 70–71; social use, 90–91; sports, 91; state language, 82; Tsinberg, Israel, 96; Ukraine, 82–83; urban public life, 86–89; youth in 1930s, 185

youth activities in the late 1930s, 185

Yung-Skoyt, 91

Zaretskii, Chayim, 43
Zayn Exelents, 68
Zelmenyaner (Kulbak), 105, 177–78
Zhenotdel, women and, 149–54
Zionism, 21–22; Bolshevik rule and, 26; Great Terror, 193; Ha-poel He-haluts, 23; influence in Minsk, 23; Kaplan, Eliezer, 24; Labor Zionism (Minsk), 26; organizations going underground, 32; Poale-Zion, 26, 47–48; Polish occupation of Minsk and, 27–28; postrevolutionary Minsk activities, 46; Provisional Government and, 24–25; publications shut down, 32; Rozin, Aron, 48–49; Russian Constituent Assembly, 24; Socialist-Zionism, 3; youth groups arrests, 47; youth groups Belorussian State University, 45–46; Zhitnitskii, Marc, 47
Zionist Workers' Movement. *See* Paole-Zion
Zvezda, 125, 150
Zviazda, 192, 204

ELISSA BEMPORAD holds the Jerry and William Ungar Professorship in Eastern European Jewish History and the Holocaust, and is assistant professor of history at Queens College, City University of New York. Born and raised in Italy, Dr. Bemporad was trained in Russian studies at the University of Bologna and in Jewish studies at the Jewish Theological Seminary of America. She received a PhD in history from Stanford University and has published studies on Russian Jewish history in a variety of academic journals. Her work has appeared in English, Italian, Russian, Belorussian, French, and Hebrew. Dr. Bemporad is a coeditor of *Conzeniana*, a series about Yiddish literature and culture that is published in Italy.

www.ingramcontent.com/pod-product-compliance
Lightning Source LLC
Chambersburg PA
CBHW061934220426
43662CB00012B/1909